W9-BRZ-931

"Bernie Baumohl has written a must-read educational and reference book that every individual investor will find indispensable for watching, monitoring, and interpreting the markets. The daily flow of high-frequency economic indicators is the stuff that makes financial markets move and that can signal the big trends that make or break investor portfolios. Most important, Bernie's long experience in reporting economics for Time Magazine *helps make the 'dismal science' lively and interesting."*
—Allen Sinai, President and Chief Global Economist, Decision Economics, Inc.

"This is the most up-to-date guide to economic indicators and their importance to financial markets in print. The coverage of less-reported indicators, especially those from nongovernment sources, is hard to find elsewhere. The inclusion of the actual published tables helps the newer student of the markets find the data in the public release. For anyone trying to follow the economic data, this should be next to your computer so that you can understand and find the data on the Internet."
—David Wyss, Chief Economist, Standard and Poor's

"Economic statistics, employment data, Federal Reserve surveys. Think they are boring? Think again! They can drive markets into a frenzy, causing billions of dollars to be made or lost in an instant. Bernie Baumohl brilliantly, clearly, and, yes, entertainingly describes what every investor and business manager should know about economic indicators: which ones move markets, how to interpret them, and how to use them to spot and capitalize on future economic trends. The Secrets of Economic Indicators *is an extraordinary and insightful work—an enormously important contribution to the body of financial literature. Read it and then keep it on your desk. Consult it the next time you are deluged with a flurry of economic statistics. Your understanding certainly will be enhanced, and your portfolio will likely be as well."*
—Robert Hormats, Vice Chairman, Goldman Sachs (International)

"Bernie Baumohl has accomplished something of real value in The Secrets of Economic Indicators. *He has successfully demystified the world of financial and economic news that bombards us in our daily lives. Both professional investors and casual observers of the world of finance and economics will be grateful for what he has done. The constant stream of heretofore bewildering news from the world of business and finance can now be easily understood. Every businessperson or investor should keep a copy of Baumohl's book close at hand as he or she catches up on the business, stock market, and economic events of the day. It is great, at long last, to have someone who has eliminated what may have been so perplexing to so many and to have done so with such remarkable clarity."*
—Hugh Johnson, Chairman and Chief Investment Officer of Johnson Illington Advisors

"If you want to make money investing, this is an essential trend-tracking tool that will help get you to the bank. This book is the real deal. Bernard Baumohl miraculously breathes life into deadly economic indicators and boring statistics . . . he knows what he's talking about, and his expertise proves it."
—Gerald Celente, Director, The Trends Research Institute

"Baumohl has a gift for taking a complicated subject and allowing it to read like a fast-moving novel. My confidence in reading and understanding economic indicators as portrayed in this book made me realize the possibilities this information holds for improving my personal net worth as well as navigating my business toward higher profits. I recommend this book if you care about your future finances."
—Morris E. Lasky, CEO, Lodging Unlimited, Inc.; Manager and consultant for $6 billion in hotel assets; Chairman, Lodging Conference; Chairman, International Hotel Conference

"I find Baumohl's writing fascinating. In addition to the famous indicators, he includes many that I hadn't heard of. I really appreciate that he tells you exactly where to find each indicator on the Web. Just about anyone who's serious about understanding which way the economy is headed will want to read this book. It could be a classic."
—Harry Domash, Columnist for MSN Money and Publisher, Winning Investing Newsletter

"I think this is an excellent book. It's well written, accessible to a variety of readers, deals with an interesting and important subject, and covers the topic well. It deserves to get a lot of notice and use."
—D. Quinn Mills, Alfred J. Weatherhead, Jr., Professor of Business Administration, Harvard Business School

DATE DUE

JUL 2 0 2016	

THE SECRETS OF
ECONOMIC

Hidden Clues to Future Economic Trends and Investment Opportunities

INDICATORS

SECOND EDITION

THE SECRETS OF
ECONOMIC

Hidden Clues to Future Economic Trends and Investment Opportunities

INDICATORS

SECOND EDITION

BERNARD BAUMOHL

Vice President, Publisher: Tim Moore
Wharton Editor: Yoram (Jerry) Wind
Executive Editor: Jim Boyd
Editorial Assistant: Pamela Boland
Associate Publisher and Director of Marketing: Amy Neidlinger
Assistant Marketing Manager: Megan Colvin
Cover Designer: Alan Clements
Managing Editor: Gina Kanouse
Project Editor: Michael Thurston
Copy Editor: Gayle Johnson
Proofreader: Harrison Ridge Editorial Services
Indexer: Lisa Stumpf
Compositor: Fastpages
Manufacturing Buyer: Dan Uhrig

© 2008 by Pearson Education, Inc.
Publishing as Wharton School Publishing
Upper Saddle River, New Jersey 07458

Wharton School Publishing offers excellent discounts on this book when ordered in quantity for bulk purchases or special sales. For more information, please contact U.S. Corporate and Government Sales, 1-800-382-3419, corpsales@pearsontechgroup.com. For sales outside the U.S., please contact International Sales at international@pearsoned.com.

Company and product names mentioned herein are the trademarks or registered trademarks of their respective owners.

Printed in the United States of America

Eleventh Printing: January 2010

ISBN-10: 0-13-244729-0
ISBN-13: 978-0-13-244729-4

Pearson Education LTD.
Pearson Education Australia PTY, Limited.
Pearson Education Singapore, Pte. Ltd.
Pearson Education North Asia, Ltd.
Pearson Education Canada, Ltd.
Pearson Educatiòn de Mexico, S.A. de C.V.
Pearson Education—Japan
Pearson Education Malaysia, Pte. Ltd.

Library of Congress Cataloging-in-Publication Data

Baumohl, Bernard.
  The secrets of economic indicators : hidden clues to future economic trends and investment opportunities / Bernard Baumohl. — 2nd ed.
      p. cm.
  ISBN 0-13-244729-0 (pbk. : alk. paper) 1. Economic forecasting. 2. Economic indicators. 3. Business forecasting. I. Title.
  HB3730.B38 2007
  330.01'12—dc22   2007005976

To my mother, Eva Baumohl, a Holocaust survivor; and in memory of my father, Naftali Baumohl

CONTENTS

ABOUT THE AUTHOR

Bernard Baumohl is managing director of The Economic Outlook Group and oversees its forecasts of economic trends and risks. He also conducts seminars on how to find and utilize economic indicators so that corporate leaders and investors can stay ahead of the business curve. Baumohl was an award-winning *TIME Magazine* economics reporter for two decades and covered the domestic and international economy from *TIME*'s New York and Washington bureaus. As an economist for European American Bank, he monitored and developed forecasts of U.S. economic activity. He also served as an analyst with the Council on Foreign Relations. A frequent guest on television and radio, he has lectured on economics at New York University, Duke University, and the New York Institute of Finance. A recipient of the John Hancock Award for Excellence in Financial Journalism, Baumohl has a master's degree in international affairs and economics from Columbia University.

What's New in the Second Edition?

From the beginning, I wanted to write a different sort of book on the economy and its ties to the financial markets. My approach was to focus on economic indicators—specifically, those key indicators that can, if read correctly, provide timely insights on where the economy is headed—and how that information can influence the value of stocks, bonds, and currencies. However, a book on economic indicators runs the risk of being antiquated unless it is periodically updated to reflect the changing universe of these market-sensitive measures. For instance, new economic indicators have been introduced since the first edition was published, and some of them show promise as useful forecasting tools. Other measures have undergone significant methodological refinements so that they can more accurately anticipate the economy's direction.

Aside from updating the collection of economic indicators, economists and investors have also had to confront several new and far-reaching issues on the workings of the U.S. and international economy. For example, there has been much discussion recently about whether the yield curve is still a reliable predictor of business cycles, or whether inflation measures adequately take into account not just changes in the price of goods and services, but also improvements in their quality.

For all these reasons, I felt the time was right for a second edition that would not only revise the list of the most important economic indicators, but would also explain their significance in a way that makes the analysis more relevant.

So what is new in this book?

In the first chapter, changes were made in the ranking of the most influential indicators. Such revisions became necessary following the introduction of new measures of economic activity, and also because of the modifications made to the way several existing indicators were computed.

I also decided to address the question I get most frequently from clients: Which economic indicators are best known for being ahead of the business curve? In response, I added a chart that lists the top ten "leading economic indicators." This list is based not just on my research, but also on the valued opinions I received from other economists. However, the chart given here, unlike the others you'll see, does not formally rank the leading indicators, because there is no agreement as to which consistently serves as "the best" crystal ball.

By far, most of the changes take place in Chapter 3. Among the most noteworthy is the addition of three measures: the *ADP National Employment Report*, the *Federal Open*

Market Committee (FOMC) *Statement*, and the release of *Treasury International Capital* (TIC) flows. The federal government has also redesigned a number of existing indicators, and that required new charts and descriptions for this book.

Chapter 4 deals with the most important international economic indicators. To keep the list current, India's GDP and inflation were added. Although this country is often referred to as the "other" giant of Asia, many experts believe India will overtake China in population and even GDP later this century.

For Chapters 5 and 6, all U.S. and foreign Internet addresses were checked to see if they were working so that you won't get that annoying "Does not exist" message. Finally, a new type of list was inserted at the end of Chapter 5—one that consists of useful "unconventional" economic indicators. These are less well-known monthly or weekly measures that gauge business activity within a specific business sector, such as the volume of railroad freight traffic, movie box office receipts, and hotel bookings—all of which help corroborate what the broader economic indicators tells us about the current and future strength of the economy.

Bernard Baumohl
March 2007
Princeton Junction, New Jersey

PREFACE

"You want to write a book about *what*? *Economic indicators*? How did you come up with this death wish?"

That was the first response I got after telling a colleague at *TIME* what I was up to. She, too, was a financial journalist, so I expected some sage advice and support. We continued our conversation over lunch. "Did I hear you correctly?" she asked, still incredulous. "We *are* talking about your writing a book on economic statistics, right?" Yes, I nodded, and then went on to explain why this idea had been percolating in my mind for months. I knew it was a tough topic to write about, but I was ready to take it on. She listened patiently to my reasoning and then let loose a barrage of suggestions.

"First, let's get real here. To make this work, a book on economic indicators has to be sexy. Edgy. Really funny. Get in some lurid details about consumer prices. Tell some lascivious tales about industrial production and capacity utilization. Toss in lots of jokes on durable-goods orders. Then there's the humor that just springs at you when writing about foreign trade and nonfarm productivity. And . . . hey, shouldn't you be taking notes on all this?"

The appetite I came to the restaurant with was suddenly gone. Not because she was poking fun at the idea. Just the opposite. Beneath all that sarcasm was a genuine message that I knew had to be taken seriously. The subject of economic indicators can be lethally boring because of its impenetrable jargon and reliance on tedious statistics. I realized from that brutal lunch encounter that my biggest challenge in writing this book was not simply to identify and describe the world's most influential economic indicators, but to make the whole subject approachable and even—dare I say it—interesting. My purpose from the start was to reach out to those who had little or no experience navigating the maze of key economic statistics and to dispel the notion that you need an economics degree, an MBA, or a CPA to understand what these indicators tell us about the economy and how we can use them to make better investment and business decisions.

The broader question, of course, is why do this book at all? Why should anyone outside the economics profession even care about economic indicators? Why is it important for the average person to know how many new homes are under construction, whether factories produced more or fewer goods in the latest month, or whether executives charged with buying raw material for their companies are increasing their orders or cutting back? Why bother with any of this stuff? Why not let the experts sort out the mishmash of economic numbers and tell us what it means?

Indeed, most Americans have little desire to follow such esoteric measures. They are content to rely on the insights of their investment advisers or hear television pundits muse endlessly about the economy and the financial markets. Other than that, few show interest in probing any further. However, that attitude changed abruptly in 2000 with the bursting of the stock market bubble and the collapse of the dot-com sector. Investors were sickened and then angered by the resulting loss of trillions of dollars in personal wealth. It made no difference whether the money was in one's personal savings, a 401(k), or a pension. No investment escaped unscathed. The decimation was universal, and for Americans, it became a painful and sobering reminder of just how much one's financial well-being was staked to the risky business of stocks and bonds.

Perhaps the most troubling revelation to come out of this awful experience was how utterly dependent ordinary investors had allowed themselves to become on so-called "experts" for virtually all investment advice. It turned out that these very "experts"—veteran portfolio managers and longtime professional market watchers—failed miserably in their responsibility to help protect the assets and curb the losses of their investing clients. Worse still, investors became justifiably furious when they realized they were also being lied to by some of the companies they had invested in and even by the brokerage firms with whom they had entrusted their hard-earned money.

The result was predictable. Disillusioned by the ineffectual advice of their brokers, the seemingly endless revelations of corporate fraud, and the biased research reports put out by some well-known Wall Street firms, a growing number of Americans have since decided to venture into the investment world by themselves, trusting their own instincts rather than someone else's. These investors are emboldened by the fact that they can now access a huge assortment of information resources from home and work. They can even access them while traveling. There is, today, an unprecedented abundance of economic and financial news and analysis instantly available to anyone, anytime. This includes virtually 24/7 radio and television coverage of business news and, of course, hundreds of useful Web sites that offer valuable data as well as varied perspectives on the outlook for the financial markets and the economy.

How do the economic indicators fit into all this? Why should investors—or business executives, entrepreneurs, and ordinary workers—pay particular attention to these reports? Because they are the vital barometers that tell us what the economy is up to and, more importantly, in what direction it is likely to go in the future. These indicators describe the economic backdrop that will ultimately affect corporate earnings, interest rates, and inflation. They can also influence the future cost of financing a car or house, the security of our jobs, and our overall standard of living. Even business leaders are under pressure to monitor economic indicators more closely. Knowledge of economic conditions in the U.S. enables CEOs to make decisions with greater confidence about whether to buy more equipment, increase inventories, hire workers, or raise fresh capital. In addition, for firms competing in the global marketplace, international economic indicators are of particular importance, because they allow executives to assess business opportunities abroad.

But how do you begin to evaluate these economic reports? There is such a bewildering variety of economic statistics in the public domain that following them all can be harmful to your health. New sets of economic numbers come out every day, week, month, and quarter, and they often tell conflicting stories about what's going on in the U.S. In addition, stocks, bonds, and currencies react differently to economic indicators. Some economic news can cause tremors in the financial markets, while other news produces no reaction at all. Many indicators have no forecasting value whatsoever, yet others have established an impressive track record of being able to predict how the economy will behave during the next 12 months.

Moreover, different indicators originate from different sources. The U.S. government pumps out loads of economic data through agencies such as the Commerce Department's Bureau of Economic Analysis and the Federal Reserve Board. However, numerous private groups also release market-moving indicators. One of the best known is The Conference Board for its Consumer Confidence and Leading Economic Indicators series. In addition, the National Association of Realtors reports monthly data on existing home sales, and Challenger, Gray and Christmas, the outplacement firm, tallies the number of announced corporate layoffs each month. Note that these sources just gauge U.S. economic activity. When you look at the assortment of economic indicators released by other countries, the quantity of information available becomes mind-numbing.

Clearly there is too much economic information out there, and not all of it is useful. So what do you focus on? How does an investor, a CEO, or even an economist decide which of the many gauges of business activity are worth tracking? Which indicators pack the greatest wallop in the financial markets? Which ones are known for doing the best job of predicting where the economy is heading? These are the key questions I try to answer in this book.

The book is organized in a way that I believe makes the most sense for you. Chapter 1, "The Lock-Up," begins with the drama that typically surrounds the release of a sensitive economic indicator. After the embargo is lifted and the economic report flashes across computer screens around the world, reaction to the latest news by global money markets can affect the financial well-being of every American.

One cannot successfully write a book on economic indicators without at least gently introducing a few basic economic terms. In Chapter 2, "A Beginner's Guide: Understanding the Lingo," I try to define as painlessly as possible those key phrases and concepts that are essential to know when reading about economic indicators.

The essence of the book begins with Chapter 3, "The Most Influential U.S. Economic Indicators." Here, all the major U.S. economic indicators are evaluated, and each one is discussed in a format designed to answer these vital questions:

- Why is this indicator important to know?
- How is it computed? (Sure, not everyone will want to get into the nitty-gritty details of how economic indicators are put together. Nevertheless, by understanding the

underlying methodology of how they are calculated, one is better able to appreciate the usefulness of these indicators, as well as their shortcomings.)

• What does the economic indicator have to say about the future? The purpose of this question is twofold. First you are shown how to interpret the official report and its accompanying tables. Particular emphasis is placed on the most interesting and useful data points in the economic release. Second, guidance is given on how to locate valuable clues in the tables that may offer you a heads-up on how the economy might perform in the months ahead. To make this task easier, copies of actual releases are included with most indicators covered in this book. Virtually all the economic releases mentioned are available on the Internet for free. You can read them on their respective Web sites or download the releases as PDF files. (Note that Internet addresses for the economic indicators are included in this book.)

• How might bonds, stocks, and the dollar react to the latest economic reports? The financial markets often respond differently to economic data. Much depends on the specific indicator released, how timely it is, whether investors are surprised by the news, and what else is going on in the economy at the time.

Chapter 4, "International Economic Indicators: Why Are They So Important?," examines the most influential foreign economic indicators. Because the U.S. economy and its financial markets are closely integrated with the rest of the world, one can no longer afford to ignore measures of economic activity in other countries. If the economies of other nations are growing, they'll buy more from U.S. producers. On the other hand, poor growth abroad bodes ill for many large U.S. companies and their employees. In addition, American investors interested in buying foreign stocks and bonds for their own portfolios should track foreign economic indicators to identify those countries and regions in the world that might offer the most attractive returns.

Chapter 5, "Best Web Sites for U.S. Economic Indicators," is evidence of how much times have changed. Not too long ago, anyone interested in obtaining a set of current and historical economic statistics had to purchase them from a private number-crunching firm. The more stats you wanted, the more costly it was. Today, nearly all this data can be accessed instantly on the Internet for free! The democratization of economic statistics gives everyone, from the experienced professional to the weekend investor, the opportunity to download, read, and analyze economic information. In this chapter, I've assembled what I think are among the best and most authoritative Web sites for economic data. Again, all are free, though some may ask users to register.

Chapter 6, "Best Web Sites for International Economic Indicators," is a compilation of Web sites that enables you to quickly locate foreign economic data that might otherwise be tough to find. However, there's one important caveat to keep in mind: No country collects and disseminates as much high-quality economic information as the U.S. Its breadth and integrity make it the gold standard in the world. Although there is a vast amount of international economic data on the Web, one has to approach such sources

with caution. There are issues concerning language (many are not in English), comprehensiveness, accuracy, and timeliness. In this chapter, I've listed sites on the Internet that
in my judgment are the best and most trustworthy for international economic data—and
that are available in English! Once again, every site listed is free (at least at the time of
this writing).

Finally, let me close by saying that this book was fun to write, largely because I
learned a great deal in the process. It is not meant to be a textbook or some intellectual
treatise on the economy. My purpose throughout is to help give you a better understanding of how to look at economic indicators, why they can be so influential, what they
might tell us about the future, and how people can best utilize all that information. If I
have accomplished this in some way, than it was worth all the swearing and temper
tantrums I went through every time my computer crashed in the course of this endeavor.

ACKNOWLEDGMENTS

One gratification that comes with completing a book is that I now get a chance to thank those whom I relied on for advice, contacts, and support along the way. To be sure, there are many people to thank—so many, in fact, that mentioning all their names would greatly lengthen this book. Still, there are some that deserve special mention because they were so giving of their time and their counsel.

I must begin by breaking with tradition. It is customary in these pages to reserve thanking your family until the end. However, that order makes little sense to me in this case. My family deserves top billing here, because I relied on their support the most these last two years. From day one I expropriated a room in our home and turned it into an impassable maze of documents, newspapers, and boxes. Indeed, we can no longer recall the color of the carpet underneath. Moreover, during the last two years, when I was writing or traveling, the burden of overseeing family and household matters fell largely on my wife, Debbie. She was the one who got our three girls off to school every morning, prepared their lunches, helped with their homework, chauffeured them to playdates, met with teachers, accompanied them to doctor checkups, got them ready for bed, paid the bills, and so much more. Without a doubt, this book would not have been possible without her support and love. Nor will I ever forget how my daughters, Ashley, Rachel, and Nicole, tried to help me in the first days by printing "Do not disturb" signs and taping them outside my door. From beginning to end, my family provided the best home environment for me to carry out this project, and for that I will always be grateful.

I am also indebted to Carolina Buia (writer and television journalist) and Marc Lieberman (NYU economics professor). Both listened to my ideas, read the initial treatment of the book, and opened some very important doors to the publishing world. I also benefited greatly from the experience and wisdom of others, including Adam Cohen (the *New York Times*), Jordan Goodman (personal finance author), Dan Kadlec (*TIME*), Jeffrey Liebenson (KMZ Rosenman), Larry Moran (Bureau of Economic Analysis, Commerce Department), Michael Panzner (HSBC Securities), David Skidmore (Federal Reserve Board), Sue Hensley and Gary Steinberg (Department of Labor), Sam Slater (Fidelity International), Chris Williamson (NTC Economics), Joel Prakken and Ben Herzon (Macroeconomic Advisers, LLC), and Douglas Offer (ADP, Inc.).

There are two people I'd like to name who were not involved in the preparation of this book, but were nevertheless enormously important to me because I learned so much from them about economic journalism. They are Bill Saporito, *TIME*'s exceptionally gifted business editor, and the late George Church (*TIME* and the *Wall Street Journal*), who was a brilliant writer on all topics, but none more so than on economics. I view both their work as the benchmark in excellent writing and editing.

Finally, one of the luckiest things to have happened to me was to work with Jim Boyd, my editor at Prentice Hall. Writing a book the first time can be a daunting experience, but Jim made the process so much easier with his intelligent guidance and sense of humor. It was a real privilege working with him. I also want to thank Michael Thurston, project editor at Pearson Education, who supervised the production of this rather complicated book.

Let me make one last note. Though I made every effort to make sure this book is accurate, I alone am responsible for any follies that might have slipped through.

CHAPTER 1

The Lock-Up

Shortly after dawn on most weekday mornings, a strange ritual takes place in Washington, D.C. Two dozen select men and women leave their homes, grab their newspapers, and rush off to spend part of the day under virtual house arrest. Yes, house arrest—as in incarceration. Precisely where they go to be confined can vary day to day. It could be in a dilapidated government building one morning and a high-tech office complex the next. Regardless of the location, what occurs in all these places is always the same. They enter a strict, prison-like setting where contact with the outside world is cut off.

One Friday morning, this same group climbs a long set of steps to the side entrance of a sleek, white-stone building on 3rd Avenue and C Street in the heart of the nation's capital. Armed guards greet them at the entrance for a security check; from this point on, everyone has to wear their ID tags at all times. The visitors proceed across a lobby and down a quiet, narrow corridor, eventually stopping in front of a locked, heavy wooden door. A government official awaits them and quickly opens the door to reveal a drab, windowless, L-shaped room 40 feet long and some 10 feet across. It is empty except for two dozen plain-looking orange and chrome chairs, each resting alongside a row of narrow cubicle-like desks. A digital clock high on the wall breaks time down to seconds. It is 7:30:15 a.m., and already 12 people have found their way into the "lock-up" room. More are expected within the next 15 minutes. All who enter dutifully sign their names on a special sheet.

Despite its austere appearance, there is an atmosphere of calm in the room, at least for now. Some visitors talk excitedly about the previous night's televised basketball game. Others are either chatting on cell phones or checking their BlackBerrys for messages. A few keep to themselves by catching up on the morning paper or downing a quick muffin and coffee. Everyone in the room, however, makes a point of always knowing the time, with some people eyeing the digital clock so frequently that their actions may be mistaken for nervous tics.

As the time approaches 8 a.m., there is a palpable change in mood. Gone now are the sounds of light conversation; these sounds are replaced by the din of laptops firing up. Everyone appears to be focused on what is about to occur.

At 7:55 a.m. sharp, a government official walks in and picks up a wall phone to call the Naval Observatory, home to the Vice President of the United States. It is also the location of the ultra-accurate atomic clock. She listens intently for a few seconds and then abruptly hangs up without saying a word. The individual then inserts a key into a lock on the wall, which allows her to adjust the digital clock to the precise second. With the correct time now set, the official then turns around to make a terse announcement.

"Please turn off all cell phones and other communication devices, and disconnect laptops from your telephone lines."

To make sure everyone complies, the official walks across the room and eyes each desk. Meanwhile, a second federal employee arrives, carrying copies of a highly sensitive government report. Each one is placed facedown on an empty desk.

Then it begins.

At precisely 8 a.m., the door to the lock-up room clicks shut. From this point on, all those inside are out of touch with the rest of the world. No one is permitted to leave. No calls or messages can come into or go out of the room. Security is tight. A guard stands by outside, ready to use force if anyone attempts to sneak out.

What secret is the government protecting? Is the CIA about to begin a classified briefing on intelligence activities? Are Congressional investigators huddling to hear the newest terrorist threat? No. All these precautions are taken for one reason. The government is about to release numbers. Statistics. More precisely, economic statistics. The visitors in the room are business reporters representing news organizations from around the world, and this morning they're working out of the Department of Labor's secure pressroom.

Why such tight secrecy? Because in the next few seconds, these journalists will be the first to lay their eyes on one of the country's most sensitive economic measures—the monthly report on employment conditions. It can shed fresh light on whether the U.S. economy is growing or facing a slowdown. Did the number of Americans who have jobs rise or fall in the latest month? Have hourly wages gone up, or did they drop? Did people work more hours or fewer? These statistics might not seem particularly earthshaking to most Americans, but they can and do whip the global stock, bond, and currency markets into a frenzy. For individual investors and professional money managers, the information in the jobs report can mean the difference between having a winning or losing portfolio. It also explains the need for the security measures. Individuals getting such hot figures ahead of time can make a quick bundle of money, because they know something about which no one else in the financial markets is yet aware of. To prevent such abuses, the government guards these and dozens of other key economic indicators as tightly as a military base. It also implements a carefully controlled procedure to disseminate sensitive economic news.

8:00:00   The instant the door is shut, reporters dive in to grab the latest release on employment conditions, which up to now has been facedown. They have just 30 minutes to read, digest, and write their stories on how the job market changed during the previous month. Most of the journalists arrived that morning with the expectation that the employment release would carry dismal economic news, with the number of people without jobs rising—a troubling sign the economy was weakening. At least that was the opinion of most professional forecasters whom these reporters had consulted just days earlier.

But on this particular morning, the employment report stuns everyone. Those in the lock-up room read with amazement that companies actually hired workers in far greater numbers than anyone expected. Moreover, other figures in the report appear to corroborate signs that the economy is doing quite well. Wages are rising, and factory overtime is increasing. Far from slowing, the latest evidence indicates the economy is actually picking up steam. It is astounding news of which the rest of the world is yet unaware.

As the digital clock continues its silent countdown, reporters working on the story suddenly face some urgent questions. What's really happening in the economy? Why were so many "experts" caught off guard? What does this mean for future inflation and interest rates? How might the stock, bond, and currency markets react to the news?

Though the latest jobs report was unexpected, these journalists are not completely unprepared. As is their routine, a day or two earlier they showered private economists with questions that covered a variety of hypothetical employment scenarios. What does it mean if the job market worsens? What if it actually improves? Now the reporters are frantically searching through their interview notes to help them file their stories.

8:28:00   A Labor Department worker in the lock-up room notifies television reporters that they can now leave under escort to prepare for their live 8:30 broadcast of the jobs report.

For the remaining journalists in the room, there is just a brief warning: "Two minutes left!" By now, most have pieced together their initial versions of the story—the headline, the opening sentences, key numbers, and the implications for the economy. All that's left are some last-minute fact-checking and a word tweak here and there.

8:29:00   "One minute. You can open your telephone lines—*BUT DO NOT TRANSMIT!*"

The level of tension is not just high in the lock-up room. At that moment, money managers and traders in New York, Chicago, Tokyo, Hong Kong, London, Paris, and Frankfurt are riveted to their computer screens, anxiously waiting for the release of the crucial jobs report. It's a stomach-churning time for them, because investment decisions that involve hundreds of billions of dollars will be made the instant the latest employment news flashes across their monitors. Why such worldwide interest in how jobs fare in America? For one thing, many foreign investors own U.S. stocks and bonds, and their values can rise or fall based on what the job report says. Second, the international economy is now so tightly interconnected that a weak or strong jobs report in the U.S. can directly impact business activity in other countries. If joblessness in America climbs, consumers will likely purchase fewer cars from Germany, wine from France, and clothing from Indonesia. In contrast, a jump in employment means households will have more income to spend on imports, and this can stimulate foreign economies.

8:29:30   "Thirty seconds!" The fingers of reporters hover over their computers' Send button, ready to dispatch the latest employment news to the world. On-air reporters are also prepared to deliver the news live.

8:29:50   An official counts the final seconds out loud:

"Ten . . . nine . . . eight . . . seven . . . six . . . five . . . four . . . three . . . two . . . one!"

8:30:00   "Transmit!" Reporters simultaneously hit the Send button on their key-boards. In seconds, electronic news carriers, including Bloomberg, AP, Reuters, and Japan's Kyodo News, release their stories. Television and cable news stations, such as CNBC, Bloomberg TV, CNN, and MSNBC, broadcast the report live. A second or two later, computer screens around the globe carry the first surprising words: "Jobs unexpect-edly rose the previous month, with the unemployment rate falling instead of rising!"

For journalists in the lock-up room, the stress-filled half-hour grind is over, and they are now free to leave. But the work has just begun for those in the investment community.

At the Chicago Board of Trade (CBOT), where U.S. Treasury bonds and notes are traded, news of the strong job growth sparks pandemonium. Bond traders were so sure they would see a deterioration in the job market that many had bet millions on such an outcome. These traders bought bonds for clients prior to the government's release on unemployment and expected to earn a quick bundle of money based on the following strategy: If the number of people employed fell, it would drag down consumer spending. That, in turn, would slow the economy, reduce inflation pressures, and cause bond prices to turn up and interest rates to fall, thereby guaranteeing traders an easy profit.

The strategy was sound, but they bet on the wrong horse. Instead of laying off workers, companies were substantially adding to their workforce. The economy was not slowing, but demonstrating remarkable strength, and those bond traders who hoped to make a fast buck for their customers now face losing lots of money. With more people getting jobs, household income increases, and that leads to greater spending and borrow-ing. The presence of a more robust economy heightens concerns about future inflation and rising interest rates. The result: Bond prices begin tumbling and interest rates start climbing. In order to cut their losses, hundreds of floor traders at the CBOT are now screaming, jumping up and down, flailing hand signals in a desperate attempt to rid themselves of bonds whose values are fast eroding.

Stock investors are also dazed by the news and jump into action. A drop in unem-ployment is bullish for the economy. More consumer spending translates into higher business sales and fatter corporate profits, which can lift share prices. However, because the New York Stock Exchange, the world's largest marketplace for equities, doesn't start trading on the floor for another hour (9:30 a.m.), money managers rush to buy stock index futures on the Chicago Mercantile Exchange (CME), where S&P 500 and NASDAQ con-tracts are traded electronically virtually 24 hours a day, five days a week. Action here occurs at lightning speed, with orders being executed in just three tenths of a second—faster than the blink of an eye. The enthusiasm of traders in the premarket hours is a harbinger of things to come. By noon that day, stocks across the board reach their highest prices in months.

At the same time, the New York Mercantile Exchange explodes into action. Commodity specialists in the cavernous trading room are also caught off guard by the jobs report and are now gesturing wildly and barking out orders to buy oil and gasoline contracts on the expectation that a resilient economy will drive up demand for fuel in the future. After all, as business activity accelerates, factories operate longer hours and use more electricity. Business and leisure travel should pick up as well. Airlines will use greater amounts of fuel. The positive jobs report will encourage more shopping and weekend getaway trips, resulting in greater gasoline consumption. Thus, moments after the Labor Department releases the news on jobs, the futures prices of gasoline, heating oil, and other types of fuel shoot up.

Meanwhile, in currency markets across Asia and Europe, news of the rebound in U.S. jobs makes the dollar a more attractive currency to own. Foreign investors are always keen on placing their money wherever they can earn a better payoff in the global marketplace. This morning, with U.S. interest rates and stocks both heading higher, owning American securities makes the most sense. Foreigners proceed to load up on U.S. equities and bonds, causing the dollar to climb in value against other currencies.

Back in Washington, hours earlier an emissary from the Labor Department delivered an advance copy of the employment release in a sealed package to the president's top economic adviser. White House officials now huddle to discuss ways to spin the positive jobs report for political gain. How should the president comment on it? Does the employment news require a change in public policy? How can it be used to support the administration's economic plan? What impact might it have on the federal budget?

Unquestionably the single most important institution to evaluate the crucial employment report is the Federal Reserve. Economists there also see the release before it goes public. They begin to scrutinize the data to detect any stress or imbalance in the labor market that could destabilize the economy. Fed experts ponder whether the unemployment rate is falling so fast that it will drive wages higher and fire up inflation pressures. As they pore over the jobs statistics, a secret but informal discussion commences inside the Fed on whether a change in interest rate policy is needed.

It has been a hectic morning for investors, policymakers, and reporters. But what about the vast majority of Americans? How did they respond to the turn of events in the employment report? Did they drop everything at 8:30 a.m. and rush off with paper and pen to the nearest television or radio to take notes on how the economy changed the month before? Not likely. In sharp contrast to all the frenetic activity in world financial markets, most households were preoccupied with carrying out the routines of daily life—getting ready for work, sending kids off to school, or doing some early shopping before the crowds show up at the supermarkets. Let's face it—the data released on jobs is just too remote and abstract to be of much interest to them. However, that doesn't mean the employment news will not affect them; everyone in the country will in some manner be touched by what transpired in the financial markets after the jobs report went public. It makes no difference whether one is a business owner, a retiree, a housewife, an employee, a homeowner, or a renter. All will eventually feel the fallout from the news that came from the Labor Department's pressroom that morning. That fallout will produce a mixture of both favorable and unfavorable developments.

What might the benefits be? Clearly, rising employment is positive for the economy. The more American workers earn, the more they have to spend on goods and services. As long as there's no danger of the economy expanding so fast that it threatens higher inflation, everyone gains from rising employment. Furthermore, the government spends less on unemployment benefits, which eases the strain on the federal budget. Now for the bad news. You'll recall that when the government released its surprisingly strong jobs report, it spooked bond traders into selling Treasury securities, which quickly drove up interest rates. With the cost of credit going up, banks and other lenders have little choice but to raise their rates on home mortgages and car loans. Even homeowners holding variable-rate mortgages now have to dig deeper into their pockets to make higher monthly payments. There's more bad news. Remember how commodity investors at the New York Mercantile Exchange reacted by bidding up the price of oil and other kinds of fuel? That will shortly spill into the retail sector, which means drivers will end up paying extra for gas, and homeowners will shell out more for heating oil. Plane travel becomes more expensive too as airlines boost fares to offset the higher cost of aviation fuel.

Now let's return to positive consequences. In foreign exchange markets, the dollar's value jumped in response to the jobs news. A stronger U.S. currency is good for American consumers because it lowers the price of imports such as foreign-made cars, home electronics, and perfumes. That, in turn, puts pressure on U.S. firms to keep their own prices down, all of which helps contain U.S. inflation. Americans traveling overseas also can purchase more with each dollar. However, here's the flip side to a muscular greenback: If your job depends on selling products in foreign markets, you could be in trouble. A strong dollar makes U.S.-made goods more expensive in other countries, and foreign buyers might want to look elsewhere for better deals.

U.S. Economic Indicators

It may be hard to believe all this action and reaction can be triggered by just a single statistic. If you multiply that by more than 50 economic indicators that are released every week, month, or quarter, you begin to understand why the stock, bond, and currency markets are in a perpetual state of motion. Among the other influential economic indicators that can rattle financial markets are consumer prices, industrial production, retail sales, and new-home construction. It is precisely because these indicators can so easily sway the value of investments that the government takes extraordinary steps to control the flow of sensitive economic information.

That wasn't always the case. Thirty years ago, barely any guidelines applied to the release of economic reports. A lock-up room was a term reserved for prisons, not press-rooms. The lack of strict ground rules on the publication of these influential statistics created the perfect climate for abuse. Politicians tried to control the release of economic news to score points with voters. When President Nixon heard that the Commerce Department was about to go public with an upbeat figure on housing starts, he pressed the agency to time the release for maximum political effect. On those occasions when economic figures turned out to be a liability, Nixon sought to hold up the report until such time he believed its release would get little notice.

Even Wall Street firms realized that big money could be made off the economic numbers given the lax supervision of their release. Some brokerages went so far as to dish out large amounts of money to reporters who were willing to leak economic news to the firm's traders before writing about it. Anyone who got an advance peek at the economic statistics stood to gain millions in a matter of minutes by knowing which stocks and bonds to trade. Eventually this blatant manipulation of the economic indicators led a furious Senator William Proxmire to schedule Congressional hearings in the 1970s on how these reports are released. Later that decade, the government set up a strict calendar that included rigid rules on how economic data would be distributed. Today, nearly every major economic indicator is released under tight lock-up conditions, which has enhanced the integrity of how the public gets such sensitive information. Trading based on inside information of economic indicators is now virtually unheard of.

This still leaves us with the most important task of all, though. How do you decipher what all these indicators actually tell us about the economy? After all, at least four key economic indicators are released on a weekly basis, 43 every month, and nine each quarter. Do we really need so many measures? Absolutely. The U.S. is the largest and most complex economy in the world. No single indicator can provide a complete picture of what the economy is up to. Nor is there a simple combination of measures that provide a connect-the-dots path to the future. At best, each indicator can give you a snapshot of what conditions are like within a specific sector of the economy at a particular point in time (see Table 1A). Ideally, when you piece together all these snapshots, they should provide a clearer picture of how the economy is faring and offer clues on where it is heading.

Yet even if you took the time to absorb every bit of economic information and monitored each squiggle in the indicators, don't expect to uncover a crystal-ball formula that can single-handedly forecast what consumer spending, inflation, and interest rates will do in the months ahead. That's because there are some important caveats when dealing with economic indicators. First, they often fail to paint a consistent picture of the economy. Different indicators can simultaneously flash conflicting signals on business conditions. One can show the economy improving, while another may point to a clear deterioration. For example, the government might report a drop in the unemployment rate, normally a bullish sign for the economy. However, a different employment survey might show a day

Table 1A: How Economic Indicators Track the U.S. Economy

The federal government and private groups release dozens of economic reports on a weekly, monthly, or quarterly basis. Each is a barometer that measures activity in a particular segment of the U.S. economy. By following these indicators, one can get the latest reading on the economy's health and valuable clues on where it is heading.

Real GDP and its Components *

Consumption (71%)

Goods (31%)

Services (40%)

Key Indicators

Retail sales

Consumer installment credit

Personal income and spending

Employment report

New claims for unemployment insurance

Consumer confidence and sentiment surveys

MBA - mortgage refinancings

ADP National Employment Report

ABC/Money consumer comfort index

Real earnings

Auto sales

Chain store sales

Business Fixed Investments (17%)

Nonresidential (12%)

Industrial production

Capacity utilization

Orders for durable goods

ISM surveys

Federal Reserve Bank regional surveys

Factory orders

Manufacturers' shipments, inventories, and orders

Housing starts

New single-family home sales

Existing home sales

MBA mortgage applications

Residential (5%)

NAHB survey on home building

* Percentages are based on how the economy performed in 2006

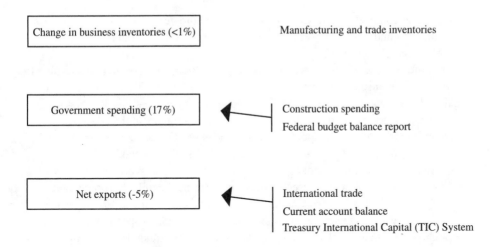

| Change in business inventories (<1%) | Manufacturing and trade inventories |

| Government spending (17%) | Construction spending |
| | Federal budget balance report |

Net exports (-5%)	International trade
	Current account balance
	Treasury International Capital (TIC) System

Signs of Price Pressures

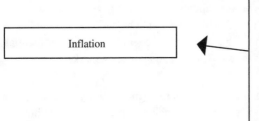

Inflation

Consumer price index
Producer price index
Employment cost index
Non-farm productivity
Unit labor costs
Import and export prices
Employer costs for employee compensation
Federal Open Market Committee (FOMC) Statement

or two later that companies are laying off workers in record numbers. You're now presented with two contradictory portraits of labor market conditions, both covering the same time period. Which should you believe?

The confusion doesn't stop there. Another complication, one especially maddening to investors and economists, is that people can behave counterintuitively. Just look at two ostensibly related reports: consumer confidence and consumer spending. The first measures the general mood of potential shoppers: If they are upbeat about the economy, it stands to reason they will spend more. If there is widespread gloom and uncertainty about the future, logic would lead you to believe people will curb their spending and save money instead. However, that's not the way it plays out in the real world. There appears to be little relationship between these two measures. During the mild 2001 recession, consumer confidence kept plummeting throughout the year, reaching levels not seen in decades. Yet these same consumers not only refused to cut back on spending that year, they bought homes and cars at a record pace. Obviously, one cannot determine the outlook for consumer spending just by monitoring the psychological state of American households. The inclination to spend is influenced by many factors, including personal income growth, job security, interest rates, and the buildup in wealth from the value of one's home and the ownership of stocks and bonds.

There is also the quandary that comes with abundance. Everyone—from the professional money manager down to the mom dabbling part time in the markets—can be overwhelmed by the statistical minutia out there. How do you discern which indicators are worth watching and which ones to view with skepticism or even ignore? How does an investor employ economic indicators to help choose which stocks and bonds to buy and sell, and when? Which measures should a business forecaster follow to spot coming economic trends? What key indicators should corporate chiefs rely on to help them decide whether to hire new workers or invest in new equipment?

You can find the answers to these questions in subsequent chapters, but clearly some economic indicators are far more telling than others. Generally, the most influential statistics—those most likely to shake up the stock, bond, and currency markets—possess some of the following attributes:

- **Accuracy:** Certain economic measures are known to be more reliable than others in assessing the economy's health. What determines their accuracy is linked to how the data is compiled. Most economic indicators are based on results of public surveys. Getting a large and representative sample is thus a prerequisite for accuracy. For instance, to measure the change in consumer price inflation, the government's Bureau of Labor Statistics sends out agents and conducts telephone interviews every month to find out how much prices have changed on 80,000 items and services at 23,000 retail outlets around the country. To calculate shifts in consumer confidence, the Conference Board, a business research organization, polls 5,000 households each month.

  Another variable is the proportion of those queried who actually came back with answers. How quickly did they respond? The bigger and faster the response, the better the quality of the data and the smaller the subsequent revisions. If an indicator has a history of suffering large revisions, it generally carries less weight in the financial markets. After all, why should an investor buy stocks or a company hire additional workers when the underlying economic statistic is suspect to begin with? The monthly construction spending report by the Commerce Department is one that gets substantially revised and is thus often ignored by the investment community. In contrast, housing starts figures are rarely revised, which is why this indicator is taken far more seriously.

- **Timeliness of the indicator:** Investors want the most immediate news of the economy that they can get their hands on. The older the data, the more yawns it evokes. The more current it is, the greater the wallop it packs on the markets. Case in point: Investors pay close attention to the employment situation report because it comes out barely a week after the month ends. In contrast, there's far less interest in the Federal Reserve's consumer installment credit report, whose information is two months old by the time it's released.

- **The business cycle stage:** There are moments when the release of certain economic indicators is awaited with great anticipation. Yet those same indicators barely get noticed at other times. Why do these economic measures jump in and out of the limelight? The answer is that much depends on where the U.S. economy stands in the business cycle. (The business cycle is a recurring pattern in the economy consisting first of growth, followed by weakness and recession, and finally by a resumption of growth. We'll take a closer look at the business cycle in the next chapter.) During a recession, when there are lots of unemployed workers and idle manufacturing capacity, inflation is less of a concern. Thus, measures such as the consumer price index, which gauges inflation at the retail level, do not have the same impact on the financial markets that they would if the economy were operating at full speed. During recessionary periods, indicators that grab the headlines are housing starts, auto sales, and the major stock indexes, because they often provide the earliest clues that an economic recovery is imminent. Once business activity is in full swing, inflation measures like the CPI take center stage again, while the other indicators recede a bit into the background.

- **Predictive ability:** A few indicators have a reputation of successfully spotting turning points in the economy well in advance. We mentioned how housing and auto sales as well as the stock indexes have such characteristics. However, other less-known measures are harbingers of a change in business activity. One such indicator is the advance orders for durable goods. Generally, economic gauges known for being ahead of the curve carry more weight with investors.

- **Degree of interest:** Depending on whether you're an investor, an economist, a manufacturer, or a banker, some indicators might be of greater interest to you than others. Business leaders, for instance, might focus on new home sales and existing home sales figures to see whether Americans are in a shopping mood. By monitoring such statistics, companies selling furniture and appliances can decide whether to expand operations, invest in new inventories, or shut down factories.

Those in the forecasting business want to know what's ahead for the economy and thus concentrate on a set of measures known as "leading indicators." These include initial unemployment claims, building permits, the ISM purchasing managers report, and the yield curve.

Investors in the financial markets also have their favorite indicators; the specific measures they watch depend on what assets are at greatest risk. Those trading stocks focus on indicators that foreshadow changes in consumer and business spending because they can affect future corporate profits and the price of shares (see Table 1B). For bond traders, the looming concern is not company profits, but the outlook for inflation and interest rates. Any evidence suggesting that inflation might accelerate can hurt bonds. (Table 1C shows the economic indicators most sensitive to the bond market.) Players in the currency markets look for economic news that can drive the dollar's value up or down. Signs pointing to a robust U.S. economy, for example, normally lure foreigners to invest in this country, especially if the other major economies show comparatively little growth. That lifts the greenback's value against other currencies. (Table 1D identifies the measures most likely to move the dollar.) Finally, we stated earlier that certain economic indicators have demonstrated over time an ability to spot turning points in the economy well in advance. Any unusual movement up or down in these forward-looking measures should tip off investors and business leaders to an upcoming shift in economic activity. The 10 indicators listed in Table 1E are particularly noteworthy, because history has shown them to be quite successful in sending early signals of a change underway in the economy. However, unlike the other tables, I have chosen not to formally rank the leading indicators, because no single one can act as the perfect crystal ball. The real value here is to see if two or more of these measures are behaving in a collective manner.

Table 1B: Economic Indicators Most Sensitive to Stocks

Rank	Indicator	Page
1	Employment Situation Report	25
2	ISM Report—Manufacturing	156
3	Weekly Claims for Unemployment Insurance	40
4	Consumer Prices	271
5	Producer Prices	273
6	Retail Sales	74
7	Consumer Confidence and Sentiment Surveys	92
8	Personal Income and Spending	63
9	Advance Report on Durable Goods	124
10	GDP	107

Table 1C: Economic Indicators Most Sensitive to Bonds

Rank	Indicator	Page
1	Employment Situation Report	25
2	Consumer Prices	271
3	ISM Report—Manufacturing	156
4	Producer Prices	283
5	Weekly Claims for Unemployment Insurance	40
6	Retail Sales	74
7	Housing Starts	178
8	Personal Income and Spending	63
9	ADP National Employment Report	55
10	GDP	107

Table 1D: Indicators That Most Influence the U.S. Dollar's Value

Rank	Indicator	Page
1	Employment Situation Report	25
2	International Trade	240
3	GDP	107
4	Current Account	254
5	Industrial Production/Capacity Utilization	145
6	ISM Report—Manufacturing	156
7	Retail Sales	74
8	Consumer Prices	271
9	Consumer Confidence and Sentiment Surveys	92
10	Productivity and Costs	303

Table 1E: Indicators That Lead the Rest of the Economy

Indicator	Page
Yield Curve	318
New Orders for Durable Goods	124
Producer Prices (crude goods without food and energy)	283
Personal Income and Spending (purchases of durable goods)	63
Housing Permits	178
Weekly Applications for Mortgages	200
Housing Market Index	196
Weekly Claims for Unemployment Insurance	40
Institute for Supply Management (manufacturing survey)	163
UBS/Gallup Survey of Investor Optimism	104

INTERNATIONAL ECONOMIC INDICATORS

Up to now, we've dealt only with U.S. economic reports. Now let's look at the growing importance of monitoring international economic indicators. During much of the twentieth century, Americans had only a remote interest in following the economic affairs of other nations. Few saw a need to take them more seriously. The U.S., after all, possessed the largest and most self-sufficient economy in the world and, by and large, had been impervious to the ups and downs of foreign economic cycles. If Germany or France or even the emerging countries of Asia suffered an economic downturn, barely anyone in the U.S. would care or even notice.

That's not the case any longer. Though the U.S. economy still reigns supreme, the international economy has undergone vast structural changes in the last three decades. These changes were brought on by a reduction in trade barriers, the modernization of global financial markets, remarkable advances in telecommunications, the Internet, computer technology, and software. The results have been profound. The world economy now operates in a more tightly integrated fashion.

For the U.S., the implications are huge. Healthy domestic economic performance depends increasingly on how well other nations are doing. Gone forever are the days when this country was immune to financial and political mishaps originating halfway around the world. When OPEC decided to sharply boost oil prices in the mid-to-late 1970s, Americans felt real pain. Indeed, U.S. inflation subsequently exploded, ultimately leading to one of the worst U.S. recessions since the Great Depression. Years later investors took another beating during the Asian financial crisis in 1997 when the Dow plummeted by the largest point loss ever on October 27 because investors were worried that problems in Asia would hurt the U.S. economy and corporate earnings. In addition, who would have imagined that a bond default by Russia in 1998—a country with an economy the size of Illinois and Wisconsin combined—would be considered so grave a threat to world financial markets that the Federal Reserve was under pressure to orchestrate a global rescue plan to calm investors worldwide?

Just how dependent have American companies become on other nations for profits and job creation? The numbers speak for themselves. Nearly half the earnings of S&P 500 firms come from business generated outside the U.S. More than 22 million American workers—nearly two in 10 jobs—are linked to foreign trade. One out of every four dollars generated in the U.S. economy is based on trade. What all this boils down to is that foreign economic indicators should be followed with the same regularity, interest, and scrutiny as the domestic indicators. If foreign economies do well, U.S. firms are in a better position to sell more exports, earn more money, and keep millions of American workers employed. By closely monitoring the international indicators, U.S. companies can seek out new foreign markets or decide whether to expand (or shut down) facilities overseas. American investors can diversify their portfolios more smartly by identifying and purchasing those foreign stocks and bonds that might offer a lucrative return.

Another important reason to monitor the performance of other major economies is that it helps us check the mood of foreign investors. As long as they view the U.S. as a safe and attractive place to invest, capital from abroad will continue to flow into this country, and that is vital to the well-being of the U.S. economy. Foreign investors play an indispensable role in financing U.S. economic growth by lending this country an average of more than $2 billion a day—money that goes into buying stocks, bonds, and other American assets. Why does the U.S. need to borrow such huge sums from other nations? Because consumers and the federal government together spend so much on cars, computers, military hardware, and health care (to name just a few items) that little domestic savings is left over. Yet savings is the lifeblood that keeps an economy healthy. It's used to finance productive investments, such as building efficient factories and funding the research and development of new and better products. Without adequate savings, the U.S. would be incapable of showing healthy long-term growth.

To make up for the shortfall in domestic savings, the U.S. has to lure the surplus savings of other countries. In addition, while all that foreign capital entering the U.S. has kept the economy humming, serious risks come with being so dependent on overseas creditors. America's net foreign debt has skyrocketed in the last decade from $50 billion to a staggering $2.5 trillion—the most of any nation in the world. In the process, foreigners have acquired an unprecedented share of U.S. assets; they own 45% of all U.S. Treasury issues, 40% of American corporate bonds, and more than 15% of all equities. Should the mood of those investors turn sour on the U.S. market—something that can occur if there is poor expectation of investment returns here as compared with other countries—it could spark a sell-off of American stocks and bonds by foreigners.

For all these reasons international economic indicators have lately taken on a more prominent role in the formulation of investment and business strategies. However, as with U.S. economic data, literally hundreds of foreign economic measures are released every month. With so much information being thrown at investors and business executives each day, how do you know which of these statistics are worthy of consideration? There is no one simple answer to this question. American companies and investors have different interests and risk exposures in the global economy.

In this book three factors are considered in determining the most influential international economic indicators. First, after the U.S., which are the largest economies in the world? Second, how liquid are the markets in those countries? That is, how easy is it to buy and sell securities on their exchanges? Third, who are the important trading partners of the U.S.? By trade, we're talking about the exchange of goods (such as the sale of trucks, pharmaceuticals, and computers) and the exchange of services (such as insurance, consulting, transportation, and entertainment). The service sector is especially important because it includes the all-important category of investment flows. Table 1F lists the "must-watch" international economic indicators.

Table 1F: Top International Economic Indicators

Indicator	Page
German Industrial Production	328
German IFO Business Survey	330
German Consumer Price Index	332
Japan Tankan Survey	336
Japan Industrial Production	342
Eurozone/Global Purchasing Managers Index	347
OECD Composite Leading Indicators (CLI)	354
China Industrial Production	357
India GDP and Wholesale Price Index	362
Brazil Industrial Production	368

CHAPTER 2

A Beginner's Guide: Understanding the Lingo

Every field of study has its own jargon, an assortment of words or phrases with which one has to grow familiar to understand the subject. Economic indicators are no different. You will regularly come across certain terms and expressions when dealing with measures of economic performance. No need to worry, though. The language of economic indicators is fairly straightforward if you give it a chance. In many cases their meaning and significance are surprisingly obvious. So let's proceed with some of the most common concepts you'll encounter when reading about these indicators.

ANNUAL RATES

You're cruising down the highway at 65 miles per hour. Whether your destination is actually 65 miles away is not important. What counts is what your speedometer tells you: If you keep up this driving pace for a full hour, you will travel about 65 miles.

The term "miles per hour" is used to measure relative speed. A similar relationship exists with economic indicators. A common way to compare how fast the economy is growing is to measure changes in activity in the form of annual rates. For instance, the government might report that autos were selling at a 14 million vehicle annual rate the previous month. That doesn't mean automakers sold 14 million cars and trucks the month before; it's how many will be sold if last month's pace were maintained for each of the next 12 months. Why do it this way? The reason is experts find it easier to look at performance on a yearly basis.

The methodology used to annualize a figure is simple enough: To turn a monthly level into an annual rate, simply multiply it by 12. If you have two months of data that you want to annualize, multiply it by 6. If it's a quarterly change—which is how the GDP is reported—multiply the three-month change in activity by 4. Thus, whenever you see an economic indicator reported in an annual rate, it is telling you what will happen if that pace were sustained for a full 12 months.

BUSINESS CYCLE

Like human nature, the economy has its ups and downs. At times the economy can grow robustly, with household income rising, consumers happily spending, and companies hiring and expanding their businesses. However, there also are periods when the economy looks tired, with growth barely perceptible. There is less consumer shopping and little, if any, new business investment is under way. In the most extreme case, the economy actually shrinks, which is what happens in a recession. Over time, however, recessions give way to a fresh round of economic activity. These swings, from good times to awful times and then eventually back to good times again, are roughly what we mean by a business cycle.

Why does the economy have such cycles? Why not have steady, continuous, nonstop growth? After all, that should make everyone happy.

The reason the economy is condemned to undergo business cycles is because it's only natural. An open economy is essentially a reflection of human behavior, with millions of people making decisions every day. What should they buy? How much can they spend? Is it time to invest in stocks? Corporate leaders face different issues. Is it time to hire workers? Rebuild inventories? Buy another company?

Occasionally consumers and businesses make mistakes that can have broader economic consequences. Households might have borrowed so much that they're having difficulty servicing their debt. Banks could see their profits slip as loan defaults rise. Retailers might miscalculate by filling their stockrooms with new goods just when consumers are cutting back on spending. If the mistakes are grave enough and widespread, they can lead to an economic downturn, with people being laid off. Fortunately, the government has several tools at its disposal to revive growth, such as lower interest rates, tax cuts, and greater federal spending.

The business cycle itself has five phases. The first phase is the highest point of output the economy achieves just before it gets into trouble and turns down. After the peak comes phase two, which is the recession itself, a painful process whereby the economy actually shrinks. It saps the wealth and confidence of households and causes all sorts of financial distress for business. Such economic contractions can last six months or as long as several years. The third phase is reached when the economy finally hits bottom, a point known as the recession trough. The fourth phase occurs after the economy stops shrinking and resumes it growth path, or recovery. Finally, when the level of economic activity (or output) pushes past the previous high point, the business cycle marks the fifth and last phase, often called the expansion.

Because a recession is an integral part of the business cycle, it's important to define just what we mean by that term. Many economists and journalists declare a recession when there are two back-to-back quarters of negative GDP growth. Those quarters equal six consecutive months where the economy is shrinking. However, that is a rough, finger-in-the-wind assessment. The real task of determining when a recession begins and ends is left to a select group of academic economists working under the National Bureau of Economic Research (NBER), a nongovernmental and nonpartisan think tank based in Massachusetts. They make the call on whether the economy has turned down or up by evaluating several key economic indicators, such as job growth, personal income, industrial production, as well as the quarterly GDP figures.

According to the NBER, there have been 32 business cycles in the U.S. since 1854, with the average recession lasting 17 months. Since World War II, there have been 10 business cycles, with recessions averaging only 10 months long—which means the economy is now achieving longer periods of growth before getting into trouble. Just why the economy has been experiencing fewer recessions lately is a topic of debate among economists, though most attribute it to improved economic policymaking in Washington, combined with a more versatile business sector.

Consensus Surveys

You're all set to go out for a leisurely walk. Weather forecasters have predicted sunny skies and warm temperatures, so you head out in shorts and leave the sweater at home. Ten minutes later a heavy thunderstorm erupts, followed by colder air. You quickly scramble back for a change of clothing, all the while cursing the forecasters. How could they have gotten it so wrong?

Money managers encounter similar experiences, except that instead of weather reports, they tend to rely on surveys that feature forecasts from experts on what an upcoming economic indicator will report. If the actual economic news falls in line with expectations, there is generally little market reaction to the news, because investors already anticipated it. By getting it right, those forecasters demonstrated that they have a good grasp on what the economy is up to. However, had the news about the economy turned out to be radically different from what private experts predicted, money managers would have rushed in to readjust their investment positions. These abrupt moves can potentially shake up the value of stocks, bonds, and currencies. Why such violent market reactions? Any major departure from expectation means that something is going on in the economy for which the experts failed to account. Naturally this creates fresh uncertainty about current and future economic conditions. The bigger the gap between consensus expectations and reality, the larger the backlash in the financial markets.

Who puts out these consensus surveys, and how are they done? Many financial wire service organizations, such as Bloomberg, Dow Jones, Reuters, and Market News International, produce their own consensus surveys by polling economists for their predictions on key upcoming economic indicators. These indicators include consumer prices, producer prices, industrial production, retail sales, capacity utilization, and others. The methodology used is fairly simple: The responses of individual business economists are basically averaged out, and that becomes the consensus forecast.

MOVING AVERAGE

There's great temptation to jump to a conclusion about the economy's health from just one month's data, but that's not a wise practice. Economic numbers can be faulty, inaccurate, or, at the very least, misleading because of unusual events such as a major labor strike or severe weather conditions. Such situations can diminish the reliability of an economic indicator in the short term, so it's important to use caution when extrapolating information from just a single month's data.

To get a truer sense of the underlying trend in the economy, it's far better to rely on a moving average of economic numbers. Simply put, a moving average is a computation in constant motion, because it always averages data for the most recent fixed number of months. As a result, the average changes with the introduction of each new monthly report. For example, let's say consumer price inflation shot up 1% in the most recent month. Obviously a rise of that magnitude could raise lots of red flags. However, before anyone panics, it's far more prudent to consider inflation's actual trend by looking at its moving average over the past three or six months. To do this, simply add up the inflation changes over the last three or six months and divide by the total number of months you considered. When the next set of inflation figures are released a month later, recalculate the moving average by including the new figure in the equation and discarding the oldest monthly data so that you are always averaging the latest three- or six-month periods. The virtue of moving averages is that they smooth out random fluctuations and make long-term trends clearer. One disadvantage of a moving average is that it's a lagging indicator. Averages are slower to respond when there's a genuine change in the economy's direction.

NOMINAL DOLLARS VERSUS REAL DOLLARS (ALSO KNOWN AS CURRENT DOLLARS VERSUS CONSTANT DOLLARS)

Anything measured in dollars can be looked at in two ways. Nominal dollars (also referred to as current dollars) represents the actual amount of money spent or earned over a period of time. You'll see stories mentioning how American factory workers received total pay hikes of $500 million, or a 5% increase, in the last 12 months. Or perhaps you read that company A reported that income from sales of sweaters climbed to $220 million that year, up from $200 million the year before, or a jump of 10%. These figures are based in nominal dollars.

However, nominal (or current) dollars gives you only part of the story. What's missing is how inflation can distort such numbers. Let's go back to the example of the earnings of factory workers. They might have seen their pay jump by 5% in nominal terms, but before anyone celebrates, someone should ask this question: "What if the price of goods and services (that is, inflation) rose by 4% during that same period?" In that case, the wages of these workers rose by a less-than-impressive 1% in real (or constant) dollars. In other words, the actual increase in purchasing power these workers gained from their pay hike was far smaller than 5%.

Let's now look at company A. It noted that sales revenue jumped by 10%. However, that doesn't necessarily mean it sold 10% more sweaters. In fact, the firm ended up selling the same number of sweaters both years. The only reason it received more money in the second year is because the company raised the price of sweaters by 10%. Thus, the increase in real (constant) dollar sales was actually zero!

Nominal dollars simply reflects the present value of goods and services exchanged in the marketplace. However, real dollars tells you the true value of goods and services produced or sold, because it strips out the effects of inflation. When economists and investors want to compare the economy's performance over different time frames, they generally look at both measures—nominal and real. They note the change in the size of the economy in nominal dollars because that points to what individuals, businesses, and the government actually spent. However, to find out if the economy genuinely expanded by producing more in quantity or volume, economists and investors look at the numbers in real-dollar terms.

REVISIONS AND BENCHMARKS

Traders and money managers are always hungry for the very latest piece of economic news. The more timely the information, the more influential it is; and the faster investors can get their hands on it, the quicker they can act.

Therein lies the problem. Government agencies and private groups that supply economic data to the public are under tremendous pressure to get it out quickly, and that's not easy. Every week or month, depending on the economic indicator, statisticians follow a rigid schedule to query sources in the field, collect the raw responses, organize the data, readjust for seasonal factors, perhaps recalculate the numbers to adjust for inflation, and then write some introductory comments about the results before finally releasing it to the public. It's a hurried process in which accuracy and completeness at times take a backseat to getting the information out on deadline. For this reason, the first release of many economic indicators contains pieces of data that are far from reliable and thus are considered preliminary.

Of course, to many investors, it makes little difference whether the initial data is reliable. They trade on these numbers anyway, because the figures represent the very latest information they can get on the economy. Later, though, as more information is received and after statisticians have had a chance to review their computations, the preliminary figures undergo one or more revisions. Though investors also see the revisions to earlier data, they generally do not spark much trading because by then the information refers to a time period that has long since passed. Investors usually focus on the future, not the past. Economists, however, take revisions more seriously because the new figures can affect their forecasts of economic activity.

Benchmark changes are different from monthly revisions. The latter are an ongoing effort to make the statistical results more accurate, especially if there was insufficient time to gather all the data. In contrast, benchmark changes occur about once a year or so, when the government introduces new seasonal adjustment factors or decides to undertake a formal change in the methodology itself. Benchmark revisions can affect economic data going back five, 10, or even more years to allow for historical comparisons.

SEASONAL ADJUSTMENTS

Before most economic indicators are released, they are calculated to reflect seasonal adjustments. What are seasonal adjustments? The simplest way to answer this question is with an example. It's no surprise that consumers do a lot more shopping during the November/December holiday period than at other times of the year. In addition, when the Christmas shopping season is over, retail sales often slow in January and February. These seasonal shifts in consumer spending patterns are quite common. They're temporary changes that have nothing to do with the business cycle.

Let's look at another example. In the spring when schools let out, the number of people getting jobs surges as students enter the workforce to earn money over the summer. By mid-August, the process is reversed, and employment drops off as students leave the workforce and return to school. Again, these fluctuations in employment are perfectly normal and do not indicate a fundamental change in the economy's health. Even industrial production tends to fall in July as automakers shut down plants that month to retool their assembly lines for the new model year. No one should conclude this slowdown in industrial output means that the manufacturing sector is in trouble. These are all routine seasonal shifts that take place in the economy.

How do you differentiate changes that are the result of normal seasonal factors from those that represent a more serious problem in the economy? That's where the seasonal adjustment process comes in. Government experts look at economic data going back five to 10 years to identify recurring trends. These trends are changes in economic activity that have nothing to do with the broader business cycle but that can be explained by short-term external factors (such as summers, winters, and major holidays). After observing such patterns, officials come up with a formula that factors out variations in the economic numbers attributable to seasonal changes. This enables private economists and investors to distinguish economic events that should be viewed as normal from those that are out of the ordinary.

Seasonal adjustments, however, are far from perfect. You could have abnormal economic data even after seasonal adjustments are considered, and it still doesn't necessarily signal a turning point in the economy. Blizzards, floods, terrorism, labor strikes, and major bankruptcies are all unpredictable shocks that can have an impact on economic output, but their effects are almost always short-lived. Moreover, these incidents are easy to identify as the cause of any sharp deviation in business activity. By and large, seasonal adjustments are important to analysts because they can help identify true deviations from the normal course of activity in the economy.

Now that we have reviewed some of the most widely used terms that accompany economic indicators, we're ready to move on to the next chapters. What are the world's most influential economic indicators, and how do you get the most out of these statistics? How do you locate them? Interpret them? Most important of all, where can you find the clues that can tip you off to how the economy might perform in the future?

CHAPTER 3

THE MOST INFLUENTIAL
U.S. ECONOMIC INDICATORS

EMPLOYMENT SITUATION

Market Sensitivity: Very high.

What Is It: The most eagerly awaited news on the economy. Are jobs being created? It has great economic and political significance.

News Release on the Internet: *http://stats.bls.gov/news.release/empsit.toc.htm*

Home Web Address: *http://stats.bls.gov/*

Release Time: 8:30 a.m. (ET); generally announced on the first Friday of each month and covers the month just concluded.

Frequency: Monthly.

Source: Bureau of Labor Statistics, Department of Labor.

Revisions: Can be major. Revisions often go back two months with each release. The government does benchmark changes for the establishment (or payroll) survey every June. Benchmark changes for the household survey are rare—about every 10 years or so.

WHY IS IT IMPORTANT?

This is the big one! No single economic indicator can jolt the stock and bond markets as much as the jobs report. The reason? To begin with, the employment news is very timely. It's released just a week after the end of the month being reviewed. Second, the report is rich in detail about the job market and household earnings, information that can help forecast future economic activity. Third, let's face it—we're talking about the well-being of American workers. Wages and salaries from employment make up the main source of household income. The more workers earn, the more they buy and propel the economy forward. If fewer people are working, spending drops off, and business suffers. Because household spending accounts for more than two-thirds of the economy's total output, you can see why the investment community and the Federal Reserve pay such close attention to the employment report.

There is another reason why it has such a hold on financial markets and policymakers. The job numbers often contain surprises. Experts have a difficult time trying to predict the unemployment figures because so little other information is out yet for that month.

The highlight of the jobs report is, of course, the unemployment rate, which is the percentage of the civilian workforce that is unemployed. What do we mean by civilian workforce? By definition it is anyone 16 years or older who is classified as employed or unemployed (excluding the population in the military, prisons, mental hospitals, and nursing homes). Economists measure monthly changes in the job market from two different sources. One is based on the *household survey*, which the government conducts by telephone and mail interviews of households. The other is the *establishment* (or *payroll*) *survey*, in which companies are directly queried about recent changes in staffing. Together, the two surveys paint a sweeping picture of the labor market and, more broadly, the state of the economy's health.

How Is It Computed?

Household Survey

It's from the household survey that we derive the widely reported unemployment rate. Each month the government contacts 60,000 homes, a population that includes farm as well as non-farm workers, the self-employed, domestic helpers, and—believe it or not—even U.S. residents who commute to jobs in Mexico and Canada. (The point of the latter is that these Americans still earn money, make payments to the IRS, and are close enough to the U.S. to spend a part of their income here.) Here's a sample of the questions asked in these surveys: Are you working? Was the job full- or part-time? If you had a part-time job, was it because you couldn't find suitable full-time work? If you are not working, how many weeks have you been unemployed? How long have you been looking for work? Did you make an attempt in the last four weeks to find a job?

The response rate from households is fairly high—about 95% of those queried do respond. Thus, out of 60,000 households, some 57,000 come back with answers, while 3,000 are not heard from. All the interviews are done either in the week that contains the 12th day of each month, or just days later. Based on the information received, the size of the civilian labor force is calculated, along with how many of these people currently have jobs. Then comes a simple equation: divide the number of those over the age of 16 who are not working by the total number of people in the civilian labor force, and voila!—you have the unemployment rate. If the size of the civilian labor force is 100 million, and 5 million of them are out of work, the nation's unemployment rate is 5%.

While it's not rocket science to identify someone who is jobless, there is a bit more confusion about who is actually included in the labor force. Normally we do not count the military because everyone in uniform has a job, which is to protect the U.S. So the civilian labor force is the main measure used to quantify the pool of labor available in the economy. However, after that, the definitions get a little cloudy. Among the unemployed, the government includes in its labor force only those who are actively looking for work. What is meant by "actively looking for work"? Simply this: the individual must have made a specific effort to find employment within the previous four weeks. Any jobless person who is so discouraged by the poor employment prospects that he or she is not actively seeking employment is excluded from the labor force count and thus is not reflected in the main unemployment rate. (To be fair, the employment report does publish a separate unemployment rate that includes even discouraged workers, but this little-known figure is buried deep in the 25-page release. You'll see precisely where in the next section, "The Tables: Clues on What's Ahead for the Economy.")

The data in the household survey can be quite valuable to anyone doing research on demographics and marketing. It breaks down the population of those who have jobs—and those who do not—by age, sex, ethnicity, educational achievement, and marital status. The highest jobless rate is usually found among teenagers, both male and female. That's followed by blacks, Hispanics, and then whites. The lowest unemployment has traditionally been married men. Another interesting pattern is the link between joblessness and education. The unemployment rate is nearly always highest for those with less than a high school diploma—and then steadily drops as the level of education increases. The workforce that consistently has the lowest unemployment rate is the group that possesses at least a four-year college degree.

Clearly, lots of useful information can be gleaned from the data. However, one should bear in mind that the household jobs survey has one serious vulnerability. Its integrity is based on the answers given by household members, and they might not always be accurate. For example, some people may be too embarrassed to admit they are unemployed and instead describe themselves as a "consultant."

Establishment Survey

The establishment survey—often referred to as the payroll survey—is considered by many to be a better employment measure than the household survey. Consequently, it has grabbed most of the attention of the press and money managers around the world. What's special about it? The information it gathers on the job market comes directly from business establishments, not households. The Bureau of Labor Statistics (BLS) gets in touch with 400,000 companies and government agencies. These entities employ more than 40 million workers, or about 45% of total non-farm employment. The information is obtained by both mail and telephone, and it is collected using the same mid-month schedule as the household survey. Given the large number of places to contact, only 60% to

70% of the responses make it back in time for the first scheduled release of the employ-ment numbers. The reason for the initial low response is that small businesses are notori-ous for being late with their replies, yet these firms traditionally are the first to hire and fire workers. As more of them eventually submit their answers, the response rate climbs to the mid-80% range, which forms the basis of subsequent revisions in each of the next two months.

The establishment survey includes all persons on the payroll of non-farm businesses; nonprofit groups; and local, state, and federal government offices. Even residents of Mexico and Canada who travel to their jobs in the U.S. are counted. That last group might strike some as bizarre. Remember, however, that all the establishment survey does is tally the number of jobs created or lost in the U.S. business and government sectors, regardless of who filled those posts. The only groups excluded from the establishment survey are farm workers, the self-employed, and domestic help.

What makes the establishment survey such a favorite among economists and investors is that it contains a veritable gold mine of data on the latest changes in employ-ment and income—information that can reveal much about how well the U.S. economic machine is working. To give you a sense of the richness of the data in the payroll num-bers, the government looks at more than 500 different industries. Among the most impor-tant statistics from the report is the net number of new jobs formed or lost in the latest month. How long did the average workweek last? How much overtime was generated? What were the average hourly and weekly earnings in the month, and how do they com-pare to earlier periods? The establishment survey also breaks down many of these issues by geographic location and specific industry, so you can quickly tell which businesses and regions in the country are doing well and which appear to be in a slump.

An interesting question arises at this point. Because the household and establishment surveys are based on two different sources, to what extent do they agree with what's hap-pening in the employment market? It should come as no surprise that they occasionally tell conflicting stories. For instance, if the unemployment rate, a figure derived from the household survey, drops one month, it gives the impression that the economy is improv-ing and that more people are finding jobs. Yet the establishment survey may simultane-ously report that tens of thousands of jobs were actually lost that month.

Why do the two measures occasionally diverge? The reason is that they each probe the job market from different perspectives. The household survey collects data on work-ing-age individuals, while the establishment survey doesn't bother with age. It merely asks companies if they hired new workers. Second, the two surveys have separate guide-lines. The household poll includes both farm and non-farm workers, the self-employed, and domestic help. In contrast, the establishment survey covers a narrower population segment by looking only at non-farm workers in the economy; it excludes the others.

Another key difference between the two surveys is that the establishment report makes no distinction between full- and part-time work. Remember, its main focus is to report how many jobs were created. If an individual has two part-time jobs, the household survey counts that as one employed person, but the establishment survey classifies it as two jobs. Thus, if 100 new positions were created according to the establishment survey, this doesn't necessarily mean that 100 people found new employment. One individual could be holding multiple part-time jobs. Another key difference is the treatment of those who are self-employed; they are counted in the household series but not in the establishment series. Thus, it is easy to see why the two reports might conflict. However, that doesn't undermine their validity. Each survey has important information about the economy that the other lacks. In any event, over the long run, both the household and establishment numbers move in tandem.

THE TABLES: CLUES ON WHAT'S AHEAD FOR THE ECONOMY

Let's look at the nuggets of information in the official release that can provide fresh insight into current labor market conditions and what they say about the economy's future direction.

- **Table A**   Major Indicators of Labor Market Activity

  This page summarizes the employment situation for the month, and it is well worth devoting some time to become familiar with how it is presented. The top half contains household data, and the bottom half is from the establishment survey.

Table A. Major indicators of labor market activity, seasonally adjusted
(Numbers in thousands)

Category	Quarterly averages 2003 III	Quarterly averages 2003 IV	Monthly data 2003 Nov.	Monthly data 2003 Dec.	Monthly data 2004 Jan.	Dec.- Jan. change [1]
HOUSEHOLD DATA			Labor force status			
Civilian labor force.....................................	146,628	146,986	147,187	146,878	146,863	422
1 ▶ Employment.....................................	137,647	138,369	138,533	138,479	138,566	496
Unemployment.................................	8,981	8,616	8,653	8,398	8,297	-74
Not in labor force..................................	74,885	75,290	75,093	75,631	75,298	-210
			Unemployment rates			
All workers..	6.1	5.9	5.9	5.7	5.6	-0.1
Adult men..	5.8	5.5	5.6	5.3	5.1	-.2
Adult women....................................	5.2	5.1	5.1	5.1	5.0	-.1
2 ▶ Teenagers...	17.5	16.3	15.7	16.1	16.7	.6
White	5.4	5.1	5.2	5.0	4.9	-.1
Black or African American	11.0	10.7	10.4	10.3	10.5	.2
Hispanic or Latino ethnicity...................	7.8	7.1	7.4	6.6	7.3	.7
ESTABLISHMENT DATA [2]			Employment			
Nonfarm employment............................	129,820	p130,005	130,027	p130,043	p130,155	p112
Goods-producing [3].............................	21,718	p21,677	21,686	p21,670	p21,677	p7
Construction................................	6,738	p6,770	6,771	p6,784	p6,808	p24
Manufacturing.............................	14,410	p14,337	14,344	p14,317	p14,306	p-11
3 ▶ Service-providing [3]............................	108,102	p108,328	108,341	p108,373	p108,478	p105
Retail trade.................................	14,912	p14,917	14,922	p14,881	p14,957	p76
Professional and business services........	16,023	p16,114	16,114	p16,159	p16,137	p-22
Education and health services.............	16,594	p16,706	16,705	p16,734	p16,756	p22
Leisure and hospitality....................	12,120	p12,173	12,178	p12,193	p12,214	p21
Government.................................	21,560	p21,548	21,544	p21,539	p21,526	p-13
			Hours of work [4]			
Total private..	33.6	p33.7	33.8	p33.5	p33.7	p0.2
4 ▶ Manufacturing.................................	40.2	p40.6	40.8	p40.6	p40.9	p.3
Overtime..	4.1	p4.5	4.5	p4.6	p4.6	p.0
			Indexes of aggregate weekly hours (2002=100) [4]			
Total private..	98.2	p98.6	99.0	p98.0	p98.8	p0.8
			Earnings [4]			
5 ▶ Average hourly earnings, total private..........	$15.41	p$15.45	$15.46	p$15.47	p$15.49	p$0.02
Average weekly earnings, total private..........	517.67	p520.26	522.55	p518.25	p522.01	p3.76

(1) This section has the latest count on the size of the civilian labor force and the number of those who are, and are not, employed. The far-right column is the change in the figures from one month to the next. Of all the numbers in this section, the most interesting to watch are changes in household employment. This can be a sensitive leading indicator of an economy turning up, because household employment also captures the self-employed and the people they hire, something the payroll survey doesn't do. Both the number of self-employed and those working for small start-up firms tend to increase at a faster rate than the rest of the labor market in the early stages of a recovery. Thus, as a recession nears its end, keep an eye on household employment; it may start to climb well before the payroll statistics do.

(2) Here you'll find the latest monthly unemployment rates for all workers, along with a demographic breakdown of that population. Many economists often refer to the unemployment rate as a lagging indicator, which means it responds slowly to changes in the economy. As a result, they say, one can divine little from it about the future. However, that's not quite the case. By and large, the unemployment rate itself is of no use in forecasting an economic recovery. Joblessness can remain stubbornly high as long as two years after a recession ends because most employers are reluctant to add to their payrolls until they're convinced the economy is genuinely on a solid growth path. Another reason for the slow rebound in job creation is that companies have made great strides in operating more efficiently. Thanks to the widespread use of computerized equipment, better inventory management, and greater foreign outsourcing of production, employers can more easily raise output without hiring back U.S. workers in the numbers they once did.

Where the unemployment rate can serve as a leading indicator is by warning of an impending downturn in economic activity. Since the early 1980s, the increased use of sophisticated software and information technologies has allowed firms to respond much more quickly than in the past to changes in the demand for goods and services. As soon as executives detect signs of a softening in business activity, they act faster to control costs. Because labor is the single largest expense for companies, layoffs are now occurring months before the onset of a recession. In the 1990–1991 recession, the jobless rate began to climb three months before business activity turned down. And when the 2001 recession started, the unemployment rate bottomed out a year earlier. Thus, this indicator can act as an early warning system that the economy may be in trouble.

One last point about the unemployment rate: Roughly 150,000 new people of working age enter the labor force every month simply because of the nation's population growth and from students who graduate. This means that the economy needs to create that many jobs each month, on average, just to keep the unemployment rate from rising. Most economists seem to agree that to produce that many new positions every month, the economy must over time expand by at least a 3–4% annual rate. Should growth fall below that pace, fewer jobs are created, and the unemployment rate will climb higher.

(3) Want to know which economic statistic generates the most excitement in the stock and bond markets every month? It's the monthly change in non-farm employment from the establishment data. All the figures in this section are derived from payroll records and represent the strongest evidence of whether the country is creating jobs. Many analysts evaluate the economy's strength on the basis of how many net new positions have been formed. However, one has to be careful about jumping to conclusions. The change in the number of non-farm jobs created includes positions in government. To find out what is happening in the private business sector, one has to subtract the government's contribution from total non-farm payroll. Here's an illustration of why that could be important. Let's say the establishment survey shows the number of non-farm jobs dropped by a net 50,000 workers in one month. A troubling sign for the economy? Not necessarily. It could be that the business community was strong enough to create 30,000 net new jobs in the month, but that was offset when the government laid off 80,000 people in the same period (30,000 – 80,000 = –50,000). In this example, the business community was healthy enough to add 30,000 workers, but that was overshadowed by cutbacks in government jobs. Thus, it's important to keep an eye on how federal, state, and local governments influence overall non-farm employment.

(4) Differences in hours worked is another advance indicator of future economic activity. If you want to get a preview of the economy's direction, follow the changes in average hours worked in a week. It correlates very closely with overall output (GDP) and also changes in personal income. If the number of hours worked increases for three consecutive months, it's a strong sign that business will soon accelerate hiring. Should the number of hours worked show a prolonged decline, expect layoffs and cutbacks in business and consumer spending. The number of hours worked in manufacturing is especially sensitive to any shift in the public's demand for goods. When average weekly manufacturing hours dips below 41, it's often an indication that the economy is struggling, while 41.5 hours and above suggests that business activity is moving into higher gear. In recent history, average hours worked in manufacturing has ranged from a recession-level 40.1 to a robust 42 hours.

Inside the employment report, you'll also find Table B-2 (not shown), which breaks down hours worked for over 30 industry groups. This information can tip off investors on the health of specific sectors in the economy. For example, if average weekly hours in the building industry drops, it could lead a fall in housing starts, cause higher unemployment among construction workers, and hurt other firms whose fortunes are linked to home building. Indeed, anyone considering whether to buy or sell stocks of homebuilding companies should monitor these economic indicators. They can signal a change in revenues and profits with major homebuilders months before these firms release their quarterly earnings statements.

Overtime hours are another excellent indicator of future employment and GDP trends. During periods of economic uncertainty, instead of hiring new workers, companies might ask existing employees to put in extra hours. If overtime increases and that pace is sustained for at least three months, firms will be under pressure to consider hiring again. Overtime can be quite costly to a company, and, let's face it, at some point you will exhaust your present employees and diminish the quality of their work. Thus, rising overtime is a precursor to new permanent hires. Weekly manufacturing overtime normally fluctuates within a narrow range of between 4 and 5 hours. If it slips below 4 hours a week for a few months, layoffs might increase. A consistent reading above 4.5 overtime hours presages new hiring.

(5) At the bottom of Table A are the average hourly and weekly earnings for the month. The value of these measures should be obvious. If worker income rises, it bodes well for future spending. More elaborate information on hourly and weekly earnings can be found in Table B-3 (not shown), which looks at pay by selected industries. Rising earnings can reveal those industries that are doing well and where there might be a growing scarcity of experienced workers.

- **Table A-5** Employed Persons by Class of Worker and Part-Time Status

(6) Figures on part-time employment tell an interesting tale that analysts often miss. When it's hard to get suitable full-time work, many people have no choice but to accept part-time employment. This table shows the number of people in the non-farm economy who have accepted part-time work for economic reasons, which means they could not locate suitable full-time positions. A steady upward trend in the numbers suggests that the economy is still weak and unable to generate enough full-time posts to satisfy job seekers. Should the number of forced part-time workers decline, it means that enough full-time jobs are becoming available to encourage part-timers to leave their posts.

- **Table A-8** Unemployed Persons by Reason for Unemployment

(7) A favorite statistic followed by Federal Reserve officials but given less coverage in the press is the "quit rate." This term is jargon for what is formally listed in the table as "job leavers." The reason this particular measure is popular with policymakers is the logic behind it. Of all those unemployed, the "job leavers" ratio represents the percentage of workers who *voluntarily* left their jobs to seek greater opportunities. These people deliberately quit one job without immediately acquiring another, confident that they will find more lucrative employment relatively quickly. Normally, job leavers in this table fluctuate between 10% and 15% of the unemployed. When the job leavers rate declines, it is a sign that fewer workers are willing to quit, because they see a deterioration in the job market. If the rate increases, it suggests that the economy is generating enough new jobs for workers to feel more comfortable about giving up their current posts and searching for something better.

- **Table A-9** Unemployed Persons by Duration of Unemployment

(8) Another very good barometer of economic activity can be found in Table A-9, which shows not just the size of the unemployed population, but how long they've been without jobs. The length of time unemployed in the table ranges from less than five weeks to 27 weeks and more. A sharp increase in the number of persons out of work five weeks or less means that companies are laying off workers in greater numbers. Also noteworthy is the other end of the jobless extreme, those unemployed 27 weeks and more. That's because by then most unemployment insurance benefits have expired, and this can have all sorts of implications for society. There is a likelihood of more crime, greater homelessness, and additional spending on public welfare programs. A falling trend in the duration of the unemployed is a portent that the worst of the economy's troubles are over and that a recovery might be under way.

Table A-5. Employed persons by class of worker and part-time status

(In thousands)

Category	Not seasonally adjusted			Seasonally adjusted					
	Jan. 2003	Dec. 2003	Jan. 2004	Jan. 2003	Sept. 2003	Oct. 2003	Nov. 2003	Dec. 2003	Jan. 2004
CLASS OF WORKER									
Agriculture and related industries	2,134	2,053	1,999	2,301	2,341	2,410	2,418	2,245	2,163
Wage and salary workers	1,091	1,168	1,087	1,215	1,437	1,465	1,440	1,294	1,220
Self-employed workers	1,014	870	900	1,062	886	938	953	919	929
Unpaid family workers	29	15	13	(¹)	(¹)	(¹)	(¹)	(¹)	(¹)
Nonagricultural industries	133,773	136,503	134,925	135,176	135,401	135,722	136,172	136,180	136,306
Wage and salary workers	124,501	126,984	125,433	125,687	125,860	126,183	126,466	126,661	126,664
Government	19,924	19,821	19,800	19,732	19,725	19,797	19,609	19,694	19,681
Private industries	104,578	107,163	105,633	105,894	106,136	106,400	106,876	107,110	107,019
Private households	692	780	811	(¹)	(¹)	(¹)	(¹)	(¹)	(¹)
Other industries	103,886	106,383	104,822	105,192	105,351	105,662	106,129	106,382	106,204
Self-employed workers	9,216	9,412	9,396	9,340	9,401	9,460	9,541	9,477	9,501
Unpaid family workers	56	107	96	(¹)	(¹)	(¹)	(¹)	(¹)	(¹)
PERSONS AT WORK PART TIME ²									
All industries:									
Part time for economic reasons	5,135	4,833	5,270	4,572	4,896	4,800	4,880	4,788	4,714
Slack work or business conditions	3,566	3,327	3,459	3,019	3,185	3,030	3,226	3,205	2,996
Could only find part-time work	1,245	1,182	1,420	1,266	1,334	1,356	1,350	1,295	1,380
Part time for noneconomic reasons	19,374	19,543	19,229	19,158	19,021	18,935	19,110	18,561	18,905
Nonagricultural industries:									
Part time for economic reasons	5,003	4,717	5,152	4,451	4,794	4,690	4,782	4,727	4,613
Slack work or business conditions	3,494	3,248	3,382	2,952	3,127	2,964	3,153	3,144	2,911
Could only find part-time work	1,224	1,178	1,416	1,239	1,335	1,349	1,353	1,279	1,399
Part time for noneconomic reasons	19,005	19,246	18,910	18,710	18,633	18,628	18,752	18,367	18,636

6

Table A-8. Unemployed persons by reason for unemployment

(Numbers in thousands)

Reason	Not seasonally adjusted			Seasonally adjusted					
	Jan. 2006	Dec. 2006	Jan. 2007	Jan. 2006	Sept. 2006	Oct. 2006	Nov. 2006	Dec. 2006	Jan. 2007
NUMBER OF UNEMPLOYED									
Job losers and persons who completed temporary jobs	3,990	3,374	4,127	3,374	3,195	3,088	3,179	3,236	3,440
On temporary layoff	1,319	1,054	1,556	874	872	958	965	958	1,021
Not on temporary layoff	2,671	2,320	2,571	2,500	2,323	2,130	2,214	2,278	2,420
Permanent job losers	1,861	1,654	1,699	(1)	(1)	(1)	(1)	(1)	(1)
Persons who completed temporary jobs	810	666	872	(1)	(1)	(1)	(1)	(1)	(1)
Job leavers	831	730	793	826	804	783	793	807	797
Reentrants	2,252	1,916	2,192	2,277	2,292	2,249	2,279	2,199	2,230
New entrants	535	471	537	619	635	593	591	601	619
PERCENT DISTRIBUTION									
Total unemployed	100.0	100.0	100.0	100.0	100.0	100.0	100.0	100.0	100.0
Job losers and persons who completed temporary jobs	52.4	52.0	54.0	47.5	46.1	46.0	46.5	47.3	48.6
On temporary layoff	17.3	16.2	20.3	12.3	12.6	14.3	14.1	14.0	14.4
Not on temporary layoff	35.1	35.7	33.6	35.2	33.5	31.7	32.4	33.3	34.1
Job leavers	10.9	11.3	10.4	11.6	11.6	11.7	11.6	11.8	11.2
Reentrants	29.6	29.5	28.7	32.1	33.1	33.5	33.3	32.1	31.5
New entrants	7.0	7.3	7.0	8.7	9.2	8.8	8.6	8.8	8.7
UNEMPLOYED AS A PERCENT OF THE CIVILIAN LABOR FORCE									
Job losers and persons who completed temporary jobs	2.7	2.2	2.7	2.2	2.1	2.0	2.1	2.1	2.2
Job leavers	.6	.5	.5	.6	.5	.5	.5	.5	.5
Reentrants	1.5	1.3	1.4	1.5	1.5	1.5	1.5	1.4	1.5
New entrants	.4	.3	.4	.4	.4	.4	.4	.4	.4

7 ▶

Table A-9. Unemployed persons by duration of unemployment

(Numbers in thousands)

Duration	Not seasonally adjusted			Seasonally adjusted					
	Jan. 2006	Dec. 2006	Jan. 2007	Jan. 2006	Sept. 2006	Oct. 2006	Nov. 2006	Dec. 2006	Jan. 2007
NUMBER OF UNEMPLOYED									
Less than 5 weeks	2,833	2,507	2,912	2,549	2,582	2,588	2,517	2,707	2,642
5 to 14 weeks	2,433	1,986	2,529	2,242	2,077	2,064	2,135	2,037	2,283
15 weeks and over	2,343	1,997	2,208	2,255	2,264	2,062	2,152	2,081	2,118
15 to 26 weeks	1,143	945	1,044	1,085	1,010	974	1,006	991	986
27 weeks and over	1,200	1,052	1,164	1,170	1,254	1,088	1,145	1,090	1,133
Average (mean) duration, in weeks	16.0	15.9	15.5	16.8	17.2	16.4	16.3	15.9	16.2
Median duration, in weeks	8.3	7.4	7.9	8.5	8.1	8.0	8.2	7.3	8.1
PERCENT DISTRIBUTION									
Total unemployed	100.0	100.0	100.0	100.0	100.0	100.0	100.0	100.0	100.0
Less than 5 weeks	37.2	38.6	38.1	36.2	37.3	38.5	37.0	39.7	37.5
5 to 14 weeks	32.0	30.6	33.1	31.8	30.0	30.7	31.4	29.8	32.4
15 weeks and over	30.8	30.8	28.9	32.0	32.7	30.7	31.6	30.5	30.1
15 to 26 weeks	15.0	14.6	13.6	15.4	14.6	14.5	14.8	14.5	14.0
27 weeks and over	15.8	16.2	15.2	16.6	18.1	16.2	16.8	16.0	16.1

8 ▶

Nearby is another important statistical clue: the average length of time of being jobless. During the booming 1990s, the average duration of unemployment was just 14 weeks; an economic slump can extend that idle period to more than 20 weeks.

- **Table A-12** Alternative Measures of Labor Underutilization

(9) The main unemployment rate gets a lot of play in the press. However, as mentioned earlier, it excludes those who are jobless and too discouraged to even look anymore. The headline unemployment rate also does not factor in full-time workers who lost their jobs and have since grudgingly accepted part-time employment just to earn a few dollars. However, this table recalculates the unemployment rate to include these other categories (see U-5 and U-6), and the results can be startling. When you add other groups of discouraged workers to the equation, the unemployment rate can be as much as 4 percentage points above the more common headline rate.

Table A-12. Alternative measures of labor underutilization

(Percent)

Measure	Not seasonally adjusted			Seasonally adjusted					
	Jan. 2006	Dec. 2006	Jan. 2007	Jan. 2006	Sept. 2006	Oct. 2006	Nov. 2006	Dec. 2006	Jan. 2007
U-1 Persons unemployed 15 weeks or longer, as a percent of the civilian labor force	1.6	1.3	1.5	1.5	1.5	1.4	1.4	1.4	1.4
U-2 Job losers and persons who completed temporary jobs, as a percent of the civilian labor force	2.7	2.2	2.7	2.2	2.1	2.0	2.1	2.1	2.2
U-3 Total unemployed, as a percent of the civilian labor force (official unemployment rate)	5.1	4.3	5.0	4.7	4.6	4.4	4.5	4.5	4.6
U-4 Total unemployed plus discouraged workers, as a percent of the civilian labor force plus discouraged workers	5.4	4.4	5.3	4.9	4.8	4.6	4.7	4.7	4.9
U-5 Total unemployed, plus discouraged workers, plus all other marginally attached workers, as a percent of the civilian labor force plus all marginally attached workers	6.1	5.0	6.0	5.7	5.4	5.3	5.3	5.3	5.6
U-6 Total unemployed, plus all marginally attached workers, plus total employed part time for economic reasons, as a percent of the civilian labor force plus all marginally attached workers	9.2	7.8	9.1	8.4	8.0	8.1	8.0	8.0	8.3

9 ▶

• **Table B-1** Employees on Non-farm Payrolls by Industry Sector and Selected Industry Detail

(10) It's well worth watching shifts in the hiring of temporary workers for clues about future employment. Companies often prefer to employ temporary help as the economy turns up before taking the more expensive step of permanently hiring and training new full-time employees. Temps are usually cheaper, and they also give firms greater flexibility to add (and reduce) staffing during uncertain economic periods.

Table B-1. Employees on nonfarm payrolls by industry sector and selected industry detail—Continued

(In thousands)

Industry	Not seasonally adjusted				Seasonally adjusted						
	Jan. 2006	Nov. 2006	Dec. 2006ᵖ	Jan. 2007ᵖ	Jan. 2006	Sept. 2006	Oct. 2006	Nov. 2006	Dec. 2006ᵖ	Jan. 2007ᵖ	Change from: Dec. 2006-Jan. 2007ᵖ
Professional and business services	16,902	17,838	17,797	17,421	17,316	17,636	17,662	17,726	17,800	17,825	25
Professional and technical services[1]	7,256.5	7,443.9	7,512.3	7,541.1	7,243.8	7,420.1	7,438.5	7,469.6	7,505.2	7,523.7	18.5
Legal services	1,162.9	1,176.8	1,180.6	1,167.6	1,171.6	1,172.6	1,173.5	1,175.9	1,179.0	1,176.3	-2.7
Accounting and bookkeeping services	961.8	862.0	918.5	1,021.1	872.8	893.1	893.7	914.5	924.6	927.0	2.4
Architectural and engineering services	1,326.9	1,410.7	1,405.3	1,395.3	1,352.2	1,399.3	1,400.6	1,407.2	1,412.4	1,421.5	9.1
Computer systems design and related services	1,238.3	1,299.0	1,309.9	1,297.6	1,242.8	1,298.4	1,300.8	1,296.2	1,303.4	1,302.5	-.9
Management and technical consulting services	881.3	955.7	966.9	951.8	892.5	926.4	944.2	949.3	958.6	961.9	3.3
Management of companies and enterprises	1,779.5	1,824.2	1,829.6	1,815.9	1,791.6	1,822.3	1,826.8	1,823.0	1,826.8	1,829.9	3.1
Administrative and waste services	7,866.2	8,570.3	8,455.4	8,063.9	8,280.1	8,393.9	8,396.2	8,433.8	8,467.9	8,471.3	3.4
Administrative and support services[1]	7,529.9	8,222.3	8,108.1	7,718.2	7,936.1	8,047.4	8,047.5	8,083.8	8,118.5	8,118.6	.1
Employment services[1]	3,424.4	3,791.0	3,741.2	3,461.4	3,646.8	3,653.3	3,641.2	3,665.5	3,678.0	3,675.5	-2.5
Temporary help services	2,456.7	2,722.7	2,703.9	2,487.3	2,631.8	2,623.5	2,621.1	2,631.3	2,651.6	2,657.3	5.7
Business support services	770.2	811.9	817.5	796.6	773.1	797.2	801.0	802.2	804.1	800.5	-3.6
Services to buildings and dwellings	1,608.6	1,813.2	1,735.5	1,661.7	1,769.4	1,803.0	1,807.9	1,811.2	1,820.5	1,825.9	5.4
Waste management and remediation services	336.3	348.0	347.3	345.7	344.0	346.5	348.7	350.0	349.4	352.7	3.3

10 ▶ (Temporary help services)

• **Table B-7** Diffusion Indexes of Employment Change (Not Shown)

The name of this table is likely to scare off many people. However, don't be intimidated by its title. The data here is quite useful if you want to assess business confidence and future employment trends. This table notes the percentage of industries that have increased their payrolls in the last 12 months, 6 months, 3 months, and 1 month. A figure of 50% means that half the industries enlarged their staff during these time periods. A 55% figure indicates that more than half have added workers. A figure below 50% says that most firms cut the number of employees.

This table improves our understanding of the economy in two ways. First, by looking at the percentage changes over the different time frames, one can get a sense of whether layoffs are subsiding and hiring is picking up. Second, it shows how widespread the changes are in the labor market.

MARKET IMPACT

Bonds

Traders get quite agitated when there's a strong jobs report, especially if it's unexpected. The news can portend accelerating inflation and rising interest rates, both of which are anathema to bondholders. Thus, be prepared for a sell-off in fixed income securities when job creation is surging. How far bond prices will fall and how much yields will rise depends on many factors, but the most important is where the economy happens to be in the business cycle. If the U.S. has just managed to climb out of recession, a jump in employment will likely have only a modest effect on bond prices, because there's no immediate danger of inflation. However, if employment accelerates when the economy is already operating at or near peak capacity, prepare to see a steep drop in bond prices and sharply higher interest rates.

In contrast, a series of weak employment reports reflects a more sluggish economy, which is bullish for bond prices and means interest rates will head lower.

Stocks

News of robust employment can make equity investors positively giddy. As the number of people holding jobs increases and the workweek expands, employees easily slip into the role of consumers and spend more money. The result: Expectations rise that business sales and profits will pick up in the future. This can set the stage for a rally in the equity market. The only exception is if the economy is overheating, with interest rates and inflation turning up. The higher cost of borrowing will hurt companies and undermine stock prices.

Little or no growth in employment is generally seen as bad for stocks. The worry is that households will be less inclined to shop. Weak sales can shrink corporate income and earnings, thereby reducing the incentive to own shares.

Dollar

Employment news can greatly influence the dollar's value in currency markets. A vigorous jobs report could drive interest rates higher, which makes the dollar more attractive to foreign investors. They can now earn more interest income by owning U.S. Treasury securities. On the other hand, an anemic jobs report softens demand for U.S. currency, because it spells trouble for American stocks and puts downward pressure on rates, both of which make the dollar less appealing to foreigners.

WEEKLY CLAIMS FOR UNEMPLOYMENT INSURANCE

Market Sensitivity: High.

What Is It: Tracks new filings for unemployment insurance benefits.

News Release on the Internet: *www.ows.doleta.gov/unemploy/claims_arch*

Home Web Address: *www.ows.doleta.gov*

Release Time: 8:30 a.m. (ET) every Thursday; covers the week ending the previous Saturday.

Frequency: Weekly.

Source: Employment and Training Administration, Department of Labor.

Revisions: Minor changes.

WHY IS IT IMPORTANT?

Experts have paid closer attention to this indicator in the last few years even though it has been around since 1967. Improved monitoring by the Labor Department has made the series more accurate in gauging labor market conditions. The main appeal of the jobless claims report is its timeliness. Figures on new filings for unemployment benefits are released every week and are based on actual reports from state agencies around the country. As a result, analysts view this statistic as a good coincident indicator, meaning it accurately reflects what is presently going on in the economy. However, its greatest value is how first-time claims for unemployment insurance can influence future economic activity. If a large number of people are losing their jobs every week and applying for unemployment compensation, this will eventually dampen consumer spirits, slash their spending, and cause business to pare back investments. For this reason, the weekly claims report for unemployment benefits is one of the components in the forward-looking Index of Leading Economic Indicators. (See the section "Leading Economic Indicators (LEI)" later in this chapter.)

But let's take a step back for a moment. What exactly do we mean by "new claims for unemployment benefits"? Whether the economy is growing or not, it's a fact of life that people lose jobs every day. Companies close money-losing factories, get bought out by competitors, and in some instances just go belly-up. Many of their former employees are eligible to collect unemployment insurance for as long as 26 weeks in most states. Occasionally laws are passed that extend the pay period by another 13 weeks or so. The real issue, however, is that if the number of people filing for unemployment benefits increases every week or remains at a high level, it's a worrying sign that the economy is ailing. In contrast, a sustained decline in initial claims for benefits points to an economy on the mend.

In addition to counting new filers for benefit payments, this report also keeps tabs on the overall number of jobless workers who are receiving state unemployment benefits, a category known as "insured unemployment." It's important to point out that not everyone who is jobless is entitled to unemployment benefits. Labor economists estimate that more than 10% of initial claim applications for benefits are rejected because they do not meet eligibility requirements. In some industries, such as agriculture, as many as half of those who have lost jobs don't qualify for such benefits. Recent graduates who have entered the workforce but are unable to find employment are also ineligible to receive benefit payments. Moreover, not all states have the same eligibility requirements; some are stricter than others. What all this means is that many who are unemployed receive no benefits at all. During the middle of 2006, 7 million people were without jobs, according to the household survey of the employment report. Of those, only 2.5 million actually collected state unemployment benefits. That's an enormous gap, one that can have significant social and economic consequences over time.

How Is It Computed?

Every state, including the District of Columbia, offers jobless insurance programs that must conform to rules set down by federal law.

The states count all first-time filers for a given week ending on Saturday and then transmit the data to the Labor Department in Washington, which releases the figures to the public the following Thursday.

Information on "insured unemployment"—that is, the total number of unemployed currently receiving benefits—is published with a two-week lag.

The Tables: Clues on What's Ahead for the Economy

The initial unemployment claims report has shown an ability to predict when the economy approaches a turning point. For instance, first-time claims can hit their peak two to three months before the economy finally bottoms out in recession and begins its recovery phase.

- **Table**   Unemployment Insurance Data for Regular State Programs

    (1) This is the number of new claims filed for unemployment insurance benefits during the most recent week covered. A general rule of thumb is that when first-time claims stand above 400,000 for several weeks, it's symptomatic of an economy that's losing steam and in danger of slipping into recession. Such a pace also drives the official unemployment rate higher. On the flip side, a number that's persistently below 375,000 suggests a recovery is under way and companies are laying off fewer workers. In addition, for the establishment survey to show any meaningful jump in payroll employment, first-time claims must remain below 325,000.

(2) Do not use a single week's data on initial claims to interpret a trend. The weekly series can be quite erratic. Weeks containing holidays can easily distort the data on filings. A four-day workweek, for example, can reduce claims by as much as 20,000, only to have them surge the following week because they now include those who didn't have a chance to apply before. The solution is to look at initial claims based on a four-week moving average, which is reported here. The four-week average smoothes out the volatility of the weekly numbers.

(3) Another big issue for economists and politicians is whether the total number of persons collecting unemployment insurance has been increasing or decreasing over time. A figure of 3 million to 3.5 million and climbing indicates a malfunctioning economy. Consumer confidence suffers in such an environment, as does business investment. Economists also wonder what effect all these benefit payments will have on federal and state budgets. Perhaps the gravest concern, though, involves those who lost their jobs and are ineligible to receive unemployment aid for one reason or another. Jobless workers collecting unemployment insurance at least have some funds to spend, which can soften the harmful effects of an economic downturn. However, if total unemployment climbs (in the household survey) at a faster rate than those collecting unemployment insurance, it means a growing proportion of people out of work may have to get by without any state financial support, and that could lead to serious social dislocations. Without the safety net of benefit payments, many turn to the underground economy or even to crime for money.

(4) The "insured unemployment rate" is another statistic worth mentioning, albeit briefly. It's the proportion of those currently collecting unemployment insurance compared with the total number of American workers who would be eligible to receive these benefits. While the investment community mostly ignores this figure, a few economists follow its performance so that they can compare it with the official unemployment rate in the household data.

UNEMPLOYMENT INSURANCE DATA FOR REGULAR STATE PROGRAMS					
WEEK ENDING	Advance March 27	March 20	Change	March 13	Prior1 Year
Initial Claims (SA)	1 ▶ 342,000	345,000	-3,000	333,000	432,000
Initial Claims (NSA)	295,820	305,243	-9,423	312,067	371,692
4-Wk Moving Average (SA)	2 ▶ 340,250	340,250	0	342,000	420,500
WEEK ENDING	Advance March 20	March 13	Change	March 6	Prior1 Year
Ins. Unemployment (SA)	3 ▶ 3,062,000	3,030,000	+32,000	3,077,000	3,572,000
Ins. Unemployment (NSA)	3,398,430	3,518,006	-119,576	3,551,292	4,939,370
4-Wk Moving Average (SA)	3,056,500	3,071,000	-14,500	3,100,250	3,534,250
Ins. Unemployment Rate (SA)[2]	4 ▶ 2.4%	2.4%	0.0	2.4%	2.8%
Ins. Unemployment Rate (NSA)[2]	2.7%	2.8%	-0.1	2.8%	3.1%

MARKET IMPACT

Bonds

The fixed income market reacts favorably when the number of new filings for unemployment insurance picks up, especially if it jumps by more than 30,000 applications. A rise in first-time claims points to a weaker economy and diminishing inflation pressures. What unnerves bond investors is a continuous drop in claims, because it hints at a sturdier economic climate ahead. That can prompt fresh concerns about future inflation and lead to lower bond prices and rising yields.

Stocks

Equities tend to fare badly when there's a persistent increase in jobless claims. Though such a report would lower interest rates, which is normally a positive for stocks, evidence of a serious deterioration in the labor market augurs poorly for the economy, corporate profits, and share prices.

Dollar

Falling interest rates make the dollar less attractive to hold, especially if yields are higher in other countries. Thus, a steady climb in initial claims that stems from a languishing domestic economy might turn foreign investors away from U.S. securities and thereby weaken the dollar's value in foreign exchange markets.

HELP-WANTED ADVERTISING INDEX

Market Sensitivity: Low.

What Is It: A measure of newspaper ads with job openings.

News Release on the Internet:
   www.conferenceboard.org/economics/helpwanted.cfm

Home Web Address: *www.conferenceboard.org*

Release Time: 10:00 a.m. (ET); released the last Thursday of the month and
   covers the previous month.

Frequency: Monthly.

Source: The Conference Board.

Revisions: Tend to be minor.

WHY IS IT IMPORTANT?

Why track help-wanted advertisements in newspapers? It turns out to be a reasonable predictor of the economy's direction. When classified ads for jobs increase, it signifies growing confidence in the business community about upcoming sales and profits. The brighter
the outlook, the more likely employers will accelerate hiring. Should the number of ads
for jobs shrink, it is an indication that companies are getting nervous about the future.
Concerns that business may turn sour in the months ahead will cause firms to postpone or
cancel hiring plans.

   This index, which has been around since the Truman Administration (1951), seems
like a natural to excite investors. It reflects business confidence and possesses some predictive value. However, the measure has lost some luster in recent years. Traders show little reaction to it because the release comes out so late in the month—long after the
employment numbers do—and they both cover the same period. Moreover, the number of
job advertisements in newspapers has waned in recent years. Firms are instead resorting
to less costly ways to find new workers, such as placing ads on their own corporate Web
pages or using online job sites.

   Nevertheless, to economists and business leaders, the index of help-wanted ads is an
effective indicator that can help corroborate other signs of whether the economy is
strengthening or ailing.

HOW IS IT COMPUTED?

The Conference Board, a New York business research group, surveys 51 leading newspapers from major cities across the country and computes a monthly index based on the
volume of such advertisements. Every job ad is given the same weight regardless of

whether it seeks one employee or several, part-time or full-time, a CEO or a minimum-wage fast-food worker. Geographically, the focus is on newspaper ads in nine regions in the country: Mountain, Pacific, West North Central, West South Central, South Atlantic, East South Central, East North Central, Middle Atlantic, and New England. In computing the index, the Conference Board gives more weight to areas with larger labor markets.

The Conference Board currently uses 1987 as its baseline year (with an index value of 100). Since the start of the 1990s, the help-wanted index, which is seasonally adjusted, has ranged from about 100 during periods of strong economic growth all the way down to the 30s when business activity showed few signs of life.

THE TABLES: CLUES ON WHAT'S AHEAD FOR THE ECONOMY

This index stands out as a fairly good early warning system of an economy stumbling toward recession. Help-wanted advertising generally peaks months before the economy does because employers shut down hiring fairly quickly if they suspect a softening business climate ahead. For instance, the index fell throughout 2000, just before the onset of the 2001 recession.

However, don't count on this indicator to give you a heads-up on when an economy will emerge from recession. Companies do not post job advertisements the instant economic activity revs up. Instead, they tend to push existing employees to work longer hours in the early stages of a recovery until it becomes obvious that to meet the surge in demand, new workers will have to be found. Yet even then, employers don't rush in with new ads. Many firms first try to rehire those who were initially laid off. Thus, any pickup in help-wanted advertising usually comes long after the recession has ended.

- **Table** National Index of Help-Wanted Advertising

THE CONFERENCE BOARD

about us · press · contact us · help · site map

| Home | Conferences | Councils | Publications | Economics | Worldwide | Membership | Change Tabs to Topics |

Search | GO Advanced Search

(members login)

Help-Wanted Advertising Index

View economic news archive

Economics
>> Economic Indicators
  · Help-Wanted Advertising
  · Leading Indicators
  · CEO Confidence
>> Economic Research
>> Consumer Research
>> Economic Outlook
>> Economic Software
>> About the Program
>> Contact Us

The Conference Board surveys help-wanted advertising volume in 51 major newspapers across the country every month. Because ad volume has proven to be sensitive to labor market conditions, this measure provides a gauge of change in the local, regional and national supply of jobs.

	Feb. 04	Jan. 04	Dec. 03	Feb. 03
▶ National Index	40	39r	37	41
Proportion of Labor Markets With Rising Want-Ad Volume	67%	57%	29%	43%
Unemployment Rate	5.6%	5.6%	5.7%	5.8%

Source: The Conference Board, used with permission.

Besides noting the latest national index, figures are also provided for the two previous months and the year-ago level. Economists have noted a correlation between the changes in help-wanted ads and changes in the employment numbers from the Bureau of Labor Statistics. When help-wanted ads pick up, the employment numbers jump one or two months later. The lag occurs because it takes a few weeks for people to respond to such advertisements, be interviewed, have their credentials checked, and finally get hired. Thus, the job ads index can serve as a leading indicator of payroll growth (from the establishment survey), which the financial markets watch very closely. This process also works in reverse; when help-wanted ads fall off, the unemployment rate starts to climb shortly thereafter. With fewer jobs being touted, the economy has a harder time absorbing all those people just entering the labor force.

MARKET IMPACT

Bonds

Not much reaction. This indicator arrives late and merely reinforces data already out there. Rarely does the index itself precipitate activity among bond traders.

Stocks

Very little impact. Stocks have already discounted economic trends from earlier statistical releases.

Dollar

Has virtually no impact on the foreign exchange markets.

CORPORATE LAYOFF ANNOUNCEMENTS

Market Sensitivity: Low.

What Is It: Counts layoffs announced by public companies.

Home Web Address: *www.challengergray.com* (data is available only through subscription).

Release Time: 7:30 a.m. (ET); published the first week after the end of the reference month.

Frequency: Monthly.

Source: Challenger, Gray & Christmas.

Revisions: No revisions are made to previously released data.

WHY IS IT IMPORTANT?

Since the 1980s, there has been a continuous wave of mergers, plant closings, restructurings, and consolidations. Such corporate changes are to be expected in an open, competitive, and dynamic economy. But one very painful by-product of all this activity has been massive layoffs. Displaced workers now must spend weeks and months, sometimes even longer, trying to find new jobs. The resulting loss of income can devastate the financial health of households and sharply curtail consumer spending. Even those still clinging to their jobs tend to grow uneasy as they wonder about their own security. Such widespread uncertainty and stress can put consumers in a very sour mood, and if this mood is felt on a large-enough scale, layoffs can even drag an economy into recession. So monitoring trends in corporate layoffs can be useful if you want to anticipate changes in the economy's performance.

One company that does precisely that is Challenger, Gray & Christmas (CGC), an outplacement firm based in Chicago. The Challenger group scans public information records for announcements on corporate layoffs and then tallies it up along with a commentary on the latest trends. (As of May 2004, the company also began tracking hiring announcements.) However, there is no free access to the Challenger corporate layoff report on the Internet. Paid clients of CGC are the first to receive the data, which is released the first week of the month. Those who seek to get the information for free will have to rely on business news Internet sites such as Bloomberg, CNBC, and CNN.

HOW IS IT COMPUTED?

CGC culls a variety of sources for announced layoffs, including press releases, newspapers, and trade papers, and then adds them up. Its research covers publicly traded firms, though a few large private companies are also counted whenever possible. The focus is on comparing the volume of layoffs on a month-to-month basis and with earlier years. The data is also divided by industry and on a regional basis.

THE TABLES: CLUES ON WHAT'S AHEAD FOR THE ECONOMY

There are no tables to review here because Challenger has not made them available to nonsubscribers. But the press obtains highlights of the report and gives it ample coverage. By and large, the investment community and economists view these layoff figures with only limited interest. For one, the numbers are not fresh. They're based on corporate statements that were made weeks earlier. Second, several other publicly released indicators on joblessness are considered more informative. These include the Weekly Claims for Unemployment Insurance, the U.S. Labor Department's own Mass Layoffs report, and the Employment Situation release.

Nor can you draw any firm conclusions from the Challenger layoff survey. Announced job eliminations are usually not carried out in a matter of weeks, but are spread out over many months or even years. Should the economy bounce back during that time, some of these announced layoffs might not happen at all. Another problem is the way the Challenger report breaks down layoffs by geographic region. It's based mostly on the location of the company's headquarters, yet many of these layoffs can take place elsewhere, even outside the U.S.

The main question is whether layoff announcements can be utilized as a leading indicator of turning points in the economy. The answer is probably not. Since the 1980s, job elimination programs have become a permanent part of the American business landscape and can now occur in significant numbers at every stage of the business cycle. Just look at the last decade: Not only did we see companies shed workers during the recession of the early 1990s, but we also saw them continue to slash payrolls during the powerful growth years later in the decade.

MARKET IMPACT

On a slow news day, investors might take note of the Challenger report. Otherwise, its impact on the market is negligible.

Bonds

Theoretically, a large and unexpected jump in layoffs can be interpreted as a bullish sign for the fixed income market. Workforce reductions on a grand scale can reinforce the notion that a slowdown in economic activity is under way. However, for more than a decade, layoffs have taken place in significant numbers without regard for the business cycle. What's more, the Challenger report is based on dated information that the market has, in all likelihood, already discounted.

Stocks

Equity investors rarely initiate trades based solely on the Challenger report. Shareholders respond to news of layoffs the moment they are first made public by the companies themselves.

Dollar

This report has no impact on the foreign exchange markets.

MASS LAYOFF STATISTICS (MLS)

Market Sensitivity: Low.

What Is It: Measures actual layoffs in business and government.

News Release on the Internet: *www.bls.gov/mls*

Home Web Address: *www.bls.gov*

Release Time: 10 a.m. (ET); this report is out four weeks after the end of the month.

Frequency: Monthly.

Source: Bureau of Labor Statistics, Department of Labor.

Revisions: Data is revised for the last two months.

WHY IS IT IMPORTANT?

There are presently two major sources of information on layoffs. One is the Challenger, Gray & Christmas survey, which was discussed in the preceding section ("Corporate Layoff Announcements"). Its data, however, covers only announced corporate layoffs; it doesn't follow up to see if these job elimination plans were fully carried out. Yet companies have been known to reduce or even cancel publicized job cuts once business improves. Thus, the more relevant issue might be tallying the layoffs that actually occurred! To locate data on actual layoffs, you have to turn to the government's own Bureau of Labor Statistics, which releases a monthly report appropriately titled "Mass Layoff Statistics (MLS)." Though the report is not widely known to investors and economic researchers, it contains information that can have a direct bearing on future household spending and economic growth.

The MLS report tracks mass layoff "events." An event is defined as each time a company or a government agency lays off 50 or more workers at a single location within a five-week period. (For example, if GM lets go 70 workers in its Detroit auto plant and another 100 at a second GM plant in Ohio, and American Airlines in Chicago cuts its payroll by 200, all in the same workweek, the BLS counts them as three "events" involving 370 jobs.) The agency totals all mass layoff events each month, along with the number of jobless workers who filed for unemployment insurance as a result of those job cuts. In addition, the agency categorizes layoffs by the length of their duration (30 days or less out of work versus 31 days or more). It then breaks down all the data by industry and geographic location. There's a lot of information here that can be of value to investors and business leaders who want to track the magnitude of actual layoffs, see which industries and regions in the U.S. are ailing, and find out where there may be a surplus of skilled, but unemployed, workers.

How Is It Computed?

The BLS first contacts state agencies for the latest initial unemployment insurance claims. It then sorts through the data to find out how many of those who filed a claim were the result of mass layoffs. Companies and government agencies are also contacted to see how many of the job eliminations lasted 31 days or longer. After compiling the numbers, the BLS publishes two reports. One is the monthly "Mass Layoff Statistics," which is what this section is about, and the other is a quarterly release known as the "Extended Mass Layoffs" report. The latter deals with employees who have been separated from their jobs for more than a month. (This quarterly report is also available on the same Web site.)

The Tables: Clues on What's Ahead for the Economy

During the last 15 years, job cutbacks involving large numbers have occurred at virtually every stage of the business cycle, thus diminishing the value of layoff reports as a forecasting tool. Nevertheless, while it lacks use as a leading indicator, the MLS report has other valuable information that cannot be found elsewhere.

- **Table 1**   Mass Layoff Events and Initial Claimants for Unemployment Insurance

    (1) The Events column tells you how many instances there were of mass layoffs in the month. Each instance is defined as a single action that led to the elimination of at least 50 employees during a five-week period, regardless of the duration of their separation.

    (2) Here's where you'll find the monthly totals for the number of persons who put in claims for unemployment insurance as a direct result of those event-triggered layoffs. This column might look puzzling at first, because monthly totals for initial claims for unemployment benefits appear way below what you would expect, given the higher number of people filing for jobless benefits each week (see the section "Weekly Claims for Unemployment Insurance"). The reason for this is that only 10% of all first-time claims for benefits are the result of mass layoff events involving at least 50 people within a five-week period. Most layoffs that lead to unemployment claims represent numbers that are less than 50 persons per incident.

    (3) The column labeled "Total" combines mass layoff activity in both the private and government sectors. To get a more accurate sense of job losses in the private business community, it's necessary to view "Private non-farm." Within that category falls manufacturing, which is highly sensitive to changes in the business cycle. Should mass layoff events in manufacturing turn substantially higher, it can corroborate other economic evidence that business activity is slowing and that factories are under pressure to slash payrolls.

1 ▼   2 ▼   3 ▼

Table 1. Mass layoff events and initial claimants for unemployment insurance, February 2003 to January 2007, seasonally adjusted

Date	Total		Private nonfarm		Manufacturing	
	Events	Initial claimants	Events	Initial claimants	Events	Initial claimants
2003						
February	1,848	192,197	1,664	178,963	650	81,370
March	1,787	174,936	1,592	159,242	610	73,015
April	1,707	172,348	1,557	162,117	634	82,756
May	1,731	184,479	1,550	170,984	635	87,049
June	1,733	164,442	1,523	147,609	638	68,976
July	1,649	164,146	1,443	148,650	567	72,023
August	1,498	169,799	1,362	156,687	546	74,509
September	1,562	147,054	1,370	132,262	479	57,332
October	1,536	158,137	1,328	140,298	420	52,105
November	1,366	138,079	1,223	126,597	377	49,716
December	1,412	139,423	1,243	127,356	445	50,923
2004						
January	1,428	146,692	1,232	128,191	394	45,544
February	1,320	134,626	1,170	122,329	367	40,849
March	1,372	139,716	1,237	130,737	401	59,987
April	1,374	140,190	1,202	124,962	349	38,197
May	1,209	113,091	1,047	99,615	330	38,965
June	1,403	141,048	1,231	128,137	366	47,015
July	1,330	137,484	1,180	126,106	372	51,424
August	1,394	127,671	1,224	113,376	345	36,963
September	1,277	125,351	1,154	115,343	338	46,955
October	1,288	132,250	1,172	122,831	362	47,571
November	1,314	130,558	1,171	118,904	378	46,276
December	1,170	114,641	1,013	103,434	301	33,022
2005						
January	1,489	160,986	1,353	150,640	383	56,133
February	1,172	123,377	1,045	112,752	358	45,794
March	1,219	132,035	1,079	122,013	377	55,061
April	1,263	137,381	1,132	126,747	398	60,826
May	1,226	133,221	1,085	120,899	382	54,886
June	1,194	126,834	1,074	117,712	359	57,018
July	1,248	131,500	1,101	118,800	353	47,136
August	1,109	123,125	986	111,879	338	46,915
September	2,217	292,177	1,998	246,227	419	56,289
October	1,098	108,665	977	99,402	321	44,666
November	1,167	115,803	1,036	104,576	330	43,307
December	1,253	135,721	1,125	124,632	372	48,592
2006						
January	1,112	109,429	984	99,277	282	29,911
February	1,065	112,742	973	105,055	329	46,548
March	1,105	120,954	1,003	112,730	335	50,149
April	1,175	121,376	1,041	111,369	365	48,038
May	1,098	113,195	982	103,839	297	42,993
June	1,130	123,558	1,007	113,037	331	40,500
July	1,160	118,843	1,038	109,509	372	49,069
August	1,218	131,105	1,083	120,923	367	58,983
September	1,158	120,795	1,043	111,876	392	46,802
October	1,186	119,914	1,069	111,036	401	55,795
November	1,220	136,340	1,111	127,286	411	60,599
December	1,201	133,818	1,099	124,526	390	53,828
2007						
January	1,237	126,368	1,095	115,615	389	51,141

- **Table 3**   Industry Distribution: Mass Layoff Events and Initial Claimants for Unemployment Insurance

This table, which is only partially shown here, tells how widespread these layoffs are across different industries and in government.

Table 3. Industry distribution: Mass layoff events and initial claimants for unemployment insurance

Industry	Mass layoff events				Initial claimants for unemployment insurance			
	January 2006	November 2006	December 2006	January 2007	January 2006	November 2006	December 2006	January 2007
Seasonally adjusted								
Total	1,112	1,220	1,201	1,237	109,429	136,340	133,818	126,368
Total, private nonfarm	984	1,111	1,099	1,095	99,277	127,286	124,526	115,615
Manufacturing	282	411	390	389	29,911	60,599	53,828	51,141
Not seasonally adjusted								
Total [1]	1,245	1,315	2,249	1,407	117,946	136,186	254,503	134,984
Total, private	1,185	1,273	2,176	1,344	112,837	132,337	248,383	129,715
Agriculture, forestry, fishing and hunting	62	101	50	81	4,136	7,328	3,600	5,240
Total, private nonfarm	1,123	1,172	2,126	1,263	108,701	125,009	244,783	124,475
Mining	4	7	28	10	309	648	3,048	769
Utilities	(^{2})	3	3	(^{2})	(^{2})	161	154	(^{2})
Construction	125	212	423	194	7,942	17,364	36,426	12,426
Manufacturing	331	455	735	456	35,097	58,473	105,462	53,615
Food	46	59	80	59	3,589	7,222	8,557	4,525
Beverage and tobacco products	9	8	6	6	599	502	468	456
Textile mills	13	14	18	16	1,214	2,247	2,480	1,703
Textile product mills	7	9	9	9	655	1,325	758	1,132
Apparel	11	6	21	12	769	820	2,323	1,020
Leather and allied products	(^{2})	(^{2})	5	(^{2})	(^{2})	(^{2})	493	(^{2})
Wood products	27	53	59	46	2,995	5,044	6,359	4,342
Paper	6	9	13	7	405	854	1,415	572
Printing and related support activities	(^{2})	(^{2})	12	13	(^{2})	(^{2})	1,178	1,110
Petroleum and coal products	–	8	14	(^{2})	–	635	1,396	(^{2})
Chemicals	8	6	7	9	531	489	608	771
Plastics and rubber products	17	24	48	22	1,305	2,716	5,674	1,513
Nonmetallic mineral products	20	17	56	28	1,318	1,991	5,824	2,059
Primary metals	11	28	38	13	946	3,154	4,714	1,687
Fabricated metal products	32	35	57	32	2,305	3,710	5,346	2,581
Machinery	12	34	38	24	899	6,563	5,676	2,309
Computer and electronic products	22	21	24	15	1,678	1,711	2,085	1,351
Electrical equipment and appliances	10	11	25	8	1,965	2,588	5,701	514
Transportation equipment	52	79	159	104	11,421	13,352	38,811	22,315
Furniture and related products	13	21	34	23	1,253	2,075	4,510	2,948
Miscellaneous manufacturing	9	9	12	6	821	1,145	1,086	454

- **Table 6**   State Distribution: Mass Layoff Events and Initial Claimants for Unemployment Insurance (Not Shown)

  This is a state-by-state breakdown of large layoff events and the number of people who filed for unemployment benefits.

MARKET IMPACT

This report has no impact to speak of on the bond, stock, or currency markets. It comes out too late in the month for money managers, who are more interested in getting cutting-edge news on economic conditions.

ADP NATIONAL EMPLOYMENT REPORT

Market Sensitivity: High.

What Is It: A new and timely report that can serve as a preview of the government's monthly employment release.

News Release on the Internet:
www.adpemploymentreport.com/report_analysis.aspx

Home Web Address: *www.adpemploymentreport.com*

Release Time: 8:15 a.m. (ET); published just two days before the Bureau of Labor Statistics puts out the Employment Situation report.

Frequency: Monthly.

Source: Automatic Data Processing, Inc. (ADP) and Macroeconomic Advisers, LLC.

Revisions: Each release will contain minor revisions in payroll numbers for just the prior month.

WHY IS IT IMPORTANT?

For space scientists, the ultimate goal is to find life elsewhere in the universe. For biblical archeologists, the supreme achievement may be to recover the Ark of the Covenant. For traders in the stock and bond markets, the great aspiration is nothing less than to accurately predict the monthly employment numbers by the Bureau of Labor Statistics (BLS).

OK, there may be some hyperbole here, but not as much as you think. Money managers have been scrambling for years to devise a statistical measure that promises to correctly forecast the government's jobs report. That endeavor has proven to be quite difficult. Yet investors keep trying because the news generated from the official employment release has a history of rocking global stock, bond, and currency markets. Traders will thus devote lots of time, money, energy, and whatever else is needed to get a heads-up on the latest developments in the U.S. labor markets.

Just look at the variety of employment indicators out there already. The Conference Board counts jobs advertised in newspapers as well as on the Internet. Other analysts seek out clues in the weekly claims for unemployment insurance. The Institute for Supply Management (ISM) tracks job activity in both its manufacturing and service surveys. Challenger, Gray & Christmas chooses to study employment trends by adding up corporate announcements on job layoffs and hiring. There's also a plethora of consumer confidence polls that include questions on job availability and security. All these reports take different approaches to determine whether labor market conditions are improving or deteriorating. Unfortunately, the signals they send often conflict with one another, or they just do not come close to serving as an effective precursor for the market-moving BLS report.

Perhaps this shouldn't come as a surprise. These indicators mostly rely on surveys, opinion polls, job advertisements, and corporate intentions—everything *but* actual payroll data. Wouldn't it be nice to have at least one early measure that is based on national payroll statistics?

Well, now there is, and this new economic indicator has quickly grabbed the attention of investors. Launched in May 2006, the *ADP National Employment Report*[SM] has all the attributes of a news-making statistic. To begin with, it is a product of what appears to be an ideal partnership between ADP, the nation's leading provider of payroll-related services—it processes the payrolls of one out of six employees in the U.S. private sector—and Macroeconomic Advisers, LLC, a major economic forecasting firm. What's unique about the ADP report is that its monthly employment estimates are based not on a survey but on a sampling of real payroll data collected from around the country. ADP's huge database, combined with the number-crunching abilities of Macroeconomic Advisers, has given the ADP jobs report credibility in its ability to anticipate the government's own job numbers. To be sure, it's not foolproof. The ADP jobs report has had a spotty record since it went public. But the fact remains that ADP, Inc. has a unique perspective on labor market conditions because of its payroll services. Moreover, the payroll services giant and Macroeconomic Advisers have recently refined their methodology to enhance the report's predictive validity. So while it had a bit of a rough start, the ADP jobs report has the potential to come closer than any other indicator in effectively predicting the BLS's own monthly estimates on private, non-farm hiring.

How Is It Computed?

The manner in which the *ADP National Employment Report* is put together has intrigued the financial markets. ADP processes payrolls for more than 500,000 firms, spanning many different industries across the country. For its *ADP National Employment Report*, however, the firm takes a sample payroll of about 350,000 private, non-farm companies that covers some 20 million workers. (In contrast, the BLS attempts to survey 400,000 establishments each month, representing roughly 50 million employees.) ADP then collects payroll information on those companies on a weekly basis, strips out all information that identifies these companies to maintain client confidentiality, and hands the data to Macroeconomic Advisers. Economists there focus specifically on the payroll data that includes the 12th of each month—the same week the BLS carries out its survey. Experts from Macroeconomic Advisers crunch the numbers to correct for volatility and seasonal adjustments and then sort the job figures by key categories—total, goods versus services, company size, and employment in manufacturing.

By tapping ADP's wealth of payroll information and replicating some methods used by the government, the giant payroll firm and Macroeconomic Advisers believe they have come up with a jobs report that should closely correlate with the BLS's "final" (net of revisions) figures for private, non-farm payrolls each month.

The Tables: Clues on What's Ahead for the Economy

The *ADP National Employment Report* available online consists of three parts:

- A summary table that contains the total level of non-farm, private employment for each of the last six months, as well as job numbers for key segments of that workforce. You should be aware that these figures by definition *do not* include government hiring, a category the BLS *does* include in its headline payroll number. Why concentrate on trends in non-government employment? The reason is that when trying to assess the economy's health, the focus should be on what's occurring in the private sector. After all, government agencies may hire or dismiss workers regardless of what's going in the overall economy. They are not concerned about making profits. But corporations do need to record profits. Given the high cost of wages and benefits, private-sector employers are likely to hire only when they have confidence in the economy's strength—specifically, in the demand for the products they sell.

- The release also comes with four graphs that record the latest percentage change in the growth of the monthly job numbers for total private non-farm employment and its key components. To gain some historical perspective, the data includes figures that go back to 2001. Comparisons can also be made between estimates computed by ADP and the official series by the BLS.

- Finally, accompanying the table and graphs is an analysis of what occurred in the labor markets the previous month.

- **Table 1a**   Employees on Non-Farm Private Payrolls by Selected Industry and Size of Payroll

  (1) *Total non-farm private:* This top heading reflects ADP's estimates of the "true" level of non-farm private employment for each of the last six months. What is meant by "true" in this case? As I pointed out earlier, the BLS tries to gather employment information from some 400,000 establishments each month, and it has to do so under a very tight deadline. This is a daunting task, because not all companies queried can respond so quickly. By the time the government announces the market-moving preliminary job numbers the first Friday of each month, it is based on a sample that usually represents just two-thirds of those establishments. It can take more than a year before the BLS has the data it needs to announce the final or "true" numbers for that month. In contrast, ADP believes its rich payroll database and proprietary methodology enables them to forecast the BLS's true employment numbers much sooner.

  The far-right column in this table contains the latest net change in private non-farm payroll employment for all the categories.

BASED ON ADP PAYROLL DATA

Table 1a. Employees on nonfarm private payrolls by selected industry sector and size
(In thousands)

Industry / Size of Payroll	Seasonally Adjusted						
	Aug. 2006	Sep. 2006	Oct. 2006	Nov. 2006	Dec. 2006	Jan. 2007p	Change from: Dec. 2006 - Jan. 2007p
1 ▶ **Total nonfarm private**............	114,365	114,432	114,557	114,815	114,933	115,059	126
Small (1-49)................	49,977	50,040	50,106	50,203	50,299	50,376	77
Medium (50-499).........	44,976	45,000	45,053	45,166	45,191	45,241	50
Large (> 499).............	19,412	19,392	19,398	19,446	19,443	19,442	-1
Goods-producing............	22,539	22,492	22,473	22,491	22,473	22,461	-12
Small (1-49)................	8,087	8,085	8,087	8,102	8,115	8,124	9
Medium (50-499).........	9,966	9,941	9,933	9,943	9,926	9,917	-9
Large (> 499).............	4,486	4,466	4,453	4,446	4,432	4,420	-12
2 ▶ **Service-providing**............	91,826	91,940	92,084	92,324	92,460	92,598	138
Small (1-49)................	41,890	41,955	42,019	42,101	42,184	42,252	68
Medium (50-499).........	35,010	35,059	35,120	35,223	35,265	35,324	59
Large (> 499).............	14,926	14,926	14,945	15,000	15,011	15,022	11
Addendum:							
Manufacturing................	14,165	14,133	14,118	14,117	14,095	14,074	-21

Source: Automatic Data Processing, Inc.; Macroeconomic Advisers, LLC; reprinted with permission. The *ADP National Employment Report* is a trademark and service mark of ADP of North America, Inc.

Broadly speaking, two groups closely follow the job numbers every month. The first are bond traders (and, to a lesser extent, equity investors), who react instantly to the employment news by buying or selling securities. Their goal is to anticipate the financial market's reaction to the job numbers and make a quick profit on the news, regardless of whether the numbers are preliminary or final. The other group consists of economists and business managers, who rely on employment reports to gain an understanding of the current health of the economy—and how it might perform in the future. The primary goal of this group is not to make a fast buck in the markets, but to get a better grasp of the fundamentals that help determine what consumer spending, business invest-ments, inflation, and interest rates will be in the months and quarters ahead.

The value of the ADP report is that from its rich database of real-world payroll information, it can offer both traders and business leaders a truer sense of labor market conditions, arguably even better than the BLS's "preliminary" release for the month. For instance, if you were to look at the percentage change in private non-farm employment growth month to month, the folks at ADP and

Macroeconomic Advisers claim their report has had a correlation of 0.88 with the BLS's final numbers since 2001. (A correlation of 1.0 means the two series move perfectly in tandem.) Though we will have to wait and see if this high correlation will stand after one or two complete business cycles, the fact is the ADP report has the potential to be the best predictor of what the final (that is, post-revisions) BLS employment numbers will be. (See Chart 1.)

(2) *Goods-producing, service-producing:* The ADP report breaks down total nonfarm private payrolls into its two major categories—the goods-producing and service-producing sectors. It then differentiates each of those by company size (small, medium, and large). What defines the size is the number of employees, with 1 to 49 employees classified as a small firm, 50 to 499 as medium, and above 499 as large.

What forecasting values does this entire subsection have? First of all, the goods-producing sector in the U.S.—particularly manufacturing—has traditionally been much more sensitive to the ups and down of the business cycle than the service sector. If the economy sours and demand weakens, it can cause inventory levels of goods to swell at retail stores, wholesalers, and factories. As stockrooms and back lots fill up with unsold microwaves, refrigerators, large-screen televisions, and cars, producers have less need to hire workers and may even lay off existing employees. In contrast, demand for services and service workers

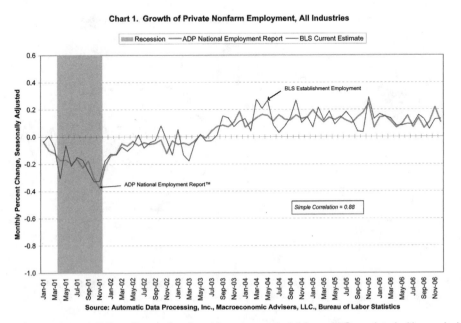

Chart 1. Growth of Private Nonfarm Employment, All Industries

Source: Automatic Data Processing, Inc., Macroeconomic Advisers, LLC., Bureau of Labor Statistics

Source: Automatic Data Processing, Inc.; Macroeconomic Advisers, LLC; reprinted with permission.

rarely experience such volatility. When households face tough economic times, they may postpone purchases of expensive consumer products, but they will still pay for the services of doctors, dentists, barbers, and public transportation. Thus, by monitoring hiring activity at goods-producing companies, you can get an early read on whether the economy is in the early stages of weakening or is entering an expansionary phase.

Moreover, since small and medium-size goods producers tend to be more nimble than large companies when it comes to hiring and layoffs, monitoring changes in their employment patterns can serve as a valuable leading indicator of turning points in the economy.

• **Chart 2**   Growth of Private Non-Farm Employment, Goods-Producing Industries

Among the graphs supplied in the *ADP National Employment Report* is one that depicts the monthly percentage change in employment in the goods-producing industries (which includes manufacturing). We noted above how hiring trends with goods-producers can help foretell changes in economic output. In Chart 2, ADP plots its payroll estimates with this sector as well as those from the BLS so that you can compare the two series since the start of 2001. What stands out is that during this time frame, ADP has demonstrated a remarkable 0.90 correlation with the

Chart 2. Growth of Private Nonfarm Employment, Goods-Producing Industries

Source: Automatic Data Processing, Inc.; Macroeconomic Advisers, LLC; reprinted with permission.

government's own series. Whether ADP can maintain such a high correlation in the future remains to be seen, but if it holds close to this relationship, the *ADP National Employment Report* will be viewed as offering the best early snapshot of what's going on in the labor market and in the overall economy.

MARKET IMPACT

Bonds

Though relatively new, the monthly ADP report is already making waves in the investment community. Precisely how the bond market reacts to the ADP jobs release, though, depends largely on two factors. First, how much did the report's estimate veer from consensus expectation? Investors in the fixed income market typically worry about statistical surprises, particularly with indicators linked to job creation. An unexpected surge in employment puts bonds in a vulnerable position.

Second, and perhaps more important, the ADP estimates have to be viewed in the context of where the U.S. economy stands in the business cycle. A strong report indicating lots of hiring at a time when the economy is emerging from recession or a period of weakness will probably not agitate bond traders. Remember, at this stage in the cycle, the economy still has lots of slack, and wage pressures are muted. As a result, bond values should remain fairly steady. But if that same report were issued after years of robust economic and job growth, it would unnerve fixed income traders, who would worry that the upcoming employment report by the BLS would show similar strong employment trends. Active hiring so late in the expansion puts pressure on labor and industrial resources. This normally causes higher wage and commodity price inflation, something the Federal Reserve is sure not to ignore. Such a scenario will undoubtedly be detrimental to bonds.

Stocks

Expectations of lively job growth are usually viewed as bullish for stock prices. If more people are working, household income rises, and that fosters more consumer spending and leads to greater corporate profits—all good for equities. But there is an important caveat here. Like bonds, investors in the stock market know there will come a time when persistent vigorous growth will strain the economy and rouse inflation pressures. This increases the likelihood that the Federal Reserve will intervene and raise interest rates, which of course is anathema to the stock market.

At the other extreme, if the ADP report consistently and correctly estimates that few new jobs are being created, it will slash projections of corporate earnings. In those circumstances, investors typically respond by lightening their portfolio of stocks.

Dollar

Investors in the foreign exchange market have also caught on to the significance of the ADP jobs report. Much of the focus here rests on what impact the report's estimates will have on U.S. interest rates. At the very least, international investors will use the ADP announcement to better position themselves for the BLS release on payroll jobs. Generally, when monthly non-farm, private payrolls increases by an average of 150,000 or more, it can lead to a firming of U.S. interest rates and thus make dollar-denominated assets a more attractive investment. Job growth of less than 100,000 a month suggests a soft or weakening economy, in which case foreign investors may conclude that interest rates are likely to fall in the future. This can undermine the dollar's value, particularly if investors see more lucrative returns outside this country.

PERSONAL INCOME AND SPENDING

Market Sensitivity: High.

What Is It: Records the income Americans receive, how much they spend, and what they save.

News Release on the Internet: *www.bea.gov/bea/newsrel/pinewsrelease.htm*

Home Web Address: *www.bea.gov/*

Release Time: 8:30 a.m. (ET); data is made public four weeks after the end of the reported month.

Frequency: Monthly.

Source: Bureau of Economic Analysis (BEA), Department of Commerce.

Revisions: After the initial release, data on income, spending, and savings undergoes revisions for the next several months as more complete information comes in. The magnitude of the changes is usually modest. Annual revisions normally are done every summer (in July or August), and benchmark changes occur every four or five years to incorporate new data as well as changes in methodology.

WHY IS IT IMPORTANT?

Consumers rule the economy, plain and simple. Without their active participation, business activity would quickly come to a standstill. Consumer expenditures are the main driving force of sales, imports, factory output, business investments, and job growth in the U.S. But to be able to spend, people need a reliable stream of income. As long as personal income rises at a healthy clip, so will spending. If income growth turns sluggish, consumers will curb their shopping. Though other factors, such as inflation and the change in household wealth due to stock and real estate values, can influence when and how much consumers spend, the most important determinant over time is personal income.

The government breaks down the personal income and spending report into three major categories: personal income, expenditures, and savings.

Personal Income

Personal income represents the money households receive before taking out taxes. Of course, what really counts is how much spendable money consumers have left after personal taxes and non-tax payments are removed. This is known as disposable personal income (DPI). Income itself can originate from several sources:

- *Wages and salaries*: What companies pay employees. It's the largest single contributor, representing 56% of all income.

- *Proprietors' income* (**8%**): A fancy term for self-employed that includes both farm and non-farm businesses, such as store owners, private-practice doctors, independent plumbers, lawyers, and consultants.

- *Rental income* (**0.5%**): Represents earnings people receive from renting or leasing real estate (as long as this is not their primary business).

- *Dividend income* (**4.5%**): Money stockholders get from corporations.

- *Interest income* (**9%**): Comes from investments in interest-bearing securities such as Treasury securities and corporate bonds.

- *Transfer payments* (**12.5%**): Payments received from federal and state governments, such as social security payments, unemployment benefits, and food stamps.

- *Other labor income* (**9.5%**): A catchall that includes employer-paid contributions like worker life insurance, health plans, and pensions.

Excluded from personal income are any profits households receive from the sale of assets such as stocks, bonds, or real estate.

Personal Spending, Formally Known as "Personal Consumption Expenditures"

There are just two things you can do with your income—you either spend it or save it. Traditionally, the average household spends about 95 cents of every dollar received, and this high level of consumption fuels two-thirds of all economic activity. It's the reason why personal consumption expenditures (PCE) grabs the big headlines when the personal income report comes out. PCE is not only the most comprehensive measure of consumer spending (far more than retail sales); it's also the largest component in the GDP. Thus, swings in PCE can lead to major shifts in the business cycle.

What are people spending their money on? Three broad product categories are highlighted under PCE: durable goods, nondurable goods, and services. Durable goods are often expensive products that last three or more years. They can include cars, refrigerators, washing machines, and so on. Because these items are costly and last a long while, durable goods make up the smallest share of consumer spending, some 12–14%. Nondurable goods have a life span of less than three years and cover commodities such as food, clothing, and books. Purchases of nondurable goods account for 30% of all spending. The third category—services—is the fastest-growing component of consumer purchases, jumping from 40% in the 1960s to about 60% now. Services includes medical treatment, haircuts, legal fees, movies, air travel, and so on.

Personal Savings

Savings is what's left after spending on goods, services, and interest payments on credit cards and loans. Subtract all these monthly outlays from disposable personal income, and the remainder is what's left for savings. This money usually ends up in savings accounts, bank CDs, money market accounts, stocks, and bonds.

In addition to the dollar amount of savings, it's also useful to know the percentage of disposable personal income that is saved; this is known as the personal savings rate. For instance, if you save $5 out of every $100 in disposable personal income, the savings rate is 5%. Back in the 1960s and early 1970s, households were relatively thrifty and maintained a savings rate often above 8%, which meant they saved at least $8 out of every $100 of after-tax income received. Since then, however, the savings rate has plummeted like a stone as Americans have shown little desire to set aside much of their take-home pay. In 1996, the rate slipped to 4%. By 2005 and 2006, personal savings fell into *negative* territory as households routinely spent more than their income. So in addition to spending their entire paycheck, Americans borrowed more money and then even dug into savings they had accumulated from past years to finance all that shopping. One of the most startling illustrations of how hooked consumers have become on living beyond their means can be seen by doing a simple calculation from this table. Look at the annualized amount of wages and salaries earned in a particular month, and compare that with what consumers actually spent (personal consumption expenditures) for that same period. Back in 1980, wages and salaries paid for nearly 80% of all spending, with the rest (20%) being financed by debt and from withdrawing from past savings. By the summer of 2006, wages and salaries financed barely 65% of all expenditures, which meant consumers had to borrow more than ever before as well as tap some savings to fill the gap between income and spending.

Can the deterioration in the savings rate continue indefinitely? No. Economists believe it will eventually turn up again. For instance, at some point interest rates will begin to climb. The higher cost of credit should not only curb spending but will also increase the incentive for Americans to save since they can now earn a bigger return on money invested in CDs or Treasury bills. In addition, once an economy weakens enough to cast doubt on future job security, it often motivates households to replenish their savings so they at least have some cash on hand for emergencies. Finally, with the future solvency of social security and private pension plans so uncertain, Americans are grudgingly beginning to realize they will have to rely more on their own savings to ensure a comfortable retirement.

HOW IS IT COMPUTED?

Gathering data for the personal income report is a hellish statistical task. The Bureau of Economic Analysis, the agency whose job it is to calculate personal income and spending, has to collect information from many sources in and out of government. For instance, numbers on wages and salaries come from the monthly employment report. Transfer payments, such as social security income, veterans' benefits, and unemployment insurance, are derived from the Social Security Administration, the Veterans Administration, and the Treasury and Labor Departments. Income from stock dividends is extrapolated from the U.S Census Bureau, IRS records, and quarterly income statements filed by corporations. Interest income is based on Treasury publications as well as figures from the Federal

Reserve's Flow of Funds. Money earned from self-employment and rental income has to be estimated from other government sources. All this just to compute personal income!

For numbers on personal spending, the agency looks at retail sales data (excluding autos). The amount Americans spend on motor vehicles is based partly on reports from auto manufacturers. Expenditures on services are also complicated. Consumer spending on air travel comes from the Air Transport Association; healthcare outlays are based on the Labor Department's employment data. In some cases, such as payments for dental services and haircuts, the BEA's only recourse is to do a simple straight-line calculation that assumes an automatic increase for such outlays each month. This might not be the most precise measure of consumer expenditures, but the methodology is supported by years of testing and practice. In any event, the government eventually revises all these numbers as more complete data becomes available.

Both personal income and personal consumption expenditures are seasonally adjusted and are presented in both current dollars (which is not adjusted for inflation) and constant dollars (which removes the effects of inflation). The monthly figures are also annualized to show how they would perform should the trend continue for a full year.

As for the savings level, no fancy tricks here. It's strictly a residual number; savings is whatever remains after you subtract total consumer outlays from personal disposable income.

The Tables: Clues on What's Ahead for the Economy

- **Table 1**   Personal Income and Its Disposition (Months)

    (1) This first table records monthly dollar amounts of personal income and outlays in current dollars and at annualized rates. Each of the major contributors to income is presented here: wages and salaries, other labor income (from fringe benefits at work), proprietors' income (self-employment), rental income, dividend income, and transfer payments. The latest figures on income are accompanied by seven months of previous data so that you can see how they've changed over time.

    By studying the growth in personal income, you can get some insight into future trends in consumer spending. But one has to be careful about generalizing here. The relationship between income and spending is not as simple as it once was. Since the mid-1990s, consumer outlays have also been greatly influenced by one's perception of personal wealth. Spending can accelerate if households see the value of their financial and real estate investments growing, a phenomenon known as the wealth effect. For example, economists estimate that for every dollar increase in the value of one's stock portfolio, consumers spend an additional 3 to 6 cents. A one-dollar rise in the value of other types of wealth (such as real estate) raises spending by 2 to 4 cents. Of course, when the economy looks bleak

Table 1.—Personal Income and Its Disposition (Months)

[Billions of dollars]

	2002				Seasonally adjusted at annual rates — 2003			
	Dec.	Jan.	Feb.	Mar.	Apr.ᵣ	Mayᵣ	Juneᵣ	Julyᵖ
Personal income	9,047.4	9,069.1	9,096.0	9,119.2	9,137.3	9,172.9	9,206.6	9,226.0
Wage and salary disbursements	5,039.5	5,050.9	5,074.1	5,083.4	5,082.5	5,095.7	5,109.9	5,109.4
Private industries	4,172.2	4,175.1	4,191.9	4,198.4	4,195.6	4,206.3	4,215.5	4,218.6
Goods-producing industries	1,110.0	1,109.5	1,111.0	1,113.5	1,111.7	1,114.5	1,116.9	1,114.1
Manufacturing	751.8	751.3	752.7	752.9	748.9	749.1	749.5	747.0
Distributive industries	1,116.7	1,114.5	1,117.8	1,118.5	1,118.3	1,119.7	1,121.7	1,121.5
Service industries	1,945.5	1,951.1	1,963.1	1,966.4	1,965.6	1,972.1	1,976.9	1,982.9
Government	867.3	875.8	882.2	885.0	886.9	889.4	894.4	890.9
Other labor income	634.4	637.0	639.4	641.1	642.8	645.2	646.9	647.8
Proprietors' income with inventory valuation and capital consumption adjustments	774.6	783.3	782.3	787.7	794.7	803.2	814.6	823.6
Farm	10.2	12.3	14.4	15.9	16.1	15.5	15.6	15.5
Nonfarm	764.4	771.0	767.9	771.7	778.7	787.7	798.9	808.2
Rental income of persons with capital consumption adjustment	127.9	127.5	126.9	126.2	121.7	116.0	110.6	116.4
Personal dividend income	446.0	448.6	451.2	453.7	456.4	459.1	461.5	463.9
Personal interest income	1,083.1	1,079.4	1,075.8	1,072.2	1,076.9	1,081.6	1,086.3	1,086.4
Transfer payments to persons	1,329.8	1,333.9	1,339.6	1,348.9	1,356.3	1,367.1	1,372.9	1,374.8
Old-age, survivors, disability, and health insurance benefits	717.6	718.2	722.4	727.1	729.6	737.3	738.5	740.0
Government unemployment insurance benefits	63.3	60.9	61.5	63.6	64.8	65.7	67.5	67.2
Other	548.9	554.8	555.7	558.1	561.9	564.1	566.8	567.5
Less: Personal contributions for social insurance	388.0	391.6	393.2	394.0	394.1	395.1	396.1	396.3
Less: Personal tax and nontax payments	1,092.2	1,070.1	1,078.3	1,083.1	1,083.1	1,085.9	1,089.0	988.1
Equals: Disposable personal income	7,955.2	7,998.9	8,017.7	8,036.1	8,054.2	8,087.0	8,117.6	8,237.9
Less: Personal outlays	7,704.1	7,707.7	7,705.4	7,769.8	7,776.2	7,815.4	7,863.1	7,922.4
Personal consumption expenditures	7,491.2	7,493.4	7,490.3	7,553.9	7,556.8	7,592.7	7,637.2	7,696.9
Durable goods	915.9	866.3	845.7	871.7	894.1	899.0	907.8	927.1
Nondurable goods	2,162.1	2,193.3	2,203.7	2,223.3	2,193.4	2,197.5	2,215.5	2,234.3
Services	4,413.2	4,433.8	4,441.0	4,458.9	4,469.3	4,496.2	4,513.9	4,535.4
Interest paid by persons	180.1	180.9	181.7	182.5	186.8	189.0	192.3	191.9
Personal transfer payments to the rest of the world (net)	32.8	33.4	33.4	33.4	33.6	33.6	33.6	33.6
Equals: Personal saving	251.1	291.2	312.3	266.4	278.0	271.6	254.4	315.5
Addenda:								
Disposable personal income:								
Total, billions of chained (1996) dollars [1]	7,106.9	7,131.0	7,118.2	7,109.1	7,140.6	7,176.3	7,187.9	7,279.8
Per capita:								
Current dollars	27,557	27,688	27,733	27,774	27,813	27,903	27,982	28,370
Chained (1996) dollars	24,615	24,684	24,622	24,571	24,658	24,760	24,778	25,071
Population (thousands) [2]	288,682	288,893	289,098	289,335	289,579	289,828	290,096	290,370
Personal saving as a percentage of disposable personal income	3.2	3.6	3.9	3.3	3.5	3.4	3.1	3.8

and the value of these assets starts to tank, you get the negative wealth effect, in which a loss in household wealth can result in a dramatic cutback in spending—especially if personal savings have been depleted. Thus, changes in household wealth can play an important role in determining consumer spending behavior.

Two other points need to be made about personal income. Year-end wages and salary amounts can be distorted because that is when companies distribute bonuses, which often causes a brief spike in monthly income. Second, transfer payments, such as social security, produce a blip in personal income data in January when the government tacks on extra dollars to reflect a cost-of-living adjustment (COLA). The precise increase in the COLA amount depends on the yearly change in consumer prices (see the section "Consumer Price Index (CPI)"). It is measured from October of one year through September of the next. If inflation rose by 3% over those 12 months, social security recipients will see a similar increase in their checks the following January.

(2) A better portent of future consumer demand can be found in real disposable personal income, which is labeled near the bottom of the table as chained dollars. This is monthly income left over after taxes (and other non-tax payments to the government) and then adjusted for inflation. It's the best measure of true consumer purchasing power. Here's why. Suppose disposable personal income climbed by 1% the previous month, but the general price level (or inflation) also rose by the same amount. In that scenario, one really gains nothing from the rise in income, because prices jumped by an identical rate. Thus, real disposable personal income growth is effectively zero. However, if income climbed by 1% and inflation inched up just 0.2% that month, real purchasing power grew by 0.8% $(1\% - 0.2\% = 0.8\%)$. Studies have shown that changes in real disposable personal income foreshadow changes in consumer spending patterns.

(3) Now let's look at spending details. The second half of this table deals with personal outlays by components (personal consumption expenditures, interest paid, and personal transfer payments). Personal consumption expenditures (PCE) is arguably the most important figure in the entire report. This figure represents the total amount that individuals have spent on durable and nondurable goods and services. Because consumer expenditures account for nearly 70% of the GDP, any change in spending behavior has a palpable impact on the overall economy.

(4) On occasion, households spend more than what they bring home in income, forcing families to dig into savings or borrow money to make up the difference. However, this is not sustainable in the long run, because at some point consumers will deplete their savings or acquire too much debt, or both. Any of these actions can lead to a sharp retrenchment in spending and throw a wrench in the economic expansion.

What are the warning signs? One trip wire is the amount of interest being paid to creditors. While looking at a category called Personal Outlays, you'll notice a subset labeled Interest Paid by Persons. (This measure does not include interest payments on mortgage debt or on home equity loans because such debt is viewed as more of an investment expense than a consumption expense.) Is there a point at which the interest debt becomes so burdensome that it can threaten future spending? Yes, but experts do not agree on where this threshold is. One popular barometer is based on a simple calculation of debt as a proportion of disposable personal income (interest paid ÷ DPI × 100). Historically, interest payments have stayed within the range of 2–2.5% of disposable personal income. If this exceeds 2.5% over a prolonged period of time, it means households might be experiencing financial stress, and that can depress future spending.

(5) Further down the table is the personal savings rate. This figure is interesting but not of great forecasting value. By definition, savings does not include any appreciation in the value of one's stocks, bonds, or real estate portfolio. Thus, anyone who invested in real estate or in the equity market over the last 20 years would have seen their household wealth increase, yet that wealth would not show up as part of personal savings.

Does it pay to track savings at all? Only if there's a precipitous change up or down in savings. An abrupt movement in either direction can indicate a growing concern among households over their financial future. A sudden climb in the savings rate occurs when people become increasingly nervous about their income and job security. And the more money that is put away for savings, the less that is available for shopping. By the same token, a sharp fall in the personal savings rate can be troubling as well. If spending continues to outpace income, households raid their savings to make up the difference, and that too can have ominous consequences for the economy down the road. So a sharp climb or fall in the personal savings rate should be investigated further. By itself, it's unclear what impact it will have on the economy in the short term.

- **Table 2** Personal Income and Its Disposition (Years and Quarters) (Not Shown)

This table lists the same categories as Table 1 but presents the data in year totals and quarters. This enables you to avoid the short-term volatility in the numbers.

- **Table 5** Personal Income and Its Disposition, Percent Change from Preceding Period

(6) Table 5 has one category that deserves particular attention—expenditures on durable goods. It consists of high-priced consumer products (such as cars and appliances) that last three years or more. Because they tend to be pricey and

Table 5.—Personal Income and Its Disposition, Percent Change from Preceding Period (Months)

[Percent]

	Seasonally adjusted at monthly rates							
	2002	2003						
	Dec.	Jan.	Feb.	Mar.	Apr. r	May r	June r	July p
Personal income	0.4	0.2	0.3	0.3	0.2	0.4	0.4	0.2
Wage and salary disbursements	.4	.2	.5	.2	0	.3	.3	0
Other labor income	.7	.4	.4	.3	.3	.4	.3	.1
Proprietors' income with inventory valuation and capital consumption adjustments	.5	1.1	-.1	.7	.9	1.1	1.4	1.1
Rental income of persons with capital consumption adjustment	-2.1	-.3	-.5	-.6	-3.6	-4.7	-4.6	5.2
Personal dividend income	.5	.6	.6	.6	.6	.6	.5	.5
Personal interest income	.2	-.3	-.3	-.3	.4	.4	.4	0
Transfer payments to persons	.9	.3	.4	.7	.5	.8	.4	.1
Less: Personal contributions for social insurance	.4	.9	.4	.2	0	.3	.3	.1
Less: Personal tax and nontax payments	.3	-2.0	.8	.4	0	.3	.3	-9.3
Equals: Disposable personal income	.5	.5	.2	.2	.2	.4	.4	1.5
Addenda:								
Personal consumption expenditures	1.1	0	0	.8	0	.5	.6	.8
Durable goods	6.8	-5.4	-2.4	3.1	2.6	.5	1.0	2.1
Nondurable goods	.6	1.4	.5	.9	-1.3	.2	.8	.8
Services	.2	.5	.2	.4	.2	.6	.4	.5
Disposable personal income, based on chained (1996) dollars	.4	.4	-.2	-.1	.4	.5	.2	1.3

6 ▶

often involve financing, orders for consumer durable goods are extremely sensitive to swings in the economy. Rising wages and job stability stimulate orders for durable goods, which, in turn, leads to a step-up in production by business. However, durable goods orders drop like a stone if there's just a whiff of trouble ahead for the economy. For that reason, this product group has become an excellent predictor of economic turning points. Orders for durable goods begin to trail off about 6 to 12 months before the onset of a recession, and they pick up a month or two before a recession ends and recovery begins.

- **Table 7**   Real Personal Consumption Expenditures (PCE) by Major Type of Product

(7) Up to this point, all figures on personal spending (PCE) were based on current dollars, which is not adjusted for inflation. This table presents real (inflation-adjusted) spending on a monthly basis, a subcategory that is particularly informative because it helps predict the pace of economic growth. Remember that some two-thirds of the GDP is based on real PCE. All you have to do is look at the latest three-month changes in real PCE and you can observe how the largest single component in the economy has performed. It's a good indicator of what the GDP will do in the current quarter and beyond.

- **Tables 9 and 11**   Price Index for Personal Consumption Expenditures

(8) When it comes to discussing inflation in the economy, most everyone refers to the CPI (consumer price index). However, a growing number of economists and policymakers, including those at the Federal Reserve, believe the best measure of consumer inflation in the economy is the PCE price index. It's also used to help convert personal spending from current dollars (which is not adjusted for

Table 7.—Real Personal Consumption Expenditures by Major Type of Product (Months)

	Seasonally adjusted at annual rates							
	2002	2003						
	Dec.	Jan.	Feb.	Mar.	Apr. r	May r	June r	July p
	Billions of chained (1996) dollars							
Personal consumption expenditures	6,691.4	6,680.3	6,649.9	6,682.5	6,699.6	6,737.7	6,762.6	6,801.7
Durable goods	1,062.9	1,008.7	987.6	1,019.8	1,048.6	1,060.5	1,074.3	1,099.7
Nondurable goods	1,962.0	1,984.4	1,972.0	1,980.4	1,970.8	1,986.6	1,996.1	2,008.1
Services	3,708.1	3,716.2	3,714.2	3,714.2	3,718.5	3,731.2	3,736.1	3,743.9
	Change from preceding period in billions of chained (1996) dollars							
Personal consumption expenditures	66.1	−11.1	−30.4	32.6	17.1	38.1	24.9	39.1
Durable goods	71.2	−54.2	−21.1	32.2	28.8	11.9	13.8	25.4
Nondurable goods	12.0	22.4	−12.4	8.4	−9.6	15.8	9.5	12.0
Services	−.6	8.1	−2.0	0	4.3	12.7	4.9	7.8
	Percent change from preceding period in chained (1996) dollars at monthly rates							
7 ▶ Personal consumption expenditures	1.0	−.2	−.5	.5	.3	.6	.4	.6
Durable goods	7.2	−5.1	−2.1	3.3	2.8	1.1	1.3	2.4
Nondurable goods	.6	1.1	−.6	.4	−.5	.8	.5	.6
Services	0	.2	−.1	0	.1	.3	.1	.2

Table 9.—Price Indexes for Personal Consumption Expenditures: Level and Percent Change From Preceding Period (Months)

	Seasonally adjusted							
	2002	2003						
	Dec.	Jan.	Feb.	Mar.	Apr. r	May r	June r	July p
	Chain-type price indexes (1996=100)							
Personal consumption expenditures	111.95	112.17	112.64	113.04	112.80	112.69	112.94	113.16
Durable goods	86.14	85.86	85.60	85.46	85.24	84.74	84.47	84.28
Nondurable goods	110.19	110.53	111.74	112.26	111.30	110.62	110.99	111.26
Services	119.02	119.31	119.57	120.05	120.19	120.51	120.82	121.14
Addendum:								
Personal consumption expenditures less food and energy	111.42	111.47	111.52	111.64	111.71	111.76	111.92	112.17
	Percent change from preceding period in price indexes at monthly rates							
8 ▶ Personal consumption expenditures	.1	.2	.4	.4	−.2	−.1	.2	.2
Durable goods	−.4	−.3	−.3	−.2	−.3	−.6	−.3	−.2
Nondurable goods	−.1	.3	1.1	.5	−.9	−.6	.3	.2
Services	.3	.2	.2	.4	.1	.3	.3	.3
Addendum:								
Personal consumption expenditures less food and energy	.1	0	0	.1	.1	0	.1	.2

Table 11.—Percent Change From Month One Year Ago in Chain-Type Price Indexes for Personal Consumption Expenditures

	2002	2003						
	Dec.	Jan.	Feb.	Mar.	Apr. r	May r	June r	July p
9 ▶ Personal consumption expenditures	2.0	2.1	2.3	2.4	1.7	1.7	1.8	1.8
Durable goods	−3.1	−3.1	−2.5	−2.4	−2.5	−3.1	−3.1	−3.1
Nondurable goods	2.3	2.3	3.0	2.9	1.0	1.0	1.3	1.5
Services	3.0	3.0	2.9	3.2	3.0	3.0	3.0	3.0
Addendum:								
Personal consumption expenditures less food and energy	1.7	1.6	1.4	1.5	1.3	1.2	1.2	1.4

inflation) into constant dollars (which is adjusted for inflation). Most investors and business executives, however, still prefer the CPI, which is fine. In the end, there's really not much of a statistical difference between these two inflation measures. The reason the PCE price index is mentioned at all is because the Federal Reserve considers this measure when setting interest rate policy.

(9) This table contains the yearly change in inflation for each month based on the PCE price index. On average, the annual PCE price inflation tends to be about 0.3 percentage points lower than the CPI. One reason for this divergence is the different assumptions behind the two price measures. The headline CPI, for instance, does not consider the possibility that consumers might substitute products if it's in their interests to do so. If beef were too expensive, a person might switch to less-costly chicken. The CPI does not take into account such changes in buying habits. It will continue to follow beef prices even though people might have altered their eating habits. The PCE price index, on the other hand, allows for substitution, which is why its inflation rates tend to be lower than the CPI.

MARKET IMPACT

Normally, an economic indicator that comes out as late in the month as this one does would not get much attention from the financial markets. Investors have already received some news on individual income and spending from the employment report and through the retail sales data. But one statistic in this report greatly preoccupies money managers and policymakers—the core PCE price index. The Federal Reserve has publicly stated that it wants to see this important inflation measure rise no more than 1% to 2% per year. A pace markedly above or below that range has very real implications for interest rate policy. Were it not for this critical inflation gauge, the personal income report would likely get only a lukewarm reception from the investment community.

Bonds

Fixed income investors prefer to see listless growth in both income and spending. Any data that affirms sluggishness in the economy is expected to support higher bond prices and lower yields. On the flip side, accelerating gains in income and especially in personal consumption can agitate bond traders because it suggests more rapid economic growth ahead and possibly higher inflation. Such a scenario might eventually force the Federal Reserve to raise short-term interest rates. Thus, a larger-than-expected jump in household spending can induce a sell-off in the bond market, with the price of fixed incomes dropping and yields climbing.

Stocks

Investors in the equity market can be expected to react differently from their colleagues in bonds. Higher personal income and spending are viewed favorably in the stock market because they fuel more economic activity and fatten corporate profits. That's a far better scenario than anemic income growth and weakening expenditures, which portend a struggling economy and soft profits.

Of course, there is an important caveat here. Stock investors will run from the markets if the data shows personal consumption surging when the economy is already operating at or close to maximum speed. This raises the prospect of accelerating inflation and higher interest rates, which are anathema to both stock and bond investors.

Dollar

Foreign exchange investors are likely to respond to the personal income and spending numbers. A healthy increase in both bodes well for the U.S. dollar. High consumer demand encourages more growth and puts upward pressure on interest rates. That makes the dollar more attractive to foreign investors, particularly if it results in a greater return on investment than other currencies. A weaker-than-expected report on consumer spending presages lower interest rates, and that's often bearish for the dollar.

RETAIL SALES

Market Sensitivity: High.

What Is It: The first report of the month on consumer spending; capable of big surprises.

News Release on the Internet: *www.census.gov/svsd/www/advtable.html*

Home Web Address: *www.census.gov*

Release Time: 8:30 a.m. (ET); available about two weeks after the month ends.

Frequency: Monthly.

Source: Bureau of the Census, Department of Commerce.

Revisions: Can be huge from month to month. Each release also contains broad revisions of the two previous months to reflect more complete information. Annual benchmark changes are released in March and can go back three years or more.

WHY IS IT IMPORTANT?

Remove three legs from a table and, well, it isn't much of a table after that. If you imagine the U.S. economy being the table and consumer spending accounting for three of the four legs, you'll understand why the investment community is so super-attentive to any indicator that provides insight into the mood and behavior of shoppers. Consumer spending makes up 70% of all economic activity—and retail sales account for a hefty one-third of that. If consumers can keep cash registers ringing, it is a sign of overall economic growth and prosperity. To monitor such expenditures, the Census Bureau calls on thousands of retailers each month for their latest sales numbers. As a result, investors and economists see the retail sales report as one of the best indicators of change in consumer spending patterns. An unexpected swing in its numbers can sway the price of stocks and bonds.

But retail sales also has certain shortcomings. It represents only spending on goods, such as those found at department stores, auto dealers, gas stations, and food service providers such as restaurants. The report tells us nothing about what's being spent on services such as air travel, dental care, haircuts, insurance, and movies. Yet the service business makes up about two-thirds of all personal expenditures. Furthermore, retail sales is measured only in nominal dollars, which means that no adjustment is made for inflation. That makes it difficult to tell if consumers actually purchased additional goods or simply paid more to cover the higher prices charged by merchants. Finally, the initial monthly retail sales releases, known as the advance report, tend to be extremely volatile and thus misleading. It's not unusual for the government to report that retail sales fell one month, only to revise the report later to show an increase.

Nonetheless, the government has made some progress in modernizing this economic series. For instance, the retail sales report now includes purchases made through the Internet, but it does not break down those online numbers in this release. To find how much consumers bought over the Internet, one has to look at the Commerce Department's quarterly E-Commerce report (see the next economic indicator, "E-Commerce Retail Sales").

HOW IS IT COMPUTED?

Surveys are sent out randomly to 5,000 large and small retailers around the country. These establishments receive them about three days after the month ends and are supposed to respond within a week or so. However, fewer than 50% of the retailers mail them back in time. Still, the government reviews the data to prepare the advance retail sales report—the first of three releases for that month. This advance report offers a quick and dirty assessment of changes in consumer spending patterns. Another 8,000 retailers are polled days later to develop a more complete picture of what shoppers are doing. Results from that survey lead to the first statistical revision, which is known as the preliminary version. Four weeks later comes the final report, with additional revisions based on the inclusion of all who responded. Generally, of the 13,000 surveyed, 70–75% respond.

Dollar figures are compiled from total receipts of retail sales, after subtracting for rebates and merchandise returned by customers. Also excluded are sales taxes, excise taxes, and finance charges from department store credit cards.

The dollar amounts in the report are not annualized; what you see represents the amount consumers spent on goods during that particular month. Retail sales figures, however, are adjusted for seasonal variations, such as how many holidays there were in the month and the impact winters traditionally have on retail sales.

THE TABLES: CLUES ON WHAT'S AHEAD FOR THE ECONOMY

There's a risk in relying too much on advance estimates of retail sales because they are based on a relatively small sampling. A more accurate sense of the underlying trend in consumer spending patterns can be discerned by monitoring sales on a three-month moving average basis or by looking at the last three months worth of data and comparing it with the same three-month period the year before.

• **Table 2**   Percent Change in Estimated Advance Monthly Sales for Retail and Food Services, by Kind of Business

(1) Just how much more—or less—did people buy from retailers in the last few weeks? This answer can be very revealing. Shifts in consumer spending behavior can provide useful insight into the present mood of American households. This column records the percentage change in retail spending by shoppers in each of the last two months and for the latest 12-month period. However, keep in mind that these figures are all in nominal dollars; there is no adjustment for inflation. Because economic performance is based on real (inflation-adjusted) growth rates, we have to see if there has been a genuine increase in the volume of retail goods sold. One way to do this is to use the monthly or yearly percentage change in consumer prices and subtract that from the equivalent change in retail sales. The result is a good approximation of the real percentage change in retail sales. For example, if retail sales increased by 6% in the latest 12-month period, and inflation as measured by consumer prices climbed 3% during this time frame, one could surmise that consumers actually purchased 3% more goods in the past year and that the remaining 3% rise in retail sales simply came from paying higher prices.

Aside from getting a sense of how well retailers are doing, this section also gives you a heads-up on what future GDP growth might be. Retail sales is used to compute Personal Consumption Expenditures (see the section "Personal Income and Spending"), which is the most important component in calculating the nation's GDP. In fact, changes in real GDP correlate well with changes in real retail sales.

(2) Roughly 25% of total dollars spent on retail sales goes toward purchases of motor vehicles and auto-related products. This auto category, however, can be extremely volatile from month to month and can distort the larger retail sales picture. To offset this, there is a separate line in the report ("Total, excluding motor vehicle and parts") where the government strips out the auto spending component so that one can better track the underlying trend in consumer spending.

(3) Because geopolitical events and domestic oil refining capacity can greatly influence how much drivers pay for gasoline, it is wise to monitor this category of spending as well and see how it affects total retail sales. For instance, a jump in consumer outlays is not necessarily indicative of healthy economic growth if it's the result of a surge in gasoline prices. Indeed, over time, high gas prices depress spending in other retail sales sectors.

(4) Traditional in-store purchases have always dominated the overall retail sales market. But there are other ways consumers can buy goods that do not involve going to stores or malls. In this category, called *nonstore retailers*, the government

Table 2. Estimated Change in Monthly Sales for Retail and Food Services, by Kind of Business

(Estimates are shown as percents and are based on data from the Advance Monthly Retail Trade Survey, Monthly Retail Trade Survey, and administrative records.)

NAICS code	Kind of Business	Percent Change[1]					
		Jan. 2007 Advance from --		Dec. 2006 Preliminary from --		Nov. 2006 through Jan. 2007 from --	
		Dec. 2006 (p)	Jan. 2006 (r)	Nov. 2006 (r)	Dec. 2005 (r)	Aug. 2006 through Oct. 2006	Nov. 2005 through Jan. 2006
	Retail & food services, total	0.0	2.3	1.2	5.7	0.9	4.1
	Total (excl. motor vehicle & parts)	0.3	3.4	1.3	6.0	0.9	4.6
	Retail	0.1	2.0	1.0	5.3	0.7	3.8
441	Motor vehicle & parts dealers	-1.3	-1.7	1.0	4.7	0.8	2.4
4411, 4412	Auto & other motor veh. dealers	-1.2	-1.4	1.0	5.1	1.0	2.8
442	Furniture & home furn. stores	0.8	-0.2	0.0	4.9	-0.8	2.9
443	Electronics & appliance stores	-1.2	3.5	1.8	12.6	5.9	8.0
444	Building material & garden eq. & supplies dealers	0.8	-3.1	0.7	2.5	0.2	0.2
445	Food & beverage stores	0.7	6.3	0.6	5.5	1.8	5.7
4451	Grocery stores	0.6	6.0	0.7	4.8	1.7	5.1
446	Health & personal care stores	0.6	8.1	0.2	8.2	1.9	8.3
447	Gasoline stations	-0.7	-2.9	3.6	3.6	-2.1	-0.3
448	Clothing & clothing accessories stores	1.0	4.6	1.1	6.1	0.3	5.1
451	Sporting goods, hobby, book & music stores	0.5	-3.1	-0.5	2.5	-2.3	0.9
452	General merchandise stores	1.3	5.6	1.2	5.8	2.0	5.1
4521	Department stores (ex. LD.)	1.4	0.3	0.5	-0.1	1.0	-0.5
453	Miscellaneous store retailers	-1.1	1.9	0.4	8.9	0.9	5.6
454	Nonstore retailers	0.5	8.4	-0.7	5.9	0.0	7.5
722	Food services & drinking places	-0.7	5.3	3.1	9.4	2.1	7.0

▲1
▲2
▲3
▲4
◄5

tallies up how much Americans spent buying goods from other sources, such as mail-order catalogs, the Internet, door-to-door vendors, vending machines, and the telephone (after viewing infomercials or cable shopping networks). True, these purchases still represent a small percentage of total retail sales. But given the cost of gasoline, which discourages driving to stores, and the growing popularity of shopping online, you can expect the proportion of sales from nonstore retailers to climb in the future and to play a more important role in the retail sales industry.

(5) This main column shows how various consumer-based industries fared from changes in retail sales. By looking at the performance of individual producers, you can see which sectors benefited the most in the latest period and whether one or two industries were chiefly responsible for the rise or fall in overall retail sales.

MARKET IMPACT

Though unreliable, the advance report on retail sales still manages to stir up the financial markets.

Bonds

Money managers in the fixed income market get all nervous when shoppers are having too good a time in stores. A jump in retail sales suggests that consumers are in a buying mood. This could accelerate economic growth, a scenario that's likely to lower bond prices and lift yields. A weak or falling retail sales report can set the stage for bond prices to rise.

Stocks

Participants in the equity markets closely monitor activity in the consumer sector of the economy. Healthy retail sales increase corporate revenues and profits, both of which are positive for stock prices. If retail sales are paltry, however, it raises questions about what consumers are up to and whether business earnings can be sustained. Such uncertainties place downward pressure on stock prices.

Dollar

Players in the currency markets find the retail sales report a tricky indicator to analyze. While foreigners prefer to see American consumers in a shopping mood because that firms up interest rates (which is bullish for the dollar), an overly strong retail sales number can also spell trouble for the greenback because many of these goods are imported. Given the already-massive U.S. trade deficit, a jump in imports also increases demand for non-dollar currencies to pay for all these foreign products—and that can potentially hurt the dollar.

E-COMMERCE RETAIL SALES

Market Sensitivity: Low.

What Is It: Measures sales of retail goods purchased through the Internet.

News Release on the Internet: *www.census.gov/mrts/www/ecomm.html*

Home Web Address: *www.census.gov*

Release Time: 10 a.m. (ET); released about seven weeks after the end of the quarter being covered.

Frequency: Quarterly.

Source: Census Bureau, Department of Commerce.

Revisions: Each report comes with revisions for the prior quarter.

WHY IS IT IMPORTANT?

The bursting of the Internet bubble on Wall Street in 2000 eviscerated the portfolios of many investors. However, those who thought the dot-com collapse would also scare people away from shopping online turned out to be flat wrong. Thanks to cheaper and more powerful PCs and the proliferation of wireless high-speed broadband services, Americans are finding the experience of shopping on the Internet more efficient and rewarding. There's no need to worry about traffic jams, red lights, and battling for parking spots. You can do comparison shopping as well as purchase products online right from your home or office, and many merchants provide free shipping. The government has been tracking online retail sales since late 1999, and the data shows that Internet purchases have been steadily climbing, grabbing a bigger slice of consumer dollars in the process.

There is one downside risk, however. Consumers give up a lot of personal information when ordering online and worry that their electronic identities will be either misused by vendors or stolen. This concern should eventually fade with the use of more sophisticated security software that can protect sensitive data and from new legislation that sharply restricts what online retailers can do with your personal records.

While the main monthly retail sales report by the Census Bureau already includes e-commerce sales, the government does not break out that data separately. Sales by barnesandnoble.com are counted in the general merchandise component along with all other sales made by Barnes & Noble bookstores. Sales of Internet-only stores, such as Amazon, are mixed in with other types of non-store retailers, such as mail-order catalog firms.

It's only in this quarterly e-commerce sales report where the details of online shopping are featured. One point to keep in mind is that not all online sales are included in this report. Just as the monthly retail trade data excludes services (such as travel agencies and financial services), they are also kept out of the e-commerce sales data.

Besides the Census Bureau, it's helpful to know that other private organizations occasionally provide free reports on Internet commerce:

• Forrester Research (*www.forrester.com*)
• comScore Networks (*www.comscore.com*)
• Nielsen/Netratings (*www.nielsen-netratings.com*)

How Is It Computed?

Online sales estimates by the Census Bureau are based on the same monthly survey used for the general monthly retail trade report. Some 11,000 retail firms are asked to separate their e-commerce sales. By definition, an e-commerce sale is counted only when customers place the order online. It's not necessary for them to actually pay for the items over the Internet. If they mail a personal check as payment for what was purchased online, it is still considered an e-commerce transaction. Online auctions are also classified as e-commerce sales, but only commissions and fees generated from the auction are included, not the value of the products auctioned.

The Tables: Clues on What's Ahead for the Economy

• **Table 1** Estimated Quarterly U.S. Retail Sales: Total and E-Commerce

E-commerce retail sales are expected to become an important marker for the retail trade industry. A quick study of this table tells why. By comparing total retail sales and its e-commerce component, it becomes clear that online sales are capturing an ever-increasing share of all retail sales. While e-commerce still accounts for a small percentage of total retail sales, its growth is expected to dramatically accelerate in the next five to 10 years and become an important indicator of consumer spending trends.

Table 1.   Estimated Quarterly U.S. Retail Sales: Total and E–commerce[1]
(Estimates are based on data from the Monthly Retail Trade Survey and administrative records.)

Quarter	Retail Sales (millions of dollars)		E-commerce as a Percent of Total	Percent Change From Prior Quarter		Percent Change From Same Quarter A Year Ago	
	Total	E-commerce[1]	Total	Total	E-commerce	Total	E-commerce
Adjusted [2]							
4th quarter 2006(p)	990,835	29,286	3.0	-0.2	6.3	4.6	24.6
3rd quarter 2006(r)	992,603	27,544	2.8	0.8	4.7	5.3	21.1
2nd quarter 2006	984,548	26,304	2.7	0.8	4.4	6.5	22.8
1st quarter 2006	976,652	25,190	2.6	3.1	7.2	8.2	25.2
4th quarter 2005(r)	946,903	23,506	2.5	0.4	3.3	6.2	22.8
Not Adjusted							
4th quarter 2006(p)	1,034,272	33,854	3.3	4.1	32.2	4.0	25.0
3rd quarter 2006(r)	993,749	25,608	2.6	-0.8	3.4	4.8	20.4
2nd quarter 2006	1,002,064	24,758	2.5	10.5	1.0	6.9	22.9
1st quarter 2006	906,635	24,509	2.7	-8.8	-9.5	8.0	25.5
4th quarter 2005	994,452	27,080	2.7	4.9	27.3	6.0	23.1

MARKET IMPACT

Bonds

This report has no impact on the fixed-income market.

Stocks

Generally, news of e-commerce sales produces no meaningful reaction in the equity markets. Internet purchases still represent a very small proportion of all retail sales. Yet, it would be a mistake to dismiss this release as unimportant. As e-commerce sales rise in volume, this report is expected to become much more influential, especially with tech-heavy stock indices, such as NASDAQ.

Dollar

There is no measurable reaction from currency traders to e-commerce sales.

WEEKLY CHAIN-STORE SALES

Market Sensitivity: Medium.

WEEKLY CHAIN-STORE SALES SNAPSHOT

What Is It: A weekly retail sales tracking measure of major department stores.

News Release on the Internet:
  www.chainstoreage.com/csa/industrydata/pdfs/weeklysales.pdf

Home Web Address: *www.chainstoreage.com*

Release Time: 7:45 a.m. (ET); the weekly survey is released on Tuesdays for the week ending the prior Saturday.

Frequency: Weekly.

Source: ICSC (International Council of Shopping Centers)/UBS.

Revisions: Figures are not revised on a weekly basis, but a more comprehensive set of statistics is released every month, and it may include some revisions.

THE JOHNSON REDBOOK INDEX

What Is It: A quick glance at weekly sales at key department and chain stores.

News Release on the Internet: No free access. Available only to paid clients. See press stories for the latest chain-store sales.

Home Web Address: *www.redbookresearch.com*

Release Time: 8:40 a.m. (ET) every Tuesday for the week ending the prior Saturday. The monthly report is released the first Thursday of the new month.

Frequency: Weekly.

Source: Redbook Research.

Revisions: Not on weekly figures. Redbook does release a monthly report in which the numbers are revised as more data arrives.

WHY IS IT IMPORTANT?

Want immediate feedback on how consumer spending has fared the last few days? Who wouldn't, given the critical role shoppers play in the economy? Two competing reports try to provide near-real-time weekly assessments of consumer buying activity in large retail chain stores. One is the Johnson Redbook Index, which is produced by Redbook Research. The other is a joint undertaking by the International Council of Shopping Centers and UBS, a global financial services firm, and is called the ICSC-UBS Weekly Chain-Store Sales Snapshot. Both reports take a similar approach to getting a read on consumer shopping. They contact department and discount chain stores every week for a quick assessment of sales performance. Both release their reports on Tuesday and cover the week ending the previous Saturday. Both also publish monthly chain-store sales data. The two surveys look at comparable store sales, which means that to be included in the survey, the stores have to be open for at least a year. What is different between the two surveys are the number of stores represented in their results and their precise methodologies.

One question that bubbles to the surface is how these chain-store surveys differ from the government's official monthly retail sales report. The answer is they're very different. The retail sales release put out by the Census Bureau represents a broad sample of retailers, both large and small, while the chain-store results are based mainly on purchases at department stores that have multiple outlets around the country. These stores include Macy's, Sears, Wal-Mart, and Target. A second point to consider is that while investors are always hungry for the most current news on consumer spending, department store sales make up just 10% of all household expenditures. People lay out lots more money on cars, vacations, entertainment, health care, food, and a host of other goods and services. Thus, chain-store sales, while a good gauge of current shopping trends, are not a very effective indicator of future consumer spending. Nevertheless, investors and economists like to follow the chain-store series because not many reports describe sales activity with such immediacy.

How Is It Computed?

International Council of Shopping Centers and UBS (ICSC-UBS)

This weekly report first became available in 1994 and is based on hard sales data by just two large department stores, Wal-Mart and Target. Information is then extrapolated to reflect probable sales activity for about 80 chain stores. ICSC-UBS then creates an index that reflects changes in sales for the past week and also from year-ago levels. A seasonal adjustment calculation allows for some week-to-week analysis, though year- to-year comparisons are more reliable.

Unlike the weekly report, the monthly chain-store sales survey is authored entirely by the International Council of Shopping Centers (not in collaboration with UBS) and is based on hard sales data from close to 80 establishments, including specialized chains such as The Gap and Abercrombie & Fitch. Because they have broader coverage, the monthly chain-store figures can serve as a rough leading indicator of future non-auto retail sales in the government series. The first set of numbers on the monthly sales is preliminary because not all of the retailers have released their data. A month later, however, the ICSC produces a final number that is based on more-complete data.

The Johnson Redbook Average

The Johnson Redbook Average monitors weekly sales trends by contacting a handful (the precise number is not revealed) of large general-merchandise retailers. For example, by contacting Wal-Mart, the Redbook can get sales information not only from Wal-Mart's main brand stores, but also from its affiliated discount chain, Sam's Club. All told, the Johnson Redbook Index is derived by contacting retailers that have more than $250 billion in annual sales. With the data in hand, Redbook puts together a sales-weighted average index and produces two main reports. One is weekly and is used primarily for year-on-year comparisons. Though it is possible to monitor sales performance from week to week, these numbers are not seasonally adjusted, so it is hard to make any meaningful comparison given the volatility in this series.

The monthly numbers are seasonally adjusted, making comparisons between months and for the year more meaningful. Yet even the monthly index can bounce around quite a bit, especially during key seasons, such as in August with back-to-school shopping and in December with holiday shopping. Most investors focus on the weekly figures because they are current and can provide an early glimpse of whether consumers are in a shopping mood. Those who follow the monthly reports tend to be more interested in the financial health of retailers for stock-picking purposes. They are not necessarily interested in the reports' value as a broader economic indicator.

THE TABLES: CLUES ON WHAT'S AHEAD FOR THE ECONOMY

- ICSC-UBS Weekly Chain-Store Sales Snapshot

    (1) This graph gives you an idea of how weekly sales have been performing relative to a 16-week, moving-average trend line.

    (2) The table lists the results of the latest weekly sales activity, how it compared to previous week's, and the year-ago performance.

Weekly Chain Store Sales Snapshot

International Council of Shopping Centers   FOR PUBLIC RELEASE AT 7:45 AM (ET)   **February 18, 2004**

Latest Week's Sales Snapshot

Week-to-Week Change:	**1.4%** from prior week
Year-over-Year Change for the Week:	**7.5%** from prior year

Last week was one of those weeks when the consumer said one thing, but did another. The **ABC News** and *Money* magazine weekly Consumer Comfort Index for the week ending Sunday, February 15 posted its steepest drop on record (since late 1985), while the consumers' evaluation of the "buying climate" dropped by 6 points — relative to its maximum drop of 8 points for any given week. Despite what they said, consumers continued their spending streak — this time with love in mind. With Valentine's Day falling on a Saturday, consumers were much more inclined to go shopping for that "someone special," especially on Valentine's Day itself. Sales for the week ending February 14th rose by a solid 1.4% compared with the prior week and a hefty 7.5% on a year-over-year basis, based on the **ICSC-UBS retail chain store sales index**. The latest week's year-over-year sales increase – which compared to an extremely weak 1.5% year-over-year decline for the same week of the prior year – was the strongest since December 18, 1999 (+7.9%). Both discounters and department stores participated in the Valentine's Day sales lift and the industry's monthly sales performance is now tracking at about +5% on a comparable-store year-over-year basis.

February Sales Expectations

January industry comp-store sales, on a year-over-year basis, rose by 6.0%, based on our tally of 77 retail chain stores. That performance was above expectation (ours and most retailers) and finished the fiscal year on a strong note. Easy comparisons, which helped in January, again will help even more in February, though we expect sales to moderate to a 5% pace for the four-week fiscal month.

Fiscal Month (Unadjusted, Year/Year Change)	
Current Fiscal Month (MTD) =	4.7%
Prior Fiscal Month =	4.2%
Two-Months Ago =	3.2%

Selected Monthly Comparable Store Sales Tracking Estimates

TGT = +6.0% r (+)	JCP - Eckerd. = -2.0%	
FD = +3.0%	MAY = +2.0%	
JCP - Dept. = +1.0%	S = +2.0%	WMT = +5.0% r (+)

r=revised; (-) or (+) indicate the direction of the change in monthly sales expectations from the previous week.

Chart 1

ICSC-UBS Weekly U.S. Retail Chain Store Sales Index

Through the Week Ending Saturday February 14, 2004

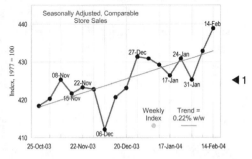

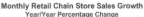

Week Ending	Index 1977=100	Year/Year Chg.	Weekly Chg.
14-Feb-04	438.9	7.5%	1.4%
07-Feb-04	432.9	5.9%	1.8%
31-Jan-04	425.3	4.0%	-1.3%
24-Jan-04	430.9	4.4%	1.1%
17-Jan-04	426.4	3.9%	-0.7%
10-Jan-04	429.2	4.9%	-0.4%
03-Jan-04	430.9	5.6%	-0.1%
27-Dec-03	431.4	5.5%	2.0%
20-Dec-03	423.1	5.7%	0.6%

Chart 2

Monthly Retail Chain Store Sales Growth
Year/Year Percentage Change

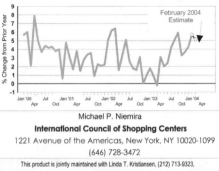

Michael P. Niemira
International Council of Shopping Centers
1221 Avenue of the Americas, New York, NY 10020-1099
(646) 728-3472

This product is jointly maintained with Linda T. Kristiansen, (212) 713-9323,
and Anurag Agarwal, (212) 713-9324, of UBS.

NOTICE: This publication is based on information ICSC believes is reliable. However, ICSC cannot guarantee its accuracy and is not liable for any damages arising out of its use. All proprietary materials and analysis are copyrighted. ©2004.

- The Johnson Redbook Index

  Survey reports and charts are available only to clients. Others can find the Redbook results in the press.

MARKET IMPACT

Bonds

Participants in the fixed-income market monitor, if casually, the Redbook and the ICSC-UBS chain-store sales reports because they are a good finger-in-the-wind measure of consumer spending behavior. If you know what consumers are doing at shopping malls, it tells you something about their appetite to spend. Strong department store sales can make bond investors queasy because of their implications for the economy and inflation. On a slow financial news day, such a report can depress bond prices and cause yields to creep higher. However, traders are usually looking at other larger economic or political news, so the chain-store sales report often slips into the background.

Stocks

Investors in equities pay more attention to chain-store numbers than their colleagues in the bond market. The weekly and monthly sales figures can set the tone for the retail industry as a whole. Healthy chain-store sales growth could result in bigger corporate profits, and that often translates into higher stock prices. Second, these statistics provide some insight into which retailers are doing well and which are ailing, allowing investors with exposure in the retail sector to shift their money accordingly.

Dollar

Currency markets do not react to the chain-store sales numbers.

CONSUMER CREDIT OUTSTANDING

Market Sensitivity: Low.

What Is It: Tracks monthly changes in consumer installment debt.

News Release on the Internet: *www.federalreserve.gov/releases/g19*

Home Web Address: *www.federalreserve.gov*

Release Time: 3:00 p.m. (ET) approximately five to six weeks after the month being reported.

Frequency: Monthly.

Source: Federal Reserve Board.

Revisions: Can be large from month to month.

WHY IS IT IMPORTANT?

The consumer installment debt release usually evokes little more than a yawn from the investment community. For one, it comes out quite late—nearly two months after the fact. By then, numerous other reports on consumer outlays for the same month have already come out. Moreover, the release itself arrives mid-afternoon, just as traders are looking to close their orders for the day. So it shouldn't be surprising if these professional investors find it hard to get worked up about news on consumer credit. Nevertheless, it would be a mistake to dismiss this report, for it has lots of useful information that can add to our understanding of the financial health of consumers and the future course of the economy.

By definition, consumer installment debt is virtually any debt taken on by individuals that is not secured by real estate. What kind of debt are we talking about? There are essentially two types. One is revolving credit, with which most everyone is familiar. It includes credit cards issued by banks, retail stores, and gasoline companies. Whether you pay all your credit card balance at once without incurring interest charges or spread the payments out for months with finance charges, it is all considered revolving credit. However, credit card usage makes up only 40% of all consumer installment debt. The rest is nonrevolving credit. This consists of outright loans to finance the purchase of autos, boats, mobile homes, vacations, home improvement, and education. It also includes the refinancing of existing debt. Consumer installment credit does not include any loan that is collateralized by real estate, so home mortgages and home equity loans are not counted in this series. Motor vehicle leases are also excluded.

If the amount of consumer credit outstanding increases for the month, it means households have borrowed more than they paid off in that period and reflects greater personal spending. When households feel secure about their jobs and income, they become more comfortable with taking on new debt. On the other hand, if the economic climate worsens, people tend to be far more cautious about borrowing. Historically, consumer borrowing and spending tend to rise and fall together. In the short term, though, personal debt can fluctuate quite a lot because of other factors, such as prices, temporary loss of income, and changes in consumer confidence levels.

However, a vital piece of information is missing in this report. The Federal Reserve does not explicitly quantify how much new credit was extended to consumers or the amount of debt that was paid off. It publishes only the net change in indebtedness. Thus, analysts are left wondering whether the monthly change in credit outstanding occurred because people took out lots more debt or cut back on their repayments, or both. For example, say the total amount of outstanding consumer debt increased from $100 billion to $103 billion in one month, a net rise of $3 billion. However, it's unclear whether people borrowed an additional $3 billion more and made no repayment on earlier loans or borrowed as much as $15 billion that month but also repaid $12 billion in old loans for a net change of, once again, $3 billion. This crucial missing piece of data keeps analysts from drawing any firm conclusion about future spending patterns.

Another factor that prevents consumer installment debt from being a reliable leading indicator of household spending is that consumers prefer using credit cards simply because they're more convenient to carry than money. If credit users pay off their entire balance every month, all they're doing is replacing cash with credit. In the data, this can register as a temporary increase in revolving credit, but it won't necessarily result in greater spending.

How Is It Computed?

To compile the consumer installment numbers, the Federal Reserve obtains information from banks, finance companies, S&Ls, credit unions, and other types of lending institutions. The data is then totaled and seasonally adjusted. The dollar amounts are not annualized; they represent the actual outstanding balance at the end of the month. Revisions on consumer installment debt can be substantial, so use the preliminary figures with caution. To better detect a genuine shift in the pace of borrowing, one has to evaluate the data over a three-to-six-month time frame.

The Tables: Clues on What's Ahead for the Economy

- **Table** Consumer Credit Outstanding

  (1) This line shows total consumer credit outstanding in dollar amounts as of the end of the last several months, quarters, and years. Below that is the breakdown of the two main components: revolving and nonrevolving debt.

  A couple of pointers here. Growth in consumer credit can have positive as well as negative consequences for the economy. We've already noted that a significant expansion in borrowing can lead to greater spending and thus stimulate

FEDERAL RESERVE statistical release

G.19

CONSUMER CREDIT
December 2003

For release at 3 p.m. (Eastern Time)
February 6, 2004

Consumer credit increased at an annual rate of 5-1/4 percent in 2003. In the fourth quarter, consumer credit grew 3-3/4 percent, down from a 6-1/4 percent rate in the third quarter. In December, consumer credit increased at an annual rate of 4 percent.

CONSUMER CREDIT OUTSTANDING[1]
Seasonally adjusted

	1999	2000	2001	2002	2003[p]	2002 Q4	Q1[r]	Q2[r]	Q3[r]	2003 Q4[p]	Oct[r]	Nov[r]	Dec[p]
Percent change at annual rate[2,3]													
Total	8.0	10.7	8.1	4.4	5.2	1.3	4.3	6.2	6.2	3.7	5.9	1.1	3.9
Revolving	4.9	11.6	6.8	1.8	3.6	-2.6	4.5	2.7	4.2	2.8	5.2	0.6	2.6
Nonrevolving[4]	10.1	10.2	8.9	6.1	6.2	3.8	4.2	8.3	7.5	4.2	6.4	1.4	4.7
Amount: billions of dollars													
Total	1,512.8	1,686.2	1,822.2	1,902.7	2,001.7	1,902.7	1,923.2	1,953.0	1,983.5	2,001.7	1,993.3	1,995.1	2,001.7
Revolving	590.5	658.9	703.9	716.7	742.5	716.7	724.8	729.7	737.3	742.5	740.5	740.9	742.5
Nonrevolving[4]	922.3	1,027.4	1,118.3	1,186.0	1,259.2	1,186.0	1,198.4	1,223.3	1,246.1	1,259.2	1,252.8	1,254.2	1,259.2

TERMS OF CREDIT AT COMMERCIAL BANKS AND FINANCE COMPANIES[5]
Percent except as noted: not seasonally adjusted

Institution, terms, and type of loan	1999	2000	2001	2002	2003[p]	2002 Q4	Q1[r]	Q2[r]	Q3[r]	2003 Q4[p]	Oct[r]	Nov[r]	Dec[p]
Commercial banks													
Interest rates													
48-mo. new car	8.44	9.34	8.50	7.62	6.93	7.34	7.11	7.05	6.75	6.82	n.a.	6.82	n.a.
24-mo. personal	13.39	13.90	13.22	12.54	11.95	12.24	11.70	12.19	11.95	11.97	n.a.	11.97	n.a.
Credit card plan													
All accounts	15.21	15.71	14.89	13.43	12.74	13.13	13.20	12.90	12.49	12.36	n.a.	12.36	n.a.
Accounts assessed interest	14.81	14.91	14.44	13.09	12.92	12.78	12.85	12.82	13.11	12.91	n.a.	12.91	n.a.
New car loans at auto finance companies													
Interest Rates	6.66	6.61	5.65	4.29	3.40	3.18	3.65	2.61	3.55	3.80	3.92	3.93	3.56
Maturity (months)	52.7	54.9	55.1	56.8	61.4	57.4	59.1	61.1	63.0	62.5	63.5	62.9	61.3
Loan-to-Value Ratio	92	92	91	94	95	96	96	97	94	94	94	94	94
Amount financed (dollars)	19,880	20,923	22,822	24,747	26,295	26,283	25,486	27,468	25,733	26,493	26,067	26,306	27,105

This release is issued around the fifth business day of each month. The exact date and time may be obtained by calling (202) 452 - 3206.
Footnotes appear on reverse.

economic activity. On the flip side, if households accumulate too much debt relative to their income growth, they slash spending and use a greater portion of their future income to pay off some of this swollen debt, a shift that can reduce sales and slow the economy. The question becomes, at what point does the level of debt get so high as to strain household finances? Experts disagree on this. One indication of trouble can be seen by comparing total consumer installment debt with the annualized amount of personal income that month (see the section "Personal Income and Spending"). Since the 1960s, consumer debt has generally settled within a range of 14% to 18% of personal income. By the 2001 recession, however, it jumped to more than 21%. Generally, when the ratio exceeds 20%, credit card delinquencies start to accelerate, and this serves as a warning that households are beginning to struggle with their debt load.

If household debt levels are high at a time when interest rates are climbing or as unemployment increases, the ramifications for the economy can be quite serious. Loan applications for nonrevolving credit will quickly plummet, because consumers are reluctant to purchase expensive items, such as a car or a boat, given the high cost of borrowing and the uncertain outlook for their income. However, there's an interesting twist here. Revolving credit will likely stay strong even under such unsettling conditions. Why is that? Because consumers initially loathe the notion they have to lower current living standards even if the economic clouds look threatening. It's not easy to suddenly cut back on discretionary activities such as dining out, taking weekend trips, and going to malls and the movies. Most of these activities are paid for with revolving credit. In addition, households can't give up spending on staples such as cell phone usage, pharmaceuticals, and food. But it is very possible to see a drop in nonrevolving credit in the early stages of economic or financial stress, even as revolving credit shows little or no slowdown.

(2) The percent change is annualized in this part of the table, and that allows you to make quick comparisons over time whether the pace of indebtedness is accelerating, slowing, or falling.

(3) Generally, the greater the demand for consumer credit, the greater the pressure on interest rates to rise. In this table, we see what level of interest rates financial institutions charge for different types of borrowing. Credit card debt carries the highest interest rate, and during difficult economic times, the burden of servicing that debt can pinch household balance sheets. The result: Credit card delinquencies and even personal bankruptcy filings begin to increase.

To get the latest reading on credit card delinquencies, go to the American Bankers Association site, which publishes this data every March, June, September, and December: www.aba.com/Press+Room/PR_ReleasesMenu.htm.

For the most current numbers on personal bankruptcy filings, check out the American Bankruptcy Institute's site: *www.abiworld.org/am/template.cfm? section=press_release.*

MARKET IMPACT

The consumer credit outstanding data arrives nearly two months late, long after other consumer spending reports are out. That's why this economic indicator doesn't set the markets on fire when it's released.

Bonds

Though fixed income investors normally do not react to these debt numbers, an unexpected jump in borrowing can upset the bond market. It means households are more willing and able to buy consumer goods, which can accelerate economic growth, raise the prospect of higher inflation, and place upward pressure on interest rates.

Stocks

The equity market's response is mostly muted. Eyebrows go up, however, if the consumer installment credit report shows a sustained contraction in borrowing. It hints of rising household financial stress, which could lead to cutbacks in spending and thus fewer sales.

Dollar

The U.S. currency is unaffected by the data on consumer installment debt. Foreign exchange traders have adjusted their portfolio well in advance of this indicator because of other, more timely reports on consumer expenditures.

CONSUMER CONFIDENCE INDEX

Market Sensitivity: Medium, but can be high at turning points in the economy.

What Is It: Examines how consumers feel about jobs, the economy, and
    spending.

News Release on the Internet: *www.conference-board.org/economics/
    consumerConfidence.cfm*

Home Web Address: *www.conference-board.org/*

Release Time: 10 a.m. (ET); announced the last Tuesday of the month being
    surveyed.

Frequency: Monthly.

Source: The Conference Board.

Revisions: Minor revisions can occur as more survey results are collected.

WHY IS IT IMPORTANT?

Happy consumers are good for business. They are more likely to shop, travel, invest, and
keep the economy on a roll. An unhappy and insecure consumer is lousy for business, and
if the number of malcontents is large enough, it can derail economic activity. Thus, any
sign of failing confidence can immediately set off alarms in Washington and Wall Street
because consumer expenditures account for well over half of the economy's total
demand. For that reason, economists, government policymakers, and professional money
managers carefully track the temperament of households.

Presently, no less than three organizations regularly check the mood of consumers.
Among the best known are the Conference Board and its monthly Consumer Confidence
Index, the University of Michigan's Consumer Sentiment Survey, and ABC News/
Washington Post's weekly Consumer Comfort Index. Of course, all these groups consider
their own data an important leading indicator of the economy. The fact is that all have
certain disadvantages that limit their effectiveness in predicting consumer spending.

The Consumer Confidence Index, which claims to be based on responses from 5,000
households, is a volatile series with a spotty link to household expenditures. The
University of Michigan's Consumer Sentiment Survey polls a much smaller population; it
queries 500 adults. ABC News/*Money* talks to 250 new people every week but asks only
about current economic conditions, not future expectations.

Furthermore, you would think that the two best-known surveys—Consumer
Confidence and Consumer Sentiment—would show similar performances month to
month, but they often don't. One might point to a pickup in confidence among consumers, while the other may show a decline. Why such conflicting signals? For one, the

surveys pursue different approaches. Conference Board questionnaires place more emphasis on household reaction to labor market conditions, while the University of Michigan gauges consumer attitudes on financial and income situations. This puts the Conference Board survey somewhat at a disadvantage as a leading indicator. The labor market is very slow to react to economic changes. For instance, just before a recession bottoms out, stock prices and consumer spending often rebound. But the unemployment rate tends to stay stubbornly high even long after the recovery has started. In addition, there might be a bias in the Consumer Confidence Index because the questionnaires are mailed out around the time the government releases the unemployment report. So there may be some psychological spillover when respondents fill out the survey. That's less an issue with the University of Michigan's Sentiment Survey, because it dwells on personal income expectations, which ultimately are the most important driving force behind consumer spending. Indeed, the University of Michigan's Consumer Expectations component is included in the Conference Board's Index of Leading Economic Indicators (see the section "Leading Economic Indicators (LEI)").

Another crucial difference between the two surveys is that the Conference Board queries an entirely new group of people every month, while the Michigan survey goes back to interview many of the same individuals it initially polled. This makes the Consumer Confidence Index more erratic on a month-to-month basis compared to the Sentiment Survey. The two also cover different time frames in their questions. The Conference Board seeks expectations over the next six months; the University of Michigan allows for a much longer period in its expectations component—one to five years.

The bottom-line question with these consumer surveys is, can they divine future household spending? Not very well, unfortunately. It's certainly reasonable to conclude that when households are uncertain about their future, they are more watchful of every dollar spent. By the same token, if Americans are upbeat about the economic outlook, it's logical to think they feel more comfortable about spending. However, it hasn't quite worked out that way, much to the chagrin of many analysts. History has shown that the relationship between consumer confidence and spending is not a close one, even though it is perfectly intuitive to think so. Perhaps this is a reminder that no methodology, mathematical construct, or statistical model can successfully predict how human beings will behave in a given circumstance. The best advice here is to put less weight on what consumers tell pollsters about their expectations of the future and focus instead on what people are doing with their money right now. The strongest evidence of confidence can be found at one place—the cash register.

That doesn't mean the Consumer Confidence Index is not without some forward-looking merit. While the short-term, month-to-month correlation between confidence and spending is a slim one, it does strengthen over the long term. A six-month or nine-month moving average of consumer confidence levels has proven to be a somewhat better indicator of future household outlays.

How Is It Computed?

The Conference Board's Consumer Confidence Index began as bimonthly in 1967 and turned monthly in 1977. It's based on an attempt to survey approximately 5,000 households nationwide every month. Rarely, however, do that many respond. About 2,500 make it in time to be included in the preliminary release of the index. A month later, a revision is published. It includes another 1,000 or so late responses. In the end, though, the difference in outcome between the first report and the follow-up revision is usually insignificant.

Here are the key questions asked in the survey:

1. How would you rate the present general business conditions in your area? Good, normal, or bad?

2. Six months from now, do you think they will be better, the same, or worse?

3. What would you say about available jobs in your area right now? Plenty, not so many, or hard to get?

4. Six months from now, do you think there will be more jobs, the same, or fewer jobs?

5. What would you guess your total family income to be six months from now? Higher, the same, or lower?

The Conference Board often throws in additional questions based on current economic conditions. For example, in a climate of falling interest rates, it might ask households if they plan to refinance their mortgage in the next six months.

With all the data in hand, the Conference Board produces three headline indices, all of which are seasonally adjusted. One is the Present Situations Index, and it reflects consumers' attitudes about current conditions. The second is the Expectations Index, which represents how consumers feel conditions might change in the next six months. Finally, you have the overall Consumer Confidence Index, which is based on a composite of the main five questions. It is weighted so that expectations make up 60% of the index while opinions about the current situation account for the remaining 40%.

The Tables: Clues on What's Ahead for the Economy

The Conference Board is a subscription-based service, so it provides only a limited amount of free information on its Web site. Those seeking more details from the latest consumer confidence survey need to subscribe. The fee-based data contains demographic breakdowns by age and income groups, responses from nine geographic regions around the country, and a list of major goods and services that consumers will purchase in the next six months.

Source: The Conference Board, used with permission.

- **Press Release on Consumer Confidence**

  The free online press release has the latest numbers for all three indexes—Consumer Confidence, Expectations, and Present Situations—along with a brief comment on how much they changed from the previous month and why.

  One of the Conference Board's most important questions to respondents each month is whether they think jobs are easier or harder to find. The percentage of people who say jobs are plentiful minus the percentage who believe jobs are hard to get is a very good statistic that can be used to corroborate other data on whether labor market conditions are becoming tighter or more lax.

MARKET IMPACT

Bonds

Though questions abound regarding its efficacy as a predictor of household spending, a sharp and sustained rise in consumer confidence is nevertheless worrisome to fixed-income investors. It could lead to an acceleration in borrowing and shopping, factors that can fuel faster economic growth and stoke inflation. Bond traders prefer to see consumer confidence less ebullient about the future or an outright decline in the index. This would suggest a retrenchment in spending and more modest economic activity ahead.

Stocks

Crumbling confidence by consumers is not favorable to equities because it can presage declining business sales and fading profits. Shareholders hope consumer confidence stays high to encourage more spending, which is bullish for stocks.

Dollar

A depressed consumer makes foreign investors with exposure in the U.S. markets a bit nervous. It raises the prospects of falling interest rates and a weakening business climate, both of which bode ill for the dollar's value. Foreign investors might sell the U.S. currency in search of higher yields and a stronger economy elsewhere. On the other hand, an upbeat consumer can lift U.S. interest rates and stock market returns to levels that promise a higher return relative to other regions in the world. This normally has the effect of increasing demand for dollars.

SURVEY OF CONSUMER SENTIMENT

Market Sensitivity: Medium, but can be high at turning points in the economy.

What Is It: Near-real-time assessment of consumer attitudes on the business climate, personal finance, and shopping.

News Release on the Internet: *www.sca.isr.umich.edu/press-release.php*

Home Web Address: *www.sca.isr.umich.edu/main.php*

Release Time: 9:45 a.m. (ET); preliminary numbers are released on the second Friday of each month. Final figures come out the last Friday of the same month. Only the results of the final survey are published on the Web site.

Frequency: Semimonthly.

Source: Reuters/University of Michigan.

Revisions: Low. Preliminary numbers, out midmonth, are revised two weeks later.

WHY IS IT IMPORTANT?

This is the granddaddy of all consumer attitude surveys. Since 1946, the University of Michigan has been interviewing consumers about their finances and their opinions on national economic conditions. Some experts believe this to be a better predictor of household spending than the Conference Board's Consumer Confidence Survey. Indeed, one component of the Michigan Sentiment survey—Consumer Expectations—is included in the Conference Board's own Index of Leading Economic Indicators. The rationale behind these attitude surveys is the widespread belief among economists that while it's virtually impossible to predict consumer behavior with any precision, Americans do seem more adept at picking up early signs of an economy that is starting to sputter than they are at identifying the beginning of a recovery. Experts think this is because households are more acutely sensitive to losing money than gaining it. Whatever the reason, over the years consumers have demonstrated a pretty good track record of predicting economic downturns. As a result, many brokerage firms, lenders, and retailers are willing to spend big bucks to subscribe to the Sentiment survey.

The University of Michigan publishes its information twice a month. A preliminary reading of the survey (incorporating about 60% of the 500 respondents) is released to clients midmonth on a confidential basis through a conference call and via fax. These results are not meant for widespread distribution, but the release is regularly leaked to the press and thus is known to the financial markets. A final report is issued on the last Friday of the month. While that comes out after the Conference Board announces its Consumer Confidence Index, the Sentiment survey arguably carries more influence among investors. Some analysts view it as a better real-time measure of consumer moods because the data includes interviews conducted up to a day or two before the official release.

How Is It Computed?

The surveys are taken on weekends with a total of 500 individuals. The University of Michigan uses a rotating interview strategy. Each month, 60% of the consumers polled are new to the survey, with the remaining 40% being interviewed a second time. The questions are broader in scope than those raised by the Conference Board. People queried are told to respond to 50 questions about their current and expected personal finance conditions and their buying plans for big-ticket items. They are also asked about the likely direction of the U.S. economy, interest rates, inflation, and jobs over the next year and for the next five years.

The main Index of Consumer Sentiment is based on the results of two subset indices: the Index of Current Economic Conditions, which explores consumers' thinking about their current finances and buying plans, and the Index of Consumer Expectations, which is designed to gauge consumers' outlook on their finances and buying plans over the coming one- and five-year periods.

The survey has five core questions, which are used to calculate all these indexes:

1. Are you and your family (living with you) better off or worse off financially than you were a year ago?

2. Do you think that a year from now you and your family living there will be better off financially, worse, or just about the same as now?

3. Do you think that during the next 12 months we'll have good times financially, bad times, or otherwise?

4. Looking ahead, what is more likely: that in the country as a whole, we'll have continued good times during the next five years or so, or that we will have periods of unemployment and depression or otherwise?

5. About the big things people buy for their homes, such as furniture, a refrigerator, stove, television, things like that. Generally speaking, do you think now is a good or bad time to buy major household items?

THE TABLES: CLUES ON WHAT'S AHEAD FOR THE ECONOMY

There does appear to be a correlation between a sustained change in the consumer "expectations" index and consumer spending in the next six months to a year—especially in the area of big-ticket items such as autos and homes.

As for accessing the actual report on the Web, most details on the monthly Consumer Sentiment Survey are reserved for subscribers. The organization does provide for free on its Web site a one-page press release of the Sentiment numbers along with a brief analysis, but only at the end of the month when the final figures are published. As for viewing historical tables and charts, nonsubscribers can see previous data, except that of the last six months.

MARKET IMPACT

Bonds

Fixed-income investors worry about consumer exuberance because that can translate into greater spending and faster economic growth.

Stocks

Equity managers prefer to see consumers upbeat because they then have a greater propensity to spend on goods and services. This can increase revenues, corporate profitability, and stock values as well.

Dollar

Foreign demand for dollars will be strong as long as the U.S. economy is growing and interest rates are attractive compared to other countries. Because consumer expenditures account for more than $6 out of every $10 spent in the economy, foreigners favor seeing a happy American consumer.

ABC News/Washington Post Consumer Comfort Index

Market Sensitivity: Low.

What Is It: A survey of consumer attitudes.

News Release on the Internet: *http://abcnews.go.com/US/PollVault/* (For the most recent survey, type "consumer comfort" in the search box.)

Home Web Address: *www.abcnews.go.com*

Release Time: 5 p.m. (ET) every Tuesday.

Frequency: Weekly.

Source: ABC News and the *Washington Post*.

Revisions: No revisions.

Why Is It Important?

The ABC News/*Washington Post* Consumer Comfort Index is not known to animate the investment community very much, especially given the existence of two major competitors—the University of Michigan's Consumer Sentiment Survey and the Conference Board's Consumer Confidence Index. However, this relatively new kid on the block does have at least one advantage: it's the only major consumer poll that comes out on a weekly basis, making it more timely than the other two.

Back in 1985, ABC News combined forces with *Money* magazine (and later with the *Washington Post*) to provide information on consumer attitudes more frequently than once a month. Persons interviewed are asked questions on matters of personal finance, the current state of the economy, and if they are in a spending mood. So how does this weekly measure stack up against its two better-known rivals? Well enough to provide an early peek at how the monthly surveys will do when they are released. Since its origin, the Consumer Comfort Index has been very highly correlated with both the University of Michigan's Sentiment survey and the Conference Board's Consumer Confidence Index. In statistics, a correlation of 1 indicates the strongest possible relationship between two variables. The correlation between ABC News/*Washington Post* and Michigan has been .88, and between ABC News/*Washington Post* and the Conference Board, .91.

How Is It Computed?

The methodology used to come up with the Consumer Comfort Index is somewhat unusual. From Wednesday through Sunday of each week, 250 new adults are interviewed by telephone. Respondents are asked to comment on three topics. The first two are whether they feel better or worse about the nation's economy and their personal finances. The third topic probes whether they are presently in a buying mood. Results from this poll are combined with the 750 responses accumulated during the previous three weeks so that in any given week, the ABC News/*Washington Post* Consumer Comfort Index is based on a rolling four-week average for a total sample of about 1,000 people.

Calculating the index is more straightforward. The negative responses to each index question are subtracted from the positive responses. The results of the three questions are then added and divided by 3. The index can range from +100 (where everyone is positive on all three measures) to –100 (everyone is negative on all three measures).

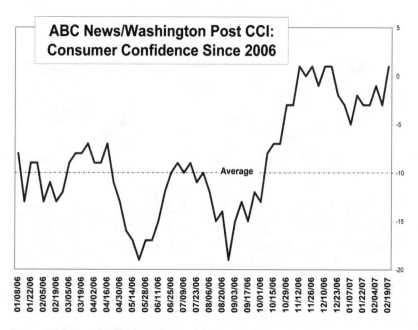

Source: ABC News/*Washington Post*, used with permission.

THE TABLES: CLUES ON WHAT'S AHEAD FOR THE ECONOMY

• ABC News/Washington Post Release

Anyone can access the complete five-page Consumer Comfort report on the ABC News Web site (http://abcnews.go.com/sections/us/PollVault/PollVault.html). It begins with the summary results from the latest survey, followed by an analysis of the data. Also available are details on how various demographic and socioeconomic groups have responded, and a table is added to provide some historical context for all the numbers.

What's useful about the Consumer Comfort measure is that it can corroborate other economic trends. Forecasters have observed how measures of consumer moods have a good track record of foreseeing the start of recessions, but they seem to fail when it comes to anticipating the beginning of recoveries. For investors, the real value in the weekly Consumer Comfort Index is that it offers a heads-up on the outcome of the more market-sensitive Consumer Confidence and Consumer Sentiment measures.

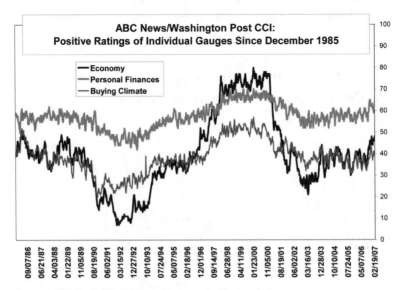

Source: ABC News/*Washington Post*, used with permission.

MARKET IMPACT

Bonds

Investors often note the results of the ABC News/*Washington Post* Comfort Index but generally don't respond to it in any measurable way. There are only two circumstances when this report can cause a stir in the bond market, and they might have to occur simultaneously. One is when the Consumer Comfort indicator comes out on an otherwise slow news day as traders are groping for a reason to trade. The second is when the survey results swing sharply in one direction or the other. Given the two events, market reaction to the Consumer Comfort news will be much the same as for the Consumer Confidence and Sentiment surveys.

Stocks

The Comfort Index is of only modest interest to equity traders. More attention is paid to the better-known monthly indices on consumer attitudes.

Dollar

Currency traders largely ignore the report. It has no appreciable impact on the dollar.

UBS/GALLUP INDEX OF INVESTOR OPTIMISM

Market Sensitivity: Low for now, but can increase in the future.

What Is It: Measures changes in investor confidence.

News Release on the Internet: *www.ubs.com/investoroptimism*

Home Web Address: *www.ubs.com*

Release Time: 8:30 a.m. (ET), with data published the fourth Monday of the month being covered.

Frequency: Monthly.

Source: UBS and the Gallup Organization.

Revisions: No revisions are done.

WHY IS IT IMPORTANT?

One of the most intriguing economic indicators also happens to be one of the least known. It's called the UBS/Gallup Index of Investor Optimism and it measures the attitude of private investors. What is special about this measure is that it has real potential to be an effective leading indicator of consumer spending. The reason for this is the remarkably close correlation that has emerged between changes in key stock market indices, such as the NASDAQ and the S&P 500, and their effect on consumer expenditures. This relationship has been firming since the 1990s, when, for the first time, stocks began to account for most of the value in household financial assets. Back in 1983, less than 20% of households in America owned stocks. Today more than 50% do. Most of these households are in the 35–64 age category, a group with the highest income levels, the most invested, and the greatest propensity to spend. Thus, you can bet with reasonable certainty that sharp swings in the stock market will affect future consumer spending behavior. This increasingly important link between stock market performance and household expenditures makes the UBS/Gallup Index of Investor Optimism a promising forecasting tool.

HOW IS IT COMPUTED?

The Index of Investor Optimism was launched in 1996 in a joint project by UBS, a global financial services firm, and the Gallup Organization, a worldwide polling company. The survey assesses the mood of a limited but growing segment of the population: households with investable assets of at least $10,000. That demographic segment accounts for nearly 40% of all U.S. households and more than 80% of the financial wealth in the U.S. Within this population group, about 800 households are randomly selected from across the country and are interviewed by phone in the first two weeks of each month. They are asked to respond along three major themes. The first consists of seven questions that form the basis of the overall Index of Investor Optimism:

1. Overall, are you optimistic, pessimistic, or neither that you will be able to achieve your investment targets over the next 12 months?

2. Overall, are you optimistic, pessimistic, or neither that you will achieve your investment goals over the next five years?

3. Overall, are you optimistic, pessimistic, or neither about your ability to maintain or increase your current income and earnings over the next 12 months?

4. As far as the general condition of the economy is concerned, how would you rate the next four areas over the next 12 months?

   4a. Economic growth

   4b. The unemployment rate

   4c. Performance of the stock market

   4d. Inflation

The other two themes provide a broader context for what investors are thinking. One is called the Topical Survey, which explores household opinions on current issues such as whether they see real estate as a good investment or how terrorist attacks have affected their investment strategy. The second is the "financial markets survey" and it contains a variety of other questions about the U.S. and foreign financial markets, such as

• Do investors think stocks are overvalued or undervalued?

• Will interest rates increase or decrease?

• What return do they anticipate on their portfolio/stocks?

• Which currencies and countries are expected to be attractive or unattractive?

The Tables: Clues on What's Ahead for the Economy

UBS provides a six-page release on its Web site that summarizes the findings of its survey. It also includes a historical table that lists the overall monthly index going back to its inception in 1996. Missing from the release, however, are some key details on the demographic breakdown of the answers, though UBS says it will e-mail that information upon request at no charge.

• UBS Report on Index of Investor Optimism (Not Shown)

While there appears to be a positive correlation between how key stock indexes perform and future consumer expenditures, precisely how much changes in equity values influence household spending depends on many factors, including the magnitude of the movement in stock values, the level of interest rates, and the growth in personal income from wages and salaries.

Though there is a link between the performance of one's stock portfolio and future spending, the UBS investor index still has to be battle-tested to see just how valid it is in the long run as a leading indicator. However, at least one recent observation can be noted: the Index of Investor Optimism peaked more than a year before the onset of the 2001 recession. By the time the economy began to turn down, the UBS index had already fallen by more than 50%.

MARKET IMPACT

The financial markets have not yet jumped on this economic indicator. That could rapidly change if its correlation with consumer spending stands the test of time.

Bonds

A rising Index of Investor Optimism reflects improved confidence in the economy and expectations that investor portfolios will rise in value. This can be construed as a negative bias against the bond market. Obviously, if the economy and stocks look more attractive, investors will move money out of fixed incomes and into equities. On the other hand, falling investor confidence suggests a widening belief of economic weakness ahead. Thus, a drop in the UBS index can stimulate more purchases of bonds and cause yields to slip.

Stocks

Higher investor optimism indicates that households are sanguine about the economy and the stock market, both of which can encourage more investments in equities and greater consumer spending.

Dollar

Participants in the foreign exchange market currently are not avid followers of this index. But if more studies show the UBS index correlating well with consumer spending, international interest in this indicator will intensify. It is expected that a precipitous drop in investor optimism will likely be viewed as a detriment to the dollar, because the survey reflects disappointment in or concern about the nation's economic strength. Conversely, a persistent climb in the index could catch the eye of foreign investors. They might consider buying U.S. assets in such instances, and this will bolster the dollar's value.

GROSS DOMESTIC PRODUCT (GDP)

Market Sensitivity: Medium to high.

What Is It: The foremost report on America's economic health, GDP measures how fast or slow the economy is growing.

News Release on the Internet: *www.bea.gov/newsreleases/national/gdp/gdpnewsrelease.htm*

Home Web Address: *www.bea.gov/*

Release Time: 8:30 a.m. (ET); advance estimates are released the final week of January, April, July, and October. Two rounds of revisions follow, each a month apart.

Frequency: Quarterly.

Source: Bureau of Economic Analysis, Commerce Department.

Revisions: Monthly revisions tend to be moderate, though they can on occasion be more substantial. Annual revisions, normally done at the end of July, reflect more complete information. Benchmark or historic revisions take place every five years or so with changes that can go back to 1929, when the GDP series began.

WHY IS IT IMPORTANT?

GDP. They are the best known initials in economics and stand for Gross Domestic Product. This is the mother of all economic indicators and is the most important statistic to come out in any given quarter. The GDP is a must-read for many, because it is the best overall barometer of the economy's ups and downs. Forecasters analyze it carefully for hints on where the economy is heading. CEOs use it to help compose business plans, make hiring decisions, and forecast sales growth. Money managers study the GDP to refine their investment strategies. White House and Federal Reserve officials view the GDP as a report card on how well or poorly their own policies are working. For these and other reasons, the quarterly GDP report is one of the most greatly anticipated.

However, trying to decipher the swell of data from the GDP may be intimidating at first. Simply put, the GDP is the total price tag in dollars of all goods and services made in the U.S. It's the sum value of all hammers, cars, new homes, baby cribs, video games, medical fees, books, toothpaste, hot dogs, haircuts, eyeglasses, yachts, kites, and computers—you get the idea—that were sold in the U.S. or exported during a specific period. Even goods that were not sold but ended up on stockroom shelves are included in the GDP because these products were still assembled. The GDP therefore reflects the final value of all output in the U.S. economy, regardless of whether it was sold or placed in inventory.

By looking at GDP performance over the last 50 years, it becomes clear that the U.S. economy has a natural predilection to grow. Business activity has expanded far more years than it has contracted. Though recessions have not disappeared, they definitely have been shorter and shallower since World War II, and that is important to the country's economic and social welfare. The faster and longer the economy grows, the higher the level of employment. With more people working, total household income goes up. This encourages Americans to spend more on goods and services. As consumer spending accelerates, companies are inclined to speed up their own production and hire additional workers. That, in turn, further increases household income—and voila!—you have a self-sustaining economic expansion. Moreover, the benefits of growth are not felt just inside the U.S. Stronger economic growth stimulates foreign businesses as well. Americans will import more cars, clothing, jewelry, wine, and home electronics from other nations, and that helps revitalize the international economy. Foreign workers also use some of their additional income to buy more goods from the U.S.

Can this self-generating cycle of growth continue indefinitely? In theory, yes. However, as a practical matter, this system is susceptible to breaking down once in a while as a result of outside shocks, like war, or in the event of a serious imbalance, such as an accumulation of excess inventories or an outbreak of inflation. Fortunately, such events are rare. And even if they occur, the U.S. government has sufficient resources and policy options at its disposal to minimize damage to the economy.

Looking at the GDP report itself, it's important to note at the outset that the government computes the size of the economy in two ways: One is in nominal dollar terms and the other is in real dollar terms. Let's review what is meant by these two concepts. Current (or nominal dollars) GDP tallies the value of all goods and services produced in the U.S. using present prices. On the other hand, real (or chained dollars) GDP counts only the value of what was physically produced. To clarify the point, suppose a hat-making factory announces that it made $1 million selling hats this year, 11% more than last year. The $1 million represents nominal company sales (or current dollars). However, something's missing. From this figure alone, it's unclear how the factory achieved the extra income. Did it actually sell 11% more hats? Or did it sell the same number of hats as the year before but simply raised prices by 11%? If the factory made more money because it increased the price tag by 11%, then in real (or constant dollar) terms, the true volume of hats sold this year was no greater than last year, at $900,000. This is an important distinction. It's vital to know if the economy grew because the quantity of products sold was greater or whether it was largely the result of price hikes, or inflation. What you want to see are real increases in economic output, which means that a greater supply of goods and services is available for consumers. Higher real GDP improves the standard of living of Americans, while GDP growth due to inflation erodes living standards because people have to pay more for the same amount of products consumed as before. These two measures of GDP thus are of fundamental importance in economics.

To appreciate what the GDP is composed of and how it is calculated, it's best to look at the tables in the release. They are not as complicated as they first appear.

- **Table 3**   Gross Domestic Product and Related Measures: Level and Change from Preceding Period

Table 3.—Gross Domestic Product and Related Measures: Level and Change From Preceding Period

	Billions of current dollars						Billions of chained (2000) dollars								
		Seasonally adjusted at annual rates						Seasonally adjusted at annual rates					Change from preceding period		
	2003	2002	2003				2003	2002	2003				2003	2003	
		IV	I	II	III	IV		IV	I	II	III	IV		III	IV
1 ► Gross domestic product	10,983.9	10,623.7	10,735.8	10,846.7	11,107.0	11,246.3	10,397.2	10,160.8	10,210.4	10,288.3	10,493.1	10,597.1	314.2	204.8	104.0
2 ► Personal consumption expenditures	7,752.3	7,501.2	7,600.7	7,673.6	7,836.3	7,898.4	7,362.2	7,198.9	7,244.1	7,304.0	7,426.6	7,474.2	221.8	122.6	47.6
Durable goods	941.8	907.3	898.2	926.2	975.1	967.8	1,027.6	963.8	965.0	1,005.1	1,069.1	1,071.4	70.4	64.0	2.3
Motor vehicles and parts	423.6	410.4	402.1	414.5	447.2	430.4	441.3	419.0	414.5	429.5	466.9	454.3	18.0	37.4	-12.6
Furniture and household equipment	334.5	325.3	321.8	329.9	339.9	346.4	400.7	373.5	374.7	391.7	412.4	424.0	36.0	20.7	11.6
Other	183.8	171.6	174.3	181.8	188.0	191.0	187.7	173.0	177.6	185.9	191.4	196.1	17.5	5.5	4.7
Nondurable goods	2,208.3	2,119.2	2,175.7	2,170.8	2,230.0	2,256.9	2,119.8	2,061.8	2,090.5	2,096.9	2,134.3	2,157.6	76.2	37.4	23.3
Food	1,064.2	1,016.4	1,037.4	1,049.7	1,074.9	1,094.7	994.6	963.9	979.6	985.4	1,002.8	1,010.7	36.4	17.4	7.9
Clothing and shoes	311.2	306.4	304.8	307.5	315.1	317.3	334.4	323.4	325.7	331.9	339.5	340.4	15.3	7.6	.9
Gasoline, fuel oil, and other energy goods	208.7	193.0	222.4	196.9	209.2	206.4	197.6	201.0	203.1	192.9	194.7	199.9	-1.7	1.8	5.2
Other	624.3	603.4	611.1	616.7	630.8	638.4	593.8	573.8	582.2	587.4	598.3	607.3	26.5	10.9	9.0
Services	4,602.1	4,474.7	4,526.8	4,576.6	4,631.2	4,673.8	4,223.8	4,175.4	4,190.7	4,208.4	4,237.2	4,259.0	82.0	28.8	21.8
Housing	1,198.6	1,167.7	1,181.5	1,191.4	1,204.9	1,216.4	1,085.4	1,071.7	1,078.0	1,082.8	1,088.7	1,092.3	23.5	5.9	3.6
Household operation	426.3	412.9	422.6	424.2	428.5	429.9	396.7	395.6	396.6	393.4	396.8	400.0	2.2	3.4	3.2
Electricity and gas	164.5	156.0	163.1	163.9	165.8	165.3	145.5	147.9	148.0	143.1	144.5	146.5	.3	1.4	2.0
Other household operation	261.8	256.9	259.5	260.3	262.7	264.6	251.2	247.6	248.5	250.5	252.4	253.6	2.0	1.9	1.2
Transportation	293.8	291.5	292.3	292.8	295.3	294.9	278.3	281.3	281.6	278.8	277.2	275.7	-6.5	-1.6	-1.5
Medical care	1,302.2	1,239.8	1,263.1	1,289.2	1,315.1	1,341.4	1,189.7	1,154.8	1,169.3	1,182.4	1,196.9	1,210.2	57.6	14.5	13.3
Recreation	319.3	309.7	312.6	317.2	321.3	326.4	291.3	287.5	287.5	290.1	291.9	295.5	6.5	1.8	3.6
Other	1,061.9	1,053.0	1,054.7	1,061.9	1,066.2	1,064.8	981.1	983.5	976.6	979.7	984.3	983.8	-2.1	4.6	-.5
3 ► Gross private domestic investment	1,667.5	1,614.7	1,605.3	1,624.3	1,689.1	1,751.5	1,635.7	1,595.8	1,581.6	1,599.9	1,656.1	1,705.3	63.7	56.2	49.2
Fixed investment	1,670.8	1,594.6	1,606.2	1,630.1	1,699.5	1,747.5	1,633.5	1,573.5	1,577.7	1,601.4	1,661.0	1,693.9	67.7	59.6	32.9
Nonresidential	1,108.0	1,074.3	1,071.8	1,086.9	1,124.4	1,148.9	1,122.8	1,088.9	1,087.3	1,105.8	1,139.5	1,158.7	30.2	33.7	19.2
Structures	258.9	256.3	256.1	259.2	259.8	260.5	237.2	239.0	236.5	238.8	237.7	235.9	-11.8	-1.1	-1.8
Equipment and software	849.1	817.9	815.8	827.7	864.6	888.4	891.0	853.9	855.0	871.6	907.7	929.6	44.3	36.1	21.9
Information processing equipment and software	463.4	424.1	436.2	451.2	477.0	488.9	522.1	468.2	487.2	506.4	537.7	557.1	62.8	31.3	19.4
Computers and peripheral equipment	97.1	84.9	86.8	93.5	101.8	106.5									
Software	181.0	169.8	173.4	177.6	185.1	187.8	182.3	169.7	174.4	178.6	185.0	191.0	14.8	6.4	6.0
Other	185.2	169.3	175.9	180.1	190.2	194.7	194.5	177.1	184.3	188.6	200.2	205.0	17.4	11.6	4.8
Industrial equipment	133.2	135.6	133.4	133.2	134.1	132.0	130.7	133.9	131.4	131.0	131.4	129.1	-5.4	-.4	-2.3
Transportation equipment	120.2	128.8	119.8	115.3	117.8	127.9	115.5	127.2	117.4	115.1	113.7	115.6	-12.7	-1.4	1.9
Other equipment	132.4	129.4	126.3	128.1	135.7	139.6	128.2	126.1	122.6	123.9	131.1	135.1	3.9	7.2	4.0
Residential	562.8	520.3	534.4	543.2	575.1	598.6	506.1	481.0	486.4	491.7	516.7	529.8	35.8	25.0	13.1
Change in private inventories	-3.3	20.2	-.9	-5.8	-10.5	4.0	-1.5	21.5	1.6	-4.5	-9.1	6.1	-7.2	-4.6	15.2
Farm	-3.1	-4.8	.2	-2.7	-4.3	-5.6	-1.6	-3.5	1.2	-2.0	-2.8	-2.7	1.7	-.8	.1
Nonfarm	-.2	25.0	-1.2	-3.0	-6.2	9.6	.4	25.4	.3	-2.4	-5.9	9.7	-8.9	-3.5	15.6
4 ► Net exports of goods and services	-491.5	-476.1	-487.6	-505.5	-490.6	-482.5	-505.5	-511.5	-490.0	-526.0	-505.2	-500.7	-34.9	20.8	4.5
Exports	1,048.1	1,017.2	1,021.0	1,020.2	1,048.5	1,102.6	1,033.9	1,017.5	1,012.4	1,009.6	1,033.7	1,079.9	19.7	24.1	46.2
Goods	724.7	698.3	707.6	707.7	722.1	761.5	719.7	703.2	706.5	703.5	718.2	750.5	12.5	14.7	32.3
Services	323.3	318.8	313.3	312.5	326.4	341.0	314.0	314.0	305.7	305.9	315.2	329.1	7.2	9.3	13.9
Imports	1,539.6	1,493.3	1,508.5	1,525.7	1,539.0	1,585.0	1,539.4	1,529.0	1,502.5	1,535.7	1,538.9	1,580.6	54.7	3.2	41.7
Goods	1,279.1	1,240.8	1,254.2	1,272.4	1,275.6	1,314.4	1,304.1	1,288.1	1,266.2	1,307.4	1,302.4	1,340.4	55.7	-5.0	38.0
Services	260.4	252.5	254.3	253.3	263.5	270.7	236.2	241.2	236.5	229.8	237.2	241.2	-.2	7.4	4.0
5 ► Government consumption expenditures and gross investment	2,055.7	1,983.9	2,017.4	2,054.2	2,072.1	2,078.8	1,899.5	1,870.8	1,869.0	1,902.8	1,911.1	1,915.0	62.6	8.3	3.9
Federal	757.2	710.0	723.0	764.7	769.6	771.5	704.3	675.8	675.5	712.0	714.3	715.4	56.3	2.3	1.1
National defense	497.0	461.1	463.3	507.3	507.2	510.1	462.6	439.5	433.2	472.8	471.2	473.4	43.8	-1.6	2.2
Consumption expenditures	436.8	404.6	408.6	447.5	443.7	447.4	401.4	382.0	377.3	411.8	406.9	409.7	39.2	-4.9	2.8
Gross investment	60.2	56.6	54.7	59.8	63.5	62.7	61.2	57.4	55.7	60.8	64.5	63.8	4.6	3.7	-.7
Nondefense	260.2	248.9	259.7	257.4	262.4	261.4	241.7	236.4	242.4	239.3	243.1	242.1	12.5	3.8	-1.0
Consumption expenditures	226.3	216.1	227.3	221.4	228.5	227.8	207.7	203.6	209.9	203.4	209.3	208.4	11.4	5.9	-.9
Gross investment	33.9	32.7	32.4	36.0	33.8	33.6	34.0	32.7	32.4	36.0	33.8	33.7	1.1	-2.2	-.1
State and local	1,298.5	1,273.9	1,294.5	1,289.6	1,302.5	1,307.4	1,195.7	1,195.3	1,193.8	1,191.4	1,197.4	1,200.2	6.6	6.0	2.8
Consumption expenditures	1,045.3	1,024.2	1,045.8	1,040.9	1,046.3	1,048.4	956.9	956.4	957.8	956.6	956.0	957.1	6.4	-.6	1.1
Gross investment	253.1	249.7	248.7	248.7	256.2	259.0	238.9	239.0	236.0	234.7	241.5	243.2	.3	6.8	1.7
Residual							-18.7	-2.5	-4.5	-11.5	-27.4	-32.2			
Addenda:															
6 ► Final sales of domestic product	10,987.2	10,603.6	10,736.7	10,852.4	11,117.4	11,242.3	10,394.9	10,138.9	10,206.4	10,289.5	10,497.7	10,585.9	318.0	208.2	88.2
7 ► Gross domestic purchases	11,475.5	11,099.9	11,223.4	11,352.2	11,597.5	11,728.7	10,899.4	10,668.0	10,697.6	10,809.9	10,995.4	11,094.9	347.9	185.5	99.5
Final sales to domestic purchasers	11,478.7	11,079.7	11,224.3	11,357.9	11,608.0	11,724.8	10,897.1	10,646.1	10,693.5	10,811.1	11,000.1	11,083.7	351.7	189.0	83.6
Gross domestic product	10,983.9	10,623.7	10,735.8	10,846.7	11,107.0	11,246.3	10,397.2	10,160.8	10,210.4	10,288.3	10,493.1	10,597.1	314.2	204.8	104.0
Plus: Income receipts from the rest of the world		304.8	296.8	299.5	312.1			291.0	283.4	285.6	296.1			10.5	
Less: Income payments to the rest of the world		266.9	269.0	266.2	274.3			256.1	256.4	253.8	260.7			6.9	
Equals: Gross national product		10,661.6	10,763.7	10,880.0	11,144.8			10,195.5	10,237.6	10,320.2	10,528.6			208.4	
Net domestic product	9,676.2	9,323.3	9,430.1	9,543.3	9,797.9	9,933.4	9,087.6	8,858.4	8,903.4	8,983.4	9,181.7	9,281.7	289.1	198.3	100.0

Note that all numbers are expressed in billions of dollars and at annual rates. (The government uses annual rates to show how the economy would perform if that quarterly pace were maintained for a full year.) Looking at this table, we see two main columns on GDP growth: billions of current dollars and billions of chained dollars. Don't worry about the jargon. "Current dollars" represents nominal GDP, or the value of economic output including price increases. (Remember the hat factory.) "Chained dollars" describes output in real (constant-dollar) terms—that is, how much the economy really produced in volume or quantity. Though both columns contain useful information, the real-dollar amount of the GDP is more closely followed to get an accurate picture of the economy's health. So unless otherwise noted, all references deal with chained (or real) dollars.

(1) *Gross Domestic Product:* The top line says it all. It's the final value of all goods and services produced in the U.S. The word "final" is intentional here; GDP does not directly include the costs of making a product during the intermediate stages. There's a logical reason for this. The value of intermediate goods is already included in the final product, so computing them separately would mean counting such costs more than once. For example, the final price of a new car already factors in all the costs of steel and rubber that went into making it. If you were to add the price of steel and rubber and wages at each stage of the assembly process, you would be counting the same production expenses several times. Thus, the government picks only the final value of goods and services to compute GDP.

Now let's look at the four major components that make up GDP:

- Personal consumption expenditures (what consumers spend)
- Gross private domestic investment (what businesses invest in plants, equipment, and construction)
- Net exports (the difference between what the U.S. sells to foreigners and what the U.S. buys from them)
- Government consumption expenditures and gross investment (how much federal, state, and local governments spend and invest)

Each of these four is further broken down into subcomponents to provide more detail and clarity on what the economy is up to.

(2) *Personal Consumption Expenditures (PCE):* This is essentially all spending by consumers on goods and services, and it accounts for 70% of total GDP. By virtue of its massive role in the economy, if households are not in a spending mood, it spells serious trouble for the economy, with a recession nearly unavoidable. For this reason, analysts closely monitor the dozen or so monthly economic indicators that report on consumer moods, income, and spending.

What are people spending money on? A broad answer can be found in one of the three subcategories that make up PCE: durable goods, nondurable goods, and services:

Durable Goods: These are big-ticket items (such as refrigerators, TVs, autos, and furniture) that by definition last three years or more. While only 15% of all consumer spending is on durable goods, they represent one of the most important measures of the economy's vitality because these types of products are more discretionary in nature. That means spending on durable goods is highly sensitive to changes in consumer income and attitudes. When income declines or consumers become concerned about the economy, they are likely to first postpone the purchase of a new car or television. Conversely, when income goes up or when consumers feel upbeat about future economic conditions, they are more comfortable buying big-ticket items. Furthermore, many durable goods are expensive and often purchased on credit, which makes their sales sensitive to interest rate movements. Once rates start to move up, consumers quickly react by cutting back spending on durable goods because of higher financing costs.

Nondurable Goods: Think vegetables, sweaters, and shoes here—items that last less than three years. Nondurables make up about 30% of all personal spending. In contrast to the volatility often found in durable goods sales, orders for nondurables grow at a more stable rate during both good and bad economic times. The reason is these products are often part of daily living, and spending for them cannot be postponed as easily as for durable goods. During uncertain economic times, households might postpone the purchase of a new car or large plasma-screen TV, but spending on food and fuel oil cannot be delayed. (That's why investors rush to buy shares of companies that produce non-durable goods when the economy is weakening and sell shares of those in the durable goods sector.)

Services: Not surprisingly, more than half of all consumer spending goes to pay for services such as medical and dental care, auto and home insurance, haircuts, mortgages, transportation, and legal costs. The service sector has grown dramatically, from 40% of all personal expenditures in 1960 to nearly 60% now. This category, too, is fairly stable because outlays for housing and medical services continue largely unabated even when income declines.

(3) *Gross Private Domestic Investment:* Business spending constitutes about 15% of GDP, but it can be extremely volatile. Much depends on the economic outlook. Business investment picks up if the economy is expected to show sustained growth, but such expenditures can drop sharply if signs emerge that economic activity is faltering.

Business expenditures fall into two broad headings: fixed investment and the change in inventory investment:

Fixed investment: The lion's share of all business spending is in fixed investment, which covers nonresidential expenditures (for example, office buildings, warehouses, computer equipment and software, machine tools, and transportation equipment)—and residential spending (constructing single-family homes and apartment buildings). Residential outlays alone can account for nearly a third of all investment spending. It makes no difference if these homes or apartments are occupied; all that matters is that they were built.

Both residential and nonresidential investment spending are highly sensitive to the business cycle. If the economy is growing and corporate earnings are increasing, this spurs spending on equipment and construction. However, the first whiff of a slowdown in economic activity can put the brakes on such investments. As demand for goods and services dries up, so will business spending. The resulting cutback in corporate expenditures can help drag an economy into recession.

Change in private inventories: Inventory changes and their relationship to GDP have been a source of much confusion, but they need not be. The relationship between inventories and economic growth is really quite a logical one. To begin with, we must understand that the GDP reflects the value of everything that is produced in the economy. To do this, the Bureau of Economic Analysis first totals all that consumers, businesses, and government have purchased. Of course, what was bought—and what was produced—are not always the same. Firms often produce a lot more goods than what is actually sold, and what's left over is classified as part of inventory. To get an accurate GDP reading of everything produced in the economy for a given period, you also have to include changes in inventories. Thus, in a simplified formula, GDP represents total demand plus the change in inventories. Here's an illustration of how the computation works. If a hat factory manufactures 1,000 hats but sells just 900, its inventory goes up by 100 hats. If you merely added up the hats that were bought, you would get an incorrect amount on the value of all the hats made by the factory. To come up with the correct figure, you need to add the 100 hats now in inventory to the 900 sold to come up with the total of what was produced.

Now let's look at the situation in reverse. If in the next quarter the same hat factory manufactures only 700 hats but sells 800, it would be inaccurate to just consider total sales, because output that quarter was less than 800. In this case, the hat factory had to dig into inventory to come up with the extra 100 hats to sell. Thus, to obtain the correct amount of what the factory produced that quarter, we'll look at our basic formula again: GDP represents total demand plus the change in inventories. Total demand for hats was 800, plus the change in inventories, which, in this case, dropped by 100. Thus, the result is real output of 700 hats.

As you can see, it's not the level of inventories that is used to compute the GDP, but the change in inventories from one period to the next.

Inventories can fluctuate wildly at turning points in the economy. In recent years, computers have made it easier to prevent inventories from getting too far out of line with sales. However, businesses still find it difficult to determine what the correct level of inventories should be when the economy nears an inflection point. If stockrooms become filled with unsold goods, companies will work off that surplus and trim production, perhaps even shutting plants and laying off workers—steps that could bring economic growth to a screeching halt. As time passes, however, with the aid of advertised sales, special discounts, and other shopping incentives, the inventory on stockroom shelves (and in car dealerships lots) eventually thins out. When consumer demand returns, retailers and whole-salers will increase their orders for goods once again. Factories, in turn, respond by cautiously gearing up production to replenish now-depleted inventories. All these steps help place the economy back on the recovery track.

(4) *Net exports of goods and services:* Foreign trade plays an increasingly important role in the economy. Exports account for about 10% of GDP, double the level of 1980. Imports have surged to 15% of GDP, up from 6.6%. As a result, as much as a quarter of all U.S. output is linked to international trade.

The GDP table lists net exports as a category that contributes to economic growth. What do we mean by "net exports," and why is it included in the GDP? To begin with, American goods and services that are exported are added to GDP for the simple reason that they are produced here in the U.S. Exports stimulate U.S. economic growth because more has to be produced in this country to satisfy both domestic and foreign demand. At the same time, we have to account for the fact that Americans do spend money on imports. Purchases of foreign goods and services by U.S. consumers are subtracted from GDP growth because Americans are satisfying some of their demand by buying products that were not made in the U.S. but represent the output of another country. The term "net exports" is simply the difference between adding exports to the GDP accounts and subtract-ing imports. Since the 1970s, the U.S. has imported much more than it has exported, which is why over the last 30 years net exports has been a negative number and thus a drag on U.S. GDP growth.

(5) *Government consumption expenditures and gross investment:* Government expenditures (federal, state, and local) represent about 18% of GDP, down from 21% in the mid-1980s. The federal component makes up a third of all govern-ment outlays, with state and local purchases accounting for the rest. The GDP table divides federal expenditures into defense spending (military hardware and salaries of military and civilian employees in the armed forces) and non-defense spending (such as highway construction, NASA, the Parks Service, and the salaries of non-defense federal employees).

State and local governments are two-thirds of all official spending and invest-ment (for example, street construction, police, and firefighting equipment), but this number can fluctuate a bit. If the regional economies are doing well, with sales and tax revenues on the rise, outlays pick up as well. However, an eco-nomic slowdown can drain state and local treasuries as official outlays increase to pay for unemployment insurance programs, while government tax revenues shrink. At such times discretionary government spending is sharply cut back.

Adding together all four of the major components—consumer spending, busi-ness investments, government outlays, and net exports—allows the Bureau of Economic Analysis to compute total GDP. However, there are other variations of the GDP that can provide additional insight into the economy's underlying health. Two such indicators extrapolated from the GDP are "final sales of domestic product" and "gross domestic purchases," both of which are listed in the GDP table under "Addenda."

(6) *Final sales of domestic product:* To get a better feel for how vigorous economic activity is, look at how many goods and services were sold that period. GDP does the same, but it also includes changes in inventories, which does not reflect pure demand in the economy. Final sales of domestic product are calculated as GDP without adding in changes in inventories. This measure is thus considered an excellent barometer of actual demand for U.S. products. There's one slight hitch, however. Final sales of domestic product include sales to foreigners as well as to U.S. consumers. To get a sense of demand just in the U.S., we have to check out the next category, gross domestic purchases.

(7) *Gross domestic purchases:* This measure adds up total purchases by U.S. con-sumers and businesses, regardless of whether the product was made here or in another country. Recall that in calculating the GDP, imports are subtracted from spending and investment. Not so with gross domestic purchases. To get a snap-shot of true demand inside the U.S., one has to exclude exports and include imports, which is what gross domestic purchases does.

Nominal and Real GDP: Adjusting for Inflation
When studying economic growth, most analysts want to know how much the econ-omy has physically expanded over time. This is not as simple to figure out as it sounds. GDP is initially calculated based on the current dollar (nominal) value of all goods and services made in the U.S. It is valuable for measuring the size of the U.S. economy, how large it is compared to the economies of other countries, and for learning the relative sizes of the industries that contribute to GDP. However, the problem with using current dollars is that it can be hard to discern whether an increase in GDP came about from greater output of goods and services or simply because of higher prices. People benefit by having more goods and services to pur-chase, not by paying higher prices for them.

So how can you determine how much of the rise in GDP was due to real expansion and how much was the result of inflation? The way to do this is to collect the current dollar value of all goods and services and then strip out the effects of price changes. The Bureau of Economic Analysis in 1996 put into effect a chain-type inflation measure that helps convert current GDP to real GDP. The methodology to accomplish this is complex and technical, but it is designed not only to remove price inflation, but also to adjust for changes in consumer shopping habits brought on by differences in product prices and in the quality of goods. (For instance, if the price of beef increases significantly, consumers might choose a less expensive cut of meat or even poultry. The chain-type calculation tries to account for these shifts.) What emerges are several different, yet quite important, inflation measures of the economy. The three major price indicators are the GDP price deflator, the gross domestic purchases deflator, and the influential PCE price index.

- **Table 4** Price Indexes for Gross Domestic Product and Related Measures: Percent Change from Preceding Period

(8) *GDP Price Index and GDP Implicit Price Deflator:* These are the main inflation gauges for the economy as a whole. Economists and other players in the financial markets watch these indicators carefully to see if inflation is in check. The GDP price index and the GDP implicit price deflator measure changes in prices for the goods and services produced by the U.S. economy. However, the two inflation markers highlighted here have one significant disadvantage. They do

Table 4.—Price Indexes for Gross Domestic Product and Related Measures: Percent Change From Preceding Period

				Seasonally adjusted at annual rates															
	2001	2002	2003	2000				2001				2002				2003			
				I	II	III	IV	I	II	III	IV	I	II	III	IV	I	II	III	IV
Gross domestic product (GDP)	2.4	1.5	1.6	3.4	2.0	1.9	1.8	3.2	3.2	1.6	1.6	1.1	1.5	1.5	1.7	2.3	1.1	1.6	1.1
Personal consumption expenditures	2.0	1.4	1.8	3.5	2.0	1.9	1.8	3.2	2.5	.5	.4	.7	2.9	2.0	1.7	2.8	.5	1.8	.6
Durable goods	-1.9	-2.9	-3.7	-1.8	-.5	-2.5	-1.0	-1.3	-3.1	-2.8	-2.2	-3.5	-2.9	-3.0	-3.0	-4.4	-3.9	-4.0	-3.8
Nondurable goods	1.5	.5	2.1	5.2	3.7	3.4	1.4	1.3	3.7	-.9	-4.3	-.1	5.7	1.4	1.0	5.1	-2.1	3.8	.4
Services	3.2	2.7	2.8	3.9	1.7	2.1	2.6	5.1	3.2	1.8	3.3	2.0	2.8	3.4	3.1	3.2	2.7	2.0	1.6
Gross private domestic investment	1.1	0	.9	2.0	1.2	1.9	.8	.3	1.3	2.3	0	-.7	-.7	-1.0	1.6	1.3	0	2.0	3.2
Fixed investment	1.1	.1	1.1	2.3	1.2	1.9	.9	.1	1.6	2.4	0	-.8	-.7	-.7	1.7	1.9	0	2.1	3.4
Nonresidential	-.2	-.9	-.2	.6	.3	1.4	0	-1.8	.2	.6	-1.2	-1.3	-1.5	-1.5	.4	-.3	-1.2	1.6	1.9
Structures	5.5	1.4	2.0	4.8	3.6	4.5	5.0	6.5	6.9	6.3	1.2	-.9	.5	.3	1.1	3.8	1.1	2.7	4.1
Equipment and software	-2.2	-1.7	-.9	-.8	-.8	.4	-1.7	-4.7	-2.1	-1.6	-2.1	-1.4	-2.1	-2.1	.2	-1.6	-1.8	1.2	1.3
Residential	4.6	2.4	3.8	7.1	3.9	3.2	3.4	5.3	5.1	7.0	2.9	.3	1.1	.9	4.5	6.4	2.2	3.1	6.2
Change in private inventories	....	....	....	....	....	....	....	....	....	....	....	....	....	....	....	....	....	....	....
Net exports of goods and services	....	....	....	....	....	....	....	....	....	....	....	....	....	....	....	....	....	....	....
Exports	-.4	-.4	2.1	2.7	2.1	.9	.4	-.1	-1.2	-2.1	-3.6	-1.2	2.9	3.3	.6	3.6	.8	1.6	2.7
Goods	-.7	-.7	2.0	1.3	1.6	.3	.4	-.1	-1.6	-2.6	-3.8	-1.4	2.1	3.3	.6	3.5	1.7	-.2	3.8
Services	.4	.3	2.2	6.2	3.5	2.5	.6	.6	-.3	-1.0	-3.0	-.9	4.6	3.2	.6	3.8	-1.3	5.7	.2
Imports	-2.5	-1.0	3.7	5.9	.7	4.2	.7	-2.8	-6.0	-5.3	-9.8	-1.6	10.5	3.7	.8	11.7	-4.1	2.7	1.1
Goods	-3.0	-1.7	2.9	6.8	1.2	4.5	.8	-3.7	-6.6	-6.6	-11.1	-2.1	10.7	2.7	.5	11.8	-6.8	2.6	.5
Services	.2	2.5	7.4	1.3	-2.0	2.5	.3	2.1	-3.0	1.4	-2.9	.7	9.3	8.6	2.0	11.3	10.4	3.3	4.0
Government consumption expenditures and gross investment	2.6	2.6	2.9	6.6	1.7	4.5	2.7	2.7	2.2	2.0	1.4	3.6	3.3	2.2	1.8	1.3	.1	1.7	.5
Federal	2.1	2.7	2.5	7.2	-1.1	5.0	1.6	2.0	1.6	2.4	1.7	5.9	2.3	1.2	-.5	7.7	1.4	1.3	.3
National defense	2.2	2.5	2.6	8.2	-.2	3.6	.9	3.6	1.6	2.4	.8	5.2	2.3	1.8	-.6	8.0	1.2	1.3	.4
Nondefense	1.9	3.2	2.3	5.4	-2.6	7.5	2.7	-.7	1.8	2.3	3.6	7.3	2.1	.2	-.4	7.2	1.6	1.3	.1
State and local	2.9	2.5	3.1	6.3	3.2	4.2	3.2	3.0	2.5	1.8	1.3	2.4	3.8	2.7	3.0	7.1	-.7	2.0	.6
Addenda:																			
Final sales of domestic product	2.4	1.5	1.7	3.4	2.0	1.9	1.8	3.1	3.2	1.6	1.6	1.1	1.4	1.5	1.8	2.4	1.1	1.6	1.1
Gross domestic purchases	2.0	1.4	1.9	3.8	1.8	2.3	1.8	2.6	2.3	1.0	.5	1.0	2.4	1.6	1.7	3.4	.4	1.8	1.0
Final sales to domestic purchasers	2.0	1.4	1.9	3.8	1.8	2.3	1.8	2.6	2.3	1.0	.5	.9	2.4	1.6	1.7	3.5	.4	1.8	1.0
Gross national product (GNP)	2.4	1.5	....	3.3	2.0	1.9	1.8	3.2	3.1	1.6	1.6	1.1	1.5	1.5	1.7	2.3	1.1	1.7	....
Implicit price deflators:																			
GDP	2.4	1.5	1.6	3.6	1.7	2.1	1.6	3.1	3.2	1.6	1.9	.7	1.9	1.0	1.8	2.3	1.1	1.6	1.0
Gross domestic purchases	2.0	1.4	1.9	4.1	1.6	2.5	1.6	2.6	2.3	1.0	.8	.6	2.9	1.2	1.8	3.4	.4	1.8	.9
GNP	2.4	1.5	....	3.6	1.7	2.1	1.6	3.1	3.2	1.6	1.9	.7	2.0	1.0	1.8	2.3	1.1	1.6	....

not provide a full picture of the inflation pressures on U.S. consumers and businesses. The reason? They include prices of exports but exclude prices of imports. A better measure of inflation in the economy, it is often argued, is the price index for gross domestic purchases, which is discussed in the next paragraph.

(9) *Deflator for Gross Domestic Purchases:* This inflation measure takes into account price changes from all purchases, including imports. If oil prices jump higher, that increase in cost is fully incorporated in the gross domestic purchase price index, unlike the GDP inflation indicators. Generally, the price indexes for gross domestic purchases and for the GDP move in tandem—except for periods when the cost of imports surges. That can happen when oil prices shoot up or if the dollar plummets in value, which automatically makes imports more expensive. In such instances, gross domestic purchases turns out to be a better gauge of inflation in the economy.

(10) *Deflator for Personal Consumption Expenditures (PCE):* Which of the major inflation measures should you rely on to help predict monetary policy or consumer spending behavior? The consumer price index (CPI) has traditionally been the main indicator of choice for the financial markets and labor unions. However, several studies have concluded that the most comprehensive and accurate measure of price changes at the consumer level is the PCE price index. Whereas the CPI merely compares price changes for a basket of goods and services whose items remain fixed for years, the PCE price index is sensitive to ongoing changes in consumer spending patterns. Even the Federal Reserve has gone on record saying it will rely more on the PCE price index and less on the CPI when setting interest rate policy. The government uses the PCE index to convert current dollar estimates of personal spending into real, inflation-adjusted dollars. Historically, the PCE tends to be about 0.5 percentage points below the CPI per year, which suggests that Americans actually have more purchasing power than what the consumer price index indicates.

How Is It Computed?

The GDP report has been a work in progress since the late 1930s, which makes it one of the longest running economic indicators around. Calculating the GDP is a mammoth undertaking because we're talking about a $13.5 trillion economy (as of 2007). The main responsibility for this task falls on the nonpartisan Bureau of Economic Analysis, which is well suited for the job given its history and experience.

The GDP series is really part of a marvelous national accounting system known as the National Income and Product Accounts (NIPA). That may be a mouthful to say, but the idea behind it is actually quite simple. In essence, the NIPA is composed of two complementary methods of estimating GDP. One side of the ledger is the product account, which tallies all goods and services sold. The other side is the income account, which looks at where all the monies generated from the production of GDP end up. After all, if consumers, businesses, and the government are spending $13.5 trillion a year, someone must be getting this income. That's where the income side of the ledger comes in. It tries to record the disposition of the money that came from the production of those products and services. (How much went to wages and salaries? Proprietor income? Interest income? Profits?) Theoretically the product and income measures should be equal. However, discrepancies between the two often crop up mainly because of how the statistics are collected. But the differences tend to be minor. By and large, the establishment of America's NIPA is an extraordinary accomplishment and the envy of the world because of its remarkable accuracy, comprehensiveness, and detailed accounting of America's massive economy.

So how does the bureau compute GDP? It collects and assimilates economic data from thousands of government and private sources. Among the information types sought are monthly retail sales, auto sales, and home purchases. To be sure, not all of the economic data is available at the time of collection. As a result, agency staffers work up reasonable estimates for the first GDP report. Why not wait until all the numbers come in before releasing it? Because investment managers and policymakers want to get information on the economy's health as quickly as possible, even if some of its components have to be estimated. Few want to wait a full three months to get the final quarterly GDP report. Thus, the BEA runs the quarterly GDP numbers through its computers three times for the public. The first GDP report, known as the advance release, is published four weeks after the quarter ends. It offers a rough preview of how the economy behaved in the quarter just ended. A month later, the preliminary GDP report is announced. It contains some revisions based on information not available at the time of the advance release. It's only at the very end of the subsequent quarter that we see a final GDP report with additional changes in the numbers to reflect more complete information.

However, it doesn't end there. On top of these revisions, the BEA takes another pass at the GDP statistics once a year, usually in July, when it further refines the numbers.

THE TABLES: CLUES ON WHAT'S AHEAD FOR THE ECONOMY

Embedded in the GDP report are numerous hints on how the economy, inflation, and the job market will perform in the months ahead.

- **Table 1** Real Gross Domestic Product and Related Measures: Percent Change from Preceding Period

(11) This table provides the latest quarterly growth rates for GDP and its chief components, along with about three years of previous quarterly data, to help you gain perspective on what the economy has been up to lately. When looking at the table, it's important to keep in mind that a real 3%–3.5% annual growth rate is considered the pace at which the economy has to grow for people to get a feeling of prosperity. For a $13.5 trillion economy, this means the U.S. must increase its output of goods and services by more than $400 billion every year. If it expands less than 3% on average, the economy may not grow fast enough to absorb all the new workers entering the labor force, and the result usually is higher unemployment.

However, this leads to an obvious question. If 3% growth is the minimum required to lower unemployment, wouldn't 4%, 6%, or 10% growth be even better? How fast can the economy grow before it gets so overheated that it causes an eruption in inflation? There is no simple answer to this question. Much depends on the supply of labor and material resources at the time. Assuming the economy is operating at a low level of unemployment, it is believed the economy's maximum rate of growth without breaking into an inflationary sweat is

Table 1.—Real Gross Domestic Product and Related Measures: Percent Change From Preceding Period

		2001	2002	2003	2000 I	2000 II	2000 III	2000 IV	2001 I	2001 II	2001 III	2001 IV	2002 I	2002 II	2002 III	2002 IV	2003 I	2003 II	2003 III	2003 IV
11 ▶	Gross domestic product (GDP)	0.5	2.2	3.1	1.0	6.4	-0.5	2.1	-0.2	-0.6	-1.3	2.0	4.7	1.9	3.4	1.3	2.0	3.1	8.2	4.0
	Personal consumption expenditures	2.5	3.4	3.1	6.5	2.5	3.9	3.4	.5	2.3	1.9	6.2	4.1	2.6	2.0	2.2	2.5	3.3	6.9	2.6
	Durable goods	4.1	6.5	7.4	24.4	-9.5	6.0	.7	1.7	9.8	.7	27.3	1.6	.5	5.0	.3	.5	17.7	28.0	.9
	Nondurable goods	1.9	3.0	3.7	.3	5.7	2.3	3.7	.4	-1.1	2.9	4.7	6.1	.4	.2	4.6	5.7	1.2	7.3	4.4
	Services	2.4	3.0	2.0	6.0	3.9	4.3	3.9	.3	2.4	1.6	2.8	3.8	4.1	2.2	1.5	1.5	1.7	2.8	2.1
	Gross private domestic investment	-8.4	-1.2	4.1	-6.9	29.1	-9.9	-23	-11.1	-16.4	-8.5	-17.7	11.1	4.6	11.4	-.6	-3.5	4.7	14.8	12.4
	Fixed investment	-3.2	-3.7	4.3	11.5	9.5	-.6	.7	-2.7	-9.2	-5.2	-10.8	-2.5	.6	.6	2.1	1.1	6.1	15.8	8.1
	Nonresidential	-4.5	-7.2	2.8	14.3	14.8	2.2	.9	-4.5	-13.6	-8.4	-14.0	-7.0	-3.0	-1.1	-.1	-.6	7.0	12.8	6.9
	Structures	-2.5	-18.4	-4.7	7.0	18.0	9.6	1.2	-5.9	-5.6	2.2	-35.3	-23.9	-14.5	-14.6	-5.6	-4.0	3.9	-1.8	-3.0
	Equipment and software	-5.2	-2.8	5.2	16.9	13.7	-.2	.8	-4.0	-16.4	-12.2	-4.1	-.2	1.2	3.7	1.7	.5	8.0	17.6	10.0
	Residential	.4	4.9	7.6	4.1	-3.5	-8.0	.4	2.6	3.7	3.1	-2.5	8.7	8.9	4.2	6.8	4.5	4.5	21.9	10.6
	Change in private inventories																			
12 ▶	Net exports of goods and services																			
	Exports	-5.2	-2.4	1.9	6.6	12.3	10.7	-27	-4.5	-13.4	-17.7	-9.8	4.4	8.7	4.3	-3.7	-2.0	-1.1	9.9	19.1
	Goods	-6.1	-4.0	1.8	8.7	13.8	18.3	-5.4	-5.4	-18.1	-18.9	-7.6	-2.6	12.0	4.3	-9.1	1.9	-1.7	8.6	19.2
	Services	-3.1	1.4	2.3	1.4	8.5	-6.6	4.4	-2.0	-.6	-14.7	-15.0	22.8	1.6	4.5	9.4	-10.1	.2	12.7	18.9
	Imports	-2.6	3.3	4.5	16.7	16.5	14.1	-1.6	-6.2	-8.6	-10.8	-3.8	8.4	17.1	4.1	8.2	-6.8	9.1	.8	11.3
	Goods	-3.2	3.7	4.5	16.0	17.7	14.1	-1.6	-6.8	-12.2	-9.2	-3.2	6.3	21.9	4.8	7.4	-6.6	13.7	-1.5	12.2
	Services	.4	1.4	-.1	20.8	10.7	14.1	-1.9	-3.1	12.5	-18.2	-6.9	19.2	-3.6	.7	12.2	-7.5	-10.9	13.4	7.0
	Government consumption expenditures and gross investment	2.8	3.8	3.4	-3.0	5.5	-2.1	1.3	5.8	5.8	-4.1	7.4	4.6	4.0	2.5	7.1	-.4	7.4	1.8	.8
	Federal	3.7	7.9	8.7	-13.9	17.2	-8.2	-1.0	8.9	6.7	0	9.9	8.4	10.5	3.9	18.2	-.2	23.5	1.2	.7
	National defense	3.9	8.9	10.5	-21.3	17.0	-7.4	1.7	7.7	2.6	2.4	14.2	8.2	9.5	4.5	22.1	-5.6	41.9	-1.3	1.8
	Nondefense	3.5	6.2	5.4	1.2	17.6	-9.7	-5.7	11.2	14.4	-4.3	2.6	8.7	12.2	2.9	11.4	10.5	-5.0	6.5	-1.6
	State and local	2.2	1.8	.6	3.2	.1	1.3	2.5	4.3	5.3	-6.1	6.1	2.7	.7	1.7	1.5	-.5	-.8	2.1	.9
	Addenda:																			
13 ▶	Final sales of domestic product	1.4	1.8	3.2	4.2	3.3	1.3	2.6	1.4	.7	-.7	3.2	2.6	1.3	1.8	1.7	2.7	3.3	8.3	3.4
	Gross domestic purchases	.7	2.8	3.3	2.5	7.2	.4	2.1	-.7	-.4	-.8	2.4	5.2	3.1	3.4	2.7	1.1	4.3	7.0	3.7
	Final sales to domestic purchasers	1.6	2.4	3.3	5.6	4.2	2.1	2.6	.9	.9	-.3	3.6	3.2	2.5	1.8	3.1	1.8	4.5	7.2	3.1
	Gross national product (GNP)	.5	2.1	......	.8	6.6	-.7	3.0	-1.3	-.6	-1.9	4.6	2.6	1.3	3.8	2.0	1.5	3.3	8.3	......
	Disposable personal income	1.8	3.8	2.5	9.2	2.7	5.2	.6	-.3	-1.4	12.2	-4.4	10.6	4.1	-.9	.6	2.4	4.9	6.3	-.5
	Current-dollar measures:																			
14 ▶	GDP	2.9	3.8	4.8	4.7	8.3	1.6	3.8	2.9	2.6	.3	3.9	5.4	3.9	4.4	3.1	4.3	4.2	10.0	5.1
	Final sales of domestic product	3.9	3.3	4.9	7.8	5.4	3.2	4.5	4.5	4.0	.9	4.8	3.8	2.8	3.3	3.5	5.1	4.4	10.1	4.6
	Gross domestic purchases	2.7	4.2	5.2	6.6	8.9	2.9	3.7	1.9	1.9	.2	3.3	5.8	6.1	4.6	4.5	4.5	4.7	8.9	4.6
	Final sales to domestic purchasers	3.6	3.8	5.3	9.7	6.1	4.5	4.4	3.5	3.3	.7	4.1	4.2	5.0	3.5	4.8	5.3	4.8	9.1	4.1
15 ▶	GNP	2.8	3.6	......	4.4	8.4	1.4	4.7	1.8	2.5	-.3	6.5	3.3	3.3	4.9	3.9	3.9	4.4	10.1	......
	Disposable personal income	3.8	5.2	4.4	13.0	4.7	7.2	2.4	2.9	1.1	12.8	-4.1	11.4	7.2	1.1	2.3	5.3	5.6	8.1	.1

Seasonally adjusted at annual rates

equal to the rise of non-farm productivity (see the section on Productivity and Costs) plus the growth in the labor force (from the Employment Situation report). A high level of productivity growth along with an ample supply of new workers coming into the labor force keeps the economy well-oiled and out of danger of overheating. Because the labor force has been growing at an annual average rate of about 1% for years, it all comes down to improvements in labor productivity. During the 1970s and 1980s, U.S. productivity grew an average of 1.5% per year. If you add that to the 1% growth in the labor force, it means the economy's top long-term speed without generating inflation was about 2.5%. Since the mid-1990s, however, there has been a dramatic—and, some say, permanent—improvement in productivity growth as companies employ computerized technology and software to operate more efficiently. As a result, productivity increases have averaged above 2.5% in recent years, lifting the red zone for economic growth to about 3.5%. (Calculation: Productivity increase of 2.5% plus 1% for the rise in the labor force equals 3.5%.) However, should the economy expand significantly above the 3.5% rate for several consecutive quarters, it could sop up excess labor and material resources, reignite inflation pressures, and force the Federal Reserve to jump in and raise interest rates.

(12) *Net exports of goods and services:* U.S. trade with other countries now accounts for $1 out of every $4 in economic activity. Indeed, so important have these international transactions become that a small change in the volume of exports or imports can markedly affect GDP growth. If U.S. exports to foreigners drop by 10% from one year to the next, it can reduce GDP growth by about 1 percentage point over 12 months. Should imports rise by 10% over the same time frame, this can slash GDP growth by as much as 1.5 percentage points.

(13) *Addendum:* Final Sales of Domestic Product: Economic forecasting is always risky because there are so many variables to ponder. Where experts seem to miss the mark most often is whenever the economy is about to turn. One early warning sign that the economy is close to switching tracks comes from real final sales, not GDP. The final sales figure is a purer measure of demand in the economy. It excludes inventories and looks at how much consumers, businesses, and the government are actually spending. If the rise in final sales slips below GDP growth for an extended period of time, it means companies have been producing much more than what people are interested in buying. As a result, inventories can swell to undesirable levels, and that will force companies to slow or halt production. Such a scenario can depress economic growth in the future or even cause a recession. Much depends on the degree to which real final sales have fallen and how much unwanted inventories have accumulated.

Conversely, if final sales are increasing at a faster clip than GDP growth, it portends strong economic growth ahead as companies accelerate production to meet the higher demand.

(14) Up to now, all references to GDP numbers were in real (inflation-adjusted) dollars. However, don't neglect growth in nominal (current-dollar) terms. After all, that's how corporate sales, revenues, and profits are recorded. Historically, S&P 500 earnings growth tended to stay in line with nominal GDP. While profits may surge ahead from time to time, over the long run they cannot increase faster than economic growth.

(15) Occasionally you hear references to both GDP and GNP (Gross National Product) and wonder what the difference is between the two. GDP covers all goods and services made in the U.S., regardless of whether it is an American company or a foreign company operating in the States. So long as it is produced within U.S. shores, the output is counted in the GDP. GNP, on the other hand, records goods and services produced only by U.S. residents, regardless of where these plants or offices are located in the world. Here's an example: GDP does not include production of autos made by General Motors if the plant is located in Europe because they were made outside the U.S., but GNP does include it. All production at a Japanese-owned Honda car plant in the U.S. is included in the GDP because these vehicles were manufactured here, but it is excluded from the GNP because of the plant's foreign ownership. GDP is a better measure of output in the U.S. and is more closely associated with U.S. employment activity.

• **Table 2** Contributions to Percent Change in Real Gross Domestic Product (Not Shown)

Simply scanning the GDP headline figures won't tell you much about what's going on in the economy. After all, even with zero economic growth, people are still spending $13.5 trillion a year. In Table 2, you can see which specific sectors in the economy have contributed most to growth and which have been a drag, and by how much. A quick study of this table can answer key questions. Was the latest pickup in economic activity due to a surge in government spending? How much has the business sector contributed to overall growth in the latest period? What role have consumers played in the economy's performance?

• **Appendix Table A** Real Gross Domestic Product and Related Aggregates and Price Indexes

(16) Some of the most intriguing numbers in the GDP report are buried in a table at the end of the release. One is final sales of computers, a key statistic because it reflects business spending on technology products. Such outlays rise when companies are optimistic about the economic outlook and sufficiently confident that they'll see a return on these investments. Sales of computers can also serve as a precursor to productivity growth in the future.

(17) The second figure is motor vehicle output. If dealership lots are filling up because of slow-selling cars and trucks, you'll see the effects in the output

Appendix Table A.—Real Gross Domestic Product and Related Aggregates and Price Indexes: Percent Change From Preceding Period

	2004	2005	2006	Seasonally adjusted at annual rates															
				2003				2004				2005				2006			
				I	II	III	IV	I	II	III	IV	I	II	III	IV	I	II	III	IV
Gross domestic product (GDP) and related aggregates:																			
GDP	3.9	3.2	3.4	1.2	3.5	7.5	2.7	3.9	4.0	3.1	2.6	3.4	3.3	4.2	1.8	5.6	2.6	2.0	3.5
Goods	4.9	4.6	6.4	3.9	1.6	16.2	2.5	3.7	3.0	5.0	4.6	4.9	3.5	6.7	3.1	12.8	3.6	3.8	7.9
Services	3.2	2.3	2.3	.1	3.6	1.9	2.8	4.5	3.0	2.5	2.5	1.8	1.8	3.5	.8	2.4	2.4	2.8	3.5
Structures	5.2	4.6	.6	-1.0	9.2	14.1	2.2	.5	13.6		-2.7	8.0	11.1	.7	3.1	2.9	.3	-7.4	-8.6
Motor vehicle output	3.5	5.9	-1.7	-11.8	10.9	8.9	-6.5	9.9	-7.1	16.6	1.9	12.0	-.7	22.6	-19.1	3.8	-9.4	27.4	-31.7
GDP excluding motor vehicle output	3.9	3.1	3.6	1.7	3.2	7.4	3.0	3.6	4.5	2.7	2.6	3.1	3.4	3.6	2.6	5.6	3.0	1.2	4.8
Final sales of computers [1]	8.2	24.5	17.1	16.9	-2.5	90.4	20.0	-16.0	-17.4	23.0	42.8	24.3	31.5	11.6	33.8	9.5	6.7	11.7	46.7
GDP excluding final sales of computers	3.9	3.1	3.3	1.1	3.5	7.0	2.5	4.0	4.2	3.0	2.4	3.3	3.1	4.1	1.6	5.6	2.5	1.9	3.2
Farm gross value added [2]	7.4	1.0	4.6	-16.1	26.6	-34.7	-36.1	120.0	-17.4	19.4	23.7	-2.0	-24.6	11.3	8.1	14.1	3.9	-2.0	-4.4
Nonfarm business gross value added [3]	4.3	3.8	3.9	1.2	4.3	11.0	1.6	3.6	5.2	3.2	2.4	4.2	4.4	4.9	1.8	6.7	2.7	1.9	4.2
Price indexes:																			
GDP	2.8	3.0	2.9	3.1	1.3	2.1	2.2	3.7	3.7	2.1	3.2	3.5	2.4	3.3	3.3	3.3	3.3	1.9	1.5
GDP excluding food and energy	2.7	3.0	2.9	2.7	1.1	1.7	2.1	3.4	3.4	2.6	3.1	3.4	2.4	2.8	3.3	3.1	3.0	2.2	2.3
GDP excluding final sales of computers	2.9	3.2	3.1	3.3	1.4	2.2	2.3	3.8	3.7	2.2	3.4	3.2	2.6	3.4	3.4	3.4	3.5	2.0	1.6
Gross domestic purchases	3.1	3.5	3.1	4.1	.6	2.2	1.9	4.3	4.1	2.6	3.6	3.2	3.3	4.4	3.5	2.7	4.0	2.2	.1
Gross domestic purchases excluding food and energy	2.7	2.8	2.7	2.6	1.3	1.8	2.0	3.5	3.3	2.5	2.9	3.4	2.3	2.5	3.0	3.0	2.9	2.2	2.3
Gross domestic purchases excluding final sales of computers to domestic purchasers	3.2	3.7	3.3	4.4	.7	2.4	2.0	4.4	4.2	2.8	3.8	3.4	3.5	4.6	3.7	2.9	4.2	2.3	.2
Personal consumption expenditures (PCE)	2.6	2.9	2.8	3.1	.7	2.4	1.5	3.7	3.6	1.9	3.0	2.3	3.1	4.1	2.9	2.0	4.0	2.4	-.8
PCE excluding food and energy	2.0	2.1	2.2	1.1	1.3	1.8	1.6	2.5	2.5	1.7	2.3	2.4	1.9	1.6	2.5	2.1	2.7	2.2	2.1
Market-based PCE [4]	2.3	2.7	2.6	3.1	.3	2.2	.9	3.3	3.4	1.5	2.9	2.1	3.1	4.3	2.5	1.7	4.2	2.2	-1.6
Market-based PCE excluding food and energy [4]	1.5	1.7	1.9	.7	1.0	1.4	.9	1.7	1.9	1.2	1.8	2.2	1.7	1.2	1.9	1.6	2.7	1.9	1.7

numbers in the table. Automakers will respond by slowing or halting production. On the other hand, if demand for autos rebounds and dealers are clamoring for more shipments, output will resume at higher levels. Because the auto industry relies on thousands of suppliers (for rubber, glass, steel, electronics, and fabrics), a change in activity in auto production can affect the fortunes of many other ancillary businesses.

(18) Aside from the main GDP growth figure, what is arguably the second most incendiary statistic in this important report is the change in inflation as measured by the Personal Consumption Expenditures (PCE) price index. Inflation at the consumer level is very closely monitored by the Federal Reserve and greatly influences their decision whether to raise, lower, or keep interest rates unchanged. What these policymakers study most carefully is the percentage change in the core PCE (that is, excluding food and energy). Some people may wonder—and legitimately so—why on earth the Fed pays so much attention to an inflation measure that completely ignores food and energy. After all, these are essential and routine expenses for households. The answer to this question may not satisfy consumers, but the Fed does have a reason for focusing on core-PCE.

We said earlier that while food and energy prices often move up or down sharply in the short run, they may do so for reasons that have nothing to do with economic fundamentals. For instance, a sudden cold spell or a severe drought can damage crops and temporarily inflate the price of certain foods. Sabotage or a hurricane can briefly interrupt the flow of oil and cause energy prices to spike for a short time. These are essentially one-time events that have little permanent impact on inflation. To be sure, consumers have to cough up more money during those periods. However, Fed officials are less concerned about such temporary blips in inflation. Their main goal is to prevent more serious imbalances in the economy that could lead to a *permanent* jump in inflation.

Here's an example: If the economy is racing ahead to the point where total demand for goods and services is growing faster than the nation's ability to supply such products, pressure builds on prices to climb. If left unchecked, this increase in prices can become permanently imbedded in inflation—and that can be very harmful for the economy! To prevent such an imbalance (between demand and supply) from materializing in the first place, the Fed raises interest rates to cool down economic activity a little. This is not an easy job. The big challenge for central bankers is to anticipate such significant imbalances and act on them *before* they become problematic and worsen inflation. Remember, it takes as long as nine to 18 months for a change in interest rates to do their therapeutic work on the economy. So rather than set interest rates based on the main PCE inflation measure, which is heavily influenced by short-run gyrations in food and energy prices, the Fed prefers to track core PCE because it better reflects the economy's true underlying rate of inflation. In this table we see the annual rate of inflation for the latest quarter. Generally speaking, the Federal Reserve prefers to see core-PCE stay within a 1% to 2% range. If inflation is markedly above that level, the central bank could decide to lift the fed funds rates until prices show evidence of retreating back to their target zone. Should the inflation rate slip below 1%, it can be symptomatic of an excessively weak economy, and then the Fed will just as quickly push down rates.

MARKET IMPACT

The GDP report lags behind many more-current monthly indicators, and its release can become a nonevent. However, you have to be careful here! Despite its dated appearance, the GDP report must not be ignored. For one, it could contain some genuine surprises. The growth rate can turn out to be hugely different from what the market expected. Second, it's essential reading for anyone who wants to identify sources of strength and weakness in the economy. Third, a close read of the GDP report can provide some hints on where the economy and corporate profits might be headed in the coming quarters. Fourth, the revisions might be large enough to completely alter your outlook on the economy and call for a new investment strategy. Finally, if the inflation statistics in this report remain stubbornly outside the Fed's comfort zone, you can expect a change in interest rate policy fairly quickly. For these reasons you should never take the GDP release for granted.

Bonds

When the actual GDP data is released, the first question on everyone's mind is how it compares with expectations. If the economy is growing at or below the pace projected by economists, the bond market is likely to react positively, especially if real final sales are anemic and unwanted inventories are ballooning.

Conversely, if GDP growth numbers exceed expectations and the inflation indexes are showing signs of accelerating, it could be a nightmare for bond holders. A strong GDP report combined with rising inflation pressures will spread fears that the Federal Reserve will sooner or later intervene and raise short-term rates to cool down the economy. Unless investors are confident that the Fed can nip inflation in the bud, chances are bond prices will plummet and cause yields to spike.

Stocks

The equity market's reaction to the GDP report will likely be less reflexive than the bond market's. Here the central question is how the latest release affects the outlook for corporate profits. A healthy economy generates more business earnings, while a sluggish business environment depresses sales and income. However, there's an important qualification here. If economic activity has been racing ahead of the 3.5% rate for several quarters, even shareholders start to get nervous about rising prices. Higher inflation will cause an erosion of household purchasing power and probably will force interest rates higher. Thus, the equity market can be as uncomfortable with an economy growing too quickly as it is when it moves too slowly.

Dollar

To foreign investors, a strong American economy is viewed more favorably than a weak one. Robust economic activity in the U.S. spurs corporate profits and firms up interest rates. Thus, foreign investors see opportunities to make money in the stock market and from higher-yielding Treasury bills and bonds. All this increases the demand for dollars. If the Federal Reserve moves quickly to preempt inflation by driving up short-term rates, odds are this would also lead to an appreciation of the dollar because of the perception that the U.S. central bank is ahead of the curve in containing price pressures.

However, if inflation accelerates and stays at a high level, it would lower U.S. competitiveness in the world and worsen the country's foreign trade deficit, a scenario that can make U.S. currency far less appealing.

Durable Goods Orders

(Also known as the Advance Report on Durable Goods Manufacturers' Shipments, Inventories, and Orders)

Market Sensitivity: High.

What Is It: A key indicator of future manufacturing activity.

News Release on the Internet: *www.census.gov/indicator/www/m3/adv/*

Home Web Address: *www.census.gov*

Release Time: 8:30 a.m. (ET); released three to four weeks after the end of the reporting month.

Frequency: Monthly.

Source: Census Bureau, Department of Commerce.

Revisions: Revisions can be major and cover the two preceding months.

Why Is It Important?

Most economic indicators tell a story about what has already happened in the economy. Only a few provide solid clues about what might occur in the future. The Advance Report on Durable Goods orders is one such statistic, and that's why it gets center-stage attention from the financial markets and the business community the moment it is released. When we are looking at "orders" for factory goods, it is about production that will take place in the months ahead. A jump in orders is a positive sign because it suggests that factories and employees will remain busy as they work to satisfy this demand from customers. By the same token, a persistent decline in orders must be viewed as a troubling omen that assembly lines might soon fall silent, leaving workers with little to do. In such a situation, manufacturers face tough choices. Either they will have to shut down some plants and possibly lay off workers, or they will continue to maintain current production levels and risk filling up stockroom shelves with inventories no one wants.

Durable goods are by definition products that have a life expectancy of at least three years (such as autos, computers, machinery, aircraft, and communications equipment), and they represent a crucial part of business investment spending. Many sectors of the economy are tied to durable goods production, including employment growth, industrial output, productivity, and profits. There is another reason why orders for durable goods are so noteworthy: they serve as a sneak preview of the more comprehensive factory orders report, which includes both durable and nondurable goods, that is released just a week later. (See the next section, "Factory Orders.")

How Is It Computed?

The advance durable goods report is based on results obtained from 4,200 manufacturers representing 89 industry categories. Firms with $500 million in annual shipments as well as a handful of smaller companies are asked for figures on new orders, shipments, unfilled orders, and inventories. For military equipment, the government relies on Defense Department data.

A new order is considered if it comes with a legally binding agreement to purchase a product for immediate or future delivery. Options on new orders are not counted. New orders are added up (with previous cancellations netted out), and the value of shipments is calculated after factoring out discounts but before freight charges and excise taxes. Inventories are priced according to their current cost basis.

All numbers are seasonally adjusted but not annualized, nor are the dollar amounts adjusted for inflation. To estimate "real" changes in durable goods orders, compare the growth rate over time with the performance of the producer price index.

The Tables: Clues on What's Ahead for the Economy

What makes the durable goods report such a high-profile indicator for investors is that it can foreshadow significant changes in economic activity far sooner than most other statistics. However, it's important to keep in mind that new durable goods orders are notoriously volatile month to month due in part to sudden large orders for defense goods and aircraft. So you must strip out some of these components to get a true reading of demand in the business sector.

Let's begin with a description of the release on durable goods. It is divided into four main components: new orders, shipments, unfilled orders, and total inventories. Studied together, they can help business leaders and investors better anticipate the future pace of manufacturing output, hiring activity, and consumer demand; all are factors that determine economic growth in the coming months.

- **Table 1** Durable Goods Manufacturers' Shipments and New Orders

  (1) *New Orders:* Orders of U.S.-made durable goods reflect the very latest demand from both American and foreign buyers. A surge in orders will keep factories busy in the future, making this statistic a good leading indicator. But beware: a single large military or aircraft order can inflate total new orders for durable goods and mislead analysts about the economy's underlying strength. To avoid any confusion, this table also contains separate data that excludes the volatile elements of defense and transportation orders.

  (2) *Orders excluding transportation:* As you can see from the title, this category records the number of new orders—but without the transportation component. Why subtract transportation from the total? Orders for civilian aircraft occur in periodic bursts and are hugely expensive. When a large order is received, it swells the total value of new orders for a brief period, greatly exaggerating the

Table 1. Durable Goods Manufacturers' Shipments and New Orders
[Millions of Dollars]

Item	Seasonally Adjusted						Not Seasonally Adjusted [1]					
	Monthly			Percent Change			Monthly			Year to Date		Percent Change
	Jan 2004 [2]	Dec 2003 [r]	Nov 2003	Dec - Jan [2]	Nov - Dec [r]	Oct - Nov	Jan 2004 [2]	Dec 2003 [r]	Jan 2003	2004	2003	Change 04/03
DURABLE GOODS												
Total:												
Shipments	188,110	188,193	184,074	0.0	2.2	0.2	168,020	189,514	159,049	168,020	159,049	5.6
New Orders [4]	180,984	184,226	181,346	-1.8	1.6	-2.4	169,335	189,869	159,786	169,335	159,786	6.0
Excluding transportation:												
Shipments	136,550	135,122	130,829	1.1	3.3	-0.4	121,500	138,690	111,676	121,500	111,676	8.8
New Orders [4]	131,468	128,935	126,831	2.0	1.7	-3.3	121,401	131,894	110,701	121,401	110,701	9.7
Excluding defense:												
Shipments	178,764	178,838	175,275	0.0	2.0	0.3	160,268	178,701	152,004	160,268	152,004	5.4
New Orders [4]	171,952	173,617	170,450	-1.0	1.9	-2.3	159,521	173,356	151,721	159,521	151,721	5.1
Manufacturing with unfilled orders:												
Shipments	128,892	126,803	124,212	1.6	2.1	0.5	114,593	129,679	107,234	114,593	107,234	6.9
New Orders [4]	128,176	128,882	127,774	-0.5	0.9	-3.1	121,853	136,404	113,107	121,853	113,107	7.7
Primary metals:												
Shipments	11,863	11,568	11,069	2.6	4.5	0.9	11,606	10,269	11,231	11,606	11,231	3.3
New Orders	11,915	11,622	11,811	2.5	-1.6	-1.1	12,335	10,715	11,665	12,335	11,665	5.7
Fabricated metal products:												
Shipments	21,308	21,047	20,423	1.2	3.1	-0.5	19,592	19,530	19,199	19,592	19,199	2.0
New Orders	22,363	21,843	21,089	2.4	3.6	-0.5	21,322	19,668	19,282	21,322	19,282	10.6
Machinery:												
Shipments	23,402	22,926	21,260	2.1	7.8	-1.1	20,410	22,734	18,230	20,410	18,230	12.0
New Orders	23,703	24,165	22,269	-1.9	8.5	2.6	21,945	23,349	19,094	21,945	19,094	14.9
Computers and electronic products:												
Shipments	38,325	37,487	36,348	2.2	3.1	-0.5	33,024	45,044	27,810	33,024	27,810	18.7
New Orders [4]	31,708	29,604	29,471	7.1	0.5	-12.5	28,482	37,965	25,234	28,482	25,234	12.9
Computers and related products:												
Shipments	8,762	8,494	8,172	3.2	3.9	-3.3	7,717	11,090	6,262	7,717	6,262	23.2
New Orders	8,503	8,686	8,139	-2.1	6.7	-0.9	7,260	11,024	5,976	7,260	5,976	21.5
Communications equipment:												
Shipments	6,977	6,742	6,667	3.5	1.1	-1.5	5,648	8,907	4,744	5,648	4,744	19.1
New Orders	7,182	4,145	5,122	73.3	-19.1	-46.4	6,676	6,168	6,642	6,676	6,642	0.5
Semiconductors:												
Shipments	6,410	6,046	6,290	6.0	-3.9	0.3	5,945	6,370	5,136	5,945	5,136	15.8
New Orders [4]	(NA)	(NA)	(NA)	(NA)	(NA)	(NA)	(NA)	(NA)	(NA)	(NA)	(NA)	(NA)
Electrical equipment, appliances, and components:												
Shipments	8,545	8,620	8,627	-0.9	-0.1	0.8	7,353	9,040	7,438	7,353	7,438	-1.1
New Orders	8,532	8,228	8,464	3.7	-2.8	-2.3	7,502	8,499	7,447	7,502	7,447	0.7
Transportation equipment:												
Shipments	51,560	53,071	53,245	-2.8	-0.3	1.6	46,520	50,824	47,373	46,520	47,373	-1.8
New Orders	49,516	55,291	54,515	-10.4	1.4	-0.2	47,934	57,975	49,085	47,934	49,085	-2.3
Motor vehicles and parts:												
Shipments	36,832	38,450	37,591	-4.2	2.3	-0.6	34,956	34,033	36,776	34,956	36,776	-4.9
New Orders	36,666	38,631	37,868	-5.1	2.0	-1.2	35,255	34,695	37,193	35,255	37,193	-5.2
Nondefense aircraft and parts:												
Shipments	5,362	5,323	5,861	0.7	-9.2	6.8	3,932	6,534	3,556	3,932	3,556	10.6
New Orders	4,398	6,098	4,930	-27.9	23.7	-12.4	3,783	8,602	4,704	3,783	4,704	-19.6
Defense aircraft and parts:												
Shipments	3,503	3,488	3,016	0.4	15.6	-10.8	2,903	4,159	2,566	2,903	2,566	13.1
New Orders	2,501	3,787	3,733	-34.0	1.4	-5.0	2,961	2,899		2,961	2,899	2.1
All other durable goods:												
Shipments	33,107	33,474	33,102	-1.1	1.1	-0.5	29,515	32,073	27,768	29,515	27,768	6.3
New Orders	33,247	33,473	33,727	-0.7	-0.8	-0.7	29,815	31,698	27,979	29,815	27,979	6.6
Capital goods:[3]												
Shipments	69,727	68,534	66,183	1.7	3.6	-0.5	59,721	77,190	52,632	59,721	52,632	13.5
New Orders	69,270	69,684	67,084	-0.6	3.9	-5.5	64,007	82,539	56,704	64,007	56,704	12.9
Nondefense capital goods:												
Shipments	61,705	60,590	58,684	1.8	3.2	0.1	52,962	68,166	46,523	52,962	46,523	13.8
New Orders	61,093	60,204	57,862	1.5	4.0	-6.2	55,280	67,865	49,791	55,280	49,791	11.0
Excluding aircraft:												
Shipments	59,653	58,120	55,823	2.6	4.1	-0.7	51,673	64,753	45,298	51,673	45,298	14.1
New Orders	59,721	57,657	55,553	3.6	3.8	-5.8	53,856	63,082	47,721	53,856	47,721	12.9
Defense capital goods:												
Shipments	8,022	7,944	7,499	1.0	5.9	-5.3	6,759	9,024	6,109	6,759	6,109	10.6
New Orders	8,177	9,480	9,222	-13.7	2.8	-1.2	8,727	14,674	6,913	8,727	6,913	26.2

Row markers at left: 1 ▶ (Total), 2 ▶ (Excluding transportation), 3 ▶ (Excluding defense), 4 ▶ (Semiconductors), 5 ▶ (Capital goods), 6 ▶ (Excluding aircraft).

underlying pace of demand for durable goods, only to plummet the next month
when it returns to a more normal level. To eliminate these erratic movements,
it's better to study the behavior of durable goods orders without transportation.

(3) *Orders excluding defense:* A similar situation exists with defense goods. The
number of orders for military goods depends entirely on preparations for
national defense and the execution of foreign policy. Given the active role of the
U.S. in the world, there are occasional spurts of official spending on tanks, guns,
aircraft, ammo, naval ships, missiles, submarines, and computers. Of course, the
economy can benefit from higher defense spending, but what we're really after
is knowledge of the underlying strength or weakness of the private business sector. Orders excluding defense turn out to be an excellent predictor of industrial
output, especially if they were not influenced by a large order for civilian aircraft. A persistent climb in new orders for nondefense durable goods lasting, say,
three to four months presages a broad improvement in manufacturing activity
and an increase in factory jobs three to six months down the road.

New durable orders excluding both defense and aircraft: You have to do the math
yourself here because there is no separate breakout for such a category, but it's
well worth the effort. What you come up with is a less well-known but very
effective gauge of consumer confidence. Durable goods are mostly high-priced
consumer products whose purchases are not pressing to most households.
Falling into this group are boats, furniture, cars, wide-screen TVs, and appliances for kitchens and laundry rooms. A common characteristic of all of them is
that consumers have some discretion as to when to buy these products. About
15% of discretionary spending goes to the purchase of durable goods. When
consumers grow uneasy about the economy's path, this is the first place they cut
spending. If new orders (aside from defense and aircraft) rebound, it shows that
households are sufficiently comfortable with their finances and the employment
outlook to resume spending again—all good signs for the industrial sector and
the economy as a whole.

(4) In addition to the broad headings just described, the Advance Report on Durable
Goods contains more details on orders for different industry groupings:

- Primary metals[*]
- Fabricated metals
- Machinery
- Computers, communications equipment, and electronic products
- Electrical equipment and appliances
- Transportation
- All other durables

*When large manufacturers gear up to increase production, their first step is to make sure they have adequate supplies of industrial raw materials. Thus, a resurgence in orders for primary materials is a portent that industrial output is about to shift into higher gear.

(5) *Capital goods orders:* Located at the bottom of this table are orders for capital goods. These are costly items not normally sold to households but to companies that use them to make other products. Purchases here include blast furnaces, machine tools, robotics, and similar equipment. Again, there's a separate listing for total capital goods orders, which includes those for defense, and for nondefense capital goods.

(6) *Nondefense capital goods, excluding aircraft:* This category, also known among economists as "core capital goods orders," might be the best leading indicator of business investment spending. Capital goods orders begin to slip six to 12 months prior to an economic downturn and generally rebound anywhere from three to 18 months after the economy hits a recession bottom.

Shipments

Shipments are, well, just that—shipments! They are products that have been ordered and are now being delivered. If you think of new orders as a leading indicator of manufacturing activity, shipments should be seen as a coincident indicator, which is a measure of what is going on in the economy right now. For that reason, the value of durable goods shipments are used to calculate GDP.

As a rule, shipments are far less volatile than orders. An aircraft maker like Boeing can receive a major order in one month for 40 passenger jets, which will cause the dollar value for new orders to spike that month. However, the actual assembly and delivery of all those aircraft takes much longer. For instance, only two planes might be ready for delivery each month, which means that shipments of the aircraft will be spread out over 20 months. Hence, the measurement of shipments tends to be far more stable than orders.

Unfilled Orders

• **Table 2**   Durable Goods Manufacturers' Unfilled Orders and Total Inventories

(7) *Unfilled orders:* This measure is a favorite among economists for several reasons. First of all, a large backlog of orders suggests that factories will stay busy in the future. That is, orders are coming in too fast for manufacturers to satisfy them on a timely basis. But a buildup in unfilled orders can also pose a problem for the economy. For example, it can strain manufacturing resources, create significant bottlenecks in the production process, cause delays in deliveries, and

Table 2. Durable Goods Manufacturers' Unfilled Orders and Total Inventories
[Millions of Dollars]

Item	Seasonally Adjusted						Not Seasonally Adjusted [1]			Percent Change 2004/ 2003
	Monthly			Percent Change			Monthly			
	Jan 2004 [2]	Dec 2003 [r]	Nov 2003	Dec - Jan [2]	Nov - Dec [r]	Oct - Nov	Jan 2004 [2]	Dec 2003 [r]	Jan 2003	
DURABLE GOODS										
Total:										
Unfilled Orders[4]	505,232	505,948	503,869	-0.1	0.4	0.7	509,314	502,054	486,552	4.7
Total Inventories	263,022	262,827	261,414	0.1	0.5	-0.4	262,333	255,909	270,014	-2.8
Excluding transportation:										
Unfilled Orders[4]	255,370	254,042	254,183	0.5	-0.1	0.9	256,617	250,771	240,424	6.7
Total Inventories	195,307	195,394	194,396	0.0	0.5	-0.2	195,195	190,780	202,420	-3.6
Excluding defense:										
Unfilled Orders[4]	346,955	347,357	346,532	-0.1	0.2	0.4	349,543	344,345	340,987	2.5
Total Inventories	238,920	238,568	237,831	0.1	0.3	-0.5	238,553	232,274	248,811	-4.1
Manufacturing with unfilled orders:										
Unfilled Orders[4]	505,232	505,948	503,869	-0.1	0.4	0.7	509,314	502,054	486,552	4.7
Total Inventories	205,363	205,543	204,731	-0.1	0.4	-0.3	204,592	200,399	212,929	-3.9
Primary metals:										
Unfilled Orders	16,490	16,438	16,384	0.3	0.3	4.7	16,718	15,989	14,893	12.3
Total Inventories	17,464	17,300	17,276	0.9	0.1	0.7	17,607	17,420	19,246	-8.5
Fabricated metal products:										
Unfilled Orders	39,990	38,935	38,139	2.7	2.1	1.8	39,759	38,029	36,983	7.5
Total Inventories	30,864	30,979	30,995	-0.4	-0.1	-0.1	30,949	30,473	31,790	-2.6
Machinery:										
Unfilled Orders	44,203	43,902	42,663	0.7	2.9	2.4	44,399	42,864	43,284	2.6
Total Inventories	41,894	41,589	41,220	0.7	0.9	-0.6	41,967	40,527	42,979	-2.4
Computers and electronic products:										
Unfilled Orders[4]	128,958	129,165	131,002	-0.2	-1.4	-0.4	130,148	128,745	121,377	7.2
Total Inventories	47,267	47,734	47,130	-1.0	1.3	-0.1	46,927	45,928	50,148	-6.4
Computers and related products:										
Unfilled Orders	8,584	8,843	8,651	-2.9	2.2	-0.4	8,348	8,805	7,838	6.5
Total Inventories	6,022	6,145	6,021	-2.0	2.1	-0.8	5,799	5,639	6,150	-5.7

7 ►

even lead to inflation pressures. To correct this, companies have to either increase plant capacity, hire more workers, or keep production lines operating overtime. Without such changes, producers may end up losing clients who are unhappy with the chronic delays in delivery. So you can see why many experts watch unfilled orders very carefully. It serves as an early marker for new capital investments and job growth. Greater spending on plant and equipment stimulates more economic activity and improves the nation's industrial infrastructure. As factory employment rises, so does personal income, and this helps generate more household spending. The one big risk here is when the competition among corporations to acquire material resources and labor gets so intense that it drives up inflation pressures.

What happens if unfilled orders abruptly decline? This can occur for two reasons: Either companies are operating at optimal levels and thus can quickly satisfy all orders coming in, or orders themselves have markedly tapered off. The latter can hurt the economy by putting in jeopardy future production and jobs. By and large, unfilled orders tend to rise when the economy is growing robustly and drop when business activity turns anemic.

Inventories

Whenever factory output exceeds orders, it can cause inventories to balloon and lead to corporate financial headaches. A buildup of unwanted goods can be quite costly to a firm. After all, companies have to pay suppliers for the raw materials needed to manufacture goods. But if there are suddenly fewer buyers for these completed goods, producers have little choice but to store them as unwanted inventories. As these inventories mount, manufacturing executives are often forced to slash output, which can lead to plant shutdowns and layoffs.

MARKET IMPACT

Bonds

Players in the bond market have a visceral dislike for surprises. Yet the Advance Report on Durable Goods is notable for regularly catching investors off guard because it is so volatile and unpredictable. Should orders come in at a pace much greater than expected, it could pummel bond prices and kick up yields. A surge in new orders, excluding defense and aircraft orders, indicates a strengthening manufacturing sector, faster GDP growth, and possibly higher inflation in the future. Conversely, a sudden drop in orders will weaken the manufacturing sector and possibly the rest of the economy, a scenario that's generally bullish for bonds.

Stocks

It's more problematic to predict how equity investors will react to the durable goods report. Generally, a jump in orders is viewed favorably because it can lead to higher corporate profits. However, if the economy is already operating at close to full capacity, a sharp increase in orders might unnerve stock market players who fear the bond market will drive interest rates sharply higher. The rising cost of credit will cut into corporate earnings, and this could end up depressing share prices.

Dollar

The dollar frequently rallies on evidence of a strengthening U.S. economy, especially if it exceeds that of other industrialized countries. However, even currency traders might balk if the durable goods report adds to a growing body of evidence that the economy is overheating.

FACTORY ORDERS

(FORMALLY KNOWN AS MANUFACTURERS, SHIPMENTS, INVENTORIES, AND ORDERS)

Market Sensitivity: Low to medium.

What Is It: A comprehensive measure of manufacturing orders and sales.

News Release on the Internet:
www.census.gov/indicator/www/m3/prel/index.htm/

Home Web Address: *www.census.gov*

Release Time: 10 a.m. (ET); published four to five weeks following the end of the month.

Frequency: Monthly.

Source: Census Bureau, Department of Commerce.

Revisions: Revisions occur over the next two months and can be substantial.

WHY IS IT IMPORTANT?

This economic indicator is a source of some confusion. After all, just a week or so before its release, the government puts out a similar report known as the Advance Report on Durable Goods Orders (see the preceding section). At first glance, it seems to cover the same ground as Factory Orders, but that's not quite the case. The Advance Report is a quick and dirty computation of orders for durable goods (hard products such as cars, aircraft, and refrigerators). This release on Factory Orders, however, adds another important piece of information. Not only does it show the durable goods data of a week ago, but, for the first time, there's also data on nondurable goods orders—defined as soft items such as food, clothing, and fuel—which the earlier Advance Report omits. Nondurable items make up 47% of all factory orders, with durable goods accounting for the rest. By including both durables and nondurables, the Factory Orders report completes the picture on U.S. manufacturing, and this enables economists, investors, and political leaders to get the latest pulse on U.S. factory activity.

Given the comprehensiveness of Factory Orders, you might think financial markets worldwide would anxiously await its release every month. The fact is that to most investors, the report on Factory Orders is as interesting as a soap opera rerun. Why? Because the most valued aspect of this report is the change in durable goods—not non-durables. Durable goods orders are considered an excellent leading indicator of economic activity. But the curtain already opened on that statistic days earlier with the release of the Advance Report on Durable Goods. By the time Factory Order is published, all the news on durable goods has already been digested. Relatively little attention is paid to non-durables because it possesses little predictive value. Non-durable orders tend to rise at a fairly stable rate every month regardless of whether the economy is doing well or not. Consumers will always buy food, clothing, gas, and heating oil, because these products are essential for living.

Should we simply skip the Factory Orders report? No! It contains a mother lode of detailed information on manufacturing. If examined closely, these statistics can offer fresh insight into the soundness of the economy.

How Is It Computed?

The Census Bureau conducts a monthly survey that contacts 4,200 manufacturing departments covering 89 industry groups. Most of the companies queried have more than $500 million in sales a year, with only a few smaller firms included in the survey. Inquiries are made to obtain the latest figures on orders, shipments, and inventories. Not all these companies come back with answers on time. Roughly 60% do, and they are counted in the preliminary release of Factory Orders. Subsequent revisions are based on more complete information.

A new order is considered if it comes with a legally binding agreement to purchase a product for immediate or future delivery. Options on new orders are not counted. New orders are also calculated net of cancellations. For military orders, the government relies on data from the Defense Department. Shipment values are computed net of discounts but before freight charges and excise taxes. Inventory values are calculated on a current cost basis.

All figures are presented in both seasonally and nonseasonally adjusted terms, but they are not corrected for inflation; that is, the numbers are in nominal (current) dollars. To compute the amount after accounting for inflation, use the Producer Price Index for intermediate materials to make the adjustment.

The Tables: Clues on What's Ahead for the Economy

Factory orders are not a high-profile economic indicator as far as money managers are concerned. A quick scan of the headline numbers is enough to satisfy most. However, by investing a little more time in looking beyond the headline figures, you may come away with a better feel for how the economy will perform in the coming quarters.

- **Table 2**   Value of Manufacturers' New Orders for Industry Groups

   This table represents the total dollar amount and percent change of new orders received by U.S. factories from both domestic and foreign customers. New orders is an excellent leading indicator because it impacts future production activity. In this report, orders are broken down into two types of goods. One is durable goods, which we already had an advance peek at the week before, and, in this release for the first time, nondurable goods. Recall that durable goods are considered "hard" products that have a life expectancy of at least three years. Nondurable goods are products that have less than three years of useful existence. Orders for this last category tend

Table 2. Value of Manufacturers' New Orders for Industry Groups

[Millions of Dollars]

Industry	Seasonally Adjusted Monthly Dec. 2003ᵖ	Nov. 2003ʳ	Oct. 2003	Percent Change Nov.-Dec.	Oct.-Nov.	Sep.-Oct.	Not Seasonally Adjusted [1] Monthly Dec. 2003ᵖ	Nov. 2003ʳ	Oct. 2003	Dec. 2002	Year to date 2003ᵖ	2002	Percent 2003/2002
All manufacturing industries [2]	342,383	338,726	341,856	1.1	-0.9	2.4	344,296	330,467	356,785	313,957	3,947,601	3,800,930	3.9
Excluding transportation [2]	286,843	284,211	287,232	0.9	-1.1	1.6	286,573	278,096	298,300	264,507	3,322,287	3,183,832	4.3
Excluding defense [2]	331,847	327,830	330,563	1.2	-0.8	1.8	327,907	320,207	346,566	300,175	3,826,556	3,703,304	3.3
With unfilled orders [2]	126,363	127,774	131,920	-1.1	-3.1	5.5	133,978	125,009	134,875	122,398	1,475,496	1,433,824	2.9
Durable goods industries [2]	181,865	181,346	185,771	0.3	-2.4	3.9	187,373	176,103	193,408	168,525	2,098,886	2,040,581	2.9
Primary metals	11,578	11,811	11,948	-2.0	-1.1	9.8	10,753	11,018	12,200	9,706	132,866	134,089	-0.9
Iron and steel mills	5,321	5,553	5,734	-4.2	-3.2	18.6	5,024	5,135	5,619	4,487	60,943	61,884	-1.5
Aluminum and nonferrous metals	4,967	4,937	4,871	0.6	1.4	3.6	4,581	4,661	5,083	4,194	56,412	56,545	-0.2
Ferrous metal foundries	1,290	1,321	1,343	-2.3	-1.6	-0.5	1,148	1,222	1,498	1,025	15,511	15,660	-1.0
Fabricated metal products	21,043	21,089	21,191	-0.2	-0.5	2.1	19,286	20,465	22,338	18,292	246,177	249,408	-1.3
Machinery	23,053	22,269	21,705	3.5	2.6	1.4	22,303	20,893	21,779	19,538	253,139	244,559	3.5
Construction machinery	1,865	2,273	1,947	-17.9	16.7	4.1	1,862	2,063	1,964	1,754	21,691	20,074	8.1
Mining, oil field, and gas field machinery	710	840	751	-15.5	11.9	-2.2	798	809	690	661	8,727	7,561	15.4
Industrial machinery	3,004	2,612	2,798	15.0	-6.6	-10.0	3,207	2,279	3,139	2,774	34,603	32,186	7.5
Photographic equipment	955	923	918	3.5	0.5	8.1	1,006	960	1,016	907	10,321	9,821	5.1
Ventilation, heating, air-conditioning, and refrigeration equipment	3,011	2,495	2,599	20.7	-4.0	0.7	2,771	2,372	2,423	2,261	30,933	30,392	1.8
Metalworking machinery	1,444	1,519	1,593	-4.9	-4.6	-1.5	1,275	1,764	1,836	1,792	19,999	24,531	-18.5
Turbines, generators, and other power transmission equipment	3,620	3,138	2,632	15.4	19.2	9.7	3,611	3,062	2,552	1,990	30,467	27,202	12.0
Material handling equipment	1,474	1,470	1,395	0.3	5.4	-3.5	1,567	1,304	1,416	1,382	16,106	15,760	2.2
Computers and electronic products [2]	29,136	29,471	33,685	-1.1	-12.5	2.5	37,278	29,924	33,673	33,999	357,068	325,378	9.7
Computers	5,271	5,361	5,490	-1.7	-2.3	3.2	5,812	5,204	6,171	5,778	59,486	50,949	16.8
Nondefense communications equipment	3,594	4,573	8,876	-21.4	-48.5	16.3	5,811	5,469	8,961	6,728	76,372	69,868	9.3
Defense communications equipment	593	549	676	8.0	-18.8	67.3	611	522	658	412	5,665	4,327	30.9
Semiconductors [2]	(NA)	(NA)	(NA)	(NA)	(NA)	(NA)	(NA)	(NA)	(NA)	(NA)	(NA)	(NA)	(NA)
Electronic components	4,648	4,640	4,488	0.2	3.4	5.3	5,146	4,795	4,628	4,558	48,642	52,709	-7.7
Nondefense search and navigation equipment	782	808	887	-3.2	-8.9	4.5	855	824	856	886	10,246	9,726	5.3
Defense search and navigation equipment	2,443	2,795	2,881	-12.6	-3.0	6.8	4,165	2,844	2,611	4,226	31,668	24,616	28.6
Electromedical, measuring, and control instruments	7,183	6,688	6,394	7.4	4.6	-15.3	8,415	6,110	6,110	6,560	75,978	66,053	15.0
Electrical equipment, appliances, and components	8,358	8,464	8,665	-1.3	-2.3	0.8	8,625	8,389	8,877	8,661	101,129	103,013	-1.8
Electric lighting equipment	1,020	1,004	930	1.6	8.0	-13.8	1,216	967	918	1,168	12,413	12,541	-1.0
Household appliances	1,986	2,070	2,088	-4.1	-0.9	4.2	2,107	2,119	2,074	2,105	23,736	22,600	5.0
Electrical equipment	2,362	2,348	2,651	0.6	-11.4	1.5	2,406	2,203	2,696	2,544	29,951	29,891	0.2
Transportation equipment	55,540	54,515	54,624	1.9	-0.2	6.4	57,723	52,371	58,485	49,450	625,314	617,098	1.3
Motor vehicle bodies, parts, and trailers	18,229	18,297	18,759	-0.4	-2.5	0.3	16,293	17,760	20,823	14,378	215,929	222,082	-2.8
Nondefense aircraft and parts	6,296	4,930	5,625	27.7	-12.4	20.6	8,604	5,111	4,635	8,275	60,884	65,295	-6.8
Defense aircraft and parts	4,020	3,733	3,931	7.7	-5.0	7.2	5,814	3,126	3,131	4,665	44,638	40,087	11.4
Ships and boats	2,221	3,371	1,494	-34.1	125.6	-2.4	2,807	3,500	1,729	2,304	25,732	22,423	14.8
Furniture and related products	5,677	6,106	5,981	-7.0	2.1	0.6	5,082	6,158	6,289	5,261	69,752	68,959	1.1
Nondurable goods industries	160,518	157,380	156,085	2.0	0.8	0.6	156,923	154,364	163,377	145,432	1,848,715	1,760,349	5.0

to be more stable because they consist of commodities vital to our daily needs. Thus, any big movement in the total value of new orders is likely to come from changes in durable goods.

(1) *All manufacturing industries:* The best way to determine how busy major U.S. factories will be is to look at the number of new orders coming in, both in absolute dollar terms as well as the percentage change from previous months. Whether it's steel mills, autos, computers, communications, aircraft, or dozens of other industries, this is where you'll get a sense of future production trends for each of the industries featured and for manufacturing as a whole. The table lists new orders for all key manufacturing industries in the latest month and the percentage change in each of the last three months. Why is this so important to track? New orders keep the production lines going. If orders drop off, factories risk being idle, and companies owning these plants can quickly lose money. If demand for factory goods is strong, assembly lines will remain in full operation, and the manufacturer can generate sales income.

Looking solely at total new orders, however, conveys only the most general impression. Certain manufacturing industries are more important than others to the economy. Moreover, total orders can be distorted by the occasional surge in spending on civilian aircraft and defense. Both are typically expensive and cause the value of new orders to balloon, greatly exaggerating for a single month the underlying pace of demand for manufactured goods. To eliminate these erratic movements, it's more prudent to look at manufacturing orders after excluding transportation and defense orders. Fortunately, the Census Bureau adjusts for some of these categories in the same table. Finally, to smooth out the wild monthly swings in the data, one should examine orders on at least a three-month moving-average basis.

(2) *Durable goods industries:* Equity investors here will find more details on orders for an assortment of key manufacturing industries, including computers, semi-conductors, industrial machinery, electronic components, and motor vehicles. It's worth repeating here that regardless of whether you're using the Advance Durable Goods Orders of a few days ago or this revised Factory Orders release, if new orders pick up (minus aircraft and defense), it's a sign that factories will be humming for at least the next three to six months, or longer.

The most substantial shortcoming in the data for new orders is that it does not differentiate between domestic and foreign orders. Thus, it's difficult to discern how much of the new demand originates from inside and outside the U.S.

(3) *Nondurable goods industries:* Unlike durable goods, orders for nondurable goods show little fluctuation during the course of the business cycle, because many products in this group are considered household necessities. Indeed, non-durable goods account for 63% of all retail sales, with food products, pharma-ceuticals, and textiles making up the largest chunk. The one nondurable that can be subject to wide price swings is petroleum, a commodity whose cost is often influenced by geopolitical factors.

Though the total dollar amount of orders for nondurable goods orders is noted at the bottom of Table 2, you'll notice that there's no product breakdown of non-durables here. For that, you have to go to Table 1 (not shown) of this release, which lists the value of products shipped.

• **Table 3**   Value of Manufacturers' Unfilled Orders for Industry Groups

(4) Unfilled orders is one of the most trusted leading indicators of future manufac-turing activity and is a good barometer of the economy's overall health. The cat-egory represents orders to manufacturers that have yet to be filled and shipped. When the economy is growing modestly, the order backlog is minimal, because factories have enough production capacity to meet demand. However, those dynamics change if new orders begin to surge and stay at high levels. Since

[Millions of Dollars]

Industry	Seasonally Adjusted						Not Seasonally Adjusted				Percent Change
	Monthly			Percent Change			Monthly				
	Dec. 2003ᴾ	Nov. 2003ʳ	Oct. 2003	Nov. - Dec.	Oct. - Nov.	Sep. - Oct.	Dec. 2003ᴾ	Nov. 2003ʳ	Oct. 2003	Dec. 2002	Dec. 03/02
All manufacturing industries [1]	505,768	503,869	500,307	0.4	0.7	1.7	501,979	495,329	491,677	480,679	4.4
Excluding transportation [1]	253,822	254,183	251,891	-0.1	0.9	2.5	250,906	251,197	247,897	236,263	6.2
Excluding defense [1]	347,046	346,532	345,067	0.1	0.4	1.8	344,075	343,320	340,826	336,134	2.4
Durable goods industries [1]	505,768	503,869	500,307	0.4	0.7	1.7	501,979	495,329	491,677	480,679	4.4
Primary metals	16,612	16,384	15,642	1.4	4.7	6.7	16,158	15,543	14,895	14,459	11.8
Iron and steel mills	9,768	9,524	8,899	2.6	7.0	11.2	9,437	8,979	8,378	7,800	21.0
Aluminum and nonferrous metals	4,513	4,495	4,396	0.4	2.3	0.7	4,409	4,248	4,217	4,481	-1.6
Ferrous metal foundries	2,331	2,365	2,347	-1.4	0.8	2.4	2,312	2,316	2,300	2,178	6.2
Fabricated metal products	38,409	38,139	37,473	0.7	1.8	1.8	37,861	37,891	37,170	36,900	2.6
Machinery	43,530	42,663	41,654	2.0	2.4	0.5	42,524	42,249	41,182	42,420	0.2
Construction machinery	2,596	2,641	2,289	-1.7	15.4	0.0	2,568	2,509	2,111	2,009	27.8
Mining, oil field, and gas field machinery	1,099	1,117	1,004	-1.6	11.3	4.4	1,099	1,117	1,004	898	22.4
Industrial machinery	7,600	7,575	7,593	0.3	-0.2	-0.8	7,253	7,530	7,546	7,472	-2.9
Photographic equipment	843	811	784	3.9	3.4	1.2	809	819	789	554	46.0
Ventilation, heating, air-conditioning, and refrigeration equipment	4,400	4,538	4,593	-3.0	-1.2	1.1	4,196	4,408	4,433	3,996	5.0
Metalworking machinery	3,935	3,921	3,819	0.4	2.7	2.6	3,874	4,002	3,821	3,643	6.3
Turbines, generators, and other power transmission equipment	9,331	8,415	8,072	10.9	4.2	-0.6	9,305	8,411	8,050	10,730	-13.3
Material handling equipment	4,796	4,764	4,704	0.7	1.3	-0.2	4,800	4,683	4,666	4,889	-1.8
Computers and electronic products [1]	129,686	131,002	131,589	-1.0	-0.4	2.7	129,220	129,454	129,155	118,817	8.8
Computers	8,883	8,651	8,684	2.7	-0.4	-2.7	8,805	8,871	8,564	8,124	8.4
Nondefense communications equipment	46,995	49,558	51,203	-5.2	-3.2	5.3	46,525	49,206	50,151	41,805	11.3
Defense communications equipment	3,456	3,302	3,202	4.7	3.1	6.8	3,456	3,302	3,202	2,942	17.5
Semiconductors [1]	(NA)	(NA)	(NA)	(NA)	(NA)	(NA)	(NA)	(NA)	(NA)	(NA)	(NA)
Electronic components	14,140	13,934	13,602	1.5	2.4	2.2	13,964	13,684	13,525	15,484	-9.8
Nondefense search and navigation equipment	4,657	4,815	4,783	-3.3	0.7	0.9	4,581	4,745	4,685	4,489	2.0
Defense search and navigation equipment	35,651	35,632	35,405	0.1	0.6	1.0	36,028	34,675	34,445	33,634	7.1
Electromedical, measuring, and control instruments	15,904	15,110	14,710	5.3	2.7	1.4	15,861	14,971	14,583	12,339	28.5
Electrical equipment, appliances, and components	13,732	13,997	14,160	-1.9	-1.2	0.7	13,509	13,938	14,094	13,792	-2.1
Electric lighting equipment	1,366	1,408	1,463	-3.0	-3.8	-7.6	1,333	1,356	1,447	1,455	-8.4
Household appliances	766	927	964	-17.4	-3.8	4.8	767	961	882	899	-14.7
Electrical equipment	8,407	8,525	8,634	-1.4	-1.3	1.2	8,274	8,535	8,673	8,071	2.5
Transportation equipment	251,946	249,686	248,416	0.9	0.5	0.9	251,073	244,132	243,780	244,416	2.7
Motor vehicle bodies, parts, and trailers	13,378	13,304	13,027	0.6	2.1	4.0	13,432	12,958	12,407	12,133	10.7
Nondefense aircraft and parts	104,838	103,900	104,831	0.9	-0.9	0.1	105,071	103,003	104,222	111,494	-5.8
Defense aircraft and parts	62,405	61,840	61,123	0.9	1.2	0.9	60,753	59,085	59,216	55,964	8.6
Ships and boats	20,221	20,282	19,233	-0.3	5.5	-3.5	20,461	19,832	18,727	20,648	-0.9
Furniture and related products	5,454	5,603	5,518	-2.7	1.5	1.0	5,235	5,727	5,546	5,254	-0.4

production capacity can't be expanded overnight, at some point manufacturers will no longer be able to keep up with the high level of orders coming in. If orders can't be processed fast enough, deliveries get delayed. One positive outcome from such bottlenecks for the economy is that companies might invest to expand capacity and raise output. At the very least, a growing backlog of orders means high factory employment, more overtime, and busy assembly lines. The danger from unfilled orders is that they can cause a buildup of inflation pressures as both manufacturing capacity and commodities become scarce. Indeed, Federal Reserve officials closely monitor unfilled orders to detect any emerging imbalance between the demand and supply for materials and products.

Aside from warning of inflation, changes in the order backlog can send other signals. A persistent fall in unfilled orders, for instance, can warn of a slowdown in consumer and business spending that could result in a decline in factory output and even recession. Before jumping to any conclusions, however, remember to track changes in unfilled orders, excluding transportation and defense, since these two components can greatly warp the data.

- **Table 4**   Value of Manufacturers' Inventories for Industry Groups (Not Shown)

  Inventory levels is another yardstick that can be used to foretell what the economy will do. Factory inventories represent more than a third of all business inventories, with wholesale and retail filling up the rest. As an economic concept, inventories can move up or down, depending on the relative pace of demand and supply. Traditionally, inventories grow when the economy is expanding, because at such times, businesses are happy to keep stockrooms filled. The problem begins after demand unexpectedly drops and factories fail to adjust in time and slow their output. This can quickly lead to an imbalance where supplies are growing faster than demand. The result is that unwanted inventories begin to pile up as factories get stuck holding goods that no one wants to buy at the moment.

- **Table 7**   Ratios of Manufacturers' Inventories to Shipments and Unfilled Orders to Shipments (Not Shown)

  Two interesting columns are presented here. One deals with the inventory-sales (or shipments) ratio. It provides some perspective on where inventories stand relative to current sales. The second ratio, unfilled orders to shipments, tells just how bad the logjam is between orders coming in and shipments going out. The higher the ratio, the longer the delay in deliveries. Again, about a dozen industries are tracked in this table.

MARKET IMPACT

The Factory Orders report is considered old news to financial markets, so any reaction is modest, unless it contains a major revision from the Advance Report on Durable Goods, which is rare.

Bonds

Bond prices might inch higher if Factory Orders conforms with other evidence that the economy is weakening. A decline in new orders and order backlog would lower the threat of inflation and enhance the chance of an easing in monetary policy by the Federal Reserve—all bullish events for fixed income securities. On the other hand, a spike in new orders and a jump in the backlog raise the prospect of inflation, which can upset bond investors and lead to a sell-off that results in higher interest rates. As for inventories and the I/S ratio, traders generally pay little attention to them unless the economy is close to an inflection point.

Stocks

Equity investors prefer to see Factory Orders validate other signs of economic strength because this translates into higher corporate earnings. Thus, rising orders for both durable and nondurable goods and a pickup in unfilled orders are viewed as beneficial for stocks. However, its actual impact on share prices might be negligible because similar indicators have already come out by then.

Dollar

The dollar appears completely unaffected by the Factory Orders release.

BUSINESS INVENTORIES

(FORMALLY KNOWN AS MANUFACTURING AND TRADE INVENTORIES AND SALES)

Market Sensitivity: Low to medium.

What Is It: Tracks total U.S. business sales and inventories.

News Release on the Internet: *www.census.gov/mtis/www/mtis.html*

Home Web Address: *www.census.gov*

Release Time: 10 a.m. (ET); released six weeks after the month ends.

Frequency: Monthly.

Source: Census Bureau, Department of Commerce.

Revisions: Tend to be small. Annual benchmark changes come out in the spring or summer and can cover several years.

WHY IS IT IMPORTANT?

"Business inventories." The term alone is enough for many to shut this book for good. Despite its irksome title, this release by the Census Bureau offers a lot of useful information on what the economy is up to, as well as some valuable clues regarding its future path. At the heart of this report are three sets of data: total business sales, total inventories, and the inventory-sales (I/S) ratio. Let's look at them individually.

Total business sales: We don't need to spend much time on this part of the report, because a lot of the sales data on manufacturers, wholesalers, and retailers has already been released weeks before in separate economic reports. (Figures on retail sales came out four weeks earlier. Those by manufacturers were published two weeks ago, and the wholesalers' numbers the previous week.) The main virtue of this release is that all these sales numbers are now combined into one table, along with total inventories and the inventory-sales ratio, giving analysts an opportunity to connect the dots more easily and get a fuller picture of the economy.

Business inventories: Total business inventories represents the amount of goods that manufacturers, wholesalers, and retailers keep in their stockrooms. Though some of the data on inventories has been out before, new in this release are the figures on retail inventories. This is a late but very telling piece of data, because the economy often first runs into trouble at the retail level.

Understanding inventories is crucial because they can directly affect the pace of future economic growth. A company whose stockroom or back lot is filled with unsold goods can quickly find itself in a financial squeeze, especially if the economy starts to weaken. Keep in mind that inventories are often financed with short-term loans that have to be repaid even when income from sales is down. At the same time, holding a certain level of inventories is vital for businesses. A company has to have something to sell, or it can't make money. The central question for corporate managers is just how much inventory they should carry in light of present orders and expected future demand for goods and supplies. Generally speaking, stockpiles with manufacturers account for 40% of total business inventories, with retailers and wholesalers each holding about 30%.

Historically, inventory problems have been one of the main causes of economic downturns, and they usually play out in the following scenario: Retailers with bloated inventories and sleepy sales will cut back or cancel their orders to wholesalers. As a result, wholesalers, fearful that their own stockrooms will start to swell with unwanted products, start to postpone orders to factories. That leaves factories with no choice but to slow or shut down their own production, a step that may lead to plant closings and large-scale layoffs. With more people out of work, household income drops, and consumers spend less. This makes it even tougher for retailers to sell off their excess inventories, which, in turn, sets off yet another round in this entire cycle. On a wide-enough scale, such a sequence of events can easily bring on a recession.

Interestingly, changes in inventory can also rescue an economy from recession. For example, companies generally succeed in drawing down their stock of excess goods by promoting special sales, discounts, and other incentives to lure consumers back. Once firms get close to depleting their old inventories, a process that can take many months, they will at some point have to replenish their stockrooms. New orders from retailers thus become the powerful tonic that helps the economy get back on its feet. Retailers submit fresh orders to wholesalers, and the latter purchase more from factories. Plants are reopened, and workers are rehired.

To some extent, the wild inventory swings just described are becoming less common as more companies rely on technology and software to help them maintain a better balance between stockroom supplies and sales. This "just-in-time" system of inventory management is supposed to keep the economy out of trouble. But the practice isn't perfect, and corporate buyers still make mistakes.

Inventory-sales (I/S) ratio: Companies always want keep enough inventory on hand so they can sell to customers. But how much is enough? The most popular gauge for assessing whether inventory levels are too high or too low is the I/S ratio. The I/S ratio measures how many months it takes to sell off inventories based on the latest monthly sales rate. A very general rule of thumb is to stock up for no more than one and a half months worth of sales (also expressed as an I/S ratio of 1.5 months). Some industries desire less, others more. Automakers, for instance, routinely prefer to have close to two months worth of vehicles on their lots (I/S ratio = 2.0). If the I/S ratio for motor vehicle inventory at dealerships exceeds two months' supply, it's a yellow flag that they're carrying more than is prudently needed. Indeed, it might serve as fresh evidence that car purchases are waning. Too high a ratio, and companies will halt further stock building, a step that can derail production activity. Too low an I/S ratio means that sales to consumers have been growing faster than the rise in inventories. Without further action by the retailers, it would be only a matter of time before they would be left with nothing to sell. To avoid this predicament, companies rush through orders for more goods, which paves the way for faster economic growth.

HOW IS IT COMPUTED?

As mentioned, much of the data for this report has already come out. Only the retail inventory data is new here. These numbers are provided with and without seasonal adjustments. However, they are not annualized or adjusted for inflation.

UNITED STATES DEPARTMENT OF
COMMERCE
NEWS   WASHINGTON, DC 20230

ECONOMICS
AND
STATISTICS
ADMINISTRATION

U.S. CENSUS BUREAU

FOR WIRE TRANSMISSION 10:00 A.M. ET, Thursday, February 12, 2004   CB-04-18

MANUFACTURING AND TRADE INVENTORIES AND SALES

> **INTENTION TO REVISE:** Revisions to the Wholesale and Retail adjusted and unadjusted monthly estimates for sales and inventories are scheduled for release March 3 and March 30, respectively. Manufacturing estimates will be revised at a later date. Revisions to the Wholesale data will be reflected in the January 2004 Manufacturing and Trade Inventories and Sales (MTIS) press release scheduled for March 12, 2004. Revisions to the Retail data will be reflected in the February 2004 MTIS scheduled for April 13, 2004.

Sales. The Census Bureau of the Department of Commerce announced today that the combined value of distributive trade sales and manufacturers' shipments for December, adjusted for seasonal and trading-day differences but not for price changes, were estimated at $889.8 billion, up 0.9 percent (±0.2%) from November and up 7.0 percent (±0.4%) from December 2002.

Inventories. Manufacturers' and trade inventories adjusted for seasonal variations but not for price changes, were estimated at an end-of-month level of $1,190.7 billion, up 0.3 percent (±0.2%) from November and up 1.9 percent (±0.5%) from December 2002.

Inventories/Sales Ratio. The total business inventories/sales ratio based on seasonally adjusted data at the end of December was 1.34. The December 2002 ratio was 1.41.

1 ▶

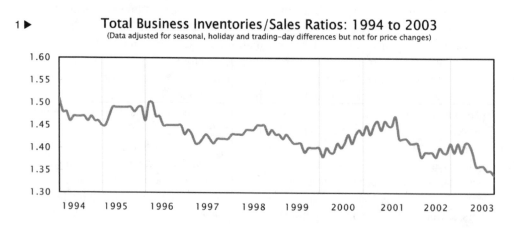

Total Business Inventories/Sales Ratios: 1994 to 2003
(Data adjusted for seasonal, holiday and trading-day differences but not for price changes)

THE TABLES: CLUES ON WHAT'S AHEAD FOR THE ECONOMY

- **Cover Page** Total Business Inventories/Sales Ratios

  (1) For the last 30 years, businesses have shown a desire to hold an average of about 1.45 months worth of goods on shelves and in stockrooms. To see where the I/S ratio presently stands, go to the graph that tracks the I/S ratio over the last 10 years. Generally, if the I/S ratio falls much below the 1.45-month trend, companies typically increase their orders to bring inventories back to preferred levels, provided the economy is not in the midst of a downturn. If the economy is sinking, firms might decide to wait until demand improves before submitting new orders.

- **Table 1** Estimated Monthly Sales and Inventories for Manufacturers, Retailers, and Merchant Wholesalers

  (2) This neatly organized table breaks down sales and inventory levels in dollar terms and lists the I/S ratio for manufacturers, retailers, and wholesalers. From here we can observe the domino effect of how changes in one sector can affect the other two over time. For example, if consumer spending slows markedly, retail sales will suffer. A buildup in unwanted retail inventories increases the I/S ratio. Wholesalers end up receiving fewer orders. As their inventory swells, wholesalers, in turn, order less from manufacturers.

  This process eventually corrects itself. Retailers will use a variety of sales promotion programs to work down all that surplus inventory. This process can take

(In millions of dollars)   3 ▼

	Sales			Inventories[1]			Inventories/Sales Ratios		
	Dec. 2003	Nov. 2003	Dec. 2002	Dec. 2003	Nov. 2003	Dec. 2002	Dec. 2003	Nov. 2003	Dec. 2002
	(p)	(r)	(s)	(p)	(r)	(s)			
Adjusted									
Total business..............	889,797	881,635	831,472	1,190,686	1,187,687	1,168,999	1.34	1.35	1.41
Manufacturers[3]...............	346,533	341,454	323,362	438,106	438,126	444,188	1.26	1.28	1.37
Retailers.......................	292,400	291,921	275,763	458,123	456,845	436,103	1.57	1.56	1.58
Merchant wholesalers..........	250,864	248,260	232,347	294,457	292,716	288,708	1.17	1.18	1.24
Not Adjusted									
Total business..............	945,296	855,100	868,285	1,178,306	1,220,733	1,155,640	1.25	1.43	1.33
Manufacturers[3]...............	344,042	333,414	316,560	427,737	439,491	433,756	1.24	1.32	1.37
Retailers.......................	343,377	286,269	319,815	453,333	485,870	431,121	1.32	1.70	1.35
Merchant wholesalers..........	257,877	235,417	231,910	297,236	295,372	290,763	1.15	1.25	1.25

from three to nine months and even longer. Once that's done, however, and the economy is rebounding, investments in new inventory resume across the pipeline—from retailers to factories.

(3) Though the I/S ratio is itself a lagging indicator, which means it tends to follow, not lead, the economy's overall pace, its performance can still have implications for the future. For instance, a low I/S ratio can set the stage for faster economic growth in the coming months as companies seek to replenish their stockrooms. Conversely, a persistent rise in the I/S ratio (where inventories are rising faster than sales) can eventually lead to a slowdown in economic activity, along with lower inflation and interest rates.

• **Table 2** Percent Changes for Sales and Inventories—Manufacturers, Retailers, and Merchant Wholesalers

(4) Keep an eye on the change in inventories in this table, because it's a key element in how GDP is calculated. GDP, which represents total output, is computed by adding up all sales in the economy plus the change in inventories. What do we mean by "change in inventories"? Suppose a U.S. company produces 100 television sets during the quarter but sells only 80. The unsold 20 sets get stored as inventory. If we now calculate the GDP for that quarter based on sales alone, we come up with just the dollar value of 80 television sets, even though the true output for that period was 100 TV sets. Thus, to get the correct GDP, we have to add a special allowance for the change in inventories, which in this case increased by 20 during the quarter. Total sales (80) plus the change in inventories (+20) brings you up to 100, the correct number for total output.

What if in the next quarter the firm sells 60 TVs but produces only 50? The same basic formula applies here too. To satisfy customer demand, the company digs into inventory to come up with the other 10. Thus, the level of inventory has fallen by 10. Again, to measure GDP output in that quarter, you count total sales (60) and the change in inventory levels (–10) to give you total output of 50 for

4
▼

	Adjusted						Not Adjusted					
	Sales			Inventories			Sales			Inventories		
	Dec. 03/ Nov. 03	Nov. 03/ Oct. 03	Dec. 03/ Dec. 02	Dec. 03/ Nov. 03	Nov. 03/ Oct. 03	Dec. 03/ Dec. 02	Dec. 03/ Nov. 03	Nov. 03/ Oct. 03	Dec. 03/ Dec. 02	Dec. 03/ Nov. 03	Nov. 03/ Oct. 03	Dec. 03/ Dec. 02
Total business.........	0.9	0.7	7.0	0.3	0.4	1.9	10.5	–5.9	8.9	–3.5	0.9	2.0
Manufacturers.........	1.5	0.5	7.2	0.0	–0.1	–1.4	3.2	–6.3	8.7	–2.7	–0.5	–1.4
Retailers..............	0.2	1.0	6.0	0.3	0.8	5.0	19.9	–0.8	7.4	–6.7	2.7	5.2
Merchant wholesalers..	1.0	0.6	8.0	0.6	0.5	2.0	9.5	–10.9	11.2	0.6	0.4	2.2

that quarter. The point is that changes in inventories play a major role in how economic growth is calculated.

By monitoring three-month changes in inventory levels in this table, one can get a heads-up on whether it will add to or subtract from GDP. There's one catch. This table measures percent changes in inventories based on nominal dollars—that is, before adjusting for the effects of inflation. GDP, however, values inventories in real (inflation-adjusted) dollars. To make a rough adjustment from nominal to real dollars, take the percent change in producer price inflation for finished goods (see the later section "Producer Price Index (PPI)") and subtract it from the percent change in total inventories. For example, if total inventories jumped 0.3% in nominal dollars in the month and the PPI rose 0.1%, the real change in inventory was up roughly 0.2%. Because the quarterly GDP report covers three months, you will have to assess real inventory changes for the last three months that data is available.

- **Table 3** Estimated Monthly Retail Sales, Inventories, and Inventories/Sales Ratios, By Kind of Business

(5) This table shows how various retailers stand in terms of sales, inventories, and the I/S ratio. Of the three, the I/S is the most meaningful in serving as a leading economic indicator of future orders and production activity. Specific emphasis is placed on motor vehicles, home furnishings, building materials, clothing, food and beverages, and general-merchandise stores.

(In millions of dollars)

NAICS Code	Kind of Business	Sales			Inventories[1]			Percent Change In Inventories			Inventories/Sales Ratios		
		Dec. 2003 (p)	Nov. 2003 (r)	Dec. 2002 (s)	Dec. 2003 (p)	Nov. 2003 (r)	Dec. 2002 (s)	Dec. 03/ Nov. 03	Nov. 03/ Oct. 03	Dec. 03/ Dec. 02	Dec. 03	Nov. 03	Dec. 02
	Adjusted [2]												
	Retail trade, total	292,400	291,921	275,763	458,123	456,845	436,103	0.3	0.8	5.0	1.57	1.56	1.58
	Total (excl. motor veh. & parts)	215,478	215,116	202,269	299,494	298,332	289,524	0.4	0.6	3.4	1.39	1.39	1.43
441	Motor vehicle & parts dealers	76,922	76,805	73,494	158,629	158,513	146,579	0.1	1.1	8.2	2.06	2.06	1.99
442,3	Furniture, home furn., elect. & appl. stores	16,887	16,869	15,509	28,583	28,401	26,373	0.6	0.9	8.4	1.69	1.68	1.70
444	Building materials, garden equip & supplies	28,413	28,244	24,875	47,285	46,746	43,109	1.2	0.9	9.7	1.66	1.66	1.73
445	Food & beverage stores	42,792	42,962	41,327	34,565	34,645	34,294	-0.2	0.1	0.8	0.81	0.81	0.83
448	Clothing & clothing access. stores	15,245	15,269	14,525	36,794	36,741	36,061	0.1	0.9	2.0	2.41	2.41	2.48
452	General merchandise stores	40,569	40,434	38,437	67,786	67,073	66,456	1.1	0.0	2.0	1.67	1.66	1.73
4521	Dept. strs. (excl. leased depts.)	18,017	18,018	18,336	35,821	36,089	37,767	-0.7	-1.3	-5.2	1.99	2.00	2.06
	Not Adjusted												
	Retail trade, total	343,377	286,269	319,815	453,333	485,870	431,121	-6.7	2.7	5.2	1.32	1.70	1.35
	Total (excl. motor veh. & parts)	270,789	219,306	252,873	290,986	326,051	281,124	-10.8	1.7	3.5	1.07	1.49	1.11
441	Motor vehicle & parts dealers	72,588	66,963	66,942	162,347	159,819	149,997	1.6	4.8	8.2	2.24	2.39	2.24
442,3	Furniture, home furn., elect. & appl. stores	23,959	18,424	21,625	28,383	32,462	26,162	-12.6	4.4	8.5	1.18	1.76	1.21
444	Building materials, garden equip & supplies	25,542	25,671	21,814	45,914	45,577	41,816	0.7	-0.6	9.8	1.80	1.78	1.92
445	Food & beverage stores	46,655	42,914	44,693	35,356	36,248	35,074	-2.5	1.8	0.8	0.76	0.84	0.78
448	Clothing & clothing access. stores	26,835	16,540	25,296	33,998	40,893	33,356	-16.9	0.6	1.9	1.27	2.47	1.32
452	General merchandise stores	61,470	45,473	58,883	63,537	79,567	62,207	-20.1	2.2	2.1	1.03	1.75	1.06
4521	Dept. strs. (excl. leased depts.)	31,243	21,082	31,854	33,170	43,595	35,010	-23.9	1.5	-5.3	1.06	2.07	1.10

A word of caution: Auto and truck inventories, which account for one-third of total retail inventories, can be quite volatile in this series. To reduce any distortions, look at the total retail I/S ratio, excluding the motor vehicle and parts components.

MARKET IMPACT

Financial markets and the press react mildly to this report because so much of the data has already been put out in separate releases. It's also hard to get excited about economic events that took place nearly two months ago. Still, on a slow business news day, the retail inventory series might draw some attention, particularly if the economy is reaching an inflection point.

Bonds

Faster-than-expected growth in retail inventory can upset traders in fixed income securities because it adds to GDP growth and can put upward pressure on interest rates. A fall in inventory investment subtracts from economic output, which is positive for bonds.

Stocks

Rarely does the stock market get excited by this release. Though a slowdown in sales and production displeases equity investors because of its implications for earnings, chances are most investors have already seen and reacted to similar evidence weeks earlier.

Dollar

The main question for foreign exchange traders is how the news on retail inventories will influence interest rates in the U.S. For them, a jump in the I/S ratio (with inventories rising at a faster pace than sales) is symptomatic of an economy in the process of slowing down. That eventually portends lower interest rates, which translates into a smaller payback for international investors. Currency traders generally look at the dollar more favorably if both sales and inventories are rising at the retail, wholesale, and manufacturing level.

INDUSTRIAL PRODUCTION AND CAPACITY UTILIZATION

Market Sensitivity: Medium.

What Is It: Records U.S. industry's output and spare capacity.

News Release on the Internet: *www.federalreserve.gov/releases/g17/current*

Home Web Address: *www.federalreserve.gov*

Release Time: 9:15 a.m. (ET); released around the 15th of the month and reports on the previous month.

Frequency: Monthly.

Source: Federal Reserve Board.

Revisions: Modest changes are made for the previous three months, followed by an annual revision in the fall that can go back several years.

WHY IS IT IMPORTANT?

Any economic indicator released by the Federal Reserve is automatically noticed by investors around the world. After all, this is the agency that conducts U.S. monetary policy and controls short-term interest rates. Two of the Fed's most closely watched reports are Industrial Production and Capacity Utilization, both published simultaneously around the middle of every month. Industrial production covers nearly everything that is physically produced or mined in the U.S. and includes the making of cars, umbrellas, paper clips, electricity, and medical equipment. It makes no difference whether these goods are for American buyers, foreign consumers, or inventory. All that matters is how much industry is actually churning out in this country. One reason experts are so keen on following industrial production is that it reacts fairly quickly to the ups and downs of the business cycle. It also has a good track record of forecasting changes in manufacturing employment, average hourly earnings, and personal income.

The capacity utilization rate is a deceptively simple and incredibly important concept. Fed economists look at how much industries in the U.S. are presently producing and then compare that output with what they could potentially produce if the industrial sector were running at maximum capability. This series is significant in three respects. First, a nation's economic power is judged by its ability to produce goods when they're needed. It reflects the strength and flexibility of the industrial sector. Second, it is useful to know how underutilized manufacturers, utilities, and the mining sectors are in case more output is needed in the future. Third, the capacity utilization rate has some predictive value. It's a good leading indicator of business investment spending and can warn of building inflation pressures.

Industrial Production

The industrial production (IP) series is like a window into the industrial part of the economy. It differs from most other economic indicators in one important respect. It measures changes in the volume of goods produced. That is, IP doesn't take the price of these products into account, so there's no need to worry about the distorting effects of inflation. That makes it a purer measure of output, so it corresponds more closely to the performance of real (inflation-adjusted) GDP. One can ask why IP figures are so influential to economic forecasters when the manufacturing sector makes up less than 20% of the economy, while the service industry gets far less attention yet contributes much more to the economic pie. The answer is that the service sector grows at a fairly stable pace regardless of whether the economy is weak or strong. People will always spend on medical and dental care, transportation, and haircuts. In contrast, manufacturing activity is highly sensitive to changes in interest rates and demand, so it closely parallels shifts in the overall economy. As a result, there is a close relationship between changes in industrial output and GDP growth.

Capacity Utilization

Capacity utilization measures the amount of slack in the economy. If a bike-making firm has the capacity to manufacture 500 bicycles a month but is currently producing only 350, it's operating at a capacity utilization rate of just 70%. Now let's assume that the rest of the bike industry is operating at the same low level. Under such circumstances, getting spare parts would be no problem. There's likely to be lots of extra bike tires and brakes available from suppliers. Nor would there be a reason to hire additional workers or invest in new bike-making machinery, because there are not enough buyers out there to purchase what can already easily be produced.

But all this changes once demand surges and the industry starts churning out bikes at close to 100% of its capacity. If that feverish pace continues for an extended period, bike makers will begin to experience shortages in parts. Prices for bike components can also rise. As the cost of assembling bicycles accelerates, shoppers will see their price tags go up as well. The lesson here is that as American industry gets closer to operating at full capacity, shortages in resources emerge, and this can generate inflation. High capacity utilization rates can also lead to new investments in factory equipment and plant expansion so that companies can increase output in the future. As you might imagine, the capacity utilization rate for manufacturing typically climbs when the economy is vibrant and falls when demand softens.

How Is It Computed?

Industrial Production

Every month, the Federal Reserve calculates an index of industrial production after collecting data on 300 industry components representing manufacturing, mining, and the electric utilities and gas industries. Each component is given a weight based on how important it is to the economy. (These weights are adjusted every year.) Most of this information is derived from government data as well as private trade associations.

The Fed first puts out a preliminary release on industrial production two weeks after the reporting month, and it is based on only 70% of the data needed. Why such a low figure? Because the investment community and policymakers want to get a read on industrial activity as quickly as possible given this sector's role in the economy and its sensitivity to turning points in the business cycle. Since it takes time to collect output figures from so many industries, some 30% of the information arrives too late for the first report. Fed economists thus fill in the gaps with estimates that are based on other economic reports. These reports include hours worked in factories (from the employment data) and the amount of electric power consumed by businesses (from power supply companies). Interestingly, both hours worked and electric power consumption seem to move in line with total industrial output, so these estimates tend to be quite accurate. Indeed, the preliminary IP index and the final revised index three months later vary by an average of just 0.3 percentage points.

Finally, data on IP is presented in two formats. One is by "major market group," which essentially reflects the demand for consumer goods, business equipment, intermediate goods, and materials. The second format is "industry group," and it measures output by industry in broad, supply-side terms.

One cautionary note: Although industrial production figures are seasonally adjusted, final numbers can occasionally be distorted because of bizarre weather, natural disasters, or a major labor strike. Thus, to discern the true underlying growth rate of industrial production in the economy, it is best to look at a three-month moving average. (Industrial production does not include output from agriculture, construction, transportation, communications, trade, finance, or service industries.)

Capacity Utilization

If you think industrial production is tough to compute, calculating capacity utilization rates is very near a crapshoot. To determine what proportion of capacity is being used, you have to know how much industry is capable of producing when it operates at full speed. However, that is impossible to determine with any precision. For one, how do you define full capacity? Industries rarely work at 100% capacity, though theoretically they can function seven days a week, 24 hours a day. Indeed, some industries do have such nonstop operations. These companies include chemical and steel manufacturers as well as petroleum refining companies. During times of war, many other U.S. industries mobilize their workforce and plants to work past 90% capacity. However, these are extreme situations. The Fed gets around this by defining capacity based on what is considered the "normal" operating time for each industry. A second difficulty in calculating capacity is that a growing number of production facilities are not even located in the U.S. Though capacity utilization in this report is based only on U.S. operations, the fact is that manufacturing capacity is increasingly being moved offshore, where costs are cheaper. Because American companies can also rely on these foreign production facilities to help meet U.S. demand, it becomes harder to define what true full capacity is. Third, manufacturers regularly invest in new plants and equipment, but it's not immediately clear whether this is done to expand production capabilities or replace aging and less-efficient equipment. Finally, mergers and acquisitions also impact capacity, because they often lead to a permanent shutdown or sale of redundant production facilities. So, trying to figure out the nation's capacity utilization rate at any given moment is like taking a snapshot of a moving target. Yet despite these difficulties, the Federal Reserve makes a valiant effort to calculate capacity utilization rates for 85 detailed industries (67 in manufacturing, 16 in mining, and two in utilities) and then comes up with an industry total.

The Tables: Clues on What's Ahead for the Economy

Manufacturing is the most cyclically sensitive part of the economy, a factor that makes industrial production a classic indicator of current business conditions. When economic activity is increasing, factory production rises with it. As the business cycle approaches its peak, factory output also tops out. And when the economy slips into recession, output drops as well. Does industrial production have any use as a predictive indicator? The answer is yes. The IP report can reveal quite a lot about the future direction of economic growth, corporate sales, inflation, and more.

- **Cover Page**   Industrial Production and Capacity Utilization: Summary

  (1) The "total index" on the front-page table summarizes the change in industrial activity during the latest four-month period. Historically, there has been a strong relationship between industrial production and quarterly GDP. By monitoring percentage changes in industrial output over the last three months, one can make a fairly good estimate of the current trend in GDP growth.

  (2) Another key set of numbers refers to the total amount of consumer goods (such as cars and trucks) produced versus that of business goods. Strong sales and a thinning of inventories encourages more production of consumer products, while the output of business equipment reflects mainly capital investment spending by companies.

  (3) Here you have the three main components of the industrial production index. The largest by far is manufacturing, which in 2006 accounted for about 80% of industrial output, with mining and utilities roughly splitting the difference.

FEDERAL RESERVE statistical release

G.17 (419)

For release at 9:15 a.m. (EST)
February 17, 2004

INDUSTRIAL PRODUCTION AND CAPACITY UTILIZATION

Industrial production rose 0.8 percent in January; output in December was revised downward and is now estimated to have been unchanged from the November reading. At 113.8 percent of its 1997 average, overall industrial output in January was 2.4 percent above its January 2003 level. Manufacturing output rose 0.3 percent, and mining output increased 0.1 percent; with unusually cold weather in January, the output of utilities rose 5.2 percent. The rate of capacity utilization for total industry increased from 75.6 percent in December to 76.2 percent in January.

(over)

INDUSTRIAL PRODUCTION AND CAPACITY UTILIZATION: SUMMARY   4 ▼
Seasonally adjusted

Industrial production	1997=100				Percent change				
	2003 Oct.ʳ	Nov.ʳ	Dec.ʳ	2004 Jan.ᵖ	2003 Oct.ʳ	Nov.ʳ	Dec.ʳ	2004 Jan.ᵖ	Jan. '03 to Jan. '04
Total index	111.8	112.9	112.9	113.8	.3	1.0	.0	.8	2.4
Previous estimates	111.9	113.1	113.2		.4	1.0	.1		
Major market groups									
Final Products	107.7	108.8	108.5	109.1	-.1	1.1	-.3	.6	1.4
Consumer goods	106.0	107.0	106.6	107.4	-.1	1.0	-.4	.8	.8
Business equipment	110.8	112.8	112.8	113.4	-.3	1.8	.0	.5	3.3
Nonindustrial supplies	109.6	110.6	110.5	111.5	.8	1.0	-.2	.9	2.1
Construction	103.1	104.1	104.2	104.5	.9	1.0	.0	.4	1.8
Materials	116.9	118.0	118.5	119.5	.5	1.0	.4	.9	3.5
Major industry groups									
Manufacturing (see note below)	112.9	114.1	114.2	114.6	.2	1.0	.1	.3	2.3
Previous estimates	113.0	114.2	114.5		.2	1.0	.3		
Mining	93.7	94.0	94.2	94.3	.2	.3	.2	.1	.9
Utilities	111.0	112.8	111.3	117.1	1.0	1.6	-1.3	5.2	4.4

Capacity utilization	Percent of capacity								Capacity growth
	Average 1972–2003	1982 low	1988–89 high	2003 Jan.	2003 Oct.ʳ	Nov.ʳ	Dec.ʳ	2004 Jan.ᵖ	Jan. '03 to Jan. '04
Total industry	81.1	70.9	85.2	75.2	75.0	75.7	75.6	76.2	1.1
Previous estimates					75.1	75.8	75.8		
Manufacturing (see note below)	80.0	68.7	85.6	73.6	73.6	74.3	74.4	74.6	.9
Previous estimates					73.7	74.4	74.5		
Mining	86.9	78.6	85.6	84.8	85.4	85.7	85.9	86.0	-.4
Utilities	86.9	77.6	92.8	85.9	82.4	83.4	82.1	86.1	4.1
Stage-of-process groups									
Crude	86.3	77.2	88.5	82.9	83.8	84.0	84.3	84.6	-1.0
Primary and semifinished	82.2	68.1	86.4	77.2	77.0	77.8	77.8	78.7	1.8
Finished	78.2	71.3	83.2	71.4	71.1	71.8	71.6	71.7	.7

Interested in developing forecasts of corporate revenues for U.S. manufacturers? One strategy used by some analysts involves taking the three-month percentage change in manufacturing output and multiplying it by the three-month percentage change in consumer price inflation. The result becomes a good proxy for nominal dollar GDP performance, which, in turn, is a reliable harbinger of factory sales growth.

(4) The percent change in production for all these groups over the past year is listed here.

(5) Moving on to capacity utilization, this table shows how much spare capacity is left at factories, mines, and utilities. In general, the utilization rate rises or falls with the business cycle, much like industrial production. If orders for products fade, factory output declines, and less capacity is utilized. If the utilization rate lingers below 80%, it tends to discourage new business investments and may even trigger a round of job dismissals.

On the other hand, strong demand for goods stimulates production. Manufacturers utilize more of their factories and plants, causing any slack in capacity to shrink or even disappear. As capacity utilization edges closer to operating at maximum levels, pressure on prices starts to build. Is there a red zone in the capacity utilization rate that usually detonates inflation? Generally speaking, the industrial sector can function safely (that is, without an eruption of higher prices) with a capacity utilization rate as high as 81%. After the utilization rate enters the 82%–85% range, however, production bottlenecks appear, and this can put fresh pressure on prices, especially at the producer price level. Look at the summary table to see the current capacity utilization rate for total industry and its three main components: manufacturing, mining, and utilities.

• **Table 1**   Industrial Production: Market and Industry Group Summary

A wealth of information on industrial output is found in Tables 1 and 2. Table 1 lists percent change in production of key products for each of the past four months, as well as the last four quarters annualized, and over the last three years.

Here are some of the most important categories:

(6) *Business equipment:* A category that tells of plans by companies to invest in new plants and equipment.

(7) *Defense and space equipment:* A broad measure of production for military and aerospace hardware.

(8) *Motor vehicles and parts:* An indication of whether automakers see enough demand to fill dealers' lots.

Table 1
INDUSTRIAL PRODUCTION: MARKET AND INDUSTRY GROUP SUMMARY
Percent change, seasonally adjusted

Item	2003 proportion[1]	Fourth quarter to fourth quarter			Annual rate				Monthly rate				Jan. '03 to Jan. '04
		2001	2002	2003	2003 Q1	Q2	Q3	Q4ʳ	2003 Oct.ʳ	Nov.ʳ	Dec.ʳ	2004 Jan.ᵖ	
Total IP	100.00	-5.2	1.3	1.4	.9	-4.0	3.8	5.4	.3	1.0	.0	.8	2.4
MARKET GROUPS													
Final products and nonindustrial supplies	58.62	-4.9	.5	1.1	1.9	-4.5	2.9	4.1	.1	1.0	-.3	.7	1.6
Consumer goods	31.18	-2.2	1.0	.2	1.4	-5.1	2.2	2.6	-.1	1.0	-.4	.8	.8
Durable	8.15	-2.9	6.0	3.1	1.6	-6.5	11.2	7.0	-.8	1.2	.1	.6	2.3
Automotive products	4.13	1.1	9.9	5.0	3.2	-8.8	20.5	7.0	-2.4	1.0	.2	.8	3.8
Home electronics	.36	-10.3	4.4	24.5	39.2	-8.7	18.6	59.7	7.1	3.3	-1.2	-4.2	3.9
Appliances, furniture, carpeting	1.42	-2.0	1.8	1.2	.2	1.7	2.8	.0	.0	1.4	-.1	1.0	2.0
Miscellaneous goods	2.24	-8.1	2.4	-2.3	-5.4	-7.2	-.5	4.1	.5	1.2	.2	.9	-.6
Nondurable	23.03	-1.9	-.8	-.8	1.2	-4.5	-.8	1.0	.2	.9	-.6	.8	.3
Non-energy	18.27	-1.0	-2.8	-.3	1.1	-1.4	-2.3	1.6	.3	.8	-.6	.0	-.5
Foods and tobacco	9.97	-.6	-3.9	-1.9	-.7	-1.7	-2.1	-3.2	-.3	.4	-.8	-.2	-2.5
Clothing	.86	-15.1	-2.4	-13.4	-18.7	-18.5	-18.2	3.9	1.7	.6	-.2	-1.0	-11.2
Chemical products	4.67	3.0	-1.8	3.3	1.7	.9	1.0	9.8	1.0	1.6	-.7	.5	4.0
Paper products	2.24	-3.2	-.9	5.6	15.6	4.2	-2.8	6.1	1.4	.7	-.4	.0	3.5
Energy	4.75	-5.8	8.7	-2.8	2.2	-16.0	5.5	-1.2	-.4	1.4	-.5	4.1	3.4
Business equipment	9.57	-12.8	-1.4	2.7	3.3	-4.8	5.3	7.3	-.3	1.8	.0	.5	3.3
Transit	1.57	-5.9	-15.2	-3.1	-11.8	-12.6	3.9	9.9	-1.5	1.5	1.1	.6	.3
Information processing	3.05	-12.8	5.5	8.3	17.8	-1.3	8.8	8.8	1.8	-.1	-.7	.5	5.2
Industrial and other	4.96	-15.0	-1.0	1.0	-.2	-4.5	3.5	5.6	-1.3	3.1	.1	.5	3.0
Defense and space equipment	1.99	12.4	3.6	4.7	9.9	1.8	6.1	1.2	.0	-.4	-.3	-.8	1.4
Construction supplies	4.23	-6.5	.4	1.1	-2.9	-4.5	4.7	7.6	.9	1.0	.0	.4	1.8
Business supplies	11.30	-5.6	1.4	1.4	3.1	-4.1	1.6	5.2	.7	1.0	-.2	1.1	2.2
Materials	41.38	-5.7	2.5	2.0	-.6	-3.4	5.0	7.2	.5	1.0	.4	.9	3.5
Non-energy	29.85	-6.6	3.0	2.6	-1.0	-3.3	5.5	9.5	.5	1.1	.7	.5	3.9
Durable	18.64	-7.2	4.2	4.4	-.8	-3.1	9.4	12.8	.8	1.2	.8	.8	6.0
Consumer parts	3.92	-7.2	6.7	2.5	.9	-9.8	8.1	12.4	-.7	.9	1.8	.8	3.3
Equipment parts	6.51	-7.4	5.9	11.8	3.0	6.8	20.4	17.9	1.2	1.5	1.0	1.6	14.4
Other	8.21	-6.8	1.5	-.5	-4.7	-7.3	1.7	9.0	1.3	1.1	.2	.2	.8
Nondurable	11.20	-5.6	.9	-.5	-1.3	-3.8	-.7	4.1	-.2	1.0	.4	.0	.5
Textile	.68	-11.6	-1.0	-10.3	-13.7	-16.5	-17.3	8.4	1.1	1.5	-.6	.3	-7.2
Paper	2.61	-6.1	1.5	-4.4	-7.6	-3.9	-3.0	-2.9	-1.0	.8	.4	.1	-1.8
Chemical	4.23	-5.1	1.7	2.7	2.2	-5.2	4.2	10.2	-.3	1.8	.8	.1	3.6
Energy	11.53	-2.9	1.0	.5	.5	-3.6	3.9	1.6	.5	.5	-.3	2.0	2.5
INDUSTRY GROUPS													
Manufacturing	82.29	-5.6	1.0	1.8	1.0	-3.2	3.7	6.0	.2	1.0	.1	.3	2.3
Manufacturing (NAICS)	76.93	-5.5	1.2	1.7	.1	-3.6	4.3	6.1	.1	1.0	.2	.3	2.3
Durable manufacturing	41.70	-7.3	3.0	3.7	1.4	-3.9	8.4	9.6	.1	1.2	.5	.6	4.4
Wood products 321	1.45	-2.2	-1.8	3.2	-2.7	-2.8	7.2	11.7	2.5	1.1	-.3	.8	4.3
Nonmetallic mineral products 327	2.26	-5.6	2.1	1.2	-2.2	-3.0	3.9	6.4	1.1	.9	.6	.6	2.1
Primary metal 331	2.16	-10.6	3.5	-.8	-1.8	-16.0	-.6	18.0	2.1	2.3	.8	-1.4	-2.4
Fabricated metal products 332	5.64	-8.4	-.1	-1.6	-5.1	-8.6	1.7	6.2	.2	.9	.7	.9	.7
Machinery 333	5.12	-17.1	-.9	2.8	-.3	-.1	2.9	9.0	-1.1	3.8	.1	.6	5.8
Computer and electronic products 334	7.91	-7.5	10.8	15.7	12.2	7.5	25.0	19.1	2.1	.8	.2	1.0	14.9
Electrical equip., appliances, and components 335	2.18	-12.7	-2.3	.8	-3.7	-3.1	1.3	9.3	.6	1.3	.4	.4	3.1
Motor vehicles and parts 3361–3	6.67	-2.8	9.9	3.9	.6	-11.2	19.3	9.2	-2.2	.5	.8	.9	3.2
Aerospace and other miscellaneous transportation equipment 3364–9	3.46	4.9	-9.7	.7	-2.9	-1.6	2.5	5.0	-.1	.9	.6	.5	2.2
Furniture and related products 337	1.65	-7.4	-.4	-2.3	-.4	-8.1	-.4	-.1	-.5	.7	.3	.3	-2.5
Miscellaneous 339	3.20	-2.8	3.5	-1.4	5.8	-6.4	-4.7	.3	-.4	.4	1.3	.3	-1.6
Nondurable manufacturing	35.23	-3.3	-.9	-.8	-1.5	-3.2	-.3	2.1	.1	.8	-.2	.0	-.2
Food, beverage, and tobacco products 311,2	11.59	-.4	-3.5	-1.6	-.6	-1.2	-1.3	-3.2	-.4	.3	-.6	-.2	-2.1
Textile and product mills 313,4	1.17	-10.3	-1.3	-7.0	-11.6	-10.8	-9.7	5.4	1.7	2.3	-1.9	1.2	-3.0
Apparel and leather 315,6	.94	-15.5	-2.0	-12.6	-17.9	-18.0	-16.7	4.3	1.6	.6	.1	-1.0	-10.4
Paper 322	2.97	-6.0	2.9	-5.8	-7.5	-.4	-2.9	-.1	.1	.7	.6	-.1	.1
Printing and support 323	2.35	-6.7	-1.7	-5.1	-4.2	-10.4	-2.4	-3.0	-.5	-.3	-.1	-.1	-5.3
Petroleum and coal products 324	2.46	-2.5	1.2	2.4	2.3	-2.6	3.4	6.7	.2	.8	.8	-1.2	1.7
Chemical 325	10.02	-1.3	-.1	2.9	2.3	-1.7	3.4	8.0	.3	1.4	.0	.5	3.8
Plastics and rubber products 326	3.72	-5.7	2.2	-.1	-1.0	-4.4	1.6	3.7	.4	.9	-.3	-.1	.5
Other manufacturing (non-NAICS) 1133,5111	5.36	-6.3	-2.2	4.3	16.4	3.1	-5.3	4.3	1.0	.8	-.8	.2	2.2
Mining 21	7.62	-1.0	-2.3	.7	.0	-.7	1.0	2.7	.2	.3	.2	.1	.9
Utilities 2211,2	10.08	-5.2	6.6	-1.1	.5	-13.3	6.8	2.6	1.0	1.6	-1.3	5.2	4.4
Electric 2211	8.32	-3.7	5.5	.0	.8	-10.9	9.2	2.2	1.3	1.7	-1.8	4.8	4.7
Natural gas 2212	1.77	-12.8	13.4	-6.6	-.5	-24.1	-3.5	4.7	-.2	1.0	1.0	7.0	2.8

6 ▶
7 ▶
8 ▶

• **Table 2** Industrial Production: Special Aggregates and Selected Detail

(9) One important way to determine if companies are taking steps to operate more efficiently is to see if they are investing in high-technology products. This table has a category labeled "selected high-technology" that measures the output of computers, sophisticated office equipment, semiconductors, and

Table 2

INDUSTRIAL PRODUCTION: SPECIAL AGGREGATES AND SELECTED DETAIL

Percent change, seasonally adjusted

Item	2003 proportion	Fourth quarter to fourth quarter			Annual rate				Monthly rate				Jan. '03 to Jan. '04
		2001	2002	2003	2003 Q1	Q2	Q3	Q4r	2003 Oct.r	Nov.r	Dec.r	2004 Jan.p	
Total industry	100.00	-5.2	1.3	1.4	.9	-4.0	3.8	5.4	.3	1.0	.0	.8	2.4
Energy	18.95	-3.6	2.9	-.2	1.1	-7.6	4.1	2.1	.5	.9	-.5	2.7	2.8
Consumer products	4.75	-5.8	8.7	-2.8	2.2	-16.0	5.5	-1.2	-.4	1.4	-.5	4.1	3.4
Commercial products	2.41	-1.6	3.5	.8	1.8	-12.1	3.4	11.8	2.4	2.0	-1.4	4.1	3.6
Oil and gas well drilling	.25	-10.9	-14.8	4.0	-1.2	18.1	-.2	.5	.5	-.4	.0	-5.2	.4
Converted fuel	3.69	-7.9	3.7	.2	3.3	-17.2	15.7	1.9	1.4	1.1	-.9	4.4	2.8
Primary materials	7.84	-.2	-.4	.8	-.9	3.7	-1.0	1.4	.1	.3	.0	.9	2.4
Non-energy	81.05	-5.6	1.0	1.8	.8	-3.2	3.7	6.2	.2	1.0	.1	.3	2.3
Selected high-technology industries	4.93	-8.4	15.3	21.6	13.8	14.4	33.3	26.0	2.4	1.3	1.3	2.6	24.6
Computers and office equipment 3341	1.17	-5.7	24.0	14.0	15.9	-4.3	20.2	26.7	2.1	1.9	1.8	2.0	14.2
Communications equipment 3342	1.31	-22.8	-5.5	5.8	27.4	2.8	-6.7	2.4	2.2	-.9	-1.8	1.9	4.2
Semiconductors and related electronic components 334412–9	2.45	.8	24.9	35.0	5.8	33.2	69.5	39.2	2.6	2.1	2.5	3.2	42.7
Excluding selected high-technology industries	76.11	-5.2	-.1	.6	-.1	-4.3	1.9	4.9	.0	1.0	.0	.2	.9
Motor vehicles and parts 3361–3	6.67	-2.8	9.9	3.9	.6	-11.2	19.3	9.2	-2.2	.5	.8	.9	3.2
Motor vehicles 3361	2.94	1.5	11.6	3.7	1.3	-14.4	28.4	3.7	-4.7	-.5	.4	1.0	1.4
Motor vehicle parts 3363	3.32	-5.3	7.8	3.1	.6	-8.9	12.2	10.0	-.9	.3	1.5	1.0	3.7
Excluding motor vehicles and parts	69.44	-5.5	-1.0	.2	-.1	-3.6	.4	4.5	.3	1.1	.0	.1	.6
Consumer goods	26.22	-1.5	-.3	.7	1.1	-3.0	1.5	3.1	.0	.9	-.4	.2	.2
Business equipment	7.29	-11.5	-4.6	.8	-.3	-5.3	4.3	4.9	-.8	2.1	.0	.1	1.9
Construction supplies	4.19	-6.4	.5	1.0	-3.2	-4.6	4.9	7.6	.8	.9	.0	.3	1.7
Business supplies	10.95	-5.5	.7	.5	2.9	-5.1	.1	4.4	.6	1.0	-.3	1.0	1.2
Materials	24.81	-7.2	.3	-.2	-2.0	-5.1	.1	6.6	.4	1.1	.4	.1	.8
Measures excluding selected high-technology industries													
Total industry	95.07	-4.9	.4	.4	.1	-5.0	2.4	4.4	.1	1.0	-.1	.7	1.2
Manufacturing[i]	77.36	-5.2	-.1	.6	.1	-4.3	1.9	4.8	.0	1.0	.1	.2	.9
Durable	36.96	-6.9	1.0	1.3	-.5	-6.4	5.1	7.4	-.1	1.2	.4	.3	1.7
Measures excluding motor vehicles and parts													
Total industry	93.33	-5.4	.8	1.3	.9	-3.5	2.8	5.1	.4	1.0	-.1	.8	2.3
Manufacturing[i]	75.62	-5.8	.3	1.6	1.0	-2.4	2.4	5.7	.4	1.1	.1	.3	2.2
Durable	35.22	-7.9	1.8	3.6	1.4	-2.5	6.3	9.7	.6	1.3	.4	.5	4.5
Measures excluding selected high-technology industries and motor vehicles and parts													
Total industry	88.40	-5.1	-.2	.1	.1	-4.5	1.2	4.0	.3	1.0	-.1	.7	1.1
Manufacturing[i]	70.69	-5.5	-.9	.3	.1	-3.6	.4	4.3	.2	1.0	.0	.1	.6
Stage-of-process components of non–energy materials, measures of the input to													
Finished processors	13.73	-7.4	5.0	4.8	-.6	-1.4	10.1	11.8	.2	1.2	1.0	1.0	6.9
Semifinished and primary processors	16.12	-5.8	1.2	.6	-1.4	-5.0	1.7	7.6	.6	1.1	.3	.0	1.4

9 ▶
10 ▶

related electronic components. Higher output in these items reflects a willingness by firms to make the necessary investments to lift productivity levels.

(10) Because of the enormous influence of motor vehicle output on the manufacturing industry, large fluctuations in this one group can greatly distort swings in industrial production overall. To find out how much manufacturers outside the auto industry are producing, look at the output measure excluding motor vehicles and parts.

- **Table 3** Motor Vehicle Assemblies

(11) No single industry is more closely identified with manufacturing than automakers. They are responsible for 7 million jobs and represent about 4% of GDP. The U.S. automotive industry produces a higher level of output than any other single industry. It is among the largest purchasers of aluminum, iron, plastics, rubber, textiles, vinyl, steel, and computer chips. It's also an industry that is highly sensitive to interest rates. High rates will dull sales and lead to lower auto production and even layoffs, while a drop in financing costs can spur purchases of motor vehicles, increase assembly line output, and fuel more economic growth. Given its unique position in American business, the Federal Reserve has dedicated a separate table on the output of cars and trucks produced every month.

Table 3
MOTOR VEHICLE ASSEMBLIES
Millions of units, seasonally adjusted annual rate

Item	2003 average	2003 Q1	Q2	Q3	Q4	2003 Oct.	Nov.	Dec.	2004 Jan.
Total	12.09	12.30	11.76	12.29	12.20	12.24	12.12	12.24	12.29
Autos	4.51	4.68	4.43	4.56	4.41	4.54	4.41	4.29	4.31
Trucks	7.58	7.63	7.32	7.73	7.79	7.70	7.72	7.95	7.99
Light	7.32	7.39	7.08	7.46	7.49	7.40	7.41	7.64	7.67
Medium and heavy	.26	.23	.24	.26	.30	.29	.30	.31	.32
MEMO Autos and light trucks	11.83	12.07	11.52	12.03	11.90	11.94	11.82	11.93	11.97

- **Table 7** Capacity Utilization

(12) This is one of the most interesting tables in the entire release. When it comes to capacity utilization rates, not all industries share the same threshold for inflation. Operating at 85% capacity might pose a serious strain for the motor vehicle industry, but it's unlikely to overtax the primary metals producers. Table 7 shows the current and historical capacity utilization rates for many key industries. The data here can help presage inflationary pressures for specific sectors. Here's one example: The computer industry operated at a peak of 86.6% of capacity during the halcyon years of 1994–1995. However, in 2003, the industry was operating at an average capacity of just 71%. With so much excess production capacity sitting idle, prices for computers and peripheral equipment were able to stay down.

This table can also give you a heads-up on which industries are likely to increase future capital investments. Producers who have been operating at high capacity utilization rates are likely to increase outlays for new facilities to relieve current production pressures and improve productivity.

Percent of capacity, seasonally adjusted

Item		2003 proportion	1972-2003 ave.	1988-89 high	1990-91 low	1994-95 high	2003 Q1	Q2	Q3	Q4r	2003 Oct.r	Nov.r	Dec.r	2004 Jan.p
Total industry		100.00	81.1	85.2	78.6	84.8	75.1	74.1	74.6	75.4	75.0	75.7	75.6	76.2
Manufacturing		84.35	80.0	85.6	77.2	84.3	73.5	72.7	73.2	74.1	73.6	74.3	74.4	74.6
Manufacturing (NAICS)		79.53	79.8	85.5	77.0	84.4	72.9	72.0	72.6	73.6	73.1	73.8	73.9	74.0
Durable manufacturing		44.99	78.3	84.5	73.4	83.7	70.3	69.1	70.1	71.4	70.8	71.5	71.8	72.1
Wood products	321	1.45	80.2	88.8	73.0	87.9	73.1	72.7	74.0	76.1	75.7	76.5	76.2	76.9
Nonmetallic mineral products	327	2.20	79.4	85.7	72.1	84.0	77.5	76.9	77.7	78.8	78.3	78.9	79.4	79.8
Primary metal	331	2.18	80.8	95.3	75.2	94.9	76.8	73.4	73.3	76.3	74.9	76.7	77.3	76.2
Fabricated metal products	332	6.26	76.9	80.3	71.1	83.8	68.8	67.2	67.3	68.2	67.7	68.3	68.7	69.2
Machinery	333	5.73	79.5	84.6	72.8	87.6	66.8	67.0	67.6	69.3	67.5	70.1	70.3	70.8
Computer and electronic products	334	9.67	79.1	81.1	76.3	85.3	63.2	62.9	65.2	66.8	66.9	67.0	66.7	66.9
Electrical equip., appliances, and components	335	2.23	83.0	87.4	75.0	92.5	73.5	73.1	73.5	75.4	74.6	75.6	75.9	76.3
Motor vehicles and parts	3361–3	6.27	77.7	89.7	56.5	87.8	80.9	77.9	80.7	81.8	81.5	81.7	82.2	82.6
Aircraft and other miscellaneous transportation equipment	3364–9	4.06	72.9	88.9	81.9	67.7	63.8	63.6	64.0	64.8	64.3	64.9	65.3	65.6
Furniture and related products	337	1.77	78.9	84.0	67.9	83.7	71.1	69.6	69.6	69.6	69.2	69.7	69.9	70.1
Miscellaneous	339	3.15	76.9	81.7	77.7	81.2	77.8	76.5	75.6	75.7	75.1	75.4	76.4	76.6
Nondurable manufacturing		34.55	82.0	87.0	81.8	85.5	76.5	76.1	76.1	76.7	76.3	76.9	76.8	76.9
Food, beverage, and tobacco products	311,2	11.18	82.1	85.5	81.3	84.5	77.4	77.3	77.2	76.8	76.7	77.0	76.6	76.5
Textile and product mills	313,4	1.23	83.3	91.4	77.2	91.0	73.2	71.7	70.4	72.0	71.2	73.0	71.8	72.9
Apparel and leather	315,6	1.13	79.6	84.2	77.3	89.2	65.2	63.4	61.9	64.0	63.3	64.1	64.6	64.5
Paper	322	2.69	88.3	93.7	85.2	92.4	83.6	83.8	83.4	83.6	82.9	83.6	84.2	84.1
Printing and support	323	2.46	84.3	91.6	82.7	86.0	73.7	71.9	71.8	71.5	71.6	71.5	71.5	71.5
Petroleum and coal products	324	2.07	86.4	88.9	82.5	90.2	88.4	87.6	87.9	89.0	88.4	89.0	89.6	88.4
Chemical	325	10.27	78.4	85.6	80.8	81.3	73.1	72.6	73.0	74.2	73.5	74.5	74.5	74.8
Plastics and rubber products	326	3.51	83.7	91.3	77.2	92.4	79.6	79.1	79.9	81.1	80.6	81.4	81.3	81.5
Other manufacturing (non-NAICS)	1133,5111	4.81	83.6	90.7	79.1	82.8	82.3	83.2	82.4	83.5	83.2	84.0	83.4	83.6
Mining	21	6.71	86.9	85.6	83.4	88.3	84.7	84.7	85.0	85.6	85.4	85.7	85.9	86.0
Utilities	2211,2	8.95	86.9	92.8	84.1	93.8	86.3	82.4	82.9	82.6	82.4	83.4	82.1	86.1
Selected high-technology industries		6.35	78.8	79.9	74.5	88.3	61.7	62.0	65.0	67.1	66.8	67.2	67.4	68.6
Computers and office equipment	3341	1.37	78.1	79.3	67.2	86.6	71.4	68.6	70.4	73.3	72.4	73.3	74.1	75.1
Communications equipment	3342	2.09	77.7	81.7	73.2	87.5	50.6	50.9	50.2	50.7	51.3	50.9	50.1	51.1
Semiconductors and related electronic components	334412–9	2.89	80.7	80.5	78.1	91.5	64.9	66.8	73.0	75.9	75.3	75.8	76.5	77.8
Measures excluding selected high-technology industries														
Total industry		93.65	81.3	85.6	78.8	84.7	76.3	75.3	75.7	76.4	76.0	76.7	76.6	77.1
Manufacturing		78.00	80.1	86.1	77.3	84.1	74.7	73.9	74.3	75.1	74.6	75.4	75.4	75.6
STAGE-OF-PROCESS GROUPS														
Crude		9.67	86.3	88.5	84.7	88.9	83.3	83.3	83.7	84.0	83.8	84.0	84.3	84.6
Primary and semifinished		48.65	82.2	86.4	77.5	87.9	77.2	75.8	76.4	77.5	77.0	77.8	77.8	78.7
Finished		41.68	78.2	83.2	77.2	80.3	71.2	70.4	70.9	71.5	71.1	71.8	71.6	71.7

MARKET IMPACT

Bonds

Traders in the fixed income market usually can anticipate changes in industrial production before the official release is out. What tips them off are earlier reports, such as factory hours worked (from the employment data), the purchasing managers report (based on the ISM survey), producer prices, and retail sales. Of course, surprises do happen from time to time. Should industrial production and capacity utilization jump by a greater than expected amount, this can prompt a sell-off in the bond market. This is particularly the case if the utilization rate climbs above 80%, a zone that can begin to drain resources, create bottlenecks, and accelerate inflation.

On the flip side, slower production along with falling utilization rates could raise bond prices and lower interest rates because the threat of inflation has subsided.

Stocks

Industrial production is not one of those high-profile indicators known to roil the equity market. Strong production is generally considered to be supportive of stock prices because it signifies more economic growth and better corporate profits. The only concern for stock investors is if higher production leads to excessively tight capacity and higher prices. Should the latter scenario emerge, stocks might react negatively to a jump in industrial output.

Dollar

Normally, the dollar reacts modestly to industrial production. Foreigners try to assess how production and capacity utilization will affect future inflation and interest rates in the U.S. Because a jump in industrial output suggests faster economic growth, it can increase foreign demand for dollar-based investments—or, at the very least, prevent U.S. currency from falling.

INSTITUTE FOR SUPPLY MANAGEMENT (ISM) MANUFACTURING SURVEY

Market Sensitivity: Very high.

What Is It: First monthly report on the economy with a focus on manufacturing.

News Release on the Internet: *www.ism.ws/ISMReport/index.cfm*

Home Web Address: *www.ism.ws*

Release Time: 10 a.m. (ET); released the first business day after the reporting month.

Frequency: Monthly.

Source: Institute for Supply Management.

Revisions: No monthly revisions are done, but every January the seasonal adjustment factors are reassessed and this can lead to changes in all the data.

WHY IS IT IMPORTANT?

You might choose to ignore this economic indicator because of its less-than-riveting name. So here's a warning: Don't! It is the first piece of news on the economy out of the gate every month and the most influential statistic released by the private sector. The organization behind this market-moving series is the Institute for Supply Management (ISM), a Tempe, Arizona-based group that represents corporate purchasing managers around the country. Indeed, prior to January 2002, it was known by the more transparent name of National Association of Purchasing Managers. The ISM puts out two major surveys each month. The first is based on comments from purchasing managers in the manufacturing sector. The second deals with their counterparts in the non-manufacturing, or service, industry. It is the manufacturing survey that grabs most of the attention in the financial markets and the press.

    This raises an immediate question. How is it that an obscure bunch of purchasing managers in manufacturing can hold such sway over the investment community? The answer can be found by understanding what corporate purchasing agents do. Manufacturing companies need lots of supplies to make products. Those in charge of procuring this material for their companies are purchasing managers. A sample of items they might order includes wiring, packing boxes, ink, and computers. If there is a pickup in demand for manufactured products, purchasing managers quickly respond by increasing orders for production material and other supplies. If manufacturing sales slow, these corporate buyers will cut back on industrial orders. Thus, by virtue of their position, purchasing managers are in the forefront of monitoring activity in manufacturing. That's important because the goods-producing industry is highly sensitive to the ebb and flow of business in the broader economy. Best of all about the ISM's Purchasing Managers Index is its timing. Survey results come out on the first business day of every month. As such, they provide the earliest clues about how the economy has fared during the previous four weeks. Indeed, the numbers are so current that Federal Reserve officials are briefed on the data before the public sees it. The ISM's non-manufacturing report (see the next major section) comes out two business days later, but it has not yet achieved the exalted status of the manufacturing release.

How Is It Computed?

The ISM's manufacturing survey has an interesting history. Its origin can be traced to Herbert Hoover. Faced with a collapsing U.S. economy during the Great Depression, President Hoover was frustrated by the lack of current data on the health of American manufacturers. He approached the ISM, then known as the National Association of Purchasing Agents, and urged them to develop a survey that would provide up-to-date information on the health of this important part of the economy. The group complied, and the survey began in 1931. It has been around ever since, except for a brief four-year interruption during World War II.

Nowadays, the ISM mails out questionnaires every month to about 400 member companies around the country, representing 20 different industries. Corporate purchasing managers are asked to assess if activity is rising, falling, or unchanged in the following fields:

- New orders: New orders by purchasing agents
- Production: Manufacturing output
- Employment: Hiring in the company
- Supplier deliveries (or vendor performance): Speed of delivery from suppliers
- Inventories: The rate of liquidating manufacturers' inventories
- Customers' inventories: Agents guess the inventory levels of their customers
- Commodity prices: Prices paid by manufacturers for supplies
- Backlog of orders: Orders not yet filled
- New export orders: Rate of new orders from other countries
- Imports: Material that agents purchased from other countries

(Seasonal adjustment factors are applied only on new orders, production, employment, supplier deliveries, inventories, export orders, and imports.)

The Purchasing Managers Index (PMI) itself is a compilation based on the answers to the first five queries in the preceding list. They are weighted as follows to compute the index: new orders (30%), manufacturing production (25%), employment (20%), supplier deliveries (15%), and inventories (10%). The bottom five provide additional coverage on how manufacturing is performing. The PMI is calculated as a so-called diffusion index, which shows changes in activity from month to month, but not actual levels of production. As the responses from members come in, the ISM takes the percentage of those who reported activity being higher in each component and adds that to half the percentage of those who reported seeing no changes. If the result is an index number above 50, it means the manufacturing sector is growing. Below 50 means it's contracting. An index of 50 represents no change in activity.

Here are two examples: Let's say 100% of those surveyed reported no change in manufacturing production. To come up with the index, take half the percentage of those who said orders were unchanged (which gives you 50%) and add it to the percentage of agents who saw higher activity (no one did, so it's 0%). The result is an index of 50, which means that purchasing managers have seen no discernible change in manufacturing output from one month to the next.

In the second example, we'll assume that 30% of the agents reported higher activity, while 50% noticed no change in business. The diffusion index in this case comes to 55% (30 plus half of 50), which is a sign that manufacturing output is expanding.

THE TABLES: CLUES ON WHAT'S AHEAD FOR THE ECONOMY

You can glean lots of information about the present health of specific industries from the ISM survey. For example, inside the ISM report, 20 different business sectors—from food to furniture manufacturers—are probed so that you can see where the greatest sources of strength and weakness are in the economy. Which sectors are growing, hiring, or feeling the inflation pinch? What makes this so valuable to equity investors is the timeliness of the results and the fact that this information came directly from industry executives. With very few exceptions over its long history, the ISM index has been an excellent leading indicator of GDP growth.

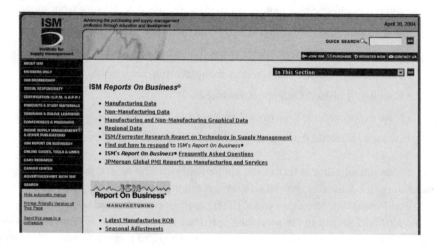

Reprinted with permission from the publisher, the Institute for Supply Management™, from the monthly ISM *Report on Business®*.

- ## ISM Manufacturing Survey at a Glance

The latest outcome of the Purchasing Managers Index and its components is the first table in the report, and it's well worth studying. The overall PMI has been effective at gauging turning points in the business cycle and thus is closely linked to movement in the GDP. For instance, a PMI reading of 50 is believed to be consistent with real GDP growth of about 2.5%. Every full point in the index above 50 can add another 0.3 percentage points or so of growth over the year.

MARCH 2004 ISM BUSINESS SURVEY AT A GLANCE

	Series Index	Direction Mar vs Feb	Rate of Change Mar vs Feb
PMI	62.5	Growing	Faster
New Orders	65.7	Growing	Slower
Production	65.5	Growing	Faster
Employment	57.0	Growing	Faster
Supplier Deliveries	67.9	Slowing	Faster
Inventories	48.3	Contracting	Faster
Customers' Inventories	39.5	Too Low	Slower
Prices	86.0	Increasing	Faster
Backlog of Orders	63.5	Growing	Faster
New Export Orders	62.0	Growing	Faster
Imports	56.8	Growing	Slower

Images in this section reprinted with permission from the publisher, the Institute for Supply Management™, from the monthly ISM *Report on Business*®.

More broadly, here is how you can interpret the results:

- Above 50: Both manufacturing and the economy are expanding.
- Below 50 but above 43: Manufacturing activity is contracting, yet the overall economy may still be growing.
- Below 43 on a sustained basis: Both manufacturing and the economy are likely to be in recession. The prospect increases that Fed officials will lower rates to spur faster economic growth.

What if the PMI surges beyond the 60 range? It depends how long it stays there and whether supplies and capacity utilization are getting tight. Three to six months above 60 in an economy already showing vigorous growth, and low unemployment, could prompt the Federal Reserve to raise interest rates.

One of the most useful leading economic indicators of future production is new orders. A jump in orders is normally followed by higher production in the months ahead. Should new orders show a persistent decline, it's an omen that activity in manufacturing, and possibly the overall economy, may soon start to sputter, if not stall.

New Orders

ISM's New Orders Index grew in March with a reading of 65.7 percent. The index is 0.7 percentage point lower than the 66.4 percent registered in February and is the 11th consecutive month the index has exceeded 50 percent. A New Orders Index above 51 percent, over time, is generally consistent with an increase in the Census Bureau's series on manufacturing orders (in constant 1987 dollars). Nineteen industries report increases for the month of March: Tobacco; Leather; Industrial & Commercial Equipment & Computers; Wood & Wood Products; Transportation & Equipment; Textiles; Paper; Primary Metals; Chemicals; Printing & Publishing; Glass, Stone & Aggregate; Miscellaneous*; Apparel; Fabricated Metals; Electronic Components & Equipment; Rubber & Plastic Products; Instruments & Photographic Equipment; Food; and Furniture.

New Orders	%Better	%Same	%Worse	Net	Index
March 2004	50	41	9	+41	65.7
February 2004	49	41	10	+39	66.4
January 2004	48	40	12	+36	71.1
December 2003	45	42	13	+32	73.1

The employment index series should be tracked to see if factories are laying off or actively hiring new workers. The ISM can thus foreshadow changes in employment conditions before the official jobs report is released.

Employment

ISM's Employment Index grew for the fifth consecutive month, following a 37-month trend of contraction. The index registered 57 percent in March compared to 56.3 percent in February, an increase of 0.7 percentage point. The last time the Employment Index registered higher than March's index was in December 1987, registering 59.1 percent. An Employment Index above 48 percent, over time, is generally consistent with an increase in the Bureau of Labor Statistics (BLS) data on manufacturing employment. The 11 industries reporting growth in employment during March are: Miscellaneous*; Transportation & Equipment; Industrial & Commercial Equipment & Computers; Apparel; Furniture; Electronic Components & Equipment; Textiles; Chemicals; Instruments & Photographic Equipment; Wood & Wood Products; and Rubber & Plastic Products.

Employment	%Higher	%Same	%Lower	Net	Index
March 2004	26	65	9	+17	57.0
February 2004	23	66	11	+12	56.3
January 2004	16	73	11	+5	52.9
December 2003	21	64	15	+6	53.5

The supplier deliveries index (also known as vendor performance) deserves close monitoring. It tracks the change in delivery times purchasing agents experience from their suppliers. An index figure racing into the high 50s and above means purchasing agents are waiting longer to receive material they ordered. This normally occurs when demand is so strong that suppliers are having trouble shipping goods in time. In such a climate, suppliers can regain pricing power, which, of course, also raises fresh concerns about future inflation. This index has proven to be such an effective predictor of economic activity that it is included in the Conference Board's Index of Leading Economic Indicators.

Supplier Deliveries

ISM's Supplier Deliveries Index indicates that delivery performance is slower when comparing March to February. March's reading of 67.9 percent is an increase of 5.8 percentage points over February's reading of 62.1 percent. A reading above 50 percent indicates slower deliveries. The 17 industries reporting slower supplier deliveries in March are: Primary Metals; Miscellaneous*; Electronic Components & Equipment; Fabricated Metals; Transportation & Equipment; Instruments & Photographic Equipment; Textiles; Apparel; Paper; Industrial & Commercial Equipment & Computers; Furniture; Printing & Publishing; Wood & Wood Products; Glass, Stone & Aggregate; Food; Chemicals; and Rubber & Plastic Products.

Supplier Deliveries	%Slower	%Same	%Faster	Net	Index
March 2004	38	59	3	+35	67.9
February 2004	28	70	2	+26	62.1
January 2004	24	72	4	+20	60.4
December 2003	17	81	2	+15	58.6

Customer inventories (table not shown) is also an interesting category in the ISM survey. Purchasing managers go on record characterizing the inventory levels of their customers. If they perceive those inventories to be low and the index falls below 50, it should be viewed as a positive development. Dwindling customer inventories can become a source of new orders in the future for manufacturers because their clients will eventually need to replenish their own stock of goods to stay in line with sales.

The price index reflects the change in prices paid by manufacturers for material. It can tell you if inflation is accelerating or decelerating early in the production process. This price index has a correlation over time with changes in monetary policy by the Federal Reserve. If the price index stays above 65, chances increase that the Fed will step in and lift rates.

Prices°°

ISM's Prices Index indicates manufacturers continued to pay higher prices in March. This is the 25th consecutive month the index has registered higher prices. March's index is at 86 percent, 4.5 percentage points higher than February's reading of 81.5 percent. The last time the index registered as high as March's index was in January 1995 when it was also 86 percent. In March, 73 percent of supply executives reported paying higher prices and 1 percent reported paying lower prices, while 26 percent reported that prices were unchanged from the preceding month.

A Prices Index below 46.9 percent, over time, is generally consistent with a decrease in the Bureau of Labor Statistics (BLS) Index of Manufacturers Prices. The 19 industries reporting paying higher prices in March are: Tobacco; Leather; Textiles; Primary Metals; Miscellaneous*; Industrial & Commercial Equipment & Computers; Food; Fabricated Metals; Wood & Wood Products; Transportation & Equipment; Furniture; Glass, Stone & Aggregate; Paper; Electronic Components & Equipment; Chemicals; Rubber & Plastic Products; Apparel; Printing & Publishing; and Instruments & Photographic Equipment.

Prices	%Higher	%Same	%Lower	Net	Index
March 2004	73	26	1	+72	86.0
February 2004	65	33	2	+63	81.5
January 2004	54	43	3	+51	75.5
December 2003	37	58	5	+32	66.0

New exports orders (table not shown) is an index with a double-edged sword. While a jump in orders from other countries can boost domestic manufacturing, encourage hiring, and fuel GDP growth, it can also heat up the pressure of inflation as buyers in the U.S. have to compete with foreigners for American products and resources. This poses little problem if the domestic economy is weak. But if the U.S. and international economies are simultaneously showing robust growth, product prices will march higher.

MARKET IMPACT

Bonds

For players in the bond market, the PMI is one of a handful of indicators that can truly shake things up. Though manufacturing plays a far smaller role in the economy than it did 50 years ago, the timing of the data and its sensitivity to economic turning points makes the ISM report one of the "big" ones to watch. Indeed, long-term bond yields have a 70% correlation with the ISM manufacturing index. Adding to its reputation as a major market-mover is the PMI's history of frustrating even the best forecasters. Economists are not very good at predicting what the PMI will be because so little other information is available on the month just concluded.

Just how the market will react to the ISM depends largely on where the economy stands in the business cycle. Normally, investors view a PMI consistently above 50 as bearish for fixed incomes, especially if the economy is well into its expansionary phase because that can aggravate inflation pressures and invite higher interest rates. An index of 45 to 50 is unlikely to cause much of a stir in the bond market. A reading below 45, however, could energize the bond market, because it denotes serious weakness in manufacturing and perhaps for the broader economy.

Stocks

The equity market will react positively to a rising PMI, particularly after a period of tepid economic growth. Of course, if the index jumps at a time when business activity is already in high gear, stock prices could drop as worries mount that the economy may be in danger of overheating. This raises the probability that the Federal Reserve will boost interest rates to cool business activity.

Dollar

If the economy is fundamentally healthy and inflation is in check, the dollar will likely bounce higher, with a PMI above 50. Conversely, should the ISM report portray a manufacturing sector teetering on recession, foreigners might sell some of their dollar-linked investments, depressing the greenback's value against other key currencies.

INSTITUTE FOR SUPPLY MANAGEMENT (ISM) NON-MANUFACTURING BUSINESS SURVEY

Market Sensitivity: Low.

What Is It: The first read on the economy's service sector.

News Release on the Internet: *www.ism.ws/ISMReport/index.cfm*

Home Web Address: *www.ism.ws*

Release Time: 10 a.m. (ET); released on the third business day following the
month being reported.

Frequency: Monthly.

Source: Institute for Supply Management.

Revisions: No monthly revisions. There are yearly reassessments of seasonal
adjustment factors. They are normally done in January and can lead to
revisions for the last four years.

WHY IS IT IMPORTANT?

This survey reminds me of Rodney Dangerfield's old lament: "I get no respect, no respect
at all." Published for the first time in June 1998, the ISM's Non-Manufacturing survey
looks at conditions in the service sector. Though it lacks the kind of recognition and grav-
itas its manufacturing counterpart has in the financial markets, this non-manufacturing
report is expected to become one of the most influential economic indicators put out
every month.

After all, not only does it spot changes in employment trends, new orders, and prices
in the non-manufacturing industries, which represent 80% of the U.S. economy, but the
survey results are published for all to see on a near-real-time basis. The data comes out on
the third business day of each month and covers the month just concluded.

So why hasn't the non-manufacturing survey caught on faster? For one, it is a relatively new report, and there has not been enough historical experience to draw a relationship with GDP performance. Several more years of tracking ISM's non-manufacturing
index will be needed to establish any reliable correlation. At the very least, one has to see
this indicator perform through one or two complete business cycles. Another reason it has
been slow to excite investment managers and forecasters is that the service sector is not as
cyclical as manufacturing. During tough economic times, Americans quickly slash spending on pricey manufactured goods (such as cars, furniture, and home entertainment systems), but they will not significantly pare back outlays on services, because there is
always a demand for medical care, transportation, and communications. That makes the
ISM's non-manufacturing index less than an ideal forecasting tool to identify turning

points in the economy. Nevertheless, the non-manufacturing index is a compelling indicator simply because it encompasses so much of the economy and provides a very current assessment of business conditions.

There are some similarities and differences between this survey and its better-known manufacturing cousin. Both look at the same components, such as backlog of orders, new orders, employment, new export orders, imports, prices, inventory sentiment, supplier deliveries, and inventories. However, since we're dealing essentially with services, these categories are defined somewhat differently. For example, the pricing component in the manufacturing survey looks at the costs of raw materials and basic supplies. In contrast, costs in the service sector are more likely to be based on purchasing finished products and other services. Furthermore, exports in the non-manufacturing sector are not about shipping goods to other countries; they are about selling financial, consulting, entertainment, and accounting services to foreign companies and individuals. Last, there is no overall composite index like the ISM manufacturing report. Instead, the non-manufacturing survey uses a "business activity index" that measures the rate and direction of change in the service sector.

How Is It Computed?

The methodology for the non-manufacturing business activity index is much the same as that used in the manufacturing survey. Questionnaires are sent to more than 370 purchasing managers in over 17 industries, including legal services, entertainment, real estate, communications, insurance, transportation, banking, and lodging. The proportion of companies queried in each industry depends on how much that sector contributes to GDP.

Respondents are asked if they are experiencing higher activity, lower activity, or no change for each of the ten components listed here:

- Business activity: Measures changes in the level of business activity in services.

- New orders: Reflects shifts in the number of new orders from customers.

- Employment: Looks at the rate of increase or decrease in employment.

- Supplier deliveries: Tells if deliveries from suppliers are faster or slower.

- Inventories: Monitors the increase or decrease in inventory levels.

- Customer inventories: Rates the level of inventories their clients have.

- Prices: Reports whether member organizations are paying more or less for products and services.

- Backlog of orders: Measures the amount of backlog of orders, whether growing or declining.

- New export orders: Reports changes in the level of orders, requests for services, and other activities to be provided outside the U.S.

- Imports: Measures the rate of change in materials and services imported.

Once the results are tallied, a diffusion index is employed to quantify each of the 10 categories listed. Seasonal adjustments are made for only four of the 10—business activity, new orders, employment, and prices.

For the main Business Activity index, a reading of 50 shows that the same percentage of purchasing managers reported higher activity as lower activity. Index values over 50 indicate growth, while below 50 means contraction. Since its inception in 1998, the ISM non-manufacturing Business Activity index has rarely dropped below 50.

THE TABLES: CLUES ON WHAT'S AHEAD FOR THE ECONOMY

There is not enough history to determine if this survey has any qualities as a leading indicator. Because the service sector is less prone to volatile cyclical swings, its predictive value might turn out to be limited. However, at least two components in the report can send up flares of trouble ahead: prices and employment.

- Report on Non-Manufacturing: Prices (Not Shown)

  The pricing component in this survey can tip us off if the inflation threat is becoming more serious. After all, services account for about 60% of the consumer price index (CPI), and it has been the main culprit behind rising prices in the past. However, be aware that the price component in this report includes the cost of both services and materials purchased by non-manufacturers, so it should not be viewed strictly as a pure inflation gauge for services. Generally speaking, when this price index exceeds 60 beyond three months, it should flag investors that price increases might be accelerating for the broad economy too.

- Report on Non-Manufacturing: Employment (Not Shown)

  This table can provide an early clue on what the monthly payroll numbers might show when the official employment report comes out for that month. Jobs in the non-manufacturing sector account for about 80% of all employment in the economy, so this table can serve as a leading indicator of labor market conditions. What's often overlooked by the press is that this table also points out which specific service industries are showing the most and least job growth.

MARKET IMPACT

So far there has been no discernible reaction in the bond, stock, and currency markets to the ISM's non-manufacturing survey. But over time, you can expect investors to take this indicator more seriously given the growing importance of services in the economy.

CHICAGO PURCHASING MANAGERS INDEX (BUSINESS BAROMETER)

Market Sensitivity: Medium.

What Is It: Measures business activity in the Midwest region.

News Release on the Internet: *www.napm-chicago.org*

Release Time: 10:00 a.m. (ET); released on the final business day of the month being covered.

Frequency: Monthly.

Source: National Association of Purchasing Management, Chicago affiliate.

Revisions: The only revision comes from changes in seasonal adjustment factors, and it is made every January.

WHY IS IT IMPORTANT?

Timing can be everything when it comes to getting the public to notice an economic indicator. Take the Chicago Purchasing Managers report. This group is an affiliate of the Institute for Supply Management, which releases the market-sensitive Purchasing Managers Index (PMI) the first business day after the reporting month ends. So what does the local Chicago chapter do to grab some of the limelight? It publishes the survey a business day before the ISM number is released. The strategy has worked well.

Money managers around the country and in the business press carefully look over the Chicago results for some tips on what the red-hot ISM manufacturing index will do a day later. On a month-to-month basis, the Chicago Business Barometer index moves in the same direction as the national PMI numbers about 60% of the time. More importantly, of the 10 local ISM chapters that publish monthly regional reports, the Chicago survey is considered by many as the most influential. It concentrates on a region considered to be the industrial heartland of the nation. After all, this area covers the auto industry, which plays a major role in the output of the U.S. economy.

HOW IS IT COMPUTED?

The parent group, long known as the National Association of Purchasing Management, changed its name in 2002 to the Institute for Supply Management. However, the Chicago affiliate decided not to follow suit, opting instead to keep the NAPM title.

The Chicago NAPM queries about 200 purchasing managers spread out across a region that includes Illinois, Indiana, and Michigan and questions them on business activity in their area. Only about half of the respondents actually return their questionnaires. Answers received are compiled, and a diffusion index is produced based on a weighted average of the five subcomponent indexes: new orders (35% weight), production (25%), order backlogs (15%), employment (10%), and supplier deliveries (15%). Aside from the overall Business Barometer index, separate measures are provided on prices paid for goods and changes in inventories.

The diffusion index, which is seasonally adjusted, functions like the manufacturing ISM survey; a reading above 50 in the Business Barometer index indicates expansion, while one below 50 suggests some contradiction in business activity in this region.

By the way, the responses received by the Chicago affiliate for this survey are not the same data sent to the national ISM group. Different samples are used for each survey.

THE TABLES: CLUES ON WHAT'S AHEAD FOR THE ECONOMY

- **Table**   Business Barometer

  (1) Some traders in the financial markets look to the latest Chicago Business Barometer index for an early heads-up on what the more influential ISM index might do the next day. The two move in the same direction on a month-to-month basis a little better than 60% of the time. However, in terms of the size of their changes (as opposed to just relative directions), the two have demonstrated a correlation over the last two decades of about 90%. That's quite high, of course. But for investors who want to make a quick trade in the market, the more relevant concern is the direction these indexes move and not so much the level of change.

- **Tables**   New Orders and Backlogs

  (2) Given the predominant influence of auto and auto parts manufacturers in this region, you can get a sense of motor vehicle demand and production by examining the new orders and orders backlog indices in the Chicago report.

- **Tables**   Supplier Deliveries and Prices Paid

  To get a check on inflationary pressures in the industrial economy, follow the trend in these two categories: prices paid and supplier deliveries. If the price index has been rising for more than three months and purchasing managers are noticing supplier deliveries taking longer, it's a warning that inflation might soon spread to other sectors of the economy.

FOR RELEASE:
27 February 2004
9am CT

The CHICAGO Report
National Association of Purchasing Management—Chicago

2004

February

BUSINESS BAROMETER™ Growth Slows

The Chicago Purchasing Managers report the growth of Business Barometer slowed to 63.6, marking the tenth month of growth.
- PRODUCTION, NEW ORDERS, and ORDER BACKLOGS slow from last month's strong rise;
- EMPLOYMENT grew for only the third time since March 2000;
- PRICES PAID remains strong;
- BUYING POLICY: Lead Times for CAPITAL EQUIPMENT are the shortest since June 1992.

The Business Barometer™ is a trademark of the National Association of Purchasing Management – Chicago

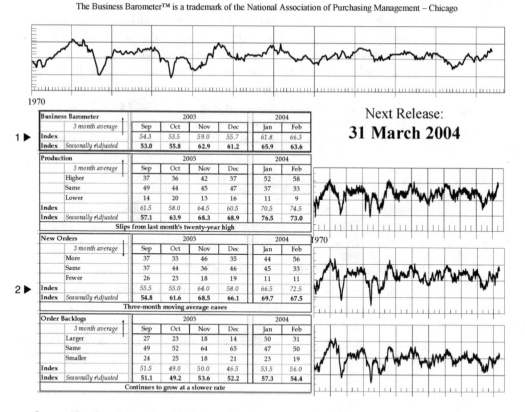

1970

Next Release:

31 March 2004

Business Barometer		2003				2004	
3 month average		Sep	Oct	Nov	Dec	Jan	Feb
Index		54.3	53.5	59.0	55.7	61.8	66.3
Index	Seasonally Adjusted	53.0	55.8	62.9	61.2	65.9	63.6

Production		2003				2004	
3 month average		Sep	Oct	Nov	Dec	Jan	Feb
Higher		37	36	42	37	52	58
Same		49	44	45	47	37	33
Lower		14	20	13	16	11	9
Index		61.5	58.0	64.5	60.5	70.5	74.5
Index	Seasonally Adjusted	57.1	63.9	68.3	68.9	76.5	73.0
Slips from last month's twenty-year high							

New Orders		2003				2004	
3 month average		Sep	Oct	Nov	Dec	Jan	Feb
More		37	33	46	35	44	56
Same		37	44	36	46	45	33
Fewer		26	23	18	19	11	11
Index		55.5	55.0	64.0	58.0	66.5	72.5
Index	Seasonally Adjusted	54.8	61.6	68.5	66.1	69.7	67.5
Three-month moving average eases							

Order Backlogs		2003				2004	
3 month average		Sep	Oct	Nov	Dec	Jan	Feb
Larger		27	23	18	14	30	31
Same		49	52	64	65	47	50
Smaller		24	25	18	21	23	19
Index		51.5	49.0	50.0	46.5	53.5	56.0
Index	Seasonally Adjusted	51.1	49.2	53.6	52.2	57.3	54.4
Continues to grow at a slower rate							

1 ▶

2 ▶

1970

Source: Kingsbury International, Ltd. (*www.kingbiz.com*); NAPM–Chicago.

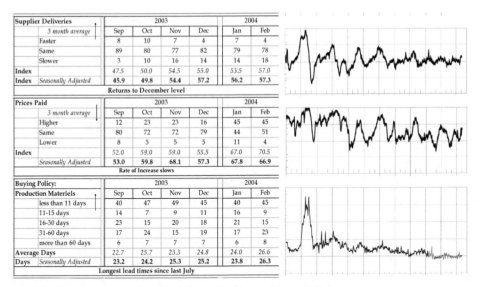

Supplier Deliveries	2003				2004	
3 month average	Sep	Oct	Nov	Dec	Jan	Feb
Faster	8	10	7	4	7	4
Same	89	80	77	82	79	78
Slower	3	10	16	14	14	18
Index	47.5	50.0	54.5	55.0	53.5	57.0
Index Seasonally Adjusted	45.9	49.8	54.4	57.2	56.2	57.3
Returns to December level						

Prices Paid	2003				2004	
3 month average	Sep	Oct	Nov	Dec	Jan	Feb
Higher	12	23	23	16	45	45
Same	80	72	72	79	44	51
Lower	8	5	5	5	11	4
Index	52.0	59.0	59.0	55.5	67.0	70.5
Seasonally Adjusted	53.0	59.8	68.1	57.3	67.8	66.9
Rate of Increase slows						

Buying Policy:	2003				2004	
Production Materiels	Sep	Oct	Nov	Dec	Jan	Feb
less than 11 days	40	47	49	45	40	45
11-15 days	14	7	9	11	16	9
16-30 days	23	15	20	18	21	15
31-60 days	17	24	15	19	17	23
more than 60 days	6	7	7	7	6	8
Average Days	22.7	25.7	23.3	24.8	24.0	26.6
Days Seasonally Adjusted	23.2	24.2	25.3	25.2	23.8	26.3
Longest lead times since last July						

Source: Kingsbury International, Ltd. (*www.kingbiz.com*); NAPM–Chicago.

MARKET IMPACT

The Business Barometer report is one of those unfortunate releases whose time in the spotlight is short-lived because it's quickly overshadowed by the national ISM story, which comes out the next business day. If the two reports diverge, market participants lean more on the ISM for the latest assessment of industrial activity in the country.

Bonds

Bond traders can be highly sensitive to this report because it is a brief forerunner to the ISM manufacturing survey. An unexpected surge in the Business Barometer will likely cause bond prices to fall in anticipation that the national survey might show similar results. Another reason for the Chicago NAPM's importance is that the Federal Reserve itself monitors this report to study conditions in the manufacturing sector and check for signs of production imbalances.

Stocks

Aside from the insight one might gain into auto industry activity from this report, equity investors are not inclined to adjust their portfolios in response to it. Obviously, if both the Chicago and ISM reports register hefty increases, the stock market might be more confident that corporate profits are on the rise. However, if the economy is already well into its expansion phase, stocks could respond perversely and retreat as expectations rise that the Fed will lift interest rates to slow the economy.

Dollar

Foreign investors usually do not take major currency positions on the basis of just the Chicago index.

INDEX OF LEADING ECONOMIC INDICATORS (LEI)

Market Sensitivity: Low to medium.

What Is It: An index designed to predict the economy's direction.

News Release on the Internet: *www.globalindicators.org/us/LatestReleases*

Home Web Address: *www.globalindicators.org*

Release Time: 10:00 a.m. (ET). The report is published three weeks after the end of the reporting month.

Frequency: Monthly.

Source: The Conference Board.

Revisions: Usually minor, but can be more significant at times.

WHY IS IT IMPORTANT?

Suppose you want to know what's ahead for the economy but you don't want to waste time going through reams of economic statistics. Is there a simpler way to find out how the economy might perform in the months ahead? One alternative is to rely on the Index of Leading Economic Indicators (LEI), which is published every month by the Conference Board, a private business research group in New York City. This index is a composite of a select group of economic statistics that are known to swing up or down well in advance of the rest of the economy. Thus, by tracking the LEI index, you'll hopefully know how the economy will perform in the coming months. Though its record is not perfect, the LEI index has been successful enough to make the measure worth watching.

Why do we need such a forecasting index in the first place? As any company executive can tell you, business cycles are not neat, well-organized affairs. If they were, it would be a lot easier to predict corporate sales, employment, and profits. Life, however, is never that simple. Dozens of economic indicators are released on a regular basis, and together they draw a remarkably unclear picture of what is happening in the economy. To make some sense of this gallimaufry of data, the Conference Board releases an index composed of 10 indicators that tend to precede changes in the economy. This index of leading economic indicators has done a fairly respectable job of signaling peaks and troughs of an economy some three to nine months down the road.

The LEI index is made up of 10 components—seven nonfinancial and three financial. They are described next, along with their relative weight in the index.

Nonfinancial Indicators

- Average hourly workweek in manufacturing (25.4%): Taken from the employment report. A sustained rise or fall in the number of hours worked is often a telling sign of whether companies will soon hire or fire workers.

- Average weekly initial claims for unemployment (3.3%): Obtained from the jobless claims report. This series is one of the most sensitive to changing business conditions. Initial claims for unemployment benefits climb when the economic climate deteriorates; the number of claims falls when the economy gets stronger.

- Manufacturers' new orders for consumer goods and materials (7.5%): Taken from the factory orders report. This inflation-adjusted series is a measure of how comfortable manufacturers are with current inventory levels and projections of future consumer demand.

- Vendor performance, or delivery times index (7%): Comes from the Institute for Supply Management's manufacturing survey. If it takes longer to deliver products to customers, this suggests that orders are flooding in so quickly that they're creating bottlenecks and products can't be shipped as fast. On the other hand, quicker deliveries are more closely associated with an economic slowdown. As orders drop, a production crunch is less likely, and the turnaround time between order and delivery becomes shorter.

- Manufacturers' new orders for nondefense capital goods (1.9%): Taken from the factory orders report. Companies are less likely to spend on new capital equipment and goods if they suspect a business slowdown is looming.

- Building permits for new private homes (2.7%): Data taken from the housing starts release. Because most builders have to file for a permit to begin construction on private homes, tracking changes in the number of permits is a good indicator of future building activity.

- Index of consumer expectations by the University of Michigan (2.9%): Changes in expectations about future economic conditions and household income can alter consumer spending behavior.

Financial Indicators

- Stock prices based on the S&P 500 stock index (3.8%): The stock market has historically been a good leading indicator of economic turning points. After all, stocks today are priced to reflect expected earnings. A rise or fall in the S&P stock index is a barometer of what investors believe the economy will do in the future.

- M2 money supply in real (inflation-adjusted) terms (35.3%): Money supply figures from the Federal Reserve. M2 is one of the broader measures of the money supply and includes currency, demand deposits, savings accounts, and bank CDs. When

M2 growth fails to keep pace with inflation, it's a sign that bank lending is slipping and the economy will soon weaken.

• <u>Interest rate spread between the 10-year Treasury bond and the federal funds rate (10.2%):</u> The difference between long-term rates and the federal funds rate (overnight borrowing rates by banks) has the best track record of the 10 components for forecasting economic activity. This is why it has been given a relatively high weight in the index. If the spread in rates increases so that long-term rates become materially higher than short-term rates, it's a sign the economy is on a growth path. However, if the spread narrows to the point where either there is no difference between the two maturities or they are inversely related (with short-term rates higher than long-term rates), it's indicative of an economy headed for trouble. This can happen when the Federal Reserve has driven short-term rates so high that the bond market is convinced economic activity will greatly weaken and bring down inflation with it.

Besides the forward-looking LEI index, the Conference Board also publishes two other measures. One is the Coincident Indicators index, which moves in line with what is currently happening in the economy. So when business activity picks up, the coincident index rises simultaneously. If economic activity is declining, so will this index. The other gauge is a Lagging Indicators index. It operates much like a rearview mirror in a car; it simply confirms that a certain part of the business cycle has passed. For instance, the lagging index would continue declining for a time even as an economy emerges from recession. "What's the point of having coincident and lagging indexes?" you might ask. "Who cares about the past or even the present? It's the future that counts!" These questions are understandable, but it's useful to know what all three indexes are doing to get a broader picture of the business cycle while it's in motion. The coincident index moves in tandem with the economy and captures its peaks and troughs in real time. The lagging indicator reassures analysts where the economy has been.

Index of Coincident Indicators

The index of coincident indicators consists of four components:

• <u>Employees in nonagricultural payrolls (52.9%):</u> Data taken from the monthly jobs report. This is the net increase or decrease in non-farm payrolls and includes full-time and part-time workers, regardless of whether they are temporary or permanent hires. This payroll series is arguably the most influential economic indicator in the financial markets.

• <u>Personal income less transfer payments (20.8%):</u> Obtained from the personal income and spending report. This is real (inflation-adjusted) personal income levels minus transfer payments. Keeping tabs on changes in income is crucial in determining the financial resources available for total spending.

- Industrial production (14.7%): From the industrial production series by the Federal Reserve. It monitors the physical output of all stages of production. A turn in economic activity quickly shows up in the manufacturing, mining, and utilities industries.

- Manufacturing and trade sales (11.6%): Obtained from the Business Inventories report. This index, which is adjusted for inflation, reflects total spending at the manufacturing, wholesale, and retail levels.

Index of Lagging Indicators

The lagging indicators index is based on a composite of seven measures:

- Average duration of unemployment (3.7%): Taken from the jobs report. The focus of attention here is the average number of weeks individuals are out of work. Employment activity—specifically, the duration of joblessness—is by nature a lagging indicator. Companies delay plans in hiring or firing workers because they are uncertain where the economy is headed. Eventually, as more economic evidence pours in, company officials get a clearer picture of business conditions, which leads to changes in employment policies.

- Inventories and sales ratio, manufacturing and trade (12.2%): Obtained from the Business Inventories report and adjusted for inflation. The inflation-adjusted inventory sales ratio is a reactive indicator. In other words, after months of weak manufacturing and retail sales, inventory levels as a proportion of sales surge. Eventually the ratio falls when sales accelerate faster than the buildup of inventories. Historically, the inventory sales ratio reaches its cyclical peak in the middle of a recession and then falls at the start of a recovery as sales pick up more rapidly than inventories.

- Change in labor cost per unit of output (6.2%): Data comes from the Productivity and Costs report. This is the six-month percentage change (annualized) of unit labor costs in the manufacturing sector. Labor costs edge up when productivity fails to keep up with compensation growth. Generally unit labor costs hit a high during the recession as output per hour drops faster than compensation.

- Average prime rate charged by banks (27.8): The prime rate is what banks charge for loans to their best corporate customers. Changes in the average prime rate generally trail changes in the rest of the economy.

- Commercial and industrial loans outstanding (11.4%): Figures are obtained from the Federal Reserve and are then adjusted for inflation. Business debt is also considered a lagging indicator because it typically peaks after a recession has started, a time when profits are slowing and debt service remains high. Such bank loans bottom out about a year after the recession ends.

• <u>Changes in the CPI for services (19.4%):</u> Comes from the CPI report. Here the Conference Board takes into account the six-month annualized rate of inflation in the service sector. For reasons not yet fully understood, service inflation actually peaks several months after the onset of recession and declines once the recovery has started.

• <u>Ratio of consumer installment credit outstanding to personal income (19.3%):</u> Figures taken from the personal income report and the Federal Reserve's consumer installment credit series. This series looks at the relationship between consumer debt and personal income. Whenever there is a prolonged drop in household income, the burden of servicing consumer debt becomes much greater. That's because a larger portion of income goes to repaying IOUs. As a result, Americans proceed to cut back on shopping and turn more cautious about using credit. Once income growth resumes and the economy is more stable, consumer spending and borrowing return to normal levels.

Of the three key business cycle indexes described—leading, coincident, and lagging—the leading indicators gauge gets most of the attention in the press, even though its forecasting performance has been short of stellar. While it has successfully predicted recessions in the past, the index has also declined on numerous occasions without a corresponding downturn in the economy. Thus, the LEI index can give off false signals about an oncoming recession too. It has a much better track record of indicating when the economy is ready to emerge from recession.

How Is It Computed?

The Commerce Department originated and first published the leading, coincident, and lagging economic indicator indexes in the 1960s. However, the government grew uncomfortable being part of the forecasting game and sold the entire series to the Conference Board in 1995. The nonprofit business group wasted little time fine-tuning the series to more accurately reflect what's going on in the economy. It jettisoned a few indicators and added new ones so that the overall indexes would send out fewer false signals.

To make the leading indicator index more timely, the Conference Board decided to advance its release date. However, this posed a problem. Some of the components that make up this index have yet to be released. In other words, the Conference Board won't have all the data it needs to come up with a complete LEI index. To get around this problem, the business group provides estimates on those missing components. Every month, three of the 10 components underlying the leading economic indicators index have to be estimated: manufacturers' new orders for consumer goods and materials, manufacturers' new orders for non-defense capital goods, and the personal consumption deflator (to calculate the "real" M2 money supply). A similar problem exists with the coincident index. The Conference Board has to do its own preliminary calculation for two of the four components: personal income less transfer payments, and manufacturing and trade sales. In the lagging indicator series, no less than five of the seven have to be estimated: the inventory sales ratio, the ratio of consumer installment debt to personal income, the change in the unit labor costs, the consumer price index for services, and the personal consumption deflator to compute real commercial and industrial loans outstanding. Because of these estimates, the leading, coincident, and lagging indexes can be substantially revised if the underlying figures turn out to be radically different from what was estimated.

THE TABLES: CLUES ON WHAT'S AHEAD FOR THE ECONOMY

Just how good is the LEI index at forecasting economic turning points? The answer depends on how high your expectations are for this or any other indicator that professes to predict future trends. Some experts poke fun at the LEI for predicting nine of the last six recessions. They criticize its failure to turn down prior to the 1990–1991 recession. In 1995, the index sent out signals of an imminent contraction in economic activity that never came to pass.

In light of this spotty record, does the LEI index really serve a useful purpose? The answer is yes, for several reasons. First, it has been more successful at predicting economic recoveries than at foreseeing recessions. Second, the Conference Board periodically refines this measure to improve its predictive performance. Third, what the LEI index offers investors and analysts is a best guess (based on underlying data) of what the economy might do in the next six to nine months. Nothing more, nothing less.

- **Table 1** Summary of Composite Indexes

  (1) This table has two parts. The top half shows how all three major indexes have changed in each of the last seven months. Let's focus on the LEI index. The old rule of thumb was that three consecutive declines in the index was a warning that an economic downturn might begin within three to nine months, and that three unbroken months of increases in the leading index portended the end of recession and the beginning of a recovery within that same time frame.

  The Conference Board, however, no longer subscribes to that three-month rule. The reason is that since 1953, the LEI index has actually fallen anywhere from two months to 20 months before the onset of recession. Not a very consistent record. So after considerable research, the business group came forward with another criterion considered to be more precise: a downward move in the LEI index of more than 2% over six months coupled with declines in a majority of the 10 components. The new rule is considered to be a more effective way of forecasting a recession. However, it has one rather important shortcoming. If you have to wait six months, it becomes less of a leading indicator, because by the end of that period, the economy may already be in recession. As a result, private economists outside the Conference Board have devised their own formulas when using the LEI. In one case, the leading index must decline at least four of the seven months, and the coincident index has to drop three consecutive months before there's a credible threat that recession is around the corner. There are probably other ways to utilize these indexes for the purpose of predicting turning points in the economy, which proves how subjective the science of forecasting can be.

Table 1.--Summary of Composites Indexes

	Jul	Aug	Sep	2003 Oct	Nov	Dec	2004 Jan
Leading index	112.8	113.2	113.3	113.9	114.2 r	114.4 r	115.0 p
Percent change	.7	.4	.1	.5	.3 r	.2	.5 p
Diffusion index	70.0	50.0	40.0	85.0	60.0	70.0	60.0
Coincident index	114.7	114.7	114.9 r	115.1 r	115.5 r	115.5 p	115.8 p
Percent change	.3	.0	.2 r	.2	.3	.0 p	.3 p
Diffusion index	87.5	37.5	100.0	100.0	100.0	50.0	100.0
Lagging index	99.6	99.6	99.0 r	99.1	98.6 r	98.2 p	98.2 p
Percent change	-.2	.0	-.6 r	.1 r	-.5 r	-.4 p	.0 p
Diffusion index	35.7	64.3	21.4	50.0	7.1	64.3	64.3
Coincident-lagging ratio	115.2 r	115.2	116.1 r	116.1 r	117.1 r	117.6 p	117.9 p

	Jan to Jul	Feb to Aug	Mar to Sep	Apr to Oct	May to Nov	Jun to Dec	Jul to Jan
Leading index							
Percent change	1.6	2.4	2.6	3.1	2.3	2.1	2.0
Diffusion index	70.0 r	90.0	85.0	100.0	90.0	90.0	80.0
Coincident index							
Percent change	.3	.4	.6	.9	1.0	1.0	1.0
Diffusion index	50.0	50.0 r	75.0	87.5	100.0	100.0	100.0
Lagging index							
Percent change	-1.5	-1.6	-2.0	-1.6	-1.9	-1.6	-1.4
Diffusion index	14.3	14.3	14.3	35.7	14.3	21.4	21.4

Source: The Conference Board, used with permission.

(2) The bottom table lays out the results of the new forecasting guideline employed by the Conference Board. It lists the latest six-month percentage change for the LEI index, as well as for the other two measures. Again, to get some historical perspective, the organization includes seven months worth of previous data.

One final note: The coincident indicator index reflects what is currently happening in the economy. When you measure the change in this index over a 12-month period, it turns out to be a good proxy for GDP growth. The yearly change in the coincident index moves in tandem with the rest of the economy about two-thirds of the time.

- **Table 2** Data and Net Contribution for Components of the Leading Index (Not Shown)

  This is a very useful table, because it breaks down the 10 components of the leading indicator index and shows how much each has contributed to the month's performance. The key here is to focus not on the magnitude of the change but on how broad-based the increase or decrease was for the individual components. There is no firm correlation between how large the change in the index is and how deep the economic upturn or downturn will be. What you want to see is if most or all of the components move in the same direction. If so, the index's predictive accuracy will be greater.

MARKET IMPACT

You would think that the investment community would stop everything just to hear the latest outcome of an index whose sole purpose is to illuminate what's ahead for the economy. While the press does devote attention to the LEI index, financial market reaction tends to be subdued. The reason for the muted response is that these leading, coincident, and lagging indicators rarely surprise investors; much of the data that underlies the indexes has already been published. It doesn't require rocket science to simulate the methodology and come up with a good guess on how the three indexes will perform in advance. Second, money managers still feel the forecasting track record of this series is short of divine. As a result, the release sparks little excitement in the markets.

Bonds

Professionals in the fixed-income markets spend little time musing over the leading indicators series because it's considered old news, and they pay virtually no attention to the coincident and lagging gauges. Perhaps these measures might generate more talk when the economy is believed to be close to a turning point, with yields possibly inching up or down a basis point or two. Otherwise, the market has largely discounted the LEI since the data underlying it has already been published.

Stocks

The LEI has a slightly greater impact on equity prices. During a recession, stock market investors search for any corroborative signs that point to a recovery and higher profits. If the LEI index posts several consecutive gains, investors feel more confident that an economic rebound is in the offing and thus raise their equity holdings. In contrast, any report that reinforces the notion that the economy is close to peaking could depress share prices, since it casts a cloud over future earnings.

Dollar

Assuming that the dollar is not being influenced by other factors, it will likely follow the same path as the stock market. Consecutive monthly rises in the LEI encourage foreign investors to buy dollar-based securities. Stronger U.S. economic growth brings with it higher interest rates and greater profits, all positive influences on the dollar. A series of falling LEI indexes would make the greenback less attractive to hold.

Housing Starts and Building Permits

Market Sensitivity: Medium.

What Is It: Records the number of new homes being built and permits for future construction.

News Release on the Internet:
www.census.gov/const/www/newresconstindex.html

Home Web Address: *www.census.gov*

Release Time: 8:30 a.m. (ET); normally released two or three weeks following the month being covered.

Frequency: Monthly.

Source: Census Bureau, Department of Commerce.

Revisions: Modest revisions occur for the preceding two months on housing starts and for just one month on permits. Seasonal adjustment changes are made every April, and they cover two years worth of data.

Why Is It Important?

Looking for a single infallible indicator that can foresee the future direction of the economy? Forget it; you won't find any. However, one comes surprisingly close—housing! Excluding one brief instance, there has never been a recession in the U.S. at a time when the housing sector stood strong. Only once since World War II did the economy contract despite a robust housing market, and that was in 2001. Even then, the recession was short-lived and not very deep. This impressive track record is why many experts view homebuilding as one of the most reliable leading indicators of economic activity. Residential real estate is among the first sectors to shut down when the economy nears recession, and it is the first to bloom when the economy starts to turn up.

What keeps housing so far ahead of the rest of the economy? Mainly its sensitivity to interest rates. An overheated economy drives interest rates higher. As mortgage rates climb, this depresses demand for homes and discourages future construction. Builders are also less likely to seek construction loans when rates are high. Conversely, when mortgage rates tumble and home prices decline—events that typically happen during periods of economic weakness—interest in home buying is rekindled now that it is more affordable. Builders, in turn, rush back to banks before the cost of borrowing rises again.

Another critical aspect of the homebuilding industry is how powerful an influence it has on the rest of the economy through what are known as "multiplier effects." By multiplier effects, we mean that changes in the pace of housing construction can have major ramifications for many other industries. Just look at who benefits when housing is strong. A jump in residential construction drives up demand for steel, wood, electricity, glass, plastic, wiring, piping, and concrete. The need for skilled construction workers such as bricklayers, carpenters, and electricians soars as well. By one estimate, for every 1,000 single-family homes under construction, some 2,500 full-time jobs and nearly $100 million in wages are generated. Moreover, while the home construction business accounts for approximately 5% of GDP, its overall impact on the economy is really much greater than that. A vibrant home-selling market also accelerates purchases of furniture, carpet, home electronics, and appliances. Housing is thus a major swing industry in the economy because it can affect so many diverse businesses.

This release presents two key gauges on the homebuilding industry: housing starts and permits.

Housing Starts

Housing starts record how much new groundbreaking occurred for residential real estate in the last month. The data on home construction is divided into three types of structures:

- The building of single-family houses: By far the largest component of the three, accounting for 75% of total home building.

- Residences with two to four apartments or units: These are usually townhouses or small condos, and they make up no more than 5% of the market.

- Structures with five or more units: This category consists mostly of apartment buildings and represents about 20% of all residential housing starts. Each apartment in a high-rise building is considered a single start. Thus, the government counts the construction of a 50-unit apartment building as 50 starts.

Housing Permits

Builders planning to construct new homes usually have to file for a permit in advance. Some 95% of all localities in the U.S. require construction firms to obtain such authorization before the first shovel touches ground. By tracking the issuance of permits, one can get a sense of how much and where future construction activity will take place. Because housing permits are such an excellent marker of future homebuilding, they are one of the 10 components that make up the Conference Board's Index of Leading Economic Indicators.

How Is It Computed?

The Census Bureau conducts telephone interviews and sends out mailers to builders in 19,000 localities across the country during the first two weeks of each month to inquire about the number of construction starts and permits filed in their regions.

A housing start occurs when excavation begins to set a new foundation for a residence. Adding a room, basement, or new roof to an existing home is not considered a housing start, although if a home is being totally rebuilt on an existing foundation, it is counted. The housing figures do not include construction of mobile homes, dormitories, rooming houses, and long-term hotels.

Permits are more straightforward. Each one represents the written authorization a builder receives from local municipalities to begin construction.

Though figures in the tables are adjusted for seasonal factors, home construction can still be extremely volatile during the winter season, so it's important not to rely too much on one or even two months worth of data. Adverse weather conditions can bring housing activity to a standstill one month, only to have it rebound vigorously the next two months to make up for earlier downtime. It's better to monitor housing activity over a three-to-four-month period to detect an underlying trend.

THE TABLES: CLUES ON WHAT'S AHEAD FOR THE ECONOMY

• Table 3   New Privately Owned Housing Units Started

For more than half a century, housing starts has been a very effective forecasting tool of future economic activity. A sharp drop-off in home construction is a telltale sign that the broad economy is on the verge of slowing, while a rebound in housing starts and home buying sets the stage for a pickup in overall business activity. Interest rates and real personal income growth are the most important forces

[Thousands of units. Detail may not add to total because of rounding]

Period	United States Total	1 unit	2 to 4 units	5 units or more	Northeast Total	1 unit	Midwest Total	1 unit	South Total	1 unit	West Total	1 unit
		In structures with --										
					Seasonally adjusted annual rate							
2003: January	1,828	1,509	(S)	278	145	115	349	327	820	646	514	421
February	1,640	1,312	(S)	298	142	98	279	247	759	602	460	365
March	1,742	1,393	(S)	313	155	112	351	281	814	680	422	320
April	1,627	1,357	(S)	239	150	130	319	283	724	589	434	355
May	1,745	1,389	(S)	329	151	116	357	293	791	620	446	360
June	1,844	1,499	(S)	317	162	106	353	290	822	683	507	420
July	1,890	1,533	(S)	321	186	121	392	321	866	728	446	363
August	1,831	1,490	(S)	309	152	110	401	325	848	711	430	344
September	1,931	1,547	(S)	339	186	112	428	345	861	705	456	385
October	1,977	1,640	(S)	308	154	112	389	330	908	748	526	450
November[r]	2,054	1,673	(S)	344	187	121	426	322	892	746	549	484
December[r]	2,067	1,670	(S)	369	172	135	404	318	968	782	523	435
2004: January[p]	1,903	1,537	(S)	339	148	110	319	275	918	716	518	436
Average RSE (%)[1]	3	3	(X)	9	10	10	8	7	4	4	6	7
Percent Change:												
January 2004 from December 2003	-7.9%	-8.0%	(S)	-8.1%	-14.0%	-18.5%	-21.0%	-13.5%	-5.2%	-8.4%	-1.0%	0.2%
90% Confidence Interval[2]	± 6.0	± 6.6	(X)	± 17.1	± 12.8	± 7.8	± 14.0	± 16.0	± 9.6	± 11.2	± 11.5	± 11.8
January 2004 from January 2003	4.1%	1.9%	(S)	21.9%	2.1%	-4.3%	-8.6%	-15.9%	12.0%	10.8%	0.8%	3.6%
90% Confidence Interval[2]	± 6.5	± 6.3	(X)	± 32.3	± 26.4	± 24.4	± 18.4	± 14.6	± 10.3	± 10.0	± 9.6	± 10.9

influencing home buying and starts. Another factor that plays a large role is tax legislation. Changes in tax laws can have a dramatic impact on homebuilding. Many apartment buildings wouldn't stand a chance of getting constructed were it not for hefty tax breaks builders receive. Moreover, the government partially subsidizes home buying by allowing owners to deduct their home mortgage interest payments on their income tax returns. Should laws ever be modified in an unfavorable way for homeowners and builders, it could put a chill on future housing activity.

(1) *Total Housing Units Started:* Check the pace of total housing starts. A healthy housing market is typically one where starts are running at a 1.5 million to 2 million unit annual range. A level that lingers close to 1 million units spells trouble for the economy; above 2 million for an extended period, and you're likely to bump up against other problems, such as shortages of supplies and skilled workers.

(2) *Single-Family Housing Starts:* Other important measures are worth noting. The performance of "single-family home starts" is a far more reliable leading indicator of the economy than "multi-family starts," which is classified as five or more units. Single-family home building is based on consumer confidence and demand, while construction of multi-unit apartment dwellings can be subject to the whims of speculative real estate investors and changes in the tax code.

(3) *Housing Starts Regionally:* This release also breaks down the number of housing starts by geographic regions (Northeast, Midwest, South, and West), which allows you to identify areas of the country that are experiencing healthy real estate (as well as economic) growth and those where activity is lagging.

- **Table 1** New Privately-Owned Housing Units Authorized in Permit-Issuing Places

Keep a close eye on building permits because they lead housing starts by roughly one to three months. While the issuance of a housing permit does not automatically result in new construction, the two series do go hand in hand over time.

In fact, you can actually track the entire construction cycle for homes by looking at Tables 1 through 5 in this release:

- Table 1 records the number of permits issued for home construction by type of home and region of the country. It's a good indicator of how confident builders are about future demand.

- Table 2 counts the number of units where construction permits have been granted but where groundbreaking has not yet started (not shown). A significant rise in these numbers suggests that builders are having trouble keeping up with the demand for new homes.

[Thousands of units. Detail may not add to total because of rounding]

Period	United States				Northeast		Midwest		South		West	
	Total	In structures with --			Total	1 unit	Total	1 unit	Total	1 unit	Total	1 unit
		1 unit	2 to 4 units	5 units or more								
					Seasonally adjusted annual rate							
2003: January	1,777	1,406	87	284	157	119	354	277	796	620	470	390
February	1,786	1,319	78	389	170	100	308	250	777	595	531	374
March	1,688	1,311	71	306	150	106	324	257	777	607	437	341
April	1,724	1,332	82	310	152	110	341	258	784	622	447	342
May	1,803	1,349	84	370	166	111	343	262	819	627	475	349
June	1,823	1,427	77	319	158	115	379	282	843	667	443	363
July	1,800	1,434	77	289	161	118	364	287	810	665	465	364
August	1,901	1,484	84	333	189	119	377	290	866	700	469	375
September	1,875	1,487	88	300	164	121	384	298	841	681	486	387
October	1,981	1,539	81	361	187	124	382	305	885	707	527	403
November	1,863	1,473	88	302	180	125	378	285	812	673	493	390
December[r]	1,953	1,530	77	346	199	123	356	278	911	722	487	407
2004: January[p]	**1,899**	**1,487**	**96**	**316**	**179**	**119**	**356**	**291**	**857**	**674**	**507**	**403**
Average RSE (%)[1]	(Z)	1	3	1	2	2	1	1	1	1	1	1
Percent Change:												
January 2004 from December 2003	*-2.8%*	*-2.8%*	*24.7%*	*-8.7%*	*-10.1%*	*-3.3%*	*0.0%*	*4.7%*	*-5.9%*	*-6.6%*	*4.1%*	*-1.0%*
90% Confidence Interval[3]	*± 0.8*	*± 0.9*	*± 1.7*	*± 1.7*	*± 1.7*	*± 2.1*	*± 3.9*	*± 4.4*	*± 1.3*	*± 1.5*	*± 1.0*	*± 1.1*
January 2004 from January 2003	*6.9%*	*5.8%*	*10.3%*	*11.3%*	*14.0%*	*0.0%*	*0.6%*	*5.1%*	*7.7%*	*8.7%*	*7.9%*	*3.3%*
90% Confidence Interval[3]	*± 1.1*	*± 1.0*	*± 3.7*	*± 1.3*	*± 2.7*	*± 3.3*	*± 3.9*	*± 4.4*	*± 1.5*	*± 1.7*	*± 1.9*	*± 2.1*

- Table 3 lists the number of units where construction began in the previous month.

- Table 4 tracks the number of new housing units undergoing construction as of the end of the previous month (not shown).

- Table 5 notes the number of homes where construction was completed in the previous month (not shown).

Overall, it takes about six months on average for a single-family house to be built, from groundbreaking to completion. The cycle for a multi-family dwelling is 10 months to a year.

MARKET IMPACT

Bonds

Good news in housing is often perceived as bad news for players in the fixed income markets. A healthy pickup in housing starts depicts an economy that is robust and where inflation pressures are likely to accelerate. That can knock down bond prices and cause yields to rise, leading to losses on bond portfolios. Traders prefer weak or falling housing starts because they portend a slackening economy with less inflation—factors that lift bond prices.

Stocks

Prolonged weakness in housing starts can alarm stock investors since it's often a precursor to a broader downturn in the economy. On the other hand, if housing activity is vibrant and inflation remains contained, shareholders will view it as a positive sign. A rebound in housing can have a beneficial impact on other businesses as well. This is bullish for corporate profits and thus for stock prices. The danger comes when housing starts surge at a time when the rest of the economy is already operating at full speed. Investors might withdraw from stocks as worries mount that the Federal Reserve will raise short-term interest rates to curb economic activity.

Dollar

Foreign investors are attracted to the U.S. if they can earn a higher rate of return here relative to what they can receive in other countries. Thus, a strong housing report is considered bullish for the dollar because it usually supports a scenario of higher corporate profits and a firming of U.S. interest rates.

The dollar's value can slip with weak housing data because it signals slower economic growth in the future and thus falling interest rates. Under such circumstances, foreigners might choose to seek out more lucrative investment opportunities outside the U.S.

EXISTING HOME SALES

Market Sensitivity: Medium.

What Is It: Measures monthly sales of previously owned single-family homes.

News Release on the Internet:

Existing Home Sales: *www.realtor.org/Research.nsf/Pages/EHSdata*

Pending Home Sales: *www.realtor.org/Research.nsf/Pages/PHSdata*

Housing Affordability Index: *www.realtor.org/Research.nsf/Pages/HousingInx*

Home Web Address: *www.realtor.org*

Release Time: 10:00 a.m. (ET); published four to five weeks after the month
being reported ends.

Frequency: Monthly.

Source: National Association of Realtors.

Revisions: Monthly revisions tend to be small. Annual revisions due to seasonal
adjustment factors take place in February and can cover the preceding three
years.

WHY IS IT IMPORTANT?

The big gorilla of the residential real estate market is existing home sales. About eight out
of every 10 homes purchased are used homes, with the rest being sales of newly constructed housing. Yet, despite its large size, the actual impact of existing home sales on
the economy is relatively modest because no new ground is broken. No physical investment in construction is made. Buyers and sellers simply transfer ownership of a deed.

If that's the case, why don't the financial markets ignore this indicator? The reason is
that sales of existing homes can indirectly stimulate economic activity. Sellers generally
use the capital gain from the sale of one house to buy a larger home to meet the needs of
an expanded family. Invariably, this means additional spending on furnishings and appliances. In other cases, buyers sell their home because it's too large and subsequently purchase a smaller house, leaving more of the capital gain available for spending on
discretionary items. A rise in existing home sales also brings in greater commissions to
real estate agents and generates higher income for both moving companies and mortgage
bankers. Equally important is that an increase in home sales is an unmistakable sign that
buyers are confident about their jobs and future income growth. All of these factors make
monitoring figures on existing home sales worthwhile.

The downside of this series is that it's not very timely. Existing home sales are
counted at the time of actual closing, which is when the deed finally gets transferred from
one owner to another. The problem is that it can take one to three months or longer

between the moment the initial contract is signed to the time buyers and sellers finally meet to close the deal. By the time existing home sales are recorded and tallied for the monthly release, market conditions in housing could already have changed. So analysts have to be careful when extrapolating data from this economic indicator. In an effort to provide more current information on housing, the National Association of Realtors (NAR), the organization that publishes existing home sales figures, recently introduced a new measure called Pending Home Sales. This series looks at the number of contracts that have been signed but not yet closed. The advantage is that we don't have to wait until the very end of the home buying process to see how the housing industry is doing.

How Is It Computed?

The NAR is a private trade group of 960,000 agents and brokers from the residential and commercial real estate market. For the monthly report, it culls information from 400 out of the 900 multiple listing boards and local Realtor boards nationwide. The raw figures are then divided into the four census regions: Northeast, South, Midwest, and West. The NAR also includes in its monthly release the median and average sale price for homes at the national level as well as for each of the four geographic regions.

Keep in mind that seasonal factors can influence selling prices; the price tag for homes is generally highest in the late spring and summer, when favorable weather conditions and the end of the school year bring increased traffic to real estate offices. In fact, demand for homes usually peaks in the summer and then declines gradually for the balance of the year.

Home sales figures are seasonally adjusted and presented in the form of annual rates.

The Tables: Clues on What's Ahead for the Economy

Each month, existing home sales data is summarized on a single page that contains two fact-filled tables: existing home Sales and Sales Price of Existing Homes.

- Existing home Sales

  (1) Monitoring the volume of sales nationwide is a good way to assess housing demand in the country. There's a strong correlation between purchases of existing homes and consumer spending, especially on durable goods such as furniture and home electronics. Furthermore, a sustained drop—or rebound—in existing home sales often portends a turning point in the economy. Finally, a big turnover in home sales produces large capital gains, which can stimulate more home buying and related shopping.

  What's the single biggest force in the economy that influences existing home sales? Interest rates. Every percentage point increase in mortgage rates can reduce existing home sales by 250,000 units.

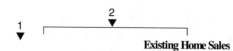

Existing Home Sales

Year	U.S.	Northeast	Midwest	South	West	U.S.	Northeast	Midwest	South	West	Inventory	Mos. Supply
2004 r	6,778,000	1,113,000	1,550,000	2,540,000	1,575,000	*	*	*	*	*	2,244,000	4.3
2005 r	7,076,000	1,169,000	1,588,000	2,702,000	1,617,000	*	*	*	*	*	2,846,000	4.5
2006 r	6,478,000	1,086,000	1,483,000	2,563,000	1,346,000	*	*	*	*	*	3,450,000	6.5
	Seasonally Adjusted Annual Rate					Not Seasonally Adjusted						.
2006 Jan	6,750,000	1,010,000	1,540,000	2,740,000	1,460,000	373,000	58,000	77,000	154,000	85,000	2,883,000	5.1
Feb	6,940,000	1,170,000	1,610,000	2,700,000	1,460,000	401,000	70,000	92,000	160,000	80,000	2,985,000	5.2
Mar	6,900,000	1,180,000	1,610,000	2,670,000	1,440,000	554,000	87,000	131,000	217,000	119,000	3,198,000	5.6
Apr	6,710,000	1,140,000	1,560,000	2,610,000	1,410,000	560,000	91,000	130,000	215,000	124,000	3,415,000	6.1
May	6,680,000	1,140,000	1,510,000	2,610,000	1,410,000	642,000	102,000	153,000	249,000	138,000	3,589,000	6.4
Jun	6,490,000	1,090,000	1,490,000	2,550,000	1,360,000	699,000	120,000	163,000	267,000	149,000	3,738,000	6.9
Jul	6,320,000	1,050,000	1,430,000	2,530,000	1,320,000	605,000	111,000	141,000	235,000	118,000	3,861,000	7.3
Aug	6,310,000	1,060,000	1,430,000	2,520,000	1,290,000	653,000	113,000	149,000	261,000	131,000	3,844,000	7.3
Sept	6,230,000	1,040,000	1,420,000	2,520,000	1,260,000	529,000	89,000	124,000	214,000	102,000	3,783,000	7.3
Oct	6,270,000	1,030,000	1,420,000	2,520,000	1,300,000	518,000	87,000	114,000	210,000	107,000	3,860,000	7.4
Nov	6,250,000	1,080,000	1,420,000	2,470,000	1,280,000	472,000	79,000	103,000	189,000	101,000	3,810,000	7.3
Dec	6,270,000	1,070,000	1,460,000	2,490,000	1,250,000	469,000	79,000	106,000	192,000	92,000	3,450,000	6.6
2007 Jan p	6,460,000	1,070,000	1,530,000	2,540,000	1,320,000	363,000	61,000	78,000	147,000	77,000	3,549,000	6.6
vs. last month:	3.0%	0.0%	4.8%	2.0%	5.6%	-22.6%	-22.8%	-26.4%	-23.4%	-16.3%	2.9%	0.0%
vs. last year:	-4.3%	5.9%	-0.6%	-7.3%	-9.6%	-2.7%	5.2%	1.3%	-4.5%	-9.4%	23.1%	29.4%
year-to-date:						0.363	0.061	0.078	0.147	0.077		

Source: National Association of Realtors, used with permission.

(2) A geographic breakdown of sales can be found for each of the four major regions, as well as their percentage changes from the previous month and year.

(3) One harbinger of future housing trends is the total number of available homes on the market for sale that month. It is listed here along with the latest percentage change from the previous month and year.

(4) Close by is the inventory sales ratio for houses. This ratio tells you how many months it takes to sell the existing inventory of used homes on the market based on the latest monthly sales rate. Generally, a 4.5- to 6-month supply of homes is considered a balanced market between buyers and sellers. If the ratio falls below 4.5 months, it's a sign that supplies may be getting tighter; that can place upward pressure on home prices. A ratio above 6 denotes a soft housing market, which may lead to lower prices.

• **Sales Price of Existing Homes**

Shifts in housing prices reflect the changing supply and demand for homes. By and large, prices of existing homes march higher from year to year, though the rate of increase depends a great deal on the economic climate and the mix of houses sold (whether they are luxury homes versus more modestly priced residences).

(5) The NAR report lists both the median (the midpoint price where half the homes sold for more and the other half sold for less) and the average sale price for both the regional and national level. This is where one can assess how residential real estate values have held up against inflation over months and years. If real estate

Sales Price of Existing Homes

Year		U.S.	Northeast	Midwest	South	West	U.S.	Northeast	Midwest	South	West
				Median					Average (Mean)		
2004		$195,400	$243,800	$154,600	$170,400	$286,400	$244,400	$273,600	$189,400	$215,600	$324,300
2005		219,600	271,300	170,600	181,700	335,300	266,600	297,000	203,800	231,700	363,800
2006 r		221,900	271,900	167,800	183,700	342,700	268,200	299,700	205,300	230,000	371,300
				Not Seasonally Adjusted					Not Seasonally Adjusted		
2006	Jan r	217,400	263,900	168,500	177,600	336,700	265,900	294,000	209,600	225,200	366,800
	Feb	217,800	280,100	160,200	182,200	333,000	263,600	301,500	191,800	229,600	363,500
	Mar	217,600	270,400	160,700	180,000	340,300	264,500	295,200	197,700	227,600	368,500
	Apr	222,600	285,200	163,500	181,600	345,300	269,100	307,100	200,200	229,300	372,800
	May	228,500	281,300	171,700	191,300	343,700	273,700	305,000	210,600	239,100	372,100
	Jun	229,300	289,100	174,400	189,400	341,300	275,800	313,300	214,800	237,400	372,200
	Jul	230,200	274,600	177,000	192,500	346,200	275,400	301,800	216,000	238,300	374,000
	Aug	224,000	272,600	171,800	184,800	345,300	270,000	302,700	210,700	230,800	372,800
	Sept	220,900	260,400	168,300	184,500	338,800	266,400	290,300	206,000	229,800	367,900
	Oct	218,900	255,400	166,600	183,700	341,800	264,600	287,900	203,200	228,100	370,000
	Nov	217,300	266,900	163,900	178,600	349,400	265,100	295,400	201,700	223,500	375,700
	Dec r	221,600	284,000	166,200	180,900	348,300	268,000	308,900	201,200	225,200	375,800
2007	Jan p	210,600	260,700	162,600	174,600	321,300	257,400	291,600	196,100	222,100	351,900
	vs. last year:	-3.1%	-1.2%	-3.5%	-1.7%	-4.6%	-3.2%	-0.8%	-6.4%	-1.4%	-4.1%

    ▲   ▲

    5   5

Source: National Association of Realtors, used with permission.

prices increase significantly faster than inflation, Americans will be inclined to view housing as an attractive investment. Of course, if home prices appreciate significantly in real (inflation-adjusted) terms, this can also be detrimental to future home buyers, especially first-time purchasers because many might not be able to afford one. This entire subject of affordability is explored in a separate release by the NAR known as the Housing Affordability Index.

- **Pending Home Sales Index (PHSI)**

A common complaint about Existing Home Sales is that it counts only "closings," and such events are based on decisions made by home buyers many months earlier. Though most closings occur within two months after a contract is signed, nearly 20% can take up to four months or even longer. To make its figures more current, the NAR in March 2005 introduced the Pending Home Sales Index, which tracks contracts that have been signed and are awaiting closing.

(6) The PHSI series is calculated as an index where "100" represents the average level of contract signings during 2001. As it turns out, that year was the first of five consecutive years of record existing home sales. By definition, these contracts include purchases of homes, condos, and co-ops. The PHSI has the potential to be a good leading indicator of housing activity, but it will take time to determine its true predictive value. Keep in mind that not all contracts to purchase a home make it to closing. Last-minute disputes could occur between buyers and sellers. Or if the economy turns sour, home buyers may suddenly get nervous and seek ways to cancel their contracts. Though the majority of

Pending Home Sales Index (PHSI)

Year		United States	Northeast	Midwest	South	West	United States	Northeast	Midwest	South	West
2004		120.9	109.7	118.6	126.8	122.9	*	*	*	*	*
2005		124.4	108.6	116.6	134.9	128.7	*	*	*	*	*
2006 p		111.8	98.5	101.5	126.8	109.6	*	*	*	*	*
		Seasonally Adjusted Annual Rate					Not Seasonally Adjusted				
2005	Dec	117.6	94.4	107.8	135.5	118.0	76.8	57.6	65.9	91.6	80.0
2006	Jan	118.6	101.0	114.3	129.4	120.0	99.4	81.2	90.4	110.1	106.4
	Feb	117.6	107.3	114.6	129.5	110.2	107.2	96.4	103.4	116.8	104.5
	Mar	116.1	112.9	106.3	127.6	111.1	134.5	132.8	123.6	146.2	129.3
	Apr	111.9	106.7	100.3	129.7	100.2	128.6	125.8	117.6	151.7	106.2
	May	113.5	106.1	101.4	127.5	110.1	135.3	129.6	123.2	153.1	124.7
	Jun	113.5	99.8	102.5	130.6	109.1	135.7	122.8	125.5	156.4	124.1
	Jul	105.6	92.1	93.8	121.9	103.2	116.6	97.3	103.7	137.6	112.3
	Aug	110.3	95.5	94.4	126.6	112.9	120.1	101.7	105.8	134.7	126.5
	Sept	109.1	89.9	96.4	125.0	112.5	100.8	84.4	91.2	113.6	103.7
	Oct	107.5	88.0	97.0	122.9	109.5	103.0	88.4	92.4	115.0	106.7
	Nov r	107.2	83.2	100.0	124.4	106.6	89.6	68.3	80.1	101.8	97.1
	Dec p	112.4	89.9	103.2	129.8	112.2	71.0	53.4	60.8	84.9	73.6
vs. last month:		**4.9%**	**8.1%**	**3.2%**	**4.3%**	**5.3%**	**-20.8%**	**-21.8%**	**-24.1%**	**-16.6%**	**-24.2%**
vs. last year:		**-4.4%**	**-4.8%**	**-4.3%**	**-4.2%**	**-4.9%**	**-7.6%**	**-7.3%**	**-7.7%**	**-7.3%**	**-8.0%**

▲
6

Source: National Association of Realtors, used with permission.

contracts do go through to closing, economists will want to monitor the Pending Home Sales a few years to see how well it can foreshadow changes in the housing market. The table itself lists the PHSI for the last 12 months for all of the U.S. and for the four major geographic regions. What we have seen so far is that the annual percentage change in the index (such as August 2006 compared with August 2005) is a better indicator of future home sales than month-to-month comparisons. Time will tell what other forecasting attributes this series has.

• Housing Affordability Index (HAI)

Just how expensive is it for Americans to buy a home? The NAR assembles a table every month that measures the affordability of purchasing a home given the existing economic climate. This series, called the Housing Affordability Index, can also be found on the NAR Web site (*www.realtor.org/research.nsf/pages/housinginx*). Though this measure has virtually no impact on the stock and bond markets, it is included here because home purchases are the single biggest investment that households make in their lifetime. A favorable combination of economic conditions, such as rising personal income and low mortgage rates, makes home buying more affordable and thus sets the stage for more real estate sales in the future.

(7) The Housing Affordability Index tells whether a typical family can qualify for a mortgage loan on a typical home. A typical home is defined here as the national

NATIONAL ASSOCIATION OF REALTORS®
Housing Affordability Index   7 ▼

Year		Median Priced Existing Single- Family Home	Mortgage Rate*	Monthly P & I Payment	Payment as a % of Income	Median Family Income	Qualifying Income**	Affordability Indexes		
								Composite	Fixed	ARM
2001		147,800	7.03	789	18.4	51,407	37,872	135.7	135.7	145.5
2002		158,100	6.55	804	18.5	52,103	38,592	135.0	132.7	148.3
2003 r		170,000	5.74	793	17.8	53,463	38,064	140.5	127.6	142.6
2003	Jan	160,000	5.96	764	17.4	52,811	36,672	144.0	142.0	156.1
2003	Feb	161,300	5.93	768	17.4	52,929	36,864	143.6	141.6	156.2
	Mar	162,100	5.80	761	17.2	53,048	36,528	145.2	143.3	158.3
	Apr	163,700	5.72	762	17.2	53,166	36,576	145.4	143.3	158.0
	May	166,400	5.62	766	17.3	53,285	36,768	144.9	143.2	155.7
	Jun	175,000	5.40	786	17.7	53,404	37,728	141.6	139.9	154.1
	July	181,600	5.39	815	18.3	53,522	39,120	136.8	135.3	148.5
	Aug	177,200	5.66	819	18.3	53,641	39,312	136.4	133.5	149.0
	Sept	171,800	5.94	819	18.3	53,759	39,312	136.7	133.8	149.3
	Oct	171,800	5.83	809	18.0	53,878	38,832	138.7	135.2	150.7
	Nov	169,900	5.85	802	17.8	53,996	38,496	140.3	136.5	151.0
	Dec r	174,800	5.82	822	18.2	54,115	39,456	137.2	133.3	148.9
2004	Jan p	168,700	5.70	783	17.3	54,395	37,584	144.7	140.8	156.5
								This Month	Month Ago	Year Ago
	Northeast	212,300	5.76	992	19.7	60,313	47,616	126.7	134.6	140.5
	Midwest	134,300	5.70	624	13.1	57,017	29,952	190.4	176.4	183.1
	South	155,500	5.75	726	17.6	49,499	34,848	142.0	135.3	139.6
	West	234,500	5.59	1,076	23.4	55,094	51,648	106.7	97.9	108.2

Source: National Association of Realtors, used with permission.

median price of an existing single-family home as calculated by NAR. The outcome can be found in the columns on the right of the page. An index value of 100 means that a median-income family has exactly enough income to qualify for a mortgage on a median-priced home. An index above 100 signifies that a family earning the median income has more than enough to qualify for a mortgage loan on a median-priced home, assuming a 20% down payment. For example, a composite index of 130 means a family earning the median family income has 130% of the income necessary to qualify for a conventional loan covering 80% of a median-priced existing single-family home.

The NAR assumes a maximum qualifying ratio of 25%, where monthly principal and interest payments cannot exceed 25% of the median family's monthly income.

MARKET IMPACT

Bonds

Reaction to existing home sales is muted unless the economy is edging closer to over-drive and facing an eruption of inflation pressures. Any unexpected jump in existing home sales could easily scare away bond investors, a scenario that will lower bond prices and raise yields.

A sudden plunge in sales might foreshadow a slowdown in economic activity in the months ahead, which would support higher bond prices and lower rates. Thus, to a large extent, the response to this release really depends on the economic backdrop.

Stocks

From the standpoint of corporate profits, investors prefer to see existing home sales stay at a high level. Housing is a major industry upon which many other businesses rely. A strong report will buoy stock values, while a weak report may undermine them. However, if strength in housing fires up inflation, the Federal Reserve will eventually intervene with higher rates, and such a prospect can upset the equity market.

Dollar

Foreign investors monitor existing home sales because it is one of the dominant indicators of consumer spending and can potentially influence interest rates. Generally, the dollar will remain firm or appreciate as long as existing home sales do not stumble into an extended downswing. A sluggish housing market would lower rates and raise uncertainties about future stock prices, both of which can weaken demand for U.S. currency.

NEW HOME SALES

Market Sensitivity: Medium.

What Is It: Tracks the sales of new single-family homes.

News Release on the Internet: *www.census.gov/newhomesales*

Home Web Address: *www.census.gov*

Release Time: 10 a.m. (ET); released about four weeks after the reporting month ends.

Frequency: Monthly.

Source: Census Bureau, Department of Commerce.

Revisions: There are frequent revisions with the data, and they can cover the preceding three months.

WHY IS IT IMPORTANT?

An abundance of economic indicators deal with housing. With every month comes news of housing starts and permits, sales of existing homes, construction spending, and now the topic of this section, new home sales. Each offers a different perspective on this all-important industry. Housing starts, or new home construction, is essentially a production figure. That is, it's less a predictor of consumer spending and more a reflection of business confidence—specifically, builder expectations of future home buying trends. Existing home sales, on the other hand, provides better insight into consumers' financial health and shopping mood. The downside of existing home sales is that its effects on the economy are rather limited. Nothing new has to be constructed since the house is already in place. Secondly, existing home sales has only limited value as a predictive indicator because it is counted only when the transaction formally closes and the title is exchanged, a process that can take several months after the initial contract.

This section looks at new home sales, which is considered a more timely measure of conditions in the housing market and a better indicator of future economic activity. For instance, the sale of a newly constructed house is recorded not at closing (as is the case with existing homes), but when the initial contract is signed. True, you don't know if all those signed contracts to purchase a home make it all the way to final closing, but those that don't are rare and are statistically insignificant. The more interesting issue is how could the sale of new homes, which makes up a tiny 15% of the residential real estate market, have such a profound effect on the economy? The answer is that they generate lots of investment, jobs, spending, and production. Builders seek construction loans; purchase property; order lumber, glass, wiring, concrete, and plumbing; and hire a variety of skilled workers to help put up a home. New homes also tend to be more expensive than existing homes because builders often include many modern amenities. In addition, when buyers move in, it triggers yet another round of spending on new furniture and other accessories for the next 12 to 18 months.

There is one other reason why top money managers closely examine this indicator on new home sales. If consumer spending is about to change direction, you'll see it turn here first. Purchasing a home is the single biggest expense a household will undertake, and unless prospective buyers are content with their income, job security, and the economic outlook, many will be reluctant to buy. Should home buying begin to wane, it sets off alarms in many sectors of the economy. Banks will cut back on construction loans for fear builders might have a hard time repaying them. Without the necessary capital, new residential investment falls, and that will suppress demand for building supplies, appliances, and construction workers. Suddenly the danger of a serious economic slowdown begins to loom.

Ironically, it is in the midst of recession that the housing sector comes back to life and helps lift the rest of the economy out of its stupor. Mortgage rates fall during an economic downturn, and at some point they drop to a level where they make housing more attractive again. As interest in home buying revives, builders find a warmer reception from bank loan officers, who, after a long dry spell of making few loans, are eager to lend again. Moreover, in a recession, there is ample supply of labor and materials. As a consequence, construction quickly picks up speed to satisfy the growing demand for new homes. Given the multiplier effects of a rebound in housing, it's only a matter of weeks before other industries benefit as well.

How Is It Computed?

To come up with figures on new home sales, the Census Bureau relies on data from its housing permits series. Why look at permits? Because builders often file for construction permits only after they've collected a deposit or received a signed contract from a home buyer.

New home sales figures generally undergo revisions, sometimes substantial ones, if parts of the country have been exposed to unusual weather patterns. As a result, it's necessary to look at the data for at least three to four months before one can decipher a trend in new home sales.

The Tables: Clues on What's Ahead for the Economy

- **Table 1**   New Houses Sold and For Sale

New home sales get center stage when the economy is believed to be near a turning point. In such instances, experts are looking for evidence that prospective home buyers are ready to jump into the housing market and lock in the lowest possible mortgage rate, a point that often occurs at the bottom of the business cycle. A pickup in new home sales is often followed a month or two later by an increase in sales of existing homes. As the pace of home buying quickens, demand for supplies and services will stimulate activity in other home-related businesses.

Table 1. New Houses Sold and For Sale
[Thousands of houses. Detail may not add to total because of rounding]

Period	Sold during period[1]					For sale at end of period					Months' supply[2]	Median sales price ($)	Average sales price ($)
	United States	North-east	Mid-west	South	West	United States	North-east	Mid-west	South	West			
	Seasonally adjusted												
2003: January	1,009	89	176	466	278	343					4.1		
February	935	50	181	442	262	343					4.5		
March	1,008	83	166	503	256	341					4.1		
April	1,004	70	174	468	292	341					4.1		
May	1,081	73	162	525	321	344					3.9		
June	1,200	85	194	552	369	343					3.5		
July	1,145	75	223	542	305	341					3.6		
August	1,190	74	255	548	313	345					3.5		
September	1,129	91	193	520	325	350					3.8		
October[r]	1,149	92	199	540	318	361					3.9		
November[r]	1,111	88	164	534	325	363					3.9		
December[r]	1,125	100	179	515	331	367					4.0		
2004: January[P]	**1,106**	**95**	**189**	**504**	**318**	**370**					**4.1**		
Average RSE (%)[3]	6	18	16	9	9	4					6		
Percent Change:													
January 2004 from December 2003	*-1.7%*	*-5.0%*	*5.6%*	*-2.1%*	*-3.9%*	*0.8%*					*2.5%*		
90% Confidence Interval[4]	*±13.6*	*±24.2*	*±28.3*	*±18.2*	*±34.3*	*±1.0*					*±11.3*		
January 2004 from January 2003	*9.6%*	*6.7%*	*7.4%*	*8.2%*	*14.4%*	*7.9%*					*0.0%*		
90% Confidence Interval[4]	*±12.8*	*±49.0*	*±34.9*	*±15.8*	*±28.0*	*±4.6*					*±12.1*		
	Not seasonally adjusted												
2002 :	973	65	185	450	273	344	36	77	161	70	(X)	187,600	228,700
2003[r] :	1,089	81	189	512	307	374	28	97	171	78	(X)	194,100	245,200
RSE (%)	2	8	7	3	3	3	12	8	5	7	(X)	3	2
2003: January	76	6	12	37	22	347	36	77	163	71	4.6	181,700	230,200
February	82	4	15	39	23	339	34	73	162	70	4.2	187,000	233,400
March	98	9	17	47	25	330	30	74	157	69	3.4	185,100	231,100
April	91	7	17	40	27	339	29	76	162	72	3.7	189,500	237,200
May	101	6	15	50	29	341	30	79	161	71	3.4	195,500	243,700
June	107	8	18	48	33	342	29	84	162	67	3.2	187,900	239,700
July	99	6	20	47	26	342	29	84	159	69	3.5	190,200	248,400
August	105	6	23	48	28	342	28	84	163	68	3.3	190,500	241,000
September	90	8	15	42	25	350	27	88	165	69	3.9	192,000	254,500
October[r]	88	7	16	40	25	368	29	92	171	76	4.2	194,100	242,800
November[r]	78	6	12	38	22	366	29	94	169	74	4.7	204,700	268,200
December[r]	76	7	11	36	21	374	28	97	171	78	5.0	195,800	254,500
2004: January[P]	**84**	**6**	**12**	**40**	**25**	**373**	**27**	**96**	**174**	**76**	**4.4**	**197,000**	**258,600**
Average RSE (%)[3]	6	18	16	9	9	4	12	9	5	6	6	5	4

That pattern is reversed if the economy has been growing at full speed for a prolonged period of time. Eventually mortgage rates will climb to painful levels and begin to push many home seekers out of the market. After new and existing home sales turn down, the broad economy begins to sputter as well.

(1) *New Houses Sold:* This is the headline number where you'll find the monthly tally of new homes sold at an annualized rate for the entire U.S. and the four

geographic regions: Northeast, Midwest, South, and West. Any discernible change in trend sales here can act as an early warning indicator that the economy is losing steam or gearing up for recovery.

(2) *New Houses for Sale at End of Period:* This table provides the latest in the supply of new homes being offered for sale. It stands to reason that the inventory of new homes ready for sale would shrink in a buoyant housing market and increase when buying turns sluggish. Of course, a great deal depends on how quickly builders are grinding out new homes during these periods. Clearly, if the inventory of unsold homes expands too much, builders will scale down future construction until the market improves again.

(3) *Months' Supply:* The all-important inventory-sales ratio of new homes tells you how many months it will take to sell the current supply of new homes based on the most recent sales pace. The I/S ratio is a good predictor of future home construction. When homes sales are brisk, the months' supply ratio usually stabilizes or falls. Generally, if it drops to four months' worth of supply or less, builders are sufficiently encouraged to keep investing in new construction. Conversely, if sales are declining or there are just not enough buyers to absorb all the new homes being built, the stock of new homes can climb past six months' worth of supply. This usually foreshadows a drop in new home construction.

(4) *Median and Average Sales Prices:* Check here to see the latest median and average price of new homes. Normally, the value of new homes appreciates faster than existing homes because they have more modern features. If prices move steadily higher over several months, it's evidence of a vibrant housing sector. It's also interesting to compare the rise in home prices with inflation. If new home prices increase significantly faster than inflation, Americans will be inclined to view housing as an attractive medium and long-term investment.

• **Table 2**   New Houses Sold, by Sales Price

New home prices can range from under $100,000 to more than $10 million. This table shows which price segment of the housing market sold the best during the past several months. Homes in the $150,000 to $200,000 category are normally the fastest-selling residences, along with high-end homes in excess of $300,000.

[Thousands of houses. Components may not add to total because of rounding. Percents computed from unrounded figures]

Period	Total	Under $100,000	$100,000 to $124,999	$125,000 to $149,999	$150,000 to $199,999	$200,000 to $249,999	$250,000 to $299,999	$300,000 and over
				Number of houses[1]				
2002 :	973	62	94	138	237	139	107	196
2003[r] :	1,089	55	98	149	264	147	112	263
RSE (%)	2	16	9	6	6	5	5	6
2003: January	76	3	9	12	19	10	8	16
February	82	5	7	13	18	12	8	18
March	98	4	11	15	25	12	11	21
April	91	6	7	14	23	11	10	20
May	101	4	10	13	25	16	10	23
June	107	5	11	16	27	14	9	26
July	99	6	9	13	25	13	10	23
August	105	6	9	14	27	13	11	25
September	90	5	7	12	23	14	8	21
October[r]	88	7	7	12	20	10	12	20
November[r]	78	3	6	10	18	10	7	23
December[r]	76	5	7	8	20	10	7	19
2004: January[p]	84	5	8	9	20	8	8	25
Average RSE (%)[2]	6	29	20	17	13	16	16	12

MARKET IMPACT

Bonds

New home sales tend to have the greatest impact on the fixed income market near the peaks and troughs of a business cycle. During periods of strong economic growth, a larger-than-expected jump in new home sales can intensify alarms of inflation and thus weaken bond prices. On the other hand, if the economy were just starting to emerge from recession, the response by traders to a rebound in new home sales will likely be more muted, because it poses far less of an inflationary threat at this stage.

A precipitous monthly drop in home sales could signal a weakening in the economy and lower inflation. In such circumstances, bond prices can edge higher, with interest rates slipping lower.

Stocks

The volatile nature of this series and its small proportion of the residential real estate market keeps it from generating much excitement among equity investors. Yet, because it is widely known as a leading indicator, the new home sales series becomes more influential whenever analysts suspect the economy is near a turning point.

Dollar

Traders in the currency markets have not shown much sensitivity to new home sales. There just isn't much of a correlation between the performance of new home sales and a change in the dollar's value.

HOUSING MARKET INDEX: NATIONAL ASSOCIATION OF HOME BUILDERS (NAHB)

Market Sensitivity: Low.

What Is It: Assesses the current market for new single-family home sales along with builder expectations of future trends.

Home Web Address: *www.nahb.org* (type "HMI" in the search box)

Release Time: 1:00 p.m. (ET); published mid-month and covers activity for the first half of the same month.

Frequency: Monthly.

Source: National Association of Home Builders; Wells Fargo

Revisions: Tend to be minor.

WHY IS IT IMPORTANT?

It is a truism in economics that as the housing industry goes, so goes the rest of the economy. That's why you'll find so many economic indicators dedicated to tracking the residential real estate market. Among the many reports, however, is one indicator that often slips below the radar screen, despite its talent for being among the best predictors of future housing activity. The Housing Market Index (HMI), published every month by the National Association of Home Builders and Wells Fargo, possesses all the characteristics of a big-time market mover. It is based on responses directly from homebuilders, who have the best pulse on current and future homebuilding trends. Furthermore, the HMI is released in the same month it reports on, long before any of the other major monthly housing reports are out. Finally, this housing index has a proven track record of being a decent leading indicator of future home sales. Given these attributes, you would think money managers would spring into action after the report is released. However, that is not the case. For one thing, the size of the statistical sample used by the association is fairly small; the survey is based on responses from 400 builders out of a total membership of 72,000. Second, the data is not broken down regionally, making it hard to identify areas of the country that are experiencing strong or weak demand for new single-family homes.

HOW IS IT COMPUTED?

For 20 years, the National Association of Home Builders has conducted a monthly survey asking roughly 900 members (about half of whom answer on time) the following questions:

- What are the current conditions for new single-family home sales? (Good, fair, or poor?)

- What are your expectations of new single-family home sales for the next six months? (Good, fair, or poor?)

- Rate the traffic of prospective home buyers you are seeing at new home sites. (High to very high, average, or low to very low?)

The survey results are based on answers received in the first 10 days of every month. Scores are calculated using a diffusion index for each question and are adjusted for seasonal factors. The index has a scale that ranges from 0 to 100, where 0 means that virtually everyone agreed that conditions were poor, and 100 indicates that everyone believed that conditions were good. An index of 50 means that the number of "good" responses received from builders is about the same as the number of "poor" responses. Thus, any index number above 50 suggests that more builders viewed conditions as "good" rather than "poor."

The centerpiece of the report is the overall Housing Market Index, which is computed as a weighted average of the results from the three main questions just listed. Answers to the first query on current conditions represent 59% of the HMI index, expected sales for the next six months accounts for 14%, and the traffic of home seekers is 27%.

THE TABLES: CLUES ON WHAT'S AHEAD FOR THE ECONOMY

The NAHB has two separate locations on its Web site for information on the Housing Market Index. One is the press release with the latest monthly analysis, and the other contains all the current and historical data points on the Housing Market Index. The easiest way to locate both is to simply type "HMI" in the search box on the NAHB's home page.

- Press Release on the Housing Market Index

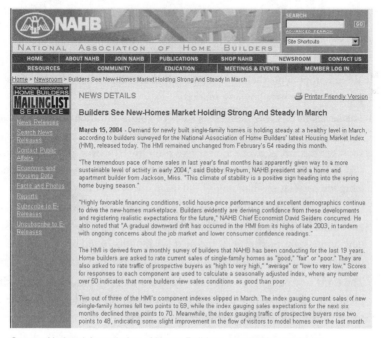

Source: National Association of Home Builders, used with permission.

Survey results and a brief analysis of the latest HMI can be found here. The index is considered a good leading indicator for the other housing reports that are released weeks later. By looking at both the HMI and the Census Bureau's housing starts figures, one can more accurately forecast the future demand and supplies for new homes and even the outlook for national economic activity given the ripple effect that home buying has on the economy.

- **Tables**   Housing Market Index and Its Components

Housing Market Index
(Seasonally Adjusted)

2002			2003												2004			
Oct	Nov	Dec	Jan	Feb	Mar	Apr	May	Jun	Jul	Aug	Sep	Oct	Nov	Dec	Jan	Feb	Mar	Apr
63	64	65	64	62	52	52	57	62	65	71	68	72	70	70	69	64	64	69

Housing Market Index Components
(Seasonally Adjusted)

2002			2003												2004			
Oct	Nov	Dec	Jan	Feb	Mar	Apr	May	Jun	Jul	Aug	Sep	Oct	Nov	Dec	Jan	Feb	Mar	Apr
Single-Family Sales: Present																		
69	71	72	69	69	59	57	62	67	69	77	73	78	78	77	76	71	70	76
Single-Family Sales: Next 6 Months																		
68	70	69	68	66	56	62	69	70	74	78	78	82	81	77	76	73	70	76
Traffic of Prospective Buyers																		
47	48	48	51	43	35	35	40	47	51	55	51	52	47	52	51	46	49	48

◀1 (Single-Family Sales: Present)   ◀2 (Single-Family Sales: Next 6 Months)   ◀3 (Traffic of Prospective Buyers)

Source: National Association of Home Builders, used with permission.

The three components that make up the HMI are shown here to provide additional perspective on the new housing market.

(1) The series in this row represents sales of single-family homes. It is actually better than the composite Housing Market Index at predicting housing starts in the short term, such as over the next two months. However, if you want to see what single-family home construction might be like beyond that period, the HMI has a higher correlation than any of the three questions individually.

(2) Builders are not likely to commit to new construction unless they expect demand to be healthy in the months ahead. This table reflects how builders assess the new home sales market over the next six months based on current assumptions of interest rates and economic growth.

(3) The third row gauges the number of buyers walking onto new home sites. A pickup in visitors to real estate showrooms can lift builder confidence because these walk-ins represent potential future sales.

MARKET IMPACT

Bonds

Economic indicators on home construction have an impact on bonds. However, the NAHB's Housing Market Index, despite its early appearance, appears to be overshadowed by other, better-known government releases on building activity. These include housing starts and new home sales, both of which are based on larger surveys. As a result, the HMI does not provoke much of a reaction in the bond market.

Stocks

Money managers might review the report, but they generally do not trade based on the information.

Dollar

Foreign exchange traders do not follow the NAHB release.

WEEKLY MORTGAGE APPLICATIONS SURVEY AND THE NATIONAL DELINQUENCY SURVEY

Market Sensitivity: Medium.

What Is It: Tracks the number of Americans applying for a mortgage to buy a home or refinance an existing mortgage.

News Release on the Internet: *www.mortgagebankers.org/NewsandMedia*

Home Web Address: *www.mortgagebankers.org*

Release Time: 7 a.m. (ET); comes out every Wednesday and covers the week ending the previous Friday. A separate report, the National Delinquency Survey, is published two and a half months after each quarter.

Frequency: Weekly.

Source: Mortgage Bankers Association (MBA).

Revisions: Few revisions are made.

WHY IS IT IMPORTANT?

The key to any forecast on the economy is the consumer. If you can correctly assess how much people will spend in the months ahead, odds are you'll do fairly well at predicting economic growth. Get consumer behavior right, and everything else usually falls into place. If you miss this critical source of demand in the economy, your projections will almost certainly be off the mark. As a result, professional forecasters look for any piece of economic data they can find that helps them foresee changes in consumer spending. One of the best pieces of information turns out to be the Weekly Mortgage Applications Survey by the Mortgage Bankers Association. A pickup in mortgage applications is very bullish for the economy in two respects. It serves as evidence that home buying interest has accelerated, which should be viewed as a positive for the residential real estate market and for the economy as a whole. Second, in a climate of falling mortgage rates, home-owners often jump at the chance to fill out a new application to refinance their existing mortgages. By switching from a high-cost mortgage to one that allows for lower monthly payments, consumers end up with a savings windfall—money that can be used to pay off other debt (such as car loans and credit card bills) or fire up a new round of consumer spending.

Reading the Weekly Mortgage Applications Survey is easy. It contains various indexes, each measuring a different part of the residential mortgage market. However, the two that grab the most attention are the purchase index and the refinance index. Because most home buyers have to apply for a mortgage before they can buy a home, changes in the purchase index can tell analysts where the housing market is headed. Rarely has the economy found itself in trouble when home buying is strong. As for the refinance index, an increase in these applications often leads to greater household spending, which in turn fuels more economic growth.

Here's a list of the main indexes in the Weekly Mortgage Applications Survey and a description of what they cover:

1. *The Market Composite Index:* This is the best indicator of total mortgage application activity. It tracks all mortgage applications during the latest week, regardless of whether they were to purchase or refinance a home. The index covers conventional and government-backed mortgage applications, as well as major types of mortgage maturities: 30-year fixed, 15-year fixed, and adjustable-rate mortgages.

2. *Purchase Index:* Refers to all mortgage applications filed for the sole purpose of buying a private home, using either a conventional or government loan.

3. *Refinance Index:* Covers all mortgage applications used to refinance an existing mortgage. It also includes conventional and government refinances.

4. *Conventional Index:* Tracks all conventional purchase and refinance mortgage applications, but excludes those with government guarantees.

5. *Government Index:* Measures activity with all Federal Housing Administration (FHA) and Veterans Administration (VA) loans. FHA and VA loans carry a federal government guarantee.

In addition to these indexes, the survey computes the latest average contract interest rate for 30-year fixed mortgages, 15-year fixed mortgages, and 1-year adjustable-rate mortgages (ARMs).

How Is It Computed?

Each week, the MBA polls 20 to 25 mortgage bankers, commercial banks, and thrifts on the latest mortgage activity. The survey manages to cover about 40% of the U.S. retail residential mortgage market.

The answers are adjusted for seasonal and holiday effects, but they are also available in a seasonally unadjusted form.

The Tables: Clues on What's Ahead for the Economy

The MBA makes the press release available on the Web at no cost. It contains a useful summary of all the key indexes, plus a brief analysis. Access to tables, however, is through subscription only. We'll stick to information that can be found in the publicly available press release for both the Weekly Mortgage Applications Survey and the National Delinquency Survey.

Source: Mortgage Bankers Association, used with permission.

- **News Release**   Weekly Mortgage Applications Survey

  The purchase index has proven to be a reliable indicator of future housing activity, especially with existing home sales, which dominate the residential real estate market. In fact, over the past 10 years there has been a 60% correlation between the annual change in the index of purchase applications and the change in sales of new and existing single-family homes in the months ahead. A sustained increase in the purchase index thus suggests the presence of a vibrant home-buying market. Moreover, the purchase index also serves as a leading indicator of consumer spending, since buyers want to outfit their new homes with furniture and appliances.

  The refinance index is the best-known measure of mortgage refinancing activity. Anyone trying to forecast consumer spending has to consider the volume of mortgage refinancing applications.

- **News Release**   National Delinquency Survey (NDS) (Not Shown)

  In addition to the Mortgage Applications Survey, the MBA publishes a quarterly report on mortgage delinquencies and home foreclosures known as the National Delinquency Survey. It's based on a sample of more than 41 million mortgage loans serviced by mortgage companies, commercial banks, thrifts, credit unions, and other lenders. Economists read it to see if economic conditions have deteriorated to the point where households have difficulty meeting their mortgage obligations.

Investors study the data to gauge the condition of the U.S. mortgage market and to check on the credit quality portfolio of banks and other mortgage lenders.

The results of the National Delinquency Survey can be found on the same MBA Web site. (To find it, go to *www.mortgagebankers.org/NewsandMedia*, and click the arrow at the bottom of the MBA News section to see the latest quarterly report.) By definition, the NDS looks at the percentage of all mortgages that are delinquent and to what extent: 30 days overdue, 60 days overdue, and 90 days overdue. Normally, after 90 days, the lender can initiate foreclosure proceedings, and the MBA includes a percentage of those as well.

Over the years, a few trends have emerged from the National Delinquency Survey. First, during moments of great financial stress, Americans place a priority on keeping their mortgage payments on time. They will usually delay payments on credit cards and other types of debts in order to have sufficient funds to keep their home. Should household finances worsen further, 30-day delinquencies on home payments will pick up, and this will shortly be accompanied by a jump in 60-day and 90-day delinquencies as well. The last to rise are foreclosure rates. Generally, banks and other mortgage lenders are reluctant to take the home repossession route, because the process can be costly and time-consuming. However, once the number of foreclosures increases, it sets in motion a process that's hard to turn around, even if the economy improves. Foreclosure rates lag behind improvements in delinquency rates because it takes so long for repossessions to work their way through the legal system.

MARKET IMPACT

Bonds

Over the last few years, the Weekly Mortgage Applications Survey has taken on greater significance among bond traders and economists for its connection to future consumer spending. The report itself tends to have only a modest impact on the financial markets. However, there are occasions when investors holding bonds might fret that a sharp increase in home buying portends greater consumer outlays and brisk economic growth—events that can lead to higher inflation. Such survey results therefore might trigger a mild sell-off, particularly if the refinancing index unexpectedly surges. As for the quarterly National Delinquency Survey, bond traders show little interest in this report.

Stocks

Equity investors regularly monitor the Weekly Mortgage Applications Survey as well as the National Delinquency Survey, but for different reasons. The former can shed light on how housing and consumer spending will perform in the months ahead, while the latter is studied to check on the quality of loan portfolios held by banks and mortgage lenders. Earnings at financial institutions can suffer if delinquencies and loan losses begin to mount.

Dollar

There's no direct reaction in foreign exchange markets to either report.

CONSTRUCTION SPENDING

Market Sensitivity: Low.

What Is It: Tallies up all spending on public and private construction.

News Release on the Internet: *www.census.gov/constructionspending*

Home Web address: *www.census.gov*

Release Time: 10 a.m. (ET); released the last business day of the month and covers construction activity for the previous month.

Frequency: Monthly.

Source: Census Bureau, Department of Commerce.

Revisions: Can be major. The two previous months are revised with each new release. In addition, annual benchmark changes occur every May that can go back two years or more.

WHY IS IT IMPORTANT?

Up to now, economic indicators that gauge construction activity have focused on residential real estate trends. The construction spending report, however, looks at both residential and nonresidential building. It is the most comprehensive barometer of building activity in the U.S. and is well worth watching because of its large contribution to GDP. The total construction industry alone accounts for nearly 9% of all economic activity. That doesn't even include all the other businesses whose fortunes are tied to the building sector, such as the home furnishings and appliance industries. Clearly construction activity is a major force in the economy. The government uses the data from this release to help compute business investment spending for the quarterly GDP report.

Construction spending is divided into three distinct categories:

- Private construction for residences (5% of GDP): Includes single-family homes and apartment buildings.

- Private nonresidential structures (2.4%): Pertains to factories, office buildings, hotels, motels, religious and educational buildings, hospitals, and other types of institutions.

- Public construction (2%): Covers public housing projects, public schools, sewer systems, and similar infrastructure development.

While many economists follow this indicator, money managers generally do not. For one, it is terribly late in coming; the data is one of the last pieces of information to be released for a given month. More than a dozen other real estate-linked indicators for the same month have been released long before, so many investors find little added value in these figures. Aside from its late arrival, the report is notorious for undergoing sizable revisions. As a result, analysts are forced to rely mostly on three- and six-month moving averages to detect a trend in the construction business.

How Is It Computed?

The government obtains the value of residential construction directly from its own surveys on housing starts and new home sales. For nonresidential structures, it relies on outside sources, such as F.W. Dodge, a division of McGraw-Hill, to contact commercial real estate builders for the estimated dollar value of the work done.

The Tables: Clues on What's Ahead for the Economy

* **Table 1**   Value of Construction Put in Place in the U.S.

    (1) Type of Construction and Amount: Private construction activity can be a telling indicator of business confidence. This table records the monthly spending (at an annual rate) on private residential and nonresidential construction for each of the past five months and also compares the latest level to that of the previous year. What separates this report from all the other previous releases on real estate activity is that we get to know for the first time how much builders are actually spending and on what type of construction (homes, hotels, schools, nursing homes, hospitals). Of great interest to analysts is the spending on home building because of the industry's reputation as being a leading indicator of economic turning points, and the fact that it accounts for nearly 70% of all private construction. Another observation worth noting is that residential construction tends to lead nonresidential construction by about a year. Thus, if home building activity peaks and then begins to weaken, commercial construction generally follows that pattern and slows within 12 months.

Market Impact

Economists and industry specialists pay more attention to this report than day-to-day traders, who do not find construction spending data particularly riveting. Even once released, this series has a history of massive revisions. In any event, it is quickly overshadowed by the more influential ISM manufacturing survey, which is released the next day.

Table 1. **Value of Construction Put in Place in the United States, Seasonally Adjusted Annual Rate**
(Millions of dollars. Details may not add to totals due to rounding.)

							Percent change Jan 2004 from -	
Type of Construction	Jan 2004ᵖ	Dec 2003ʳ	Nov 2003ʳ	Oct 2003	Sep 2003	Jan 2003	Dec 2003	Jan 2003
Total Construction	**931,178**	**934,411**	**928,657**	**925,485**	**913,824**	**883,232**	**-0.3**	**5.4**
Residential	507,146	507,068	502,732	493,377	481,735	455,960	0.0	11.2
Lodging	9,511	9,696	10,339	11,036	10,723	10,134	-1.9	-6.1
Office	39,223	40,773	41,785	42,083	40,355	40,881	-3.8	-4.1
Commercial	60,117	61,643	59,961	61,456	62,636	60,666	-2.5	-0.9
Health care	28,362	29,251	29,358	29,525	29,518	28,613	-3.0	-0.9
Educational	69,492	71,220	68,940	70,736	71,278	71,450	-2.4	-2.7
Religious	7,737	7,987	8,061	8,528	8,569	8,435	-3.1	-8.3
Public safety	8,268	8,413	8,392	9,023	8,665	8,214	-1.7	0.7
Amusement and recreation	18,361	19,215	19,010	19,614	18,751	18,922	-4.4	-3.0
Transportation	22,860	22,827	23,454	24,473	24,152	24,331	0.1	-6.0
Communication	15,994	14,727	16,245	15,218	14,961	15,309	8.6	4.5
Power	37,918	37,422	35,109	35,880	37,332	36,864	1.3	2.9
Highway and street	66,003	64,770	65,271	64,377	64,900	63,538	1.9	3.9
Sewage and waste disposal	13,270	13,166	12,679	13,162	12,943	12,033	0.8	10.3
Water supply	9,108	9,032	9,454	9,187	9,492	9,731	0.8	-6.4
Conservation and development	3,880	3,425	3,705	3,849	3,695	4,039	13.3	-3.9
Manufacturing	13,928	13,778	14,162	13,961	14,119	14,112	1.1	-1.3
Total Private Construction [1]	**715,778**	**719,336**	**712,644**	**705,215**	**692,462**	**667,636**	**-0.5**	**7.2**
Residential	501,444	501,352	496,988	487,541	475,716	450,039	0.0	11.4
Lodging	8,618	8,986	9,323	9,836	9,414	9,233	-4.1	-6.7
Office	29,286	30,885	31,692	31,587	29,812	30,839	-5.2	-5.0
Commercial	55,704	57,206	55,502	56,322	57,041	56,767	-2.6	-1.9
Health care	22,435	23,233	23,524	23,656	23,374	23,127	-3.4	-3.0
Educational	12,965	13,419	12,496	12,940	13,544	12,839	-3.4	1.0
Religious	7,736	7,983	8,056	8,526	8,565	8,431	-3.1	-8.2
Amusement and recreation	7,501	8,035	7,776	7,981	7,278	6,216	-6.6	20.7
Transportation	6,225	6,229	6,122	6,319	6,493	7,219	-0.1	-13.8
Communication	15,821	14,630	16,069	15,145	14,854	15,277	8.1	3.6
Power	32,827	32,238	29,526	30,082	30,918	32,615	1.8	0.7
Manufacturing	13,778	13,700	14,080	13,906	13,960	14,014	0.6	-1.7
Total Public Construction [2]	**215,399**	**215,076**	**216,014**	**220,270**	**221,362**	**215,595**	**0.2**	**-0.1**
Residential	5,702	5,716	5,744	5,837	6,019	5,922	-0.2	-3.7
Office	9,937	9,888	10,093	10,496	10,543	10,043	0.5	-1.1
Commercial	4,414	4,437	4,460	5,134	5,595	3,899	-0.5	13.2
Health care	5,927	6,018	5,834	5,869	6,145	5,486	-1.5	8.0
Educational	56,526	57,801	56,444	57,796	57,734	58,611	-2.2	-3.6
Public safety	8,049	8,155	8,130	8,715	8,350	8,116	-1.3	-0.8
Amusement and recreation	10,860	11,181	11,234	11,633	11,472	12,706	-2.9	-14.5
Transportation	16,635	16,598	17,333	18,155	17,659	17,113	0.2	-2.8
Power	5,090	5,184	5,583	5,798	6,414	4,249	-1.8	19.8
Highway and street	65,748	64,622	65,157	64,195	64,643	63,451	1.7	3.6
Sewage and waste disposal	12,737	12,765	12,204	12,780	12,491	11,829	-0.2	7.7
Water supply	8,858	8,708	9,130	8,738	9,080	9,123	1.7	-2.9
Conservation and development	3,699	3,114	3,388	3,792	3,639	4,014	18.8	-7.8

REGIONAL FEDERAL RESERVE BANK REPORTS

Every month, investors, economists, CEOs, and Washington policymakers are besieged by a multitude of surveys that claim to measure manufacturing activity in every nook and cranny of the country. The best known ones come from the Institute for Supply Management (ISM) and the government's own industrial production index. However, a slew of reports are also published by regional Federal Reserve Banks around the country, and some of them have begun to influence trading in the stock and bond markets. We'll focus on five of the most widely read.

The first to be released each month also happens to be among the newest of the Fed surveys, and it's already turning heads. The Federal Reserve Bank of New York first published the Empire State Manufacturing Survey in 2002, and for a few months, it went virtually unnoticed. The report began to catch the eye of investors once they realized its quick turnaround—the Empire survey comes out in the middle of the month being covered—and how well it serves as a reliable leading indicator of manufacturing activity of other Fed bank surveys.

The next to be published is the Philadelphia Fed survey, which is also released the same month it reports on. It has a reputation of predicting what the market-sensitive ISM manufacturing index will do when it comes out a few days later.

Two other noteworthy surveys come in the middle of the following month: one is from the Federal Reserve Bank of Kansas City, and the other is from the Fed Bank of Richmond.

Last on the list is the Federal Reserve Bank of Chicago, whose report is unique in comparison to the others in at least two respects. First, it's not a regional report; it instead looks at business conditions nationwide. Second, no survey is mailed. This Chicago index consists of a compilation of major economic indicators with a unique formula designed to predict inflation problems and forewarn of recessions.

The following sections discuss the five Fed bank reports in the order they are released:

- Federal Reserve Bank of New York
- Federal Reserve Bank of Philadelphia
- Federal Reserve Bank of Kansas City
- Federal Reserve Bank of Richmond
- Federal Reserve Bank of Chicago

FEDERAL RESERVE BANK OF NEW YORK: EMPIRE STATE MANUFACTURING SURVEY

Market Sensitivity: Medium.

What Is It: Tracks manufacturing activity in New York state.

News Release on the Internet:
   www.ny.frb.org/research/regional_economy/empiresurvey_overview.html

Home Web Address: *www.ny.frb.org*

Release Time: 8:30 a.m. (ET); released around the 15th of the month being reported.

Frequency: Monthly.

Source: Federal Reserve Bank of New York.

Revisions: Revisions are slight on a month-to-month basis.

WHY IS IT IMPORTANT?

If you've never heard of the Empire State Manufacturing Survey (ESMS), you're not alone. Most people haven't. Large institutional money managers have, however, and they recognize it as an up-and-coming economic indicator that could become one of the most influential reports released by the government.

The ESMS was developed by the Federal Reserve Bank of New York for internal use in July 2001, when the economy was in recession. Less than a year later, the bank went public with a monthly survey and cleverly set the timing for its release to precede other Fed surveys as a way to elbow into the financial market spotlight.

The ESMS is designed to find out the present condition of New York's manufacturing industries, as well as what company executives believe they will do in the next six months. Despite its short history, the ESMS has already demonstrated an intriguing correlation with the Philadelphia Index, which in turn has a knack for being a leading indicator of the market-shaking ISM manufacturing survey. Even the Federal Reserve Board, which sets the policy on interest rates, checks on the ESMS for any early indications of weakness or strength in manufacturing as well as any incipient signs of inflation. It is something of a surprise that the ESMS is being given such careful consideration when, in fact, New York state doesn't really have a significant amount of manufacturing.

HOW IS IT COMPUTED?

On the first business day of every month, the New York Fed polls the same group of 175 manufacturing CEOs or presidents. Respondents are asked to give their views on an assortment of issues and to return the completed forms by the 10th, though the forms still might be considered if they arrive as late as the 14th. Normally, about 100 are received on time at the New York Fed.

They are asked to describe how manufacturing conditions have changed in the month and what changes they expect to see in the next half year. Only three answers are possible: an increase in activity, a decrease in activity, or no change at all.

The survey questions are as follows:

• What is your evaluation of the level of general business activity?

• What about new orders? Shipments? Unfilled orders? Delivery times?

• Inventories? Prices paid? Prices received? Number of employees, including contract workers?

• Average employee workweek? Technology spending?

• Capital expenditures?

The responses to each question are tallied to form a diffusion index where the percentage of those who saw a decrease in activity is subtracted from the percentage who saw an increase in activity. Thus, any number above zero means that more manufacturers believe business conditions are improving rather than worsening.

THE TABLES: CLUES ON WHAT'S AHEAD FOR THE ECONOMY

• **Cover Page**   Empire State Manufacturing Survey

(1) General Business Conditions: This is the report's key index. It conveys the overall impression of manufacturing executives on whether activity is increasing or not. Note that the General Business Conditions index is not a weighted average of all the results from this survey, but is based on a distinct question on general business activity.

What can we discern from the general business condition index? Aside from its short history as an economic measure, a positive index number is a sign that factory activity is strengthening. Just how widespread that feeling is among manufacturers can be seen in the detailed tables.

• **Empire State Manufacturing Survey** (Results for the Month and for Expectations Six Months Ahead)

Detailed Tables: The numbers in each table represent the actual percentage of respondents who feel activity is higher compared with the percentage who say it is lower. The final index is merely the difference between the two. Obviously the

February
2004

Empire State Manufacturing
Survey

For release: February 17, 2004 8:30 a.m.

Summary
The *Empire State Manufacturing Survey* indicates continued improvement in New York's manufacturing sector in February. The general business conditions index reached 42.1, topping last month's record high. The indexes for new orders and shipments indicated significant improvement as well, and the unfilled orders index was also positive. For the first time in several months, the delivery time index crept above zero, and the inventories index was at its highest level in more than a year. The prices paid index rose to a new high, and the prices received index remained positive for a second consecutive month. Both employment indexes indicated improvement, with the average workweek index reaching a record high. Future indexes reflected continuing optimism.

General Business Conditions Index Breaks January's Record High
The general business conditions index rose to a new high in February, inching above January's level to reach 42.1. This reading marks the fifth consecutive month that the general business conditions index has been above 30. More than half of respondents said that conditions had improved in February, slightly more than did so last month, while 10 percent reported that conditions had deteriorated. The new orders index reached 34.9, a level very similar to those reported in the preceding

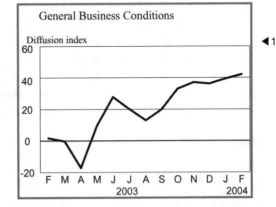

General Business Conditions

◀1

Employment indexes indicated continued improvement. The number of employees index fell several points from last month, but remained solidly positive at 16.5. Twenty-eight percent of respondents reported higher employment levels in February, while only 11 percent reported a decline. The average workweek index reached its highest level on record, 26.5, with 34 percent of respondents reporting a longer workweek and 8 percent reporting a shorter workweek.

larger the index is, the greater the consensus. One problem with this report is the volatility of these numbers. They can fluctuate wildly from month to month, which is why the graph can be helpful. It provides a snapshot of sentiments in the last 12 months. To detect an underlying trend in the data, it is advisable to calculate three-month and six-month moving averages.

(2) *New Orders:* Future production and employment in manufacturing depend on the steady flow of new orders. When orders slump, production can shift into lower gear and possibly jeopardize jobs. A sustained increase in orders is a promising sign that factories will continue to run smoothly and keep workers busy. This subcomponent can also be a harbinger of business confidence. If factories are fully operational and production orders are streaming in, firms become more comfortable about hiring new workers and increasing capital spending.

New Orders

	Higher	Same	Lower	Index	
Jan	49.03	36.75	14.21	34.82	
Feb	48.91	37.12	13.97	34.94	◀2

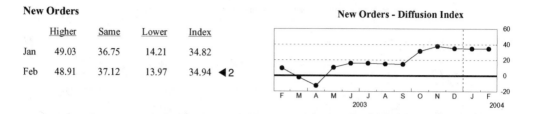

(3) *Unfilled Orders:* This indicator provides some perspective on how overburdened manufacturers are. If demand is so strong that factories are unable to match it by increasing production output, the number of unfilled orders will rise and deliveries will be delayed. Such strains can also lead to higher prices as shortages of raw materials emerge. One positive aspect of a chronic jump in unfilled orders is that it may promote new business spending by manufacturers who want to expand production capacity to satisfy customers with quicker deliveries.

Unfilled Orders

	Higher	Same	Lower	Index	
Jan	26.03	57.93	16.04	9.99	
Feb	24.39	57.70	17.91	6.48	◀3

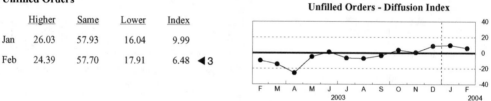

(4) *Prices Paid:* If the seeds of inflation are starting to sprout, you'll find the first evidence here, at the manufacturing level. Factories often pass on higher production costs to wholesalers; wholesalers then transfer their additional expense to retailers, and they, in turn, try to pass it on to consumers. That's how households often end up paying more for goods. The Federal Reserve carefully monitors inflation pressures at this early stage of the production process so that it can nip inflation in the bud.

Prices Paid

	Higher	Same	Lower	Index	
Jan	32.69	62.50	4.81	27.88	
Feb	38.79	56.03	5.17	33.62	◀4

Prices Paid - Diffusion Index

(chart)

(5) *Prices Received:* Corporate earnings depend not only on how well companies are able to cut operating costs, but also on their ability to set prices to achieve a decent profit margin. Global competition and a weak domestic economy can diminish a company's pricing power. On the other hand, an improving economy might return pricing flexibility to manufacturers and enhance profitability.

Prices Received

	Higher	Same	Lower	Index	
Jan	15.38	73.08	11.54	3.85	
Feb	14.66	74.14	11.21	3.45	◀ 5

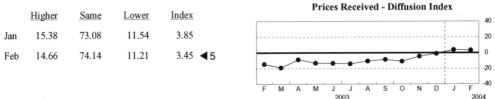

Prices Received - Diffusion Index

(6) *Number of Employees:* This is the earliest indicator available on labor market conditions for the month. It can act as a preview of changes in manufacturing jobs that could be seen in the official employment report, which is released two weeks later.

No. of Employees

	Higher	Same	Lower	Index	
Jan	35.09	54.34	10.58	24.51	
Feb	27.74	61.05	11.21	16.54	◀ 6

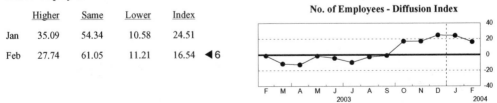

No. of Employees - Diffusion Index

MARKET IMPACT

Bonds

Keeping ahead of inflation and the interest rate curve is the main focus of bond traders. Thus, any fresh intelligence on the current and future state of the economy is looked upon with great interest. The Empire State Manufacturing Survey is seen in that light—as a timely report with current news on factory activity. The key question, however, is if traders will vigorously act on it. Here the record has been spotty. One can safely assume that this survey will be more influential when the economy is believed to be near a turning point. If the ESMS shows modest growth in manufacturing with negligible inflation, this should raise bond prices and lower interest rates. But a surge in the indexes accompanied by a persistent rise in prices paid and prices received will upset investors. The price on fixed incomes might drop as worries mount that other Fed surveys will show the same.

Stocks

The equity market is also sensitive to this report because of its positive correlation with the Philadelphia and Chicago Fed bank surveys and the ISM data. Weakness in the Empire State indexes suggests that the earnings of manufacturers are under pressure, which can dull stock prices. A healthy jump in the indexes at a time of economic softness will lift stock prices.

Dollar

There is no discernible reaction by foreign investors to this index.

FEDERAL RESERVE BANK OF PHILADELPHIA: BUSINESS OUTLOOK SURVEY

Market Sensitivity: Low to medium.

What Is It: A survey of manufacturing activity in eastern Pennsylvania, southern New Jersey, and the state of Delaware.

News Release on the Internet: *www.phil.frb.org/econ/bos/index.html*

Home Web Address: *www.phil.frb.org*

Release Time: 12:00 p.m. (ET); data is released on the third Thursday of the month being covered.

Frequency: Monthly.

Source: Federal Reserve Bank of Philadelphia.

Revisions: No monthly revisions take place, but the Philadelphia Fed does make annual benchmark changes at the start of the year.

WHY IS IT IMPORTANT?

The Philadelphia Fed regional report began in 1968 and is the longest-running survey of manufacturers by a Federal Reserve Bank. Known formally as the Business Outlook Survey (BOS), its familiarity has made it one of the most closely followed surveys by money managers and the press. The report is recognized for its timeliness because the results are published in the same month it covers. This Fed district also encompasses one of the more populated regions in the U.S. (eastern Pennsylvania, southern New Jersey, and the state of Delaware), which gives it added significance. Finally, the BOS can provide a sneak preview of what the high-profile ISM manufacturing survey might show when it comes out less than two weeks later.

HOW IS IT COMPUTED?

At the beginning of every month, the Philadelphia Fed mails questionnaires to the top executives at 250 large firms. They are asked to assess present conditions and record their expectations for the next six months. These questions can be answered in one of three ways: activity is up, down, or unchanged:

- What is your evaluation of the level of general business activity?
- What about new orders? Shipments? Unfilled orders? Delivery times?
- Inventories? Prices paid? Prices received? Number of employees?
- Average employee workweek? Capital expenditures?

Responses are received by the 10th of the month, though some of the data includes the period that bridges the current month and the previous one. All told, about half of the 250 questionnaires sent are returned on time.

Scores are tabulated for each of the questions, and seasonal adjustment factors are applied. The Philadelphia Fed then comes up with a diffusion index, which is the percentage of the positive scores minus the percentage that are negative. A zero is the break-even point, where half of the respondents report an increase and the other half a decrease. Readings above zero indicate that an expansion is under way, while an index below zero points to contraction.

THE TABLES: CLUES ON WHAT'S AHEAD FOR THE ECONOMY

• Business Outlook Survey

February 2004

1 ▶   Activity in the region's manufacturing sector continues to expand, according to firms surveyed for this month's *Business Outlook Survey.* Although indicators for general activity, new orders, and shipments fell from their January readings, they remain at relatively high levels. For the fifth consecutive month more firms reported increases in employment than reported declines, and a larger percentage of firms reported higher average work hours this month. Firms reported an increase in input prices again this month and some upward pressure on prices of their own manufactured goods. Expectations for overall growth over the next six months remain very positive, and about one-third of the firms expect employment to increase.

Growth Continues but Some Indicators Fall Back
The diffusion index of current general activity, the survey's broadest measure of manufacturing conditions, decreased from 38.8 in January to 31.4 and has now been positive for nine consecutive months (see chart). Although some current indicators fell this month, they continue to reflect solid growth in the region's manufacturing sector. The new orders index fell nearly 9 points, and the shipments index fell almost 14 points. Still, both indicators remain at relatively high levels. Firms reported an increase in unfilled orders and essentially steady inventories this month. The delivery times index, at 7.2, is at its highest reading since January 1999.

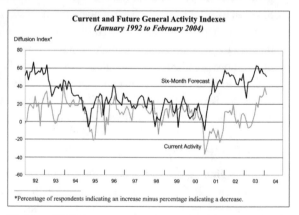

Current and Future General Activity Indexes
(January 1992 to February 2004)

*Percentage of respondents indicating an increase minus percentage indicating a decrease.

Price Indexes Drift Higher
Firms reported higher costs again this month. Over 46 percent reported higher input prices, and only 3 percent reported lower prices. The prices paid diffusion index increased for the seventh consecutive month. Twenty-four percent of firms reported that prices for their own manufactured goods were higher this month, while 5 percent reported lower prices. The current prices received index is now at its highest reading since January 1995.
Firms' expectations regarding future price increases continue to drift higher. The future prices paid index has now

decreased from 53.9 in January to 51.4 this month, but it remains at a relatively high level (see chart). The future new orders index actually increased 6 points and the future shipments index was mostly unchanged. Firms expect unfilled orders to increase over the next six months, and delivery times to be longer. More firms (39 percent) expect inventories to increase over the next six months than to decrease (25 percent). The future inventory index has trended higher over the last six months and is now at its highest reading since 1984. In response to the special questions this month (see Special Questions), 37 percent

(1) *Summary of Results:* The BOS is considered one of the better indicators of change in the industrial sector. Though it portrays only conditions in its district, changes in the indexes can foreshadow shifts in the broader the economy as well, especially with respect to prices and employment. Moreover, if you want a heads-up on what might appear in the "Beige Book," the much-studied publication from the Federal Reserve Board in Washington (see the section "The Federal Reserve Board's Beige Book"), read the Philadelphia Fed's Business Outlook Survey; portions of it make their way into the broader national report.

- Details of the Business Outlook Survey

(2) *General Business Activity Index:* Grabbing all the headlines in this release is the General Business Activity index, which has maintained a fairly close correlation with the manufacturing ISM series. They move in tandem about 70% of the time. Still, one has to be cautious here. The index can be quite volatile on a month-to-month basis because it is limited in geographic scope and reflects the answers to a single question. Thus, any conclusions about a trend should be based on a three-month moving average.

BUSINESS OUTLOOK SURVEY
Summary of Returns
February 2004

	February vs. January					Six Months from Now vs. February				
	Previous Diffusion Index	Increase	No Change	Decrease	Diffusion Index	Previous Diffusion Index	Increase	No Change	Decrease	Diffusion Index
2 ▶ What is your evaluation of the level of general business activity?	38.8	42.3	46.9	10.8	31.4	53.9	60.7	26.5	9.3	51.4
Company Business Indicators										
New Orders	36.5	40.7	46.5	12.8	27.8	49.8	63.8	25.7	8.5	55.3
Shipments	33.1	35.2	46.9	15.9	19.3	49.7	58.7	28.0	10.2	48.6
Unfilled Orders	10.7	20.4	62.3	16.0	4.4	17.2	33.6	51.7	7.9	25.7
Delivery Times	-2.0	19.2	68.7	12.1	7.2	11.5	21.5	67.9	7.9	13.6
Inventories	-3.9	24.9	50.3	24.1	0.8	8.7	39.1	30.9	25.2	14.0
Prices Paid	35.3	46.2	49.9	2.5	43.7	44.3	57.2	37.7	3.5	53.8
Prices Received	9.4	23.6	70.2	4.7	18.9	29.8	42.2	48.5	4.9	37.3
Number of Employees	17.5	20.9	68.9	8.4	12.5	15.1	32.7	51.3	13.2	19.5 ◀
Average Employee Workweek	12.9	26.7	63.8	3.1	23.6	16.7	22.0	65.0	6.6	15.4 ◀ 3
Capital Expenditures	—	—	—	—	—	26.0	30.1	36.5	6.0	24.1 ◀

Notes:
(1) Items may not add up to 100 percent because of omission of respondents.
(2) All data seasonally adjusted.
(3) Diffusion indexes represent the percentage indicating an increase minus the percentage indicating a decrease.
(4) Survey results reflect data received through February 13, 2004.

(3) *Six-Month Outlook:* Also of interest in this report are the respondents' answers to the six-month outlook. Of the 11 business indicator questions asked, two warrant particular attention. What's the half-year projection for capital expenditures? And second, will the number of manufacturing employees grow or shrink in that time frame? Clearly these two factors are related. Manufacturers will increase business expenditures only if they are confident that private demand has been resuscitated. Similarly, factories and plants are unlikely to hire permanent workers if there's still uncertainty about the economy's future direction.

MARKET IMPACT

Bonds

The Business Outlook Survey by the Philadelphia Fed isn't a huge market mover. Yet, traders of fixed income securities do track it because this report can tip off analysts about the results of the more influential national ISM survey when it is released days later.

Stocks

Investors keep an eye on the Business Outlook Survey, but they usually do not initiate major trades based on its information alone.

Dollar

Foreign exchange traders largely disregard this release.

FEDERAL RESERVE BANK OF KANSAS CITY: MANUFACTURING SURVEY OF THE 10TH DISTRICT

Market Sensitivity: Low.

What Is It: Measures manufacturing activity in a region that includes Colorado, Kansas, Nebraska, Oklahoma, Wyoming, western Missouri, and northern New Mexico.

News Release on the Internet: *www.kc.frb.org/mfgsurv/mfgmain.htm*

Home Web Address: *www.kc.frb.org*

Release Time: 11 a.m. (ET); the report is released about two weeks after the month being examined.

Frequency: Monthly.

Source: Federal Reserve Bank of Kansas City.

Revisions: No revisions. There are no annual benchmark changes at this time because of its brief history.

WHY IS IT IMPORTANT?

It's safe to say that this survey is not routinely in the business spotlight. The Kansas City Fed Manufacturing Survey is relatively new, having been launched in 1995, and it lacks a solid track record on how well it correlates with other major economic indicators and with the economy as a whole. Still, this survey has some noteworthy virtues. There's a relatively short lag from the time the survey is conducted to its release date. This quick turnaround enables the Kansas City Fed manufacturing report to come out before other key indicators, such as industrial production, business inventories, producer prices, and durable goods. Thus, by merely being ahead of the pack, the Kansas City Fed survey is looked at with interest.

HOW IS IT COMPUTED?

The Kansas City Fed queries about 150 manufacturers who represent the district's geographic and industrial distribution. Respondents are asked about changes in business conditions for three time periods: over the past month, versus a year ago, and the expected change in six months. Questions are posed on the following issues:

- Change in volume of production
- Volume of shipments
- New orders
- Order backlog

• Number of employees

• Average employee workweek

• Prices received for finished products

• Prices paid for raw materials

• Capital expenditures

• New orders for exports

• Supplier deliveries

• Inventory for raw materials and for finished goods

Responses are compiled, corrected for seasonal adjustment factors, and presented in the form of a diffusion index. That is, the percentage of those who reported a decrease for a specific category is subtracted from the percentage of those who claimed an increase. Thus, the index can range from −100 (all those queried see activity declining) to +100 (everyone sees activity as increasing). If half see activity rising and the other half see it falling, the index is zero. So any figure above zero indicates that manufacturing activity is expanding, and any figure below zero suggests it's contracting.

THE TABLES: CLUES ON WHAT'S AHEAD FOR THE ECONOMY

• **Table 1**   Summary of Tenth District Manufacturing Conditions

Though the results of this survey pertain to economic activity inside one Federal Reserve district, they still can provide fresh clues on how the rest of the country is performing. Here are some key indicators to track in the report:

(1) *Production and shipments:* Trends here reflect current manufacturing conditions as well as expectations for the near-term future.

(2) *New orders and the backlog of orders:* The numbers tell you how busy factories will be in the future.

(3) *Prices paid and received:* Changes presage inflationary or deflationary pressures.

(4) *Capital expenditures index:* Looks at business spending plans in the region, but can also be seen as a harbinger of such investments in other parts of the country.

Table1

Summary of Tenth District Manufacturing Conditions, January 2004

Plant Level Indicators	January vs. December (percent, not seasonally adjusted)				January vs. Year Ago (percent)				Expected in Six Months (percent, not seasonally adjusted)			
	Increase	No Change	Decrease	Index*	Increase	No Change	Decrease	Index*	Increase	No Change	Decrease	Index*
Production	40	36	23	17	52	18	28	24	51	29	18	33
Volume of shipments	40	29	28	12	53	18	26	27	56	25	17	39
Volume of new orders	47	24	26	21	55	16	25	30	54	26	16	38
Backlog of orders	31	40	24	7	42	31	20	22	41	38	16	25
Number of employees	21	64	12	9	30	34	32	-2	29	51	17	12
Average employee workweek	27	53	18	9	38	43	18	20	27	53	18	9
Prices received for finished product	17	74	8	9	30	47	22	8	26	61	11	15
Prices paid for raw materials	42	52	3	39	56	32	8	48	49	42	7	42
Capital expenditures					22	55	16	6	28	54	12	16
New orders for exports	14	71	5	9	14	69	6	8	21	65	4	17
Supplier delivery time	11	79	7	4	17	69	11	6	9	81	6	3
Inventories:												
Materials	28	50	19	9	28	36	33	-5	22	46	31	-9
Finished goods	18	56	24	-6	23	44	30	-7	18	50	30	-12

1 ▶ (Production, Volume of shipments)
2 ▶ (Volume of new orders, Backlog of orders)
3 ▶ (Prices received for finished product, Prices paid for raw materials)
4 ▶ (Capital expenditures)

MARKET IMPACT

Bonds

Players in the fixed income markets follow the regional Federal Reserve Bank surveys because they portray economic conditions in various parts of the country. Any surprise on the upside can make investors edgy because they can portend changes in the more influential manufacturing reports, including the ISM series and industrial production.

Stocks

Equity investors take notice but generally don't trade on the survey results.

Dollar

There is no noticeable response in the currency market to the Kansas City Fed survey.

FEDERAL RESERVE BANK OF RICHMOND: MANUFACTURING ACTIVITY FOR THE FIFTH DISTRICT

Market Sensitivity: Low.

What Is It: Measures manufacturing performance in a region encompassing the District of Columbia, Maryland, North Carolina, South Carolina, Virginia, and most of West Virginia.

News Release on the Internet:
*www.richmondfed.org/research/regional_conditions/manufacturing_
conditions/activity.cfm*

Home Web Address: *www.rich.frb.org*

Release Time: 10:00 a.m. (ET); the report is released on the fourth Tuesday of every month and reports on activity during that month.

Frequency: Monthly.

Source: Federal Reserve Bank of Richmond.

Revisions: No monthly revisions. The survey is subject to annual revisions in the fall that stem from changes in seasonal adjustment factors.

WHY IS IT IMPORTANT?

Since the Federal Reserve Bank of Richmond's manufacturing survey comes out near the end of the month, it may offer fresh insights into what the more influential ISM national manufacturing report will say when it is released just days later. The Richmond survey has a decent historical correlation of 70% with the ISM. Analysts also closely follow the inflation measures to see if price pressures are rising or diminishing in the Fifth District, which covers rural areas as well as politically sensitive urban communities.

HOW IS IT COMPUTED?

This release is known for having a quick turnaround from when the survey is taken to the time the results are published. Every month, the Richmond Fed surveys about 200 plant managers, purchasing managers, and financial controllers whose firms make up a cross section of the industrial activity in the mid-Atlantic Fed district. Typically, about 50% of those queried mail back their responses in time. About a week later, the Richmond Fed releases the results.

It presents the information a little differently than other regional Fed banks. For most of the questions, the Richmond Fed uses a diffusion index, where the percentage of respondents reporting decreases in activity is subtracted from the percentage of those reporting increases in activity. Thus, on every topic queried, a diffusion index is given for each of the last three months, along with a three-month moving average index. The moving average smoothes out the month-to-month volatility and enables one to more easily spot an underlying trend. The headline manufacturing index is a composite of three major categories, with each assigned a different weight: shipments (33%), new orders (40 %), and employment (27%). When it comes to recording swings in prices, the Richmond Fed follows a different procedure. No diffusion index is employed here. The Fed records actual changes in prices paid and prices received in the region—specifically, the average annual rate at which prices have moved during the month.

The questions asked are similar to those of other Fed banks. They want to know about changes in activity that occurred in the latest month and what is expected to happen over the next six months.

Specific topics covered in these questionnaires include the following:

Based on a diffusion index:

- Shipments
- Volume of orders
- Backlog of orders
- Capacity utilization
- Vendor lead time
- Number of employees
- Average workweek
- Wages
- Inventory levels (latest month only) for finished goods and raw materials
- Capital expenditures (expectations over the next six months only)

Based on percent change in prices (annualized):

- Prices paid
- Prices received

THE TABLES: CLUES ON WHAT'S AHEAD FOR THE ECONOMY

- Business Activity Indexes

   This survey provides a more detailed assessment of current and future price pressures than the other regional Fed bank reports. The Richmond Fed focuses on some of the most sensitive inflation detectors, such as changes in manufacturing wages and capacity utilization. By looking at the survey results, investors might get a heads-up on what the nationwide CPI, PPI, and capacity utilization measures will report when they're published a few weeks later.

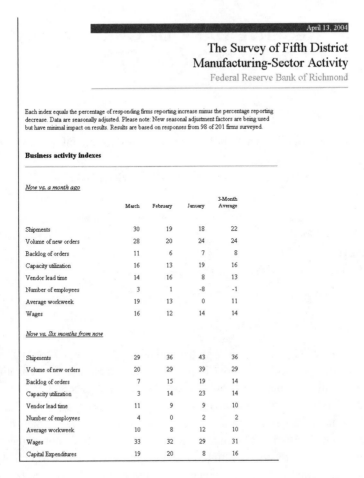

April 13, 2004

The Survey of Fifth District
Manufacturing-Sector Activity

Federal Reserve Bank of Richmond

Each index equals the percentage of responding firms reporting increase minus the percentage reporting decrease. Data are seasonally adjusted. Please note: New seasonal adjustment factors are being used but have minimal impact on results. Results are based on responses from 98 of 201 firms surveyed.

Business activity indexes

Now vs. a month ago

	March	February	January	3-Month Average
Shipments	30	19	18	22
Volume of new orders	28	20	24	24
Backlog of orders	11	6	7	8
Capacity utilization	16	13	19	16
Vendor lead time	14	16	8	13
Number of employees	3	1	-8	-1
Average workweek	19	13	0	11
Wages	16	12	14	14

Now vs. Six months from now

	March	February	January	3-Month Average
Shipments	29	36	43	36
Volume of new orders	20	29	39	29
Backlog of orders	7	15	19	14
Capacity utilization	3	14	23	14
Vendor lead time	11	9	9	10
Number of employees	4	0	2	2
Average workweek	10	8	12	10
Wages	33	32	29	31
Capital Expenditures	19	20	8	16

MARKET IMPACT

Bonds

A small but growing cadre of traders track the Richmond Fed survey for its ability to sniff out price pressures in the economy.

Stocks

Investors pay little attention to this survey.

Dollar

Currency traders do not follow this report.

FEDERAL RESERVE BANK OF CHICAGO: NATIONAL ACTIVITY INDEX (CFNAI)

Market Sensitivity: Low.

What Is It: A nationwide measure of economic activity and inflation pressures.

News Release on the Internet:
   www.chicagofed.org/economic_research_and_data/cfnai.cfm

Home Web Address: www.chicagofed.org

Release Time: 10 a.m. (ET); usually released four to five weeks after the reporting month.

Frequency: Monthly.

Source: Federal Reserve Bank of Chicago.

Revisions: Substantial revisions can occur in the monthly data.

WHY IS IT IMPORTANT?

Economists are always coming up with new calculations that they hope will improve their ability to predict how the economy will perform. They might tweak an equation here and there, change some assumptions, and occasionally add or toss certain indicators—all with the intent of coming up with a more refined method of forecasting U.S. business activity. Most of the time, these formulations go unnoticed in the financial markets because they're new and untested. Every once in a while, though, an indicator comes along that stands out because of its potential to foresee economic problems. In March 2001, the Federal Reserve Bank of Chicago launched a monthly index designed to better assess the health of the national (not regional) economy, warn of upcoming inflationary pressures, and predict the beginning and end of recessions. Called the Chicago Fed National Activity Index (CFNAI), it has emerged as one of the most promising measures to come out in recent years.

HOW IS IT COMPUTED?

Here's how it works. The index reflects the performance of 85 monthly national economic indicators drawn from four broad categories:

- Production and income
- The job market and hours worked
- Personal consumption and housing
- Sales, inventories, and orders

By using a weighted average involving all 85 measures, a single index figure is computed so that a value of 0 indicates that the economy is growing at its full potential. In other words, business is humming along at the fastest pace possible without aggravating inflation pressures. A value above 0 indicates that the economy is expanding at a rate above its safe speed, with total demand outstripping supplies to such an extent that it can lead to an outbreak of inflation. An index with a negative number points to an economy growing below potential, a development that may be benign for inflation but can also cause unemployment to rise. A three-month moving average of the index is also supplied to smooth out the volatility caused by short-term factors.

Due to the schedule of the release and the large number of components needed for the index, about a quarter of the data sought is not available in time to contribute to the monthly report. Therefore, estimates are used for the missing indicators.

THE TABLES: CLUES ON WHAT'S AHEAD FOR THE ECONOMY

The main purpose of setting up the CFNAI is to advise investors and policymakers on whether the economy is (a) growing at a healthy pace with inflation nicely in check, or (b) racing ahead at a speed that threatens a buildup of inflationary pressures, or perhaps (c) functioning way below par and in danger of slipping into recession.

- Chicago Fed National Activity Index

  The two main indexes in this report are identified as CFNAI (the report's acronym) for the latest monthly index, and CFNAI-MA3, which represents the index's three-month moving average. Trying to interpret the latest monthly reading is a useless exercise because it tends to fluctuate a great deal. It is also subject to substantial revisions the next month. The three-month moving average index is far more valuable because it is less volatile and based on more complete information.

  (1) Track the CFNAI-MA3 index to see the outlook for inflation and economic growth. A moving average that falls below –0.7 indicates that the chance of a recession has risen substantially. How does the Chicago Fed know that? Looking back over the period of 1967–2001, the CFNAI has fallen below –0.7 on seven occasions, with six of these periods actually leading to a recession. That's a success rate of 86%. When the index drops to –1.5, the economy is probably in the midst of a recession.

  A three-month moving average above 0.2 is a signal that the recession is likely over. If the index rises above 0.7 more than two years into the economic expansion, it is a warning that inflation is in danger of accelerating. A number above 1.0 when the economy is already well into the expansion means there's a clear threat that business activity may be overheating and that a sustained period of rising inflation could follow.

News Release

Embargoed for release:
10:00 am Eastern Time
9:00 am Central Time
January 29, 2004

Contact:
James Pieper
Coordinator, Media Relations
312-322-2387

Federal Reserve Bank of Chicago
230 South LaSalle Street
Chicago, IL 60604

Chicago Fed National Activity Index

CFNAI indicates above-trend economic growth again in December

The Chicago Fed National Activity Index was +0.13 in December, the fourth consecutive positive monthly reading. November's CFNAI was revised up from +0.55 to +0.68, the highest value since October 1999. Three of the four broad categories of indicators that comprise the index (see sidebar) made positive contributions in December; only the employment-related category made a negative contribution. The three-month moving average, CFNAI-MA3, fell moderately in December, to +0.35, from an upward-revised November reading of +0.46. CFNAI-MA3 readings above zero are associated with above-trend economic growth; accordingly, the CFNAI-MA3 value of +0.35 suggests that growth in national economic activity was above its historical trend in December. With regard to inflation, CFNAI-MA3 values above zero signal increased inflationary pressures over the coming year.

Most of the December decrease in the CFNAI can be attributed to a smaller contribution from output-related measures that month (+0.05) relative to November (+0.54). Industrial production (IP) growth slowed from 1.0 percent in November to 0.1 percent in December; manufacturing IP showed a similar-sized deceleration. The slowing in IP growth was largely offset by strong results from the Institute for Supply Management's survey of manufacturers: That survey's Purchasing Managers' Index rose from 61.3 in November to 63.4 in December, the highest reading in 20 years.

The employment-related category, which has not made a positive contribution to the monthly index since January 2003, contributed –0.13 to the CFNAI in December. Nonfarm payroll employment was up by just 1,000 in December, a much smaller gain than November's

The monthly CFNAI index, a weighted average of 85 indicators of national economic activity, is constructed to have an average value of zero and a standard deviation of one. A zero value for the index indicates that the national economy is expanding at its historical trend rate of growth; negative values are associated with below-trend growth, while positive values indicate above-trend growth. Month-to-month movements in the CFNAI can be volatile, so a three-month moving average version, the CFNAI-MA3, provides a more consistent picture of national economic growth. The 85 economic indicators that comprise the CFNAI are drawn from four broad categories of data: 1) production and income; 2) employment, unemployment, and hours; 3) personal consumption and housing; and 4) sales, orders, and inventories.

The next CFNAI will be released:
February 25, 2004
10:00 am Eastern Time
9:00 am Central Time

FEDERAL RESERVE BANK
OF CHICAGO

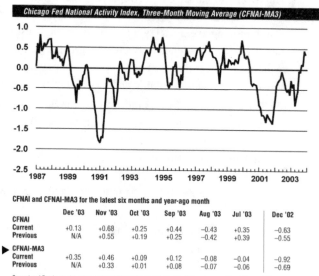

Chicago Fed National Activity Index, Three-Month Moving Average (CFNAI-MA3)

CFNAI and CFNAI-MA3 for the latest six months and year-ago month

	Dec '03	Nov '03	Oct '03	Sep '03	Aug '03	Jul '03	Dec '02
CFNAI							
Current	+0.13	+0.68	+0.25	+0.44	−0.43	+0.35	−0.63
Previous	N/A	+0.55	+0.19	+0.25	−0.42	+0.39	−0.55
CFNAI-MA3							
Current	+0.35	+0.46	+0.09	+0.12	−0.08	−0.04	−0.92
Previous	N/A	+0.33	+0.01	+0.08	−0.07	−0.06	−0.69

Current and Previous values reflect index values as of the January 29, 2004, release and December 18, 2003, release, respectively. N/A indicates not applicable.

MARKET IMPACT

Few participants in the financial markets follow this indicator. That could change in the future as investors begin to take note of its usefulness as a forecasting tool.

THE FEDERAL RESERVE BOARD'S BEIGE BOOK

Market Sensitivity: Medium.

What Is It: A summary of economic conditions around the country compiled for
the Federal Reserve Board.

News Release on the Internet: *www.federalreserve.gov/frbindex.htm* (see the
listing under Beige Book)

Home Web Address: *www.federalreserve.gov*

Release Time: 2:00 p.m. (ET); released two Wednesdays before each Federal
Open Market Committee (FOMC) meeting.

Frequency: Eight times a year.

Source: Federal Reserve Board.

Revisions: None.

WHY IS IT IMPORTANT?

Among the most important determinants of future U.S. economic growth are interest
rates. Their effects are pervasive. Changes in interest rates can impact consumer spending, business expenditures, corporate profits, government budgets, stock and bond prices,
and the value of the dollar. Movements in interest rates often precede recession and economic recoveries. Controlling this mighty tool in the short run is the Federal Reserve
Board, or, more precisely, a group within the Fed known as the Federal Open Market
Committee (FOMC).

The FOMC consists of 19 members (which consists of the seven Federal Reserve
Board Governors and the 12 regional Federal Reserve Bank presidents). Though all 19
members can deliberate on monetary policy, only 12 are allowed to vote. They are the
seven Fed Governors, the president of the Federal Reserve Bank of New York (who has
permanent voting status), and four regional Fed bank presidents who rotate among the
remaining 11 for voting privileges.

The FOMC meets eight times a year (and also confers by telephone when necessary)
to assess the economy's health and to decide what the appropriate level of short-term
interest rates should be. On days when FOMC officials gather behind closed doors to
debate monetary policy, anxiety levels in the financial markets tend to be at their highest.
So much is riding on the outcome of these deliberations that traders and money managers
wait nervously on the sidelines, doing very little until the Fed issues a statement briefly
explaining its decision to either raise the cost of credit, lower it, or keep it unchanged.

Can we determine beforehand how the FOMC might rule? No. Precious few clues
guide outside observers. Indeed, a whole cottage industry of specialists, known as "Fed

watchers," has emerged over the years. Their job is to pick up every possible nuance from speeches, side comments, and writings by FOMC members that might tip off how they will vote at the next interest rate policy meeting. So far the track record of "Fed watchers" has been less than stellar, which is of little surprise. As famed economist John Kenneth Galbraith once said, "There are two types of interest rate forecasters: those who don't know, and those who don't know they don't know."

Nonetheless, the Fed does release to the public at least one relevant document in advance of each FOMC meeting, and it serves as an economic backdrop for these closed-door sessions. Two weeks prior to an FOMC gathering, the Fed puts out the Beige Book, so called because of its tan cover. Two factors make the Beige Book special. First, it provides up-to-date information on economic conditions around the country. Second, and more importantly, this book is given to each member of the FOMC to help set the stage for the debate on interest rate policy.

The Beige Book, known formally as the Summary of Commentary on Current Economic Conditions by Federal Reserve District, is not a collection of statistical data. Far from it. The report is mostly a compilation of anecdotal information from each of the 12 Federal Reserve Districts. It is based on interviews with local businesspeople and academics who are asked to describe the economic climate in their region. It's then put together with a summary by one of the Federal Reserve District banks in preparation for the next FOMC meeting.

The Beige Book is not the only report read by FOMC officials. Two other key "books" are produced, but these are not available to the public. There's the Green Book, which is prepared by top economists at the Federal Reserve Board and contains their view of current and future domestic and international economic conditions. Finally, there is the Blue Book, the most sensitive of the three documents, written by key Fed staff members. It offers a set of interest rate policy alternatives and their likely consequences.

All three documents are distributed to FOMC members before each meeting. The Beige Book arrives two weeks before the monetary policy debate commences. The Green Book is available on the Thursday before the FOMC confers. The super-secret Blue Book is hand-delivered to FOMC members' homes on the Friday before a meeting.

How Is It Computed?

About three weeks prior to each FOMC conference, staff from all 12 regional Federal Reserve banks interview local business executives, private economists, bankers, academics, and others to get their assessment of the economic and business climate in their region. A standard set of questions is asked. How is consumer spending holding up? Is the labor market getting tighter? Are wage pressures rising? Has demand for financial services diminished? Is housing or commercial construction slowing or accelerating? Have manufacturers detected a change in order volume? One of the Federal Reserve banks, chosen on a rotating basis, summarizes all the anecdotal information and organizes the findings by district level to create the Beige Book.

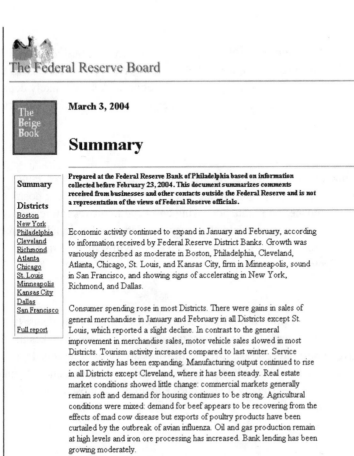

The Federal Reserve Board

March 3, 2004

The
Beige
Book

Summary

Summary

Prepared at the Federal Reserve Bank of Philadelphia based on information collected before February 23, 2004. This document summarizes comments received from businesses and other contacts outside the Federal Reserve and is not a representation of the views of Federal Reserve officials.

Districts
Boston
New York
Philadelphia
Cleveland
Richmond
Atlanta
Chicago
St. Louis
Minneapolis
Kansas City
Dallas
San Francisco

Full report

Economic activity continued to expand in January and February, according to information received by Federal Reserve District Banks. Growth was variously described as moderate in Boston, Philadelphia, Cleveland, Atlanta, Chicago, St. Louis, and Kansas City, firm in Minneapolis, sound in San Francisco, and showing signs of accelerating in New York, Richmond, and Dallas.

Consumer spending rose in most Districts. There were gains in sales of general merchandise in January and February in all Districts except St. Louis, which reported a slight decline. In contrast to the general improvement in merchandise sales, motor vehicle sales slowed in most Districts. Tourism activity increased compared to last winter. Service sector activity has been expanding. Manufacturing output continued to rise in all Districts except Cleveland, where it has been steady. Real estate market conditions showed little change: commercial markets generally remain soft and demand for housing continues to be strong. Agricultural conditions were mixed: demand for beef appears to be recovering from the effects of mad cow disease but exports of poultry products have been curtailed by the outbreak of avian influenza. Oil and gas production remain at high levels and iron ore processing has increased. Bank lending has been growing moderately.

THE TABLES: CLUES ON WHAT'S AHEAD FOR THE ECONOMY

Since there are no tables in the Beige Book, the question becomes whether one can divine from the anecdotes and summary how the Fed might rule on interest rates. The short answer is no. The Beige Book is not a good leading indicator of interest rates or anything else, for that matter. Still, it's the only game in town that permits outsiders to know what Fed governors will be reading as they prepare to discuss whether to change the benchmark Federal funds rate.

MARKET IMPACT

Though the Beige Book has no predictive value of its own, stock and bond traders are still anxious to see what it says, if only because Federal Reserve officials get this material before their all-important gathering. Moreover, the information in the Beige Book is quite timely, because it comes out sooner than most of the statistical data for the period.

Bonds

Widespread anecdotal signs of a softening in the economy are considered bullish for fixed incomes because this might move the Fed closer to lowering interest rates. On the other hand, reports of strong business activity and tight labor markets will likely depress bond prices and raise interest rates because investors expect the central bank to intervene and cool the economy.

Stocks

If the Beige Book portrays a soft economy with few inflation pressures, equity investors might look to the Fed to keep interest rate levels low. Normally this is a positive for stocks because it reduces corporate borrowing costs and improves future profits. In contrast, if economic growth is too rapid at a time when labor and material resources are becoming scarce, this heightens concerns that the Fed will soon hike rates, and this often causes stocks to retreat.

Dollar

The dollar might rise in value if the Beige Book agrees with other evidence that economic activity is robust. It portends firmer interest rates in the U.S., which makes the dollar more attractive to hold. In contrast, foreign investors are leery of reports depicting a fragile economy, since the Fed might be inclined to lower interest rates, and that might undermine the dollar's value, especially if U.S. rates end up below those of other major industrialized countries.

THE FEDERAL OPEN MARKET COMMITTEE STATEMENT

Market Sensitivity: Very high.

What Is It: A press release by the Federal Open Market Committee (FOMC) that announces its decision on where the crucial federal funds rate has been set.

News Release on the Internet: *www.federalreserve.gov/newsevents.htm* (click "monetary policy" under Press Releases)

Home Web Address: *www.federalreserve.gov*

Release Time: 2:15 p.m. on the day the FOMC concludes its meeting. A schedule of its meetings can be found at *www.federalreserve.gov/fomc/*.

Frequency: The FOMC formally gathers eight times a year and issues a statement on the results of its deliberations at the conclusion of each meeting. (Only in the most extraordinary circumstances might the FOMC choose to act between scheduled meetings.)

Source: Federal Reserve Board.

Revisions: No revisions.

WHY IS IT IMPORTANT?

Here's a report that fills barely a single page, contains virtually no numbers, and comes out just eight times a year. It is by far the briefest of all the economic releases. So why all the fuss over this statement? Simple. The brevity of this report belies the enormous impact it has around the world. On mornings when the FOMC convenes to discuss whether to raise, lower, or keep unchanged the federal funds rate, trading everywhere comes to a near standstill. This genuflect by the financial markets toward the Fed is understandable. Investors are extremely reluctant to commit large amounts of money until after the FOMC announces the results of its deliberations on interest rates. Once that statement is released, stocks, bonds, and currencies react instantly. But it is not just the investment community that feels the full frontal impact of the Fed's action on rates. Business leaders also eagerly await the news because they have to evaluate the implications that a sudden change in the cost of credit will have on their corporate balance sheets, profitability, future sales, hiring plans, and capital spending projects. Consumers are deeply affected as well, since shifts in monetary policy influence other short-term rates, such as those for bank deposits, personal loans, credit cards, home equity loans, and adjustable-rate mortgages.

At the epicenter of all this activity is a decision by the Federal Reserve on where to target a rather obscure monetary tool known as the "federal funds rate," or by its shortened version, the fed funds rate. This is the interest rate that banks charge one another for overnight loans. Why do these institutions make such short-term loans? The reason is that the Federal Reserve requires banks to keep a certain amount of cash (or reserves) either in their vaults or as deposits with their local Federal Reserve branch. (Without such a requirement, banks would happily lend out every dollar they could, and history has shown that this can pose risks to the banking system and to the economy.) However, from time to time banks find themselves short of meeting their reserve requirements. Perhaps they lent too much to customers or had an unexpected surge in withdrawals. Whatever the circumstance, these banks quickly need to acquire additional funds to meet the required reserves. At the same time, other banks may be holding more reserves than they need to. These excess funds can be lent overnight to banks that lack sufficient reserves. The rate charged on such overnight loans is dictated by the Federal Reserve's fed funds rate. History has shown that by controlling the cost of credit for these overnight loans, the Federal Reserve can over time influence the level of economic activity in the U.S.

How so? A higher federal funds rate makes banks more reluctant to be in a position to borrow overnight funds. Thus, they will either lend out less money or continue to make loans but charge their business and consumer clients a higher rate to offset the more costly fed funds rate. In both instances, loans become more expensive. The private sector responds by borrowing less, and that sets the stage for a slowdown in the economy.

If the FOMC decides to lower the fed funds rate, the process works in reverse. Banks tend to lend more, and borrowers are willing to take advantage of cheaper credit. This can stimulate more consumer spending and give the economy an extra jolt. Thus, a change in the feds fund rate will reverberate through the entire economy, since many transactions are financed by credit.

The biggest challenge for the Fed is to peg the fed funds rate at just the right level so that it permits maximum growth in jobs and economic output *without* firing up inflation. This is not an easy task. After all, the $13.5 trillion U.S. economy is buffeted every day from millions of decisions made by consumers, corporate leaders, and lawmakers. As a result, the economy is in a constant state of motion. Secondly, since we are living in an increasingly globalized environment, the actions of foreign investors and geopolitical shocks overseas can have a profound impact on business conditions in the U.S. Finally, it's important to bear in mind that the economy doesn't turn on a dime once there is a change in monetary policy. There's usually a nine- to 18-month lag from the moment there is a shift in the fed funds rate to when the real economy acts in response. That's why Federal Reserve economists devote so much time to forecasting how the economy will perform in the next year or so.

It all boils down to this: If the economy is expanding too quickly and inflation is in danger of accelerating, a key antidote is to lift the fed funds rate because the higher cost of borrowing will cool overall spending and defuse price pressures. On the other hand, if the economy is visibly weakening, with joblessness rising and inflation all but absent, the FOMC will likely choose to lower the fed funds rate to help revive growth. The point here is that controlling the direction of short-term rates (via the fed funds rate) is one of the most powerful weapons the Federal Reserve has in its arsenal to keep the economy out of serious trouble.

How Is It Computed?

The Federal Open Market Committee schedules eight regular meetings during the year. Most of the time these sessions last a day, but a few are planned for two days to allow a more wide-ranging discussion. The powerful FOMC is made up of 12 voting members, eight of whom have permanent voting status. They consist of the seven Fed Governors and the president of the New York Federal Reserve Bank. The other four seats are taken from the remaining 11 regional Federal Reserve Bank presidents, who rotate every January for a one-year stint as voting members. (The rotating 11 Fed bank presidents come from Boston, Philadelphia, Richmond, Cleveland, Chicago, Atlanta, St. Louis, Dallas, Minneapolis, Kansas City, and San Francisco.) It's important to note that *all* Federal Reserve Bank presidents fully participate in the closed-door deliberations on monetary policy. But when it comes to voting, only four of the 11 are permitted to do so with the eight permanent members.

How is a typical FOMC meeting conducted?

On the day of a meeting, all Fed governors and bank presidents, along with a few key staffers, gather in a large conference room just outside the Fed Chairman's office. The deliberations normally start at 9 a.m.

- The first item on the agenda is a presentation by a key manager at the New York Fed, who describes what has transpired in the domestic financial and foreign exchange markets since the last FOMC meeting.

- The next speaker is the Federal Reserve Board's Director of Research and Statistics, who discusses in detail the Fed's latest forecast for the U.S. economy.

- After that begins the first of two "go around the table" sessions. In the first go-around, members of the FOMC present their opinions on the regional and national outlook. Bank presidents start off this round, because they have more timely information on the health of the economy and key industries operating in their local area.

- Next comes the most important phase of the meeting. The Federal Reserve's Director of Monetary Affairs takes over and introduces a variety of possible policy actions and the likely impact each may have on the economy. The options are no change in interest rates at this time, an increase in rates (and by how much), or a decline in rates. This official explains the advantages and disadvantages of each step.

- Now it is the Fed Chairman's turn to speak. He presents his view of the economic outlook and then makes a specific recommendation on which option he favors and why.

- Once the Chairman concludes, the next and final go-around takes place. Each member of the FOMC makes a case for what he or she believes is the best target for the fed funds rate at this time. Here the members voice their agreement or disagreement with the Fed Chairman's view.

- At the end of this crucial phase, the Fed chief takes the floor again and summarizes his analysis of and recommendation for setting interest rates.

• Now it's time for the critical vote. The Fed Chairman votes first, followed by the Vice Chairman, and then the rest of the FOMC members are called in alphabetical order for their vote.

• The last stage of the meeting is the wording of the all-important FOMC statement. Crafting this press release is not an easy task. Federal Reserve officials want to announce to the world what was decided and why, along with some sense of the risks they see ahead for the economy. Given how closely the public scrutinizes the statement and its effect on global money markets, Fed officials know they have to choose their words carefully. The statement is finally released to the press and posted online at 2:15 p.m.

THE TABLES: CLUES ON WHAT'S AHEAD FOR THE ECONOMY

Once released, the FOMC statement is studied word by word by economists and the business press. Even words or phrases that showed up in previous releases but are omitted in the current statement are studied to capture all the nuances on how the Fed presently views the economy. Does it believe inflation is a bigger risk than recession? What are the most serious threats facing the economy? The answers to these questions might provide hints on whether the central bank is biased toward lowering or raising rates when it convenes the next FOMC meeting.

So how does one read the FOMC statement? The Fed has kept the layout of the press release largely unchanged for several years. Each paragraph conveys a specific message.

• Federal Reserve Press Release

(1) A short sentence that tells the outcome of the FOMC vote on interest rates.

(2) This brief section describes the economy's current state based on the latest economic indicators.

(3) The next two paragraphs are the most carefully studied in the release. This part highlights the Fed's assessment of inflation and growth. What trends do they display, and what are the underlying forces that propel both?

(4) This paragraph is more forward-looking and offers some insight into what the FOMC will monitor most closely between now and the next meeting. Here's where economists and investors get a sense of what the Fed will be inclined to do when it meets next.

(5) This lists the names of FOMC members who participated in the meeting that morning and how they voted. Generally speaking, participants on the FOMC will align their votes with that of the Fed chairman. On matters as important as setting interest rates, the preference is to have unanimity among the members. But there are occasions when certain participants disagree so strongly with the Fed chairman's recommendation they will formally register their disapproval

Federal Reserve Release

Press Release

Release Date: August 8, 2006

For immediate release

1 ▶ The Federal Open Market Committee decided today to keep its target for the federal funds rate at 5-1/4 percent.

2 ▶ Economic growth has moderated from its quite strong pace earlier this year, partly reflecting a gradual cooling of the housing market and the lagged effects of increases in interest rates and energy prices.

3 ▶ Readings on core inflation have been elevated in recent months, and the high levels of resource utilization and of the prices of energy and other commodities have the potential to sustain inflation pressures. However, inflation pressures seem likely to moderate over time, reflecting contained inflation expectations and the cumulative effects of monetary policy actions and other factors restraining aggregate demand.

4 ▶ Nonetheless, the Committee judges that some inflation risks remain. The extent and timing of any additional firming that may be needed to address these risks will depend on the evolution of the outlook for both inflation and economic growth, as implied by incoming information.

5 ▶ Voting for the FOMC monetary policy action were: Ben S. Bernanke, Chairman; Timothy F. Geithner, Vice Chairman; Susan S. Bies; Jack Guynn; Donald L. Kohn; Randall S. Kroszner; Sandra Pianalto; Kevin M. Warsh; and Janet L. Yellen. Voting against was Jeffrey M. Lacker, who preferred an increase of 25 basis points in the federal funds rate target at this meeting.

2006 Monetary policy

Home | News and events
Accessibility
Last update: August 8, 2006

and vote to dissent. Such instances tend to occur when the economy enters a state of transition, for that is when economic indicators are most likely to send mixed signals about the future and raise honest differences of opinion about the economic outlook and the risk of inflation.

MARKET IMPACT

Bonds

The reaction in the bond market to a change in the federal funds rate has been the subject of much research. That's because the two historically have had a complicated relationship. Sometimes a rise in the fed funds rate confirms that inflation is on the rise. In such instances, traders may flee the long bond (usually maturities of 10 to 30 years) and purchase shorter-term securities. The latter are less risky and may also offer more attractive returns now that the Fed is tightening monetary policy. As the sale of bonds accelerates, their yields rise. While fixed income investors normally seek out higher yields, those returns may not provide sufficient protection from current and future inflation.

It may take some time and several hikes in the fed funds rate before the economy slows and inflation pressures diminish. Once investors grow more confident that monetary policy is working and inflation appears more benign, they may quickly switch to buying bonds again in order to lock in the highest possible yield.

It is important to add a few caveats to the bond/fed funds rate relationship. First, other factors can influence how the bond market responds to monetary policy. For example, much depends on whether investors believe the Federal Reserve has the competence and commitment to achieve price stability. Is the Fed behind or ahead of the curve in combating inflation? If it is slow to react, the fed funds rate may ultimately have to go much higher, possibly even causing a recession, before finally subduing inflation. The second point is that foreign demand for U.S. bonds can also sway yields and add liquidity to (or drain liquidity from) the economy. This can complicate the Fed's job of achieving price stability.

In the final analysis, it is the perceived direction of inflation and the expected "total" real rate of return on bonds (interest income, adjusted for inflation, plus price appreciation) that most affect trading in the fixed income market. As a result, the language used in the FOMC to describe economic conditions may actually be more important to bond traders than the Fed's latest decision on rates.

Stocks

The relationship between stock prices and the fed funds rate is more direct. Whenever the Fed raises rates, or hints that it will, the news is not received kindly in the equity markets. Sure, higher rates might help dampen inflation pressures, but such action also hurts companies in two major ways. Once credit becomes more expensive, it can slow economic activity, and that can reduce future sales and profits. Rate hikes also increase the cost of doing business and that too can cut into profit margins.

Stock investors typically celebrate a drop in rates because such action can stimulate business and consumer spending and improve the outlook for corporate earnings. For these reasons, traders carefully monitor the FOMC meetings and parse every word in the press release.

Dollar

The U.S. currency will rally if the Federal Reserve shows an inclination to raise interest rates, since such a move promises higher returns on fixed income securities. How much the dollar will actually rise in value depends on the degree to which the foreign exchange market has already taken these hikes into consideration. If international investors have already priced in the next rise in the fed funds rate, then the dollar's appreciation will be minimal, if at all. Expectations of a rate cut in the U.S. could prompt investors to sell dollars, especially if central bankers in other countries are taking steps to tighten monetary policy.

Should the FOMC decide to leave rates unchanged, the outlook for the dollar will be determined by the explanation found in the Fed's press release on why it chose not to act. For example, if the latest pause comes after a series of rate increases, chances are the U.S. economy is starting to slow, and the dollar will consequently weaken since additional rate hikes are now less likely in the near future. However, if the decision to keep rates steady comes after a bout of monetary easing, it suggests that economic conditions are improving and that the risk of inflation will become greater in the future. Such circumstances should be perceived as either bullish or neutral for the dollar.

INTERNATIONAL TRADE IN GOODS AND SERVICES

Market Sensitivity: Medium.

What Is It: A monthly report on U.S. exports and imports of goods and services.

News Release on the Internet: *www.bea.gov/newsreleases/international/trade/ tradnewsrelease.htm*

Home Web Address: *www.bea.gov*

Release Time: 8:30 a.m. (ET); data is released the second week of the month and refers to trade that occurred two months earlier.

Frequency: Monthly.

Source: Census Bureau and Bureau of Economic Analysis, Department of Commerce.

Revisions: Each release comes with revisions that go back several months to reflect more complete information. Changes are usually small in magnitude, though they can be sizable at times. The annual benchmark revisions normally come out in June and can span several years.

WHY IS IT IMPORTANT?

Up until the early 1970s, the U.S. was viewed as having a closed economy. International trade was dismissed as a useful but not particularly vital part of overall domestic business activity. Back then, exports made up just 5.5% of total U.S. output, and imports accounted for 5.3%. These percentages were small enough that foreign economic events had only minimal impact on the American economy. Yet, within a decade, all of that would change. The Bretton Woods Agreement, which was formed at the end of World War II to establish a stable foreign exchange system, collapsed in 1971. As a result, currency values in the world financial markets began to float freely, sometimes moving wildly up or down. At the same time, world trade grew faster than ever. Cheaper foreign goods, often of better quality, increasingly found their way into the U.S. market and started to pose serious competition for U.S. producers. American companies responded by operating more efficiently, lowering prices, and seeking out new markets overseas. Trade has since evolved to become one of the most important forces shaping the U.S. economy. Today, the business of buying and selling products in foreign markets represents as much as a quarter of all U.S. economic activity.

Indeed, international trade plays such an important role in the U.S. that the government issues two major releases on this topic. The first report is the International Trade in Goods and Services report, which is a collection of monthly data on U.S. exports and imports. It's partly from these numbers that the "net export" figure is derived for use in the GDP account. The other report is known as the International Transactions account (see the next section, "Current Account Balance (Summary of International Transactions)"). It is released quarterly and covers not only trade in goods and services, but also foreign investment entering the U.S. and the amount of investment capital flowing out of the U.S. to other countries. Though both of these reports are valuable economic indicators, investors pay more attention to the monthly trade data since it's more current. The international transaction account comes out every three months; by then, much of the news is considered quite old for trading purposes.

What makes the monthly international trade report a must-read? First, exports reflect U.S. competitiveness in world markets, create American jobs, and improve corporate profits. Exports also contribute directly to domestic economic growth. To satisfy both American and foreign demand, U.S. firms have to produce more. Greater production translates into faster GDP growth. Third, by looking at imports, one can tell how strong demand is in the U.S. Consumers and businesses tend to import much more when the economy is expanding. The downside of rising imports is that it subtracts from GDP growth since these products are made by foreign, not U.S.-based, companies.

One potential risk to America's growing dependence on global trade is that the U.S. economy is no longer immune to financial and economic disruptions abroad. Relatively distant and seemingly modest events, such as the Asian financial meltdown of 1997, Russia's default on its foreign loans in 1998, and China's efforts to cool its speculative stock market in early 2007, can have a detrimental impact on U.S. stocks, bonds, and even the economy. Some of these effects might be short-lived, but others can last much longer.

What key forces shape the country's trade balance? Broadly speaking, America's trade performance is determined by two primary factors: the relative differences in growth rates between the U.S. and other countries, and the changing value of the dollar against other major currencies. Let's look at them separately. Obviously, where the economy stands in the business cycle can influence how much we buy from other nations. By the same token, how much foreigners buy from the U.S. depends on how well those economies are doing. If the U.S. is growing at a faster rate than most other countries, imports to the U.S. will increase by a greater amount than exports, thus ensuring a deficit in the trade account. What further deepens the deficit, however, is that Americans have also shown a greater propensity to import than shoppers in other countries. So, even if both the U.S. and other major industrial countries were growing at the same rate, the trade deficit would still worsen because Americans are inherently inclined to spend proportionally more on imports. This hunger for foreign goods has locked the U.S. into annual trade deficits every year since 1976.

The second major factor shaping the trade balance is exchange rates. Changes in currency values can alter the price of imports and exports and thus affect their demand. A strong dollar worsens the trade balance because it lowers the price of imports, thus making them more desirable to Americans. At the same time, it raises the cost of U.S.-made goods sold in international markets. This encourages foreign buyers to look elsewhere for less expensive products. It's been estimated that a 1% rise in the dollar's value against its main trading partners can worsen the trade deficit by $10–15 billion over two years. On the flip side, a falling U.S. currency makes imports more expensive and Americans might think twice about purchasing foreign goods. The upside of a weaker dollar is that it lowers the price of American exports in foreign markets, which can increase overseas demand for U.S. goods and services. Thus, changes in exchange rates over time have a profound effect on international commerce.

It should be noted that differences in inflation rates among countries could also influence trade patterns. A high U.S. inflation rate can price American-made goods out of foreign markets. In such a situation, demand for U.S. products will drop both here and abroad. In contrast, if inflation in other countries climbs at a faster rate than in the U.S., imports might become more expensive relative to what consumers will pay for American-made products. In that case, shoppers—both here and abroad—will be tempted to buy more from the U.S., where prices are rising more slowly, if at all. So, low inflation has a beneficial impact on this country's trade flows.

Could the U.S. return to a positive trade balance or, at the very least, sharply slash its deficits in the future? Sure, but it won't be easy. One solution is for America's major trading partners to grow much faster than the U.S. for several years so that they can accelerate their purchases of American products. However, such a plan is difficult to achieve because of the structural difference between the economies of the U.S. and, say, Europe or Japan. For example, the U.S. economy has a larger capital market, lower tax rates, and fewer regulatory obstacles than most other industrial countries. All these factors help promote faster growth here than overseas.

Another approach to cutting the trade deficit, at least theoretically, is to induce a prolonged recession in the U.S. because that will surely reduce imports. But this approach is a nonstarter as a policy option, since a recession will only generate other problems, including larger budget deficits, higher unemployment, a loss in income, and slower productivity growth.

A third way to correct the trade imbalance is to significantly devalue or cheapen the dollar and make imports too expensive for many Americans. Yet this solution also carries grave risks, such as rising inflation and interest rates. In the final analysis, the only reasonable way to end the chronic trade deficits is a twofold approach. First, Americans must learn to save more and consume less. Second, policymakers in Europe and Japan need to lower trade barriers, accelerate regulatory reforms, and reduce tax rates so that their citizens can have more money to spend on U.S. goods and services. So far, these regions have been agonizingly slow at making such changes.

How Is It Computed?

Each month, the Commerce Department tallies figures on U.S. exports (such as corn, telecommunications equipment, musical instruments, and computers) and imports (cars, steel, rugs, caviar, wine, and copper). Normally, they reflect transactions that actually took place in the reported month, though a small number of trades are included from previous months. Exports are reported based on what is called "free alongside ship" (FAS) value. This means that the price of the commodity includes freight transport, insurance and other charges connected with shipping the goods to the U.S. port of exportation. Imports, however, are valued on a "customs basis" (CIF), which is essentially the price of the product without the cost of insurance, freight, or import duties.

Trade in services is handled differently. Here the Commerce Department depends entirely on monthly surveys taken by businesses and associations in the service sector to see how much revenue these firms raised by selling services abroad, and, on the other side of the ledger, how much American firms paid for services provided by foreigners.

Trade figures in the report are presented in both nominal (current) dollars and real (adjusted for inflation) dollars. The conversion from nominal to real is based on the monthly import and export price indexes (see the section "Import and Export Prices"). While the nominal figures get all the immediate press attention, it's more important to follow the inflation-adjusted numbers because they reflect the actual volume of goods traded, which is what ultimately impacts real GDP.

Trade statistics are given in both seasonally- and non-seasonally-adjusted terms. Normally they are not annualized, but anyone can do so by simply multiplying the monthly trade figure by 12.

THE TABLES: CLUES ON WHAT'S AHEAD FOR THE ECONOMY

This nearly 50-page release has dozens of informative tables. Some of the most useful are highlighted in the following pages. It should be pointed out that international trade has few qualities as a leading indicator. The reason is that trade patterns change slowly due to the long lag between the time contracts are signed and when goods actually get shipped. Does that diminish the value of this release to investors and forecasters? Absolutely not. The Commerce Department provides amazingly detailed information in this report on America's foreign trade position, including its transactions with virtually every country in the world.

- **Exhibit 1**   U.S. International Trade in Goods and Services

  (1) The first table summarizes the U.S. trade balance for the latest period, along with about three years of monthly data so that readers can spot any departure from recent trends in exports and imports as well as the total trade balance. A one-month aberration is not significant, but a continuous divergence spanning at least three months can indicate that a more significant change is under way in the U.S. or international economy.

  (2) Look to see whether the departure in trade patterns stems from changes on the export or import side. An abrupt drop in the export growth rate can occur because of deteriorating economic conditions in other countries, an overly muscular dollar, or sharply rising U.S. inflation. A marked decline in imports can take place if domestic demand has plunged due to a weakened U.S. economy, or

Exhibit 1. U.S. International Trade in Goods and Services

In millions of dollars. Details may not equal totals due to seasonal adjustment and rounding. (R) - Revised.

Period	Balance			Exports			Imports		
	Total	Goods (1)	Services	Total	Goods (1)	Services	Total	Goods (1)	Services
2002									
Jan.- Dec.	-418,038	-482,872	64,834	974,107	681,874	292,233	1,392,145	1,164,746	227,399
Jan.-	-28,299	-33,495	5,196	78,580	55,228	23,352	106,879	88,723	18,156
January	-28,299	-33,495	5,196	78,580	55,228	23,352	106,879	88,723	18,156
February	-31,049	-35,876	4,827	78,579	54,988	23,591	109,628	90,864	18,764
March	-30,704	-36,661	5,957	79,286	55,083	24,203	109,990	91,744	18,246
April	-34,225	-39,773	5,548	80,674	56,871	23,803	114,899	96,644	18,255
May	-35,097	-40,830	5,733	81,050	56,848	24,202	116,147	97,678	18,469
June	-35,563	-40,683	5,120	81,974	57,702	24,272	117,537	98,385	19,152
July	-34,069	-39,304	5,235	82,954	58,638	24,316	117,023	97,942	19,081
August	-36,249	-42,070	5,821	82,566	57,870	24,696	118,815	99,940	18,875
September	-36,663	-41,938	5,275	82,294	57,807	24,487	118,957	99,745	19,212
October	-35,154	-40,647	5,493	82,159	57,301	24,858	117,314	97,949	19,365
November	-38,629	-44,147	5,518	82,917	57,765	25,152	121,545	101,911	19,634
December	-42,332	-47,447	5,115	81,075	55,774	25,301	123,406	103,220	20,186
2003									
Jan.-Dec. (R)	-489,911	-549,156	59,245	1,018,720	713,788	304,932	1,508,632	1,262,945	245,687
Jan.- (R)	-40,007	-44,833	4,826	82,058	57,156	24,902	122,065	101,989	20,076
January (R)	-40,007	-44,833	4,826	82,058	57,156	24,902	122,065	101,989	20,076
February (R)	-38,589	-43,628	5,039	82,691	57,920	24,771	121,280	101,548	19,732
March (R)	-42,952	-47,482	4,530	82,639	58,309	24,330	125,591	105,791	19,800
April (R)	-41,971	-46,334	4,363	81,103	57,243	23,860	123,074	103,577	19,497
May (R)	-41,772	-46,628	4,856	82,261	57,774	24,487	124,033	104,402	19,631
June (R)	-40,357	-45,050	4,693	84,132	59,269	24,863	124,489	104,319	20,170
July (R)	-40,613	-45,006	4,393	85,627	60,367	25,260	126,240	105,373	20,867
August (R)	-39,781	-44,695	4,914	83,385	57,691	25,694	123,166	102,386	20,780
September (R)	-41,254	-46,548	5,294	85,836	59,719	26,117	127,090	106,267	20,823
October (R)	-41,705	-47,088	5,383	88,250	61,655	26,595	129,955	108,743	21,212
November (R)	-38,220	-43,944	5,724	90,633	63,722	26,911	128,853	107,666	21,187
December (R)	-42,692	-47,921	5,229	90,103	62,962	27,141	132,795	110,883	21,912
2004									
Jan.-	-43,057	-48,392	5,335	89,045	61,907	27,138	132,102	110,299	21,803
January	-43,057	-48,392	5,335	89,045	61,907	27,138	132,102	110,299	21,803
February									
March									
April				▲			▲		
May				2			2		
June									
July									
August									
September									
October									
November									
December									

1 ▶

perhaps as a consequence of a serious erosion of the dollar's value in currency markets, which would make foreign goods much more expensive.

When it comes to trade in services, the story is slightly different. Service transactions rarely show much fluctuation. They usually grow at a stable rate month to month. By and large, the U.S. market faces little competition in services, which is why inflation tends to rise faster in this sector. (Let's face it—American dentists know that they can increase their fees without fear of losing their patients to dentists in Spain.)

- **Exhibit 2**   U.S. International Trade in Goods and Services—Three-Month Moving Averages

(3) Like many economic indicators, trade can be subject to periodic distortions. A sharp swing up or down in petroleum prices in a single month can exaggerate the overall trade picture. Large auto shipments from overseas might on occasion cause statistical shocks too. To smooth out such month-to-month volatility, the

Exhibit 2. U.S. International Trade in Goods and Services
Centered Three-Month Moving Averages
(R)-Revised

Center Month of Moving Average	Balance			Exports			Imports		
	Total	Goods (1)	Services	Total	Goods (1)	Services	Total	Goods (1)	Services
2002									
January	---	---	---	---	---	---	---	---	---
February	-30,018	-35,344	5,327	78,815	55,099	23,715	108,832	90,444	18,389
March	-31,993	-37,437	5,444	79,513	55,647	23,866	111,506	93,084	18,422
April	-33,342	-39,088	5,746	80,337	56,267	24,069	113,679	95,355	18,323
May	-34,962	-40,429	5,467	81,233	57,141	24,092	116,194	97,569	18,625
June	-34,910	-40,272	5,363	81,993	57,729	24,263	116,902	98,002	18,901
July	-35,294	-40,686	5,392	82,498	58,070	24,428	117,792	98,756	19,036
August	-35,660	-41,104	5,444	82,605	58,105	24,500	118,265	99,209	19,056
September	-36,022	-41,552	5,530	82,340	57,659	24,680	118,362	99,211	19,151
October	-36,815	-42,244	5,429	82,457	57,624	24,832	119,272	99,868	19,404
November	-38,705	-44,080	5,375	82,050	56,947	25,104	120,755	101,027	19,728
December (R)	-40,323	-45,476	5,153	82,017	56,898	25,118	122,339	102,374	19,965
2003									
January (R)	-40,309	-45,303	4,993	81,941	56,950	24,991	122,251	102,253	19,998
February (R)	-40,516	-45,314	4,798	82,463	57,795	24,668	122,979	103,110	19,869
March (R)	-41,171	-45,815	4,644	82,145	57,824	24,320	123,315	103,639	19,676
April (R)	-42,231	-46,814	4,583	82,001	57,776	24,226	124,233	104,590	19,643
May (R)	-41,367	-46,004	4,637	82,499	58,096	24,403	123,866	104,100	19,766
June (R)	-40,914	-45,561	4,647	84,007	59,137	24,870	124,921	104,698	20,223
July (R)	-40,250	-44,917	4,667	84,381	59,109	25,272	124,632	104,026	20,606
August (R)	-40,549	-45,416	4,867	84,949	59,259	25,690	125,499	104,675	20,823
September (R)	-40,913	-46,110	5,197	85,824	59,688	26,135	126,737	105,799	20,938
October (R)	-40,393	-45,860	5,467	88,240	61,699	26,541	128,633	107,559	21,074
November (R)	-40,872	-46,317	5,445	89,662	62,780	26,882	130,534	109,097	21,437
December	-41,323	-46,752	5,429	89,927	62,864	27,063	131,250	109,616	21,634

government presents trade data in three-month moving averages. In such a calculation, the latest monthly figures are added to the two prior months, and the sum is divided by 3.

To gain some additional perspective on trade, separate tables are broken out for two of the most volatile commodities: energy and motor vehicle imports. Exhibit 17 is devoted to imports of petroleum and petroleum products, and Exhibit 18 focuses on motor vehicle imports and exports. Both are discussed in more detail in the following sections.

• Exhibit 17   Imports of Energy-Related Petroleum Products, Including Crude Oil

Even though the U.S. is one of the world's largest producers of oil, it still supplies less than half of what this country consumes. The rest has to be imported. Imports of energy-related petroleum products represent 15% to 20% of Americans' total import bill for merchandise goods, so even a moderate change in oil prices can have a

Exhibit 17. Imports of Energy-Related Petroleum Products, Including Crude Oil

Details may not equal totals due to rounding.

Period	Total energy-related petroleum products (1)		Crude oil			
	Quantity (thousands of barrels)	Value (thousands of dollars)	Quantity (thousands of barrels)	Thousands of barrels per day (average)	Value (thousands of dollars)	Unit price (dollars)
2003						
Jan.- Dec.	4,654,638	129,580,947	3,673,596	10,065	99,094,675	26.97
Jan.-	360,017	10,180,337	268,431	8,659	7,444,163	27.73
January	360,017	10,180,337	268,431	8,659	7,444,163	27.73
February	316,557	9,995,440	247,105	8,825	7,526,491	30.46
March	395,753	12,482,600	300,689	9,700	9,101,197	30.27
April	396,513	10,743,443	314,662	10,489	8,188,808	26.02
May	407,791	10,167,192	320,541	10,340	7,727,416	24.11
June	401,212	10,560,977	311,946	10,398	7,955,140	25.50
July	426,696	11,670,580	339,669	10,957	9,068,389	26.70
August	397,015	11,270,137	319,337	10,301	8,797,303	27.55
September	394,328	10,733,700	316,193	10,540	8,371,844	26.48
October	402,340	10,856,961	327,444	10,563	8,594,549	26.25
November	363,893	9,953,160	290,205	9,674	7,695,589	26.52
December	392,524	10,966,420	317,375	10,238	8,623,786	27.17
2004						
Jan.-	388,549	11,405,335	309,437	9,982	8,835,252	28.55
January	388,549	11,405,335	309,437	9,982	8,835,252	28.55
February						
March		▲	▲		▲	▲
April		7	5		6	4
May						
June						

marked effect on the U.S. trade balance and on economic activity. A jump in the cost of crude oil can eventually depress consumer spending, for example. By having to pay more for gasoline and heating oil, households will have less spendable income for vacations, movies, and restaurants. Conversely, a drop in oil prices stimulates the economy, because households have more cash available for discretionary spending.

(4) This column lays out the average cost of oil per barrel imported into the U.S. for the latest month.

(5) Here one finds the quantity of oil imported to the U.S. by month.

(6) This is the monthly bill for importing crude.

(7) Located in this column is the total monthly cost of crude oil, plus other energy-related imports, including liquefied propane and butane gas.

For purposes of comparison, all this data is also presented on a historical basis that goes back more than 18 months.

- **Exhibit 9** Exports, Imports, and Balance of Goods, Petroleum, and Non-Petroleum End-Use Category Totals (Not Shown)

Given how much oil can exaggerate the cost of imports, it is also useful to see trade figures with petroleum excluded from the calculation. Exhibit 9 does just that; it sums up U.S. international trade minus petroleum imports.

- **Exhibit 18** Exports and Imports of Motor Vehicles and Parts by Selected Countries

By dedicating a table to motor vehicle trade, the Commerce Department demonstrates how singularly important this industry is to the economy. Nearly 7 million American workers are tied to the automotive manufacturing business, encompassing 1 out of 20 jobs. Imports of cars and trucks make up more than 15% of all merchandise goods brought into this country, while exports of U.S.-built motor vehicles represent about 12% of all goods sold internationally. Exhibit 18 breaks down motor vehicle shipments by countries the U.S. exports to and imports from. This table serves three purposes. First, purchases of such big-ticket items can offer insights into the health of consumer demand in the U.S. Second, the level of exports provides information on how well the domestic manufacturing sector is performing. Finally, by analyzing the export data, one can get a few clues on the strength of demand in foreign countries.

- **Exhibit 10** Real Exports and Imports of Goods by Principal End-Use Category (Adjusted for Inflation) (Not Shown)

It is best to look at trade in real terms. This is the only way one can determine changes in the actual volume of goods traded. It strips away the distortional effects of price inflation and gives you a picture of the quantity of goods and services traded. Exhibit 10 adjusts both exports and imports for inflation, but only for

Exhibit 18. Exports and Imports of Motor Vehicles and Parts By Selected Countries: 2004

In millions of dollars. Details may not equal totals due to rounding. (X) Not applicable. (-) Represents zero or less than one half of the measurement shown.

Country	Total		Cars		Trucks		Parts	
	January 2004	December 2003	January 2004	December 2003	January 2004	December 2003	January 2004	December 2003
TOTAL	5,776	6,335	1,189	1,915	718	922	3,870	3,498
Australia	95	122	25	33	23	34	47	55
Austria	32	49	1	1	(-)	(-)	30	47
Belgium	25	33	3	5	1	3	21	25
Brazil	38	37	1	(-)	(-)	(-)	37	36
Canada	3,201	3,487	474	925	470	608	2,258	1,954
Germany	288	356	196	271	6	3	86	82
Japan	151	186	30	36	2	2	119	148
Korea	36	31	1	4	1	1	33	26
Mexico	1,115	1,009	197	263	86	69	832	677
Saudi Arabia	58	84	32	56	10	10	16	18
Sweden	23	27	3	3	(-)	(-)	20	24
Taiwan	15	23	4	4	2	6	9	13
United Kingdom	163	162	79	78	3	7	81	77
Other	538	729	144	235	112	179	281	315
TOTAL	15,842	18,265	8,362	10,571	1,414	1,735	6,066	5,958
Australia	64	66	45	46	(-)	(-)	19	21
Austria	45	99	36	88	(-)	(-)	9	10
Belgium	84	167	67	136	11	22	7	9
Brazil	156	155	27	26	9	6	121	123
Canada	4,470	4,950	2,192	2,517	747	963	1,531	1,470
Germany	1,654	2,695	1,240	2,241	(-)	1	413	453
Japan	3,598	3,897	2,486	2,607	57	65	1,055	1,225
Korea	1,061	1,022	918	896	(-)	(-)	143	126
Mexico	2,981	2,914	746	861	553	621	1,681	1,432
Saudi Arabia	(-)	(-)	(-)	(-)	(-)	(-)	(-)	(-)
Sweden	152	346	132	318	3	5	17	23
Taiwan	132	122	2	6	(-)	(-)	129	115
United Kingdom	360	692	264	571	16	31	80	91
Other	1,085	1,141	206	258	18	22	861	860

merchandise goods. Inflation-adjusted trade in services is available only on a quarterly basis with the GDP report.

What's valuable about this table is that net exports (exports minus imports) are a key component of the GDP account. Thus, monitoring real net exports can offer an early glimpse of upcoming changes in the quarterly GDP growth rate.

- **Exhibits 6, 7, and 8**   Exports and Imports of Goods by Principal End-Use Category and Commodity (Exhibits 7 and 8 Not Shown)

The minutiae of trade statistics in this report can easily scare away many readers, and that's perfectly understandable. However, a few moments of study will show that there is a veritable gold mine of information in these tables that can be helpful to investors and business leaders.

Exhibit 6. Exports and Imports of Goods by Principal End-Use Category

In millions of dollars. Details may not equal totals due to seasonal adjustment and rounding. (R) Revised.

Period	Total Balance of Payments Basis	Net Adjust-ments	Total Census Basis(1)	End-Use Commodity Category					
				Foods, Feeds, Beverages	Industrial Supplies(2)	Capital Goods	Auto-motive Vehicles, etc.	Consumer Goods	Other Goods
				Exports					
2003									
Jan.-Dec. (R)	713,788	-10,241	724,030	55,096	172,969	293,047	80,121	89,895	32,901
Jan.- (R)	57,156	-747	57,903	4,434	14,077	22,922	6,643	7,319	2,509
January (R)	57,156	-747	57,903	4,434	14,077	22,922	6,643	7,319	2,509
February (R)	57,920	-857	58,777	4,436	13,976	24,093	6,653	6,990	2,629
March (R)	58,309	-973	59,282	4,412	14,414	23,612	6,663	7,299	2,882
April (R)	57,243	-1,026	58,269	4,372	14,212	22,983	6,641	7,167	2,894
May (R)	57,774	-888	58,662	4,327	14,260	23,268	6,756	7,173	2,878
June (R)	59,269	-885	60,154	4,506	14,465	24,111	6,553	7,684	2,835
July (R)	60,367	-855	61,222	4,650	14,821	24,710	6,812	7,542	2,687
August (R)	57,691	-916	58,607	4,392	14,020	23,891	6,116	7,447	2,742
September (R)	59,719	-774	60,493	4,598	14,069	24,665	6,748	7,716	2,696
October (R)	61,655	-782	62,437	4,828	14,731	25,576	6,928	7,547	2,828
November (R)	63,722	-750	64,472	5,189	14,650	27,214	6,670	8,098	2,651
December (R)	62,962	-790	63,752	4,952	15,275	26,002	6,937	7,915	2,671
2004									
Jan.-	61,907	-975	62,882	4,563	15,208	25,803	6,776	7,747	2,785
January	61,907	-975	62,882	4,563	15,208	25,803	6,776	7,747	2,785
February									
March									
April									
May									
June									
July									
August									
September									
October									
November									
December									
				Imports					
2003									
Jan.-Dec. (R)	1,262,945	3,460	1,259,485	55,834	316,330	295,678	210,217	333,634	47,791
Jan.- (R)	101,989	195	101,795	4,534	24,981	24,457	16,969	26,975	3,879
January (R)	101,989	195	101,795	4,534	24,981	24,457	16,969	26,975	3,879
February (R)	101,548	207	101,341	4,417	25,933	23,224	16,826	26,942	3,999
March (R)	105,791	249	105,542	4,630	28,371	23,216	17,333	28,057	3,936
April (R)	103,577	266	103,311	4,671	26,051	24,064	16,872	27,729	3,924
May (R)	104,402	350	104,053	4,612	25,559	24,466	17,786	27,758	3,872
June (R)	104,319	468	103,852	4,462	25,880	24,407	18,227	26,719	4,156
July (R)	105,373	203	105,169	4,586	26,719	24,459	17,964	27,334	4,107
August (R)	102,386	466	101,920	4,536	26,758	24,041	15,570	27,220	3,796
September (R)	106,267	307	105,960	4,786	26,902	25,296	17,400	27,608	3,967
October (R)	108,743	269	108,474	4,788	26,799	25,478	18,335	29,047	4,026
November (R)	107,666	257	107,409	4,869	25,616	25,659	18,208	28,966	4,090
December (R)	110,883	223	110,659	4,942	26,761	26,911	18,725	29,280	4,040
2004									
Jan.-	110,299	248	110,050	4,838	27,420	26,824	17,721	29,327	3,920
January	110,299	248	110,050	4,838	27,420	26,824	17,721	29,327	3,920
February									

Exhibit 6 divides the import and export of goods into six broad categories: foods and beverages, industrial supplies, capital goods, automotive vehicles (plus parts and engines), consumer goods, and other goods. This table offers a quick wrap-up of the sectors most responsible for the latest changes in the trade balance. For example, if imports surged, was it the result of consumers buying more cars, televisions, and wine, or because companies spent more on capital goods? It is preferable to have imports rise as a result of purchases of capital goods rather than consumer goods. Capital goods imports can help U.S. firms and factories operate more efficiently, create more jobs, and reduce the risk of future inflation. Imports of mostly consumer goods simply go to satisfy consumption, and by doing so, they exacerbate the trade deficit and add very little to the economy's long-term health.

Exhibits 7 and 8 go a step further. Here you can identify 150 specific commodity categories that have been imported and exported, including telecom equipment, computers, leather and furs, tractors, TVs, pleasure boats, drilling equipment, and textile sewing machines. The data can help identify U.S. industries that are showing stronger sales overseas as well as reveal those domestic sectors possibly headed for trouble because of inroads foreign competitors are making in the U.S. market.

- **Exhibit 14**   Exports, Imports, and Trade Balance by Selected Countries and Areas

If you are looking for a breakdown of trade patterns between the U.S. and its three dozen major trading partners, you will find it in this chart. A chronic trade imbalance with certain countries not only puts pressure on currency rates but even affects foreign economic policy, especially when unfair or illegal trading practices by other nations end up hurting U.S. producers.

- **Supplemental Section: Exhibit 6-a**   Exports, Imports, and Trade Balance by Country and Area (Not Shown)

Perhaps the most remarkable set of tables on this topic can be found in the supplemental section of the release. Supplemental Exhibits 6 and 6a show trade between the U.S. and virtually every nation in the world.

Exhibit 14. Exports, Imports, and Balance of Goods By Selected Countries and Areas--2004

In millions of dollars. Details may not equal totals due to rounding. (-) Represents zero or less than one half of measurement shown. (R) - Revised. (X) - Not applicable. (Note: This exhibit is not additive. See footnote (2))

Item (1)	Balance		Exports		Imports	
	January 2004	December 2003	January 2004	December 2003	January 2004	December 2003
Total Balance of Payments Basis	-45,754 (R)	-47,164	58,181 (R)	62,366	103,935 (R)	109,529
Net Adjustments	-1,223 (R)	-1,013	-975 (R)	-790	248 (R)	223
Total Census Basis	-44,531 (R)	-46,151	59,156 (R)	63,155	103,687 (R)	109,306
North America	-8,198	-7,588	21,541	22,031	29,740	29,620
Canada	-5,223	-4,447	13,348	13,749	18,571	18,196
Mexico	-2,975	-3,141	8,193	8,283	11,168	11,424
Western Europe	-6,579	-11,103	13,583	13,914	20,163	25,017
Euro Area (2)	-4,748	-8,191	9,337	9,597	14,086	17,788
European Union	-5,940	-10,290	12,527	12,827	18,468	23,116
Austria	-204	-308	121	153	325	462
Belgium	365	320	1,264	1,266	899	945
Finland	-270	-91	136	165	407	256
France	-776	-1,415	1,485	1,465	2,261	2,880
Germany	-2,796	-4,134	2,311	2,386	5,107	6,520
Italy	-1,221	-1,371	784	984	2,005	2,355
Netherlands	777	999	1,629	1,853	852	854
Spain	66	-158	560	510	494	668
Sweden	-662	-858	235	308	896	1,166
United Kingdom	-431	-1,055	2,812	2,791	3,243	3,846
Other EU	-787	-2,219	1,192	946	1,979	3,164
European Free Trade Association	-552	-667	722	817	1,274	1,484
Norway	-325	-288	107	125	432	413
Switzerland	-204	-332	603	668	807	1,000
Other EFTA	-23	-47	13	24	36	70
Other Western Europe	-87	-145	334	271	421	417
Eastern Europe/FSR	-754	-748	586	727	1,340	1,474
Hungary	-192	-93	99	102	291	194
Poland	-50	-45	65	80	115	125
Former Soviet Republics	-360	-461	298	364	658	826
Russia	-291	-485	159	184	450	669
Other FSR	-69	24	139	180	208	156
Other EE	-152	-149	124	181	276	330
Pacific Rim Countries	-20,657	-18,488	15,145	17,886	35,802	36,374
Australia	424	522	1,018	1,094	594	572
China	-11,477	-9,874	2,593	3,320	14,070	13,194
Japan	-5,252	-5,700	3,985	4,502	9,238	10,201
Newly Industrialized Countries(NICS)	-2,289	-1,606	5,617	6,778	7,906	8,384
Hong Kong	264	691	1,071	1,367	807	676
Korea	-1,529	-1,403	1,817	2,154	3,346	3,557
Singapore	93	-46	1,233	1,291	1,140	1,337
Taiwan	-1,117	-849	1,497	1,966	2,613	2,815
Other Pacific Rim(3)	-2,064	-1,830	1,930	2,192	3,994	4,022
South/Central America	-2,332	-2,892	4,437	4,533	6,769	7,425
Argentina	12	-49	278	259	266	308
Brazil	-357	-530	1,034	1,054	1,391	1,584
Colombia	-229	-127	356	349	585	476
Other S/C A (3)	-1,757	-2,186	2,769	2,871	4,526	5,057
OPEC	-4,735	-4,619	1,419	1,599	6,153	6,218
Indonesia(3)	-582	-413	187	262	769	676
Nigeria	-766	-1,000	117	77	882	1,077
Saudi Arabia	-1,065	-802	383	447	1,448	1,249
Venezuela(3)	-1,500	-1,513	280	298	1,779	1,811
Other OPEC	-822	-890	453	515	1,275	1,405
Other Countries	-3,359	-2,906	2,911	2,981	6,270	5,887
Egypt	221	143	287	208	66	64
South Africa	-220	-90	194	333	413	423
Other	-3,360	-2,959	2,430	2,440	5,790	5,399
Uniden. ctys (4)	(-)	21	(-)	21	(X)	(X)
Timing Adjustments	(X)	244	(X)	23	(X)	-221

MARKET IMPACT

Financial market reaction to the monthly trade data is tough to predict. Everyone recognizes the growing importance of international commerce to the U.S. economy and how flows of imports and exports can tip off investors to domestic demand, industry earnings, pricing power, and potential changes in currency values. What lessens the value of the international trade report is its late arrival. The trade balance is the last economic release by the Census Bureau each month, and it reports on activity that took place two months back. So it's hard to get worked up when this report comes out. One factor that might provoke a sharp reaction is if the trade numbers significantly diverge from what the market or policymakers expected that month. Sudden changes in export or import flows could have implications for GDP growth estimates and the dollar, and that could startle market participants.

Bonds

Anticipating how bond investors might respond to trade data can be very tricky. There's no consistent pattern of response because much depends on the factors behind the latest trade news. Let's take a look at a sample of the scenarios investors might face.

If the monthly trade deficit turns out to be smaller than expected, this could be viewed as good news for fixed incomes. The reason? The dollar often rallies in such cases because foreign investors prefer to see the U.S. trade gap shrink. A stronger dollar will help reduce inflation pressures in the U.S., and this can lift bond prices.

Note, however, that the same report can also be viewed negatively by bondholders, because a shrinking deficit can boost GDP growth. Greater exports or fewer imports—both of which can reduce the red ink in trade—means that less is subtracted from the GDP account. If the cause is a surge in exports, this will further pump up the U.S. economy, and that can unnerve fixed-income investors and lead to a sell-off in bonds. On the other hand, if the reason for the smaller deficit turns out to be a drop in imports, it suggests the U.S. economy might be weakening. This is considered good news for bond investors.

Now suppose that the trade deficit suddenly balloons. You might conclude that is bad news for bond investors. After all, this would normally put downward pressure on the dollar, which might raise both inflation and interest rates in the U.S. An increase in the trade shortfall means that the U.S., which is already the world's largest debtor nation, will have to borrow even more money from foreign investors to finance these additional deficits. Ah, but there might also be good news here for bonds. A higher trade deficit could also mean less economic growth, because a jump in imports will subtract from the GDP account.

With such a dizzying assortment of possible outcomes in the bond market, what is one to do? First, don't just look at the headline trade figures, but focus instead on the dynamics going on behind the scenes. If the trade balance improves, bond investors prefer the reason to be a fall in imports rather than a surge in exports. If the deficit climbs, traders hope the cause is a plunge in exports, which would at least ease economic output.

Stocks

This is not an easy call for equity players either. Basically, they prefer to see the deficit shrink as a result of vibrant demand for exports. That will keep U.S. factories humming, improve the outlook for corporate profits, and bolster the dollar's value. The only wrinkle here would come from the bond market. Should export growth be so strong that it heightens fears of inflation, interest rates would edge higher and spoil the party for stock investors. In the final analysis, though, stocks tend to do better if the trade balance improves due to an increase in sales overseas.

Dollar

While investors in the bond and stock markets agonize over how to respond to the latest international trade figures, currency traders take a more direct approach. Unless caused by a deep recession in the U.S., any improvement in the trade balance is viewed favorably for the dollar. The more goods and services foreigners buy from the U.S., the more dollars they'll need to pay for these American products.

In contrast, a worsening trade deficit can undermine the dollar. To purchase foreign goods and services, Americans have to sell dollars so they can pay for these products in local currencies. The problem is that foreign exchange traders are already swimming in a sea of surplus dollars. Flooding the market with even more dollars can only further depress the greenback's value.

CURRENT ACCOUNT BALANCE (SUMMARY OF INTERNATIONAL TRANSACTIONS)

Market Sensitivity: Low to medium.

What Is It: The broadest accounting of America's trade and investment relationship with the rest of the world.

News Release on the Internet: *http://bea.gov/newsreleases/international/ transactions/transnewsrelease.htm*

Home Web Address: *http://bea.gov/*

Release Time: 8:30 a.m. (ET); data is released two and a half months after the reference quarter ends.

Frequency: Quarterly.

Source: Bureau of Economic Analysis, Commerce Department.

Revisions: Usually moderate. Annual benchmark changes are made in June.

WHY IS IT IMPORTANT?

The explosion in world trade over the last several decades has fundamentally altered the U.S. economic landscape. More than 12 million American jobs are now tied to the exports sector; some 10 million are supported by importers. About a quarter of all U.S. business activity is now linked in some fashion to international commerce.

Given its importance to the U.S. economy, we need to delve a little deeper into precisely what we mean here by trade. One aspect of it deals with the basic exchange of goods and services between the U.S. and other countries, an area that was explored in the preceding section on international trade. However, the International Transactions release provides a more comprehensive accounting of where the U.S. stands in its economic ties with the rest of the world. For instance, besides selling and buying goods and services in foreign markets, we need to keep in mind that the U.S. also imports and exports investment capital. Every day, foreigners buy and sell U.S. stocks, bonds, and other types of assets, and Americans are major buyers of similar assets overseas. Moreover, U.S. investors get paid a return (usually in the form of dividends and interest payments) on their investments abroad—income that flows back into this country. By the same token, foreigners get a return from their investment stake in U.S. assets. The quarterly U.S. international transactions report attempts to track all these cross-border movements of physical goods and services, income flows from investments, and the purchases and sales of assets. It might sound complicated, but it really isn't.

Let's take a look at the international transactions release and see how all this information is laid out. The report is divided into two sections. The first deals with the Current Account, which includes the merchandise trade, services, investment income flows, and unilateral transfers. The second part is titled the Capital and Financial Accounts, and it tracks the movement of actual investments and loans into and out of the U.S.

Current Account

The current account balance summarizes the net change in four components: Merchandise Trade, Services, Income Flows, and Unilateral Transfers:

1. *Merchandise Trade Account:* This refers to goods or "visible" trade, such as the export and import of cars, home electronics, bananas, bicycles, and calculators. The trade balance is the net difference between the value of goods Americans sell to other countries (exports) and the goods Americans buy from other countries (imports). Since the mid-1970s, the U.S. has recorded annual deficits by importing far more products than it exported. Indeed, the gap is so large it is the prime reason the U.S. has suffered deficits in the overall current account.

2. *Services Trade Account:* The services account, or "invisible" trade, is the net result of what Americans pay for services sold by foreigners (considered an import) and what foreigners spend on U.S. services (listed as an export). This kind of cross-border business includes insurance, engineering, investment banking, public relations, accounting, and advertising services. Fees from patents, copyrights, and movies also belong to this category. The balance in the services account is the only component of the current account that has consistently shown a surplus, though it is not big enough to offset the gaping shortfall from the merchandise trade account.

3. *Income Account:* A subcategory of the service account is the net income received from investing in foreign assets. When Americans invest in assets outside the U.S., such as in European or Japanese stocks and bonds, the earnings received from those assets are classified as export income because they are earned from investments Americans made abroad. Conversely, payments Americans make to foreigners who invest in U.S. assets are considered an import because they're based on capital shipped here. An income deficit occurs when the investment income paid to foreigners exceeds the income foreigners pay U.S. investors. For most of the post-World War II period, the U.S. maintained a surplus in the income account, but since 2002, it too has slipped into the deficit column.

4. *Unilateral Transfers:* These represent one-way transfers of foreign aid, government grants, pension payments, and worker remittances (which occur when foreigners working in the U.S. send money back to their families in another country). By definition, unilateral transfers show up as a negative in the current account because they always involve money leaving U.S. shores.

The contribution that each component makes in the current account breaks down as follows (based on 2006 data):

Total Exports of Goods, Services, and Investment Income	100%(+)
Exports of Goods	50%
Exports of Services	20%
Income Receipts	30%

Total Imports of Goods and Services and Income Payments	100% (–)
Imports of Goods	65%
Imports of Services	13%
Income Payments	22%

Unilateral Transfers (Net)	100% (–)
U.S. Government Grants	24%
U.S. Government Pensions and Other Transfers	9%
Private Remittances and Other Transfers	67%

Capital and Financial Accounts

As the title suggests, this category is subdivided into the Capital Account and the Financial Account. The capital account is usually small and consists mostly of uncommon flows of certain money. For example, if the U.S. issues a loan to another country and then later decides that the borrower need not repay it (a form of debt forgiveness), the amount is entered as an import on the capital account. Another example of an entry in the capital account is the case of a U.S. resident who emigrates permanently to another country and takes along all his assets. This would be classified as an import as well.

Of far greater importance is the financial account. This table is filled with numbers showing the movement of investment capital and loans into and out of the U.S. Here is where you'll find changes in U.S. ownership of foreign stocks and bonds and in other assets (such as an American firm acquiring an overseas company) during a given period, as well as shifts in foreign ownership of U.S. securities and private assets. Also included in this category are U.S. government agency (like the Federal Reserve) holdings of foreign currencies and securities. It also includes the reverse—what foreign central banks own of U.S. financial assets.

Taken together, the current account and the financial and capital accounts make up America's balance of payments, which represents all economic transactions between the U.S. and the rest of the world.

So how does the U.S. stack up in its trade and financial affairs? Not too well! Americans love to spend and borrow, even if it is beyond their means to do so. Since the 1980s, the U.S. has consistently consumed far more than it produces, which means that Americans increasingly rely on imports to satisfy their enormous appetites. However, to finance all this consumption, the U.S. has to borrow, on average, more than $2 billion every day from other nations. Total U.S. gross debt to foreigners is an astounding $14 trillion. (Net foreign debt, which adjusts for the $11.5 trillion of U.S.-owned foreign assets, was $2.5 trillion.) Can such a buildup in debt continue indefinitely? No. The problem is that no one is sure at what point this massive and still-growing debt will begin to seriously destabilize the U.S. and global economy.

HOW IS IT COMPUTED?

Since the International Transactions account has numerous elements, the Bureau of Economic Analysis (BEA) has to rely on many sources for data. Trade in goods and services comes essentially from the monthly international trade report. Investment earnings are calculated using estimates of holdings, dividend-payout ratios, and interest rates, based on information from corporate reports and the U.S. Treasury. Travel receipts and payments are derived from two places. The BEA gets U.S. and foreign travel data directly from the Mexican and Canadian governments. For travel to Europe, Asia, and elsewhere, the agency relies on surveys taken by passengers while in flight either arriving in or leaving the U.S.

The data in the current account and the capital and financial accounts is seasonally adjusted, but it is not annualized. The data represents quarterly changes in trade and investment flows, or the year-end totals. The current account is not adjusted for inflation.

THE TABLES: CLUES ON WHAT'S AHEAD FOR THE ECONOMY

- **Table 1**   U.S. International Transactions—Current Account

  To get a snapshot of where the U.S. stands in its trade and financial relationship with the rest of the world, go directly to the memoranda section at the very end of Table 1 and review lines 71 to 76. The result is the current account balance for the latest quarter. A negative figure reflects how much the U.S. has to borrow from overseas to help finance the appetite of American consumers, business, and government.

  Can the U.S. afford to sink deeper into debt with the rest of the world? This is no academic question. There has been a vigorous debate in the economics profession about how dangerous the unending stream of current account deficits is to the future health of the U.S. economy. Many are raising alarms that if the red ink continues, sooner or later foreign creditors will decide to lessen their exposure to the U.S.

Table 1. U.S. International Transactions
[Millions of dollars, quarters seasonally adjusted]

(Credits +, debits -)	2002	2002 I	2002 II	2002 III	2002 IV	2003 I	2003 II^r	2003 III^p	Change 2003 II-III
Current account									
1 Exports of goods and services and income receipts	1,229,649	297,074	307,616	313,939	311,015	310,278	311,794	322,014	10,220
2 Exports of goods and services	974,107	236,442	243,696	247,815	246,151	247,377	247,484	254,670	7,186
3 Goods, balance of payments basis	681,874	165,298	171,421	174,315	170,840	173,346	174,247	177,858	3,611
4 Services	292,233	71,144	72,275	73,500	75,311	74,031	73,237	76,812	3,575
5 Transfers under U.S. military agency sales contracts	11,943	2,785	2,751	3,418	2,989	2,827	3,014	3,381	367
6 Travel	66,547	16,295	16,030	16,217	18,005	16,089	14,543	16,569	2,026
7 Passenger fares	17,046	4,224	4,279	4,288	4,255	3,736	3,456	4,059	603
8 Other transportation	29,166	7,102	7,075	7,307	7,682	7,837	7,853	7,789	-64
9 Royalties and license fees	44,142	10,373	11,221	11,389	11,157	11,630	11,944	12,155	211
10 Other private services	122,594	30,170	30,720	30,681	31,022	31,710	32,225	32,656	431
11 U.S. Government miscellaneous services	795	195	199	200	201	202	202	203	1
12 Income receipts	255,542	60,632	63,920	66,124	64,864	62,901	64,310	67,344	3,034
13 Income receipts on U.S.-owned assets abroad	252,379	59,821	63,140	65,339	64,077	62,094	63,496	66,524	3,028
14 Direct investment receipts	142,933	32,058	34,874	37,264	38,735	37,508	39,635	42,400	2,765
15 Other private receipts	106,143	26,950	27,560	27,225	24,408	23,700	22,620	22,882	262
16 U.S. Government receipts	3,303	813	706	850	934	886	1,241	1,242	1
17 Compensation of employees	3,163	811	780	785	787	807	814	820	6
18 Imports of goods and services and income payments	-1,651,657	-387,864	-416,962	-422,666	-424,165	-431,716	-434,248	-440,736	-6,488
19 Imports of goods and services	-1,392,145	-326,499	-348,584	-354,795	-362,267	-369,006	-371,668	-375,987	-4,319
20 Goods, balance of payments basis	-1,164,746	-271,331	-292,707	-297,627	-303,081	-309,364	-312,335	-314,090	-1,755
21 Services	-227,399	-55,168	-55,877	-57,168	-59,186	-59,642	-59,333	-61,897	-2,564
22 Direct defense expenditures	-19,245	-4,394	-4,668	-4,990	-5,193	-5,674	-6,121	-5,900	221
23 Travel	-58,044	-14,453	-14,252	-14,314	-15,025	-14,168	-12,895	-14,464	-1,569
24 Passenger fares	-19,969	-4,874	-4,874	-4,829	-5,392	-4,960	-4,720	-5,335	-615
25 Other transportation	-38,527	-8,891	-9,580	-9,787	-10,271	-10,873	-11,249	-11,282	-33
26 Royalties and license fees	-19,258	-4,728	-4,902	-5,036	-4,592	-4,698	-4,697	-4,874	-177
27 Other private services	-69,436	-17,087	-16,876	-17,487	-17,984	-18,524	-18,902	-19,289	-387
28 U.S. Government miscellaneous services	-2,920	-741	-725	-725	-729	-745	-749	-753	-4
29 Income payments	-259,512	-61,365	-68,378	-67,871	-61,898	-62,710	-62,580	-64,749	-2,169
30 Income payments on foreign-owned assets in the United States	-251,108	-59,271	-66,246	-65,820	-59,771	-60,527	-60,461	-62,705	-2,244
31 Direct investment payments	-49,458	-8,134	-13,464	-15,350	-12,510	-15,431	-17,426	-18,419	-993
32 Other private payments	-127,735	-32,512	-33,773	-31,802	-29,648	-28,245	-26,769	-27,960	-1,191
33 U.S. Government payments	-73,915	-18,625	-19,009	-18,668	-17,613	-16,851	-16,266	-16,326	-60
34 Compensation of employees	-8,404	-2,094	-2,132	-2,051	-2,127	-2,183	-2,119	-2,044	75
35 Unilateral current transfers, net	-58,853	-15,938	-13,481	-13,997	-15,436	-17,269	-16,940	-16,319	621
36 U.S. Government grants	-17,097	-6,397	-3,287	-3,075	-4,338	-5,813	-5,654	-5,309	345
37 U.S. Government pensions and other transfers	-5,125	-1,271	-1,279	-1,282	-1,292	-1,320	-1,335	-1,328	7
38 Private remittances and other transfers	-36,631	-8,270	-8,915	-9,640	-9,806	-10,136	-9,951	-9,682	269

economy and its stock and bond markets. The consequences of such a step could be disastrous. The dollar could dramatically weaken, and both inflation and interest rates will be driven higher.

Others argue that while these deficits cannot go on indefinitely, the U.S. economy is not in any imminent danger. If the U.S. imports a lot more, it just reflects how much stronger and healthier the American economy is compared with other countries. In addition, the U.S. is perceived as a stable and attractive place to invest because of its liquidity, credit-worthiness, and robust productivity growth—all of which mean that foreign lenders are not about to abandon the U.S. anytime soon. Finally, some will argue there is no direct link between a country's current account balance and its economic health. Just look at Japan: It had current account surpluses in the 1990s, yet its economy was stuck in a virtual depression throughout that decade.

Who's right here? That's a tough question to answer because economic theory provides little guidance on the consequences of long-term current account deficits. Practically speaking, current account deficits cannot be sustained because foreign investors will, at some point, conclude that their loan portfolios have far too many assets in dollars. In the interest of prudence, these investors could decide to shun U.S. financial assets and diversify into other currencies. Precisely when this shift will take place and by what magnitude are unknown. However, the prospect of a significant reversal in sentiment against the dollar is unsettling enough. To keep foreign investors interested in the U.S. and increase their holdings of dollar-denominated securities and loans, interest rates in this country would have to rise high enough to reward foreign creditors for the extra risk they face for carrying all those dollars. Of course, the downside of that scenario is that high interest rates can also derail economic growth in the U.S.

A couple of key components in the current account are worth noting because of their impact on certain U.S. business sectors:

- *Travel:* Money spent by foreign tourists in the U.S. is considered an export item, and expenditures by Americans in other countries are classified as an import. (Think of this in terms of who gets the revenues from tourism.) Since the U.S. is a popular tourist destination for people from all over the world, this country has traditionally had a surplus in the travel account. Compare lines 6 (travel by foreigners to the U.S.) and 23 (travel by Americans to other countries), and you can see whether foreign tourists have spent more in the U.S. than American travelers did in other countries, and by how much. The results have business implications for the lodging and transportation sectors.

- *Income Receipts and Payments:* Two main categories are listed here. Line 13 (Income receipts on U.S.-owned assets abroad) shows how much income Americans received from their international investments, such as interest income and dividends, as well as returns from other types of assets owned in other countries. Line 30 (Income payments on foreign-owned assets in the U.S.) represents what the U.S. paid to foreigners for their investments in this country.

• **Table 1**   U.S. International Transactions—Capital and Financial Accounts

Table 1. U.S. International Transactions
[Millions of dollars, quarters seasonally adjusted]

(Credits +, debits -)	2002	2002 I	2002 II	2002 III	2002 IV	2003 I	2003 II[r]	2003 III[p]	Change 2003 II-III
Capital and financial account									
Capital account									
39 Capital account transactions, net	-1,285	-277	-286	-364	-358	-388	-1,553	-795	758
Financial account									
40 U.S.-owned assets abroad, net (increase/financial outflow (-))	-178,985	-35,227	-128,567	29,712	-44,902	-101,331	-112,818	-4,891	107,927
41 U.S. official reserve assets, net	-3,681	390	-1,843	-1,416	-812	83	-170	-611	-441
42 Gold									
43 Special drawing rights	-475	-109	-107	-132	-127	897	-102	-97	5
44 Reserve position in the International Monetary Fund	-2,632	652	-1,607	-1,136	-541	-644	86	-383	-469
45 Foreign currencies	-574	-153	-129	-148	-144	-170	-154	-131	23
46 U.S. Government assets, other than official reserve assets, net	-32	133	42	-27	-180	-70	427	530	103
47 U.S. credits and other long-term assets	-5,611	-853	-565	-1,375	-2,818	-2,578	-1,454	-1,515	-61
48 Repayments on U.S. credits and other long-term assets	5,684	994	566	1,452	2,672	2,472	1,955	2,027	72
49 U.S. foreign currency holdings and U.S. short-term assets, net	-105	-8	41	-104	-34	36	-74	18	92
50 U.S. private assets, net	-175,272	-35,750	-126,766	31,155	-43,910	-101,344	-113,075	-4,810	108,265
51 Direct investment	-137,836	-39,083	-35,459	-31,623	-31,670	-34,405	-29,863	-37,525	-7,662
52 Foreign securities	15,801	5,367	-5,843	21,641	-5,364	-27,146	8,654	-28,826	-37,480
53 U.S. claims on unaffiliated foreigners reported by U.S. nonbanking concerns	-31,880	-1,886	-16,210	-11,862	-1,922	-11,998	-19,101	22,206	41,307
54 U.S. claims reported by U.S. banks, not included elsewhere	-21,357	-148	-69,254	52,999	-4,954	-27,795	-72,765	39,335	112,100
55 Foreign-owned assets in the United States, net (increase/financial inflow (+))	706,983	146,813	221,242	141,478	197,448	242,004	262,819	128,200	-134,619
56 Foreign official assets in the United States, net	94,860	6,106	47,552	8,992	32,210	40,978	57,000	43,895	-13,105
57 U.S. Government securities	73,521	6,257	21,706	12,300	33,258	31,768	38,639	19,611	-19,028
58 U.S. Treasury securities	43,144	-1,039	15,138	1,415	27,630	22,288	35,349	16,271	-19,078
59 Other	30,377	7,296	6,568	10,885	5,628	9,480	3,290	3,340	50
60 Other U.S. Government liabilities	137	-597	365	464	-95	-437	-16	-41	-25
61 U.S. liabilities reported by U.S. banks, not included elsewhere	17,594	-280	24,575	-4,607	-2,094	8,321	17,628	22,879	5,251
62 Other foreign official assets	3,608	726	906	835	1,141	1,326	749	1,446	697
63 Other foreign assets in the United States, net	612,123	140,707	173,690	132,486	165,238	201,026	205,819	84,305	-121,514
64 Direct investment	39,633	10,607	-456	14,199	15,281	34,386	22,391	8,139	-14,252
65 U.S. Treasury securities	96,217	11,789	14,218	57,505	12,705	14,568	55,037	49,868	-5,169
66 U.S. securities other than U.S. Treasury securities	291,492	74,461	104,187	45,880	66,964	55,574	55,964	9,626	-76,338
67 U.S. currency	21,513	4,525	7,183	2,556	7,249	4,927	1,458	2,768	1,310
68 U.S. liabilities to unaffiliated foreigners reported by U.S. nonbanking concerns	72,142	46,771	24,610	-8,102	8,863	74,848	4,147	6,772	2,625
69 U.S. liabilities reported by U.S. banks, not included elsewhere	91,126	-7,446	23,948	20,448	54,176	16,723	36,822	7,132	-29,690
70 Statistical discrepancy (sum of above items with sign reversed)	-45,852	-4,581	30,438	-48,102	-23,602	-1,578	-9,054	12,527	21,581
Memoranda:									
71 Balance on goods (lines 3 and 20)	-482,872	-106,033	-121,286	-123,312	-132,241	-136,018	-138,088	-136,232	1,856
72 Balance on services (lines 4 and 21)	64,834	15,976	16,398	16,332	16,125	14,389	13,904	14,915	1,011
73 Balance on goods and services (lines 2 and 19)	-418,038	-90,057	-104,888	-106,980	-116,116	-121,629	-124,184	-121,317	2,867
74 Balance on income (lines 12 and 29)	-3,970	-733	-4,458	-1,747	2,966	191	1,730	2,595	865
75 Unilateral current transfers, net (line 35)	-58,853	-15,938	-13,481	-13,997	-15,436	-17,269	-16,940	-16,319	621
76 Balance on current account (lines 1, 18, and 35 or lines 73, 74, and 75)	-480,861	-106,728	-122,827	-122,724	-128,586	-138,707	-139,394	-135,041	4,353

[r] Revised.   [p] Preliminary.

NOTE: Details may not add to totals because of rounding.   Source: U. S. Bureau of Economic Analysis

- Line 40. *Net U.S.-owned assets abroad:* Americans frequently buy and sell assets in other countries. This line shows the change in the amount of foreign assets held by the U.S. government and private Americans.

- Line 50. *Net U.S. private assets:* Here you'll find the net change in the private ownership of assets outside the U.S. This is further segmented into two groups: direct investments (as in buying a foreign company or factory) and foreign securities, on lines 51 and 52, respectively.

- Line 55. *Net foreign-owned assets in the United States:* This is the foreign side of the transaction—specifically, the total change in foreign ownership of U.S. assets. It combines both private and government holdings.

- Line 63. *Other net foreign assets in the United States:* A subset of line 55, this looks at the change in private foreign sector holdings of U.S. assets. This is further divided into direct investments (line 64), U.S. Treasuries (line 65), and other securities (line 66).

MARKET IMPACT

Bonds

There is little tradable value in the international transaction report. It is a quarterly indicator with a headline that carries few surprises for the fixed income market because other, more timely monthly measures, such as international trade, have already told much of the story. Nor does the current account balance stand out as some sort of leading indicator. This report, however, does get a lot of attention from economists and policymakers in Washington because of concerns that mounting current accounts deficits could at some point jeopardize U.S. economic growth.

Stocks

This release has virtually no impact on equity prices.

Dollar

Traders in the foreign exchange markets look over the report. A deterioration in the U.S. current account balance will over time erode the value of the dollar. However, no one knows with any certainty when these burgeoning deficits will tip the greenback over the cliff. Conversely, if America's trade balance reverses course and begins to move closer to surplus, it would be considered highly bullish for the U.S. currency, though much depends on what's behind this improvement. If it's the result of a deep recession in the U.S., with import demand plummeting, foreigners will likely shy away from the dollar. If current account deficits were to narrow as a result of greater international demand for U.S. goods and services, the dollar should appreciate in value in the currency markets.

TREASURY INTERNATIONAL CAPITAL (TIC) SYSTEM

Market Sensitivity: Medium.

What Is It: A report that tracks flows of investment funds entering and leaving the U.S.

News Release on the Internet: *www.treas.gov/press/international.html* (seek out "TIC Data" around mid-month)

Home Web Address: *www.treas.gov*

Release Time: 9 a.m. (ET); published near the 15th of the month and reports on cross-border capital flows that took place a month and a half earlier. (Efforts are under way to accelerate the release of this report.)

Frequency: Monthly.

Source: U.S. Department of Treasury.

Revisions: Data is subject to revisions.

WHY IS IT IMPORTANT?

It's no secret that Americans love to shop—so much so that they routinely spend more than what is in their paychecks. Nor should it be a surprise to anyone these days that the federal government regularly pays out far more than the revenues it collects from tax receipts. After all, that's why the U.S. suffers annual budget deficits. To make up for this gap between expenditures and income, both households and the federal government have to borrow. But borrow from whom? In order to borrow funds, someone else first has to save. The savings generated by one party become the funds that are available to finance spending and investment by another. Such savings also drive the stock and bond markets and give American banks the resources to lend money to their customers. However, if American households and the federal government aren't savers, who is?

To be fair, American workers actually do contribute some savings. For instance, retirement accounts, like 401k plans and similar corporate pension plans, are a form of forced savings, since many employers automatically deduct certain amounts from worker paychecks at the outset. Another source of savings in the economy are American corporations, especially when profits are strong. Companies rarely spend all their earnings, so what's left is either set aside in corporate bank accounts, returned to shareholders in the form of higher dividends or stock buybacks, or invested in the financial markets. So, yes, some savings are generated in the U.S. The problem is that the amount of national savings accumulated domestically is *nowhere* near enough to fill the gap between national spending and income in this country.

The pitifully small and inadequate savings in the U.S. stands in stark contrast to other nations that find themselves flush with excess savings because households in those countries do not have the same propensity to spend as U.S. consumers. (Workers in Europe, Japan, and China are known to save from 5% to 40% of their income.) What's more, the budget deficits of many foreign governments are more moderate, with some even managing to show surpluses.

Given the important role the U.S. plays in the world economy, foreign creditors have for years been very willing to hand over some of their excess savings to this country. By purchasing U.S. stocks, bonds, and other dollar assets, foreigners provide the U.S. with the capital it needs to keep domestic interest rates low and for economic growth to continue. An expanding American economy, in turn, means U.S. consumers will continue to buy more goods and services from other countries. So it appears everyone benefits from this arrangement.

Unfortunately, there is a serious downside to this relationship. America's reliance on foreign borrowing has turned into an addiction. In just the last 10 years, U.S. net foreign debt has ballooned from $50 billion to $2.5 trillion. Indeed, the U.S. now (2007) borrows from foreign creditors an average of $1.7 million *every minute* of the day, every day of the year!

Can the pace of such borrowing continue indefinitely? Absolutely not. There will come a time when foreign creditors will find their portfolios to be so heavily exposed toward one currency—the dollar—that they will begin to scale back on new investments in the U.S. At the start of 2007, foreigners already owned 45% of the U.S. Treasury market, more than 40% of the U.S. corporate bonds, 40% of the government agency bonds, and nearly 20% of the U.S. stock market. At some point foreign investors may choose to reduce their exposure to dollars by diversifying into other currencies. For Americans who are hooked on money flows from abroad, such a trend can have disastrous consequences. If the supply of foreign funds entering the U.S. diminishes, capital becomes more scarce, and that will drive up interest rates. Higher interest rates can dull economic activity in the U.S. and conceivably even bring on a recession.

How close is the U.S. to reaching the end of its credit line with foreigners? Are international creditors growing reluctant to keep underwriting America's profligacy?

If foreign investors begin to back away from purchasing dollar assets, the signs will show up in the monthly Treasury International Capital (TIC) report. It measures net capital flows crossing U.S. borders—that is, how much capital comes into the U.S. from other countries and, on the other side of the ledger, how much capital leaves the U.S. for other countries. The difference between the two reflects our current account balance (see the earlier section "Current Account"), which has been in deficit every year but one since 1982. The annual current account deficit recently climbed to 7% of this country's GDP, which means Americans are consuming 7% more than what the U.S. produces. Foreigners have (so far) picked up the tab to cover this red ink by taking the excess dollars they receive and reinvesting them back into the U.S.

HOW IS IT COMPUTED?

The TIC reporting system can be traced back to 1934, when the government sought out information on cross-border flows of capital. To get the data, the government asks financial institutions (such as banks, brokerage firms, broker/dealers, nonbank organizations, and mutual fund firms) as well as nonfinancial firms (including exporters, importers, industrial firms, insurance companies, and pension funds) to fill out specific forms that inquire about cross-border transactions involving stocks, treasury securities, corporate bonds, government agency type bonds, deposits, and loans.

While TIC data is the property of the Treasury, it is actually the Federal Reserve that has responsibility for collecting and verifying the information. And it's no easy task. The combined data take weeks to receive and confirm, and the investment transactions are also broken down by country and market value. The figures are eventually given to the Treasury, which then publishes the TIC report with a 45-day lag each month.

- The main press release on the monthly TIC report can be found here: *www.treas.gov/press/international.html* (seek out "TIC Data")

- To find the major foreign owners of U.S. securities, go to: *www.treas.gov/tic/mfh.txt*

- To view a detailed breakdown of ownership of U.S. securities by country, visit: *www.treas.gov/tic/country-longterm.html*

THE TABLES: CLUES ON WHAT'S AHEAD FOR THE ECONOMY

Before we sift for clues on what the TIC table says about the future course of the economy, it is first necessary to grow familiar with the report itself.

Though the TIC report looks quite daunting at first sight, it is well organized and easy to read and interpret. Two key points must be understood at the outset when examining this table. *It is written from the perspective of what foreign investors are doing in the U.S.* Are they buying or selling securities? The other important consideration is to know which direction capital ultimately flows. Does the transaction result in money entering or leaving the U.S.? When foreign investors buy a U.S. security, money flows into the U.S. When they sell securities here, money generally flows out of the U.S.

Let's break down the report using the numerical headings on the left.

- TIC Monthly Reports on Cross-Border Financial Flows

1.   Gross Purchases of Domestic U.S. Securities: This is the gross amount of U.S. securities foreign investors bought during the period. Since this results in money flowing into this country, it is given a positive (+) value.

2.   Gross Sales of Domestic U.S. Securities: The gross amount of U.S. securities foreign investors sold in the period. Such sales result in money leaving the U.S. and thus are presented as a negative (–) number.

TIC Monthly Reports on Cross-Border Financial Flows

(Billions of dollars, not seasonally adjusted)

		2004	2005	2006	Sep-06	Oct-06	Nov-06	Dec-06
	Foreigners' Acquisitions of Long-term Securities							
1	Gross Purchases of Domestic U.S. Securities	15178.9	17157.5	21100.8	1750.4	1875.2	1928.1	1850.4
2	Gross Sales of Domestic U.S. Securities	14262.4	16145.9	19958.7	1649.9	1766.6	1805.9	1787.4
3	**Domestic Securities Purchased, net** (line 1 less line 2) /1	**916.5**	**1011.5**	**1142.1**	**100.5**	**108.6**	**122.2**	**63.0**
4	**Private, net /2**	**680.9**	**891.1**	**956.5**	**83.7**	**83.3**	**115.7**	**39.0**
5	Treasury Bonds & Notes, net	150.9	269.4	136.0	-6.1	6.2	33.1	4.5
6	Gov't Agency Bonds, net	205.7	187.6	202.0	17.3	10.9	11.8	12.5
7	Corporate Bonds, net	298.0	353.1	474.4	57.1	38.8	61.8	33.1
8	Equities, net	26.2	81.0	144.1	15.3	27.4	9.1	-11.1
9	**Official, net /3**	**235.6**	**120.4**	**185.6**	**16.7**	**25.3**	**6.5**	**24.0**
10	Treasury Bonds & Notes, net	201.1	68.7	62.5	7.7	18.5	1.0	6.1
11	Gov't Agency Bonds, net	20.8	31.6	88.8	7.9	5.3	4.0	15.5
12	Corporate Bonds, net	11.5	19.1	28.5	1.8	2.0	3.6	2.9
13	Equities, net	2.2	1.0	5.8	-0.7	-0.4	-2.1	-0.5
14	Gross Purchases of Foreign Securities from U.S. Residents	3123.1	3700.0	5568.4	427.1	509.2	533.5	521.3
15	Gross Sales of Foreign Securities to U.S. Residents	3276.0	3872.4	5814.5	449.9	524.2	570.9	568.7
16	**Foreign Securities Purchased, net** (line 14 less line 15) /4	**-152.8**	**-172.4**	**-246.0**	**-22.8**	**-15.0**	**-37.4**	**-47.4**
17	Foreign Bonds Purchased, net	-67.9	-45.1	-139.7	-13.6	-6.7	-17.6	-28.5
18	Foreign Equities Purchased, net	-85.0	-127.3	-106.3	-9.2	-8.4	-19.8	-18.9
19	**Net Long-Term Securities Transactions** (line 3 plus line 16):	**763.6**	**839.1**	**896.1**	**77.7**	**93.5**	**84.9**	**15.6**
20	**Other Acquisitions of Long-term Securities, net /5**	**-38.8**	**-140.0**	**-165.7**	**-11.9**	**-10.4**	**-32.6**	**-13.1**
21	**Net Foreign Acquisition of Long-Term Securities** (lines 19 and 20):	**724.8**	**699.1**	**730.4**	**65.7**	**83.1**	**52.2**	**2.5**
22	**Increase in Foreign Holdings of Dollar-denominated Short-term U.S. Securities and Other Custody Liabilities: /6**	**190.1**	**-47.6**	**125.7**	**-10.3**	**0.6**	**17.0**	**6.5**
23	**U.S. Treasury Bills**	**60.0**	**-58.9**	**-9.0**	**-14.5**	**4.1**	**9.5**	**-4.9**
24	Private, net	26.8	-15.6	16.0	-3.9	5.0	1.8	4.4
25	Official, net	33.2	-43.3	-25.0	-10.6	-0.9	7.7	-9.3
26	**Other Negotiable Instruments and Selected Other Liabilities: /7**	**130.1**	**11.4**	**134.7**	**4.1**	**-3.4**	**7.5**	**11.5**
27	Private, net	77.4	10.6	154.5	5.9	7.4	9.3	4.7
28	Official, net	52.8	0.8	-19.8	-1.7	-10.8	-1.8	6.7
29	**Change in Banks' Own Net Dollar-Denominated Liabilities**	**63.9**	**16.4**	**-28.2**	**13.6**	**-7.5**	**1.2**	**-20.0**
30	**Monthly Net TIC Flows** (lines 21,22,29) /8	**978.9**	**667.9**	**827.9**	**69.1**	**76.3**	**70.5**	**-11.0**
	of which							
31	Private, net	637.2	580.6	699.3	57.1	83.2	61.1	-42.5
32	Official, net	341.6	87.3	128.7	11.9	-6.9	9.4	31.5

3.   Domestic Securities Purchased, net: It's the difference between lines 1 and 2. A positive number indicates that foreigners have purchased more domestic U.S. securities than they sold.

There are two types of foreign buyers. One is the private investor, such as individuals, professional traders, and foreign brokerage firms. The other represents "official" transactions, by which we mostly mean foreign central banks.

4.   Private, net: Listings 5 through 8 tell the net amount that private foreign investors bought of (5) Treasury notes and bonds, (6) Government agency bonds, (7) Corporate bonds, and (8) Equities. Line 4 aggregates this category.

5.   Official, net: Lines 10 through 13 indicate the net purchase by foreign central banks of the same four asset classes described above.

Up to now, we have discussed foreign transactions involving domestic U.S. securities. The next three lines refer to foreign investors buying or selling foreign securities in the U.S.

14.   Gross Purchases of Foreign Securities from U.S. Residents: When foreigners buy "foreign" securities in the U.S., it results in money flowing into the U.S. Here's an example: If a U.S. brokerage firm sells Mexican government bonds to a foreign investor, the proceeds flow to the U.S.

15.   Gross Sales of Foreign Securities to U.S. Residents: Now let's reverse the example above. Suppose a foreign investment firm sells Mexican bonds to Americans. This leads to an outflow of dollars and thus a debit on the TIC balance sheet.

16.   Foreign Securities Purchased, net: The difference between lines 14 and 15.

17.   Foreign Bonds Purchased, net   ⌐⎯⎯⎯⎯⎯⎯   These two lines differentiate

18.   Foreign Equities Purchased, net   ⎯⎯⎯⎯⎯⎯⎯⌐→   the asset classes in line 16.

19.   Net Long-Term Securities Transactions: Now we come to one of the important subtotals in the TIC report. It reflects net capital flows into the U.S. based on foreign purchases and sales of long-term securities in this country. This figure is the sum of lines 3 and 16. Long-term in the TIC report is defined as securities with an original maturity of more than one year. Equities are also considered long-term investments.

Why so much focus on long-term securities? Capital flows of long-term securities are considered a more accurate gauge of foreign confidence in the U.S. economy. These flows help finance the U.S. current account deficits. In contrast, transactions of short-maturity securities (like Treasury bills) often consist of "hot money," where investors buy and sell the same security in a matter of days or even minutes. Such volatile trading, while providing important liquidity to the global investment community, is less meaningful in conveying how foreign investors view the overall strength and durability of the U.S. economy.

20.   Other Acquisitions of Long-Term Securities: These involve essentially "non-market" transactions, usually between private parties. This includes stock swaps, trades in asset-back securities, and changes in holdings of nonmarketable Treasury bonds and notes. Again, a negative figure here signifies a net outflow of money from the U.S.

21.   Net Foreign Acquisition of Long-Term Securities: Now we simply add lines 19 and 20 to get the aggregate net foreign purchases of long-term securities in the U.S.

22.   Increase in Foreign Holdings of Dollar-Denominated Short-Term U.S. Securities and Other Custody Liabilities: Up until now, the TIC report has dealt with U.S. cross-border transactions of long-term securities—that is, securities with an original maturity of more than a year. This line, however, reports on monthly flows of "short-term" capital, such as Treasury bills, commercial paper, bankers' acceptances, short-maturity government agency instruments, and short-term corporate bonds.

23.   U.S. Treasury Bills: Of the amount in line 22, the figure here singles out net purchases of Treasury bills, followed by those who carried out the transactions: private investors (line 24) and central banks (line 25).

26.   Other Negotiable Instruments and Selected Other Liabilities: This is simply the residual of line 22 less line 23, and their two primary sources: private investors (line 27) and central banks (line 28).

29.   Change in Banks' Own Net Dollar-Denominated Liabilities: This aggregates the net flow of money being deposited in U.S. bank accounts by foreigners, their purchase of bank CDs, and money that American banks have borrowed from foreign institutions—versus claims that American banks have on deposits in other countries and loans to foreigners. By the way, aside from commercial banks, this line includes other types of depository institutions, such as savings-and-loans associations and credit unions, financial holding companies, and securities brokers and dealers.

30.   Monthly Net TIC Flows: Now we get to the net grand total of all monthly capital flows—short- and long-term—into the U.S. This is the sum of lines 21, 22, and 29. It's important to realize that this entire report deals only with cross-border movement in "portfolio investments and cash deposits." It does not include foreign direct investment from abroad, by which we mean capital entering the U.S. for the purpose of purchasing another company (a merger or acquisition) or the construction of new facilities.

31.   Total net flows from foreign private investors

32.   Total net flows from foreign central banks

OK, so what do we do with all this information? The TIC report offers some fresh insights into how foreign investors view the U.S. economy and financial markets. Since we depend so much on capital flows from other nations to fuel economic activity in this country, any evidence that foreign interest in the U.S. is waning could spell big trouble for the American economy.

Line 19: Net Long-Term Securities Transactions

Let's begin with the most critical issue. If the U.S. is consuming more than it produces, it means this country has to rely on foreign suppliers to satisfy America's excess demand. This gap between consumption and production makes up the current account deficit, and the shortfall has to be financed by foreign creditors if the U.S. economy is to continue growing.

Are foreign investors blithely willing to finance this deficit? That appears to be the case of the last few years. The current account deficits in 2004 and 2005 came to $665 billion and $792, respectively. (See the earlier section "Current Account" for how to get these numbers.) The TIC release shown here suggests that foreigners have been more than willing to cover that debt. In line 19, we see net foreign capital inflows of $763 billion and $838 billion those years on long-term U.S. securities. These numbers show that the U.S. has been able to entice more than enough capital from around the world. All that extra liquidity has kept U.S. interest rates low those years and has even led to rallies in the real estate and stock markets.

But are foreign investors becoming weary of financing the U.S. current account deficit year after year? Clearly there will come a time when their portfolios will appear top-heavy with dollar-based securities, and that could prompt foreign investors to rebalance their risks and diversify into non-U.S. assets. Or perhaps they may simply find more lucrative returns in markets outside the U.S. and decide to exchange their dollar holdings for other, more profitable investments. Whatever the reason, any recent retrenchment from U.S. investments by foreigners will show up in the far-right monthly column of the TIC release. As you can see from the table, net domestic securities purchased in August and September were $114.4 billion and $65.1 billion, respectively. How does that stack up with the U.S. current account deficit those months? Since the current account comes out only quarterly, we will instead use the monthly U.S. trade deficits. The trade imbalance (see the section on International Trade) jumped to $64 billion and $69 billion those two months. So, again, it doesn't appear that foreign investors are turning away from the U.S.

However, the picture looks less benign when viewed from a different perspective. If you examine the ratio of capital flows to the trade deficit, a disturbing trend emerges. The rate at which capital flows are covering the trade deficit has steadily been slipping. For instance, the total U.S. trade deficit in 2004 came to $611 billion, while capital inflows (according to line 19 of the TIC report) amounted to $763.6 billion. Thus, the ratio of cross-border investment flows to the U.S. trade deficit was 1.25 that year. In 2005, this ratio fell to 1.17. When you look at capital inflows during the latest 12-month period (see $874.5 billion in the center column) and match it to the trade shortfall for the same 12-month period (from the International Trade report), the ratio fell further, to 1.12. A disturbing trend appears to be under way that suggests the dollar might come under increasing pressure in the months ahead.

Line 4: Private, Net and Line 9: Official, Net

When looking at total net purchases of securities in the U.S., it's important to discern who the buyers are. Are foreign central banks or foreign private investors conducting most of the transactions? If a large majority of purchasers are foreign private investors, it's a sign of broad confidence in the dollar and in the future course of the U.S. economy. After all, private investors are motivated by profits. They want to be assured of making a real return on their investments in the U.S. If foreign investors become dissatisfied with their returns, they will be less inclined to buy additional U.S. stocks and bonds. Should overseas demand for dollar assets taper off, the greenback's value will fall. That could potentially destabilize world trade and become a hot international political issue. Remember, a weakened dollar may be good for U.S. exporters (and for producers in countries whose own currencies are linked to the dollar) because it lowers the price of their products in foreign markets. However, foreign firms in Europe, Japan, and several emerging countries may yell and scream at this turn of events. A cheaper dollar automatically kicks up the value of the euro, the yen, and a host of other floating currencies, and that will hurt exporters in those countries. It would mean fewer sales abroad, higher domestic unemployment, and weaker economies.

To prevent that from happening, foreign central banks often jump in and accelerate purchases of U.S. securities to keep their local currency from appreciating too much or too rapidly. Thus, when looking at the TIC report, compare the ratio of purchases from private investors (line 4) versus official institutions (line 9). Generally speaking, if net private purchases make up more than 75% of the total in line 3 (net domestic securities purchased by foreigners), this should be viewed as a positive for the U.S. economy. It's a sign that private capital inflows are strong and that interest rates will remain low. On the flip side, if private investors begin to shun the U.S. market and force foreign central banks to pick up the slack, it can foreshadow tough times for the U.S. Remember, foreign central banks may be able to impact currency values in the near term, but they do not have the resources of foreign private investors in the long run. If the global community of private investors is fundamentally shifting away from dollars, foreign central banks can only temporarily stave off a sharp decline in the U.S. currency.

MARKET IMPACT

Bonds

Traders in the bond market prefer to see monthly foreign capital inflows exceed the funding needs of the U.S. trade deficit. If not enough dollars were coming into this country to match our external deficits, the consequences could be a depreciation in the dollar, which can heighten inflation pressures. Such results will hurt bond prices and raise interest rates over time.

Stocks

Investors in the equity market may initially respond favorably to a weakened dollar, because it can boost the earnings of U.S. exporters and American companies with foreign subsidiaries. But a precipitous fall in net foreign private inflows can greatly unnerve these traders too. Without those capital flows, liquidity could dry up in the U.S. and lift interest rates to levels that could threaten economic activity. Moreover, the large majority of foreign buyers of U.S. stocks are private investors, not central banks. So if the TIC reports point to a drop-off in foreign investor interest in the U.S., common stocks in this country could face significant pressure.

Dollar

Large currency traders monitor the TIC reports closely because they have to react fairly quickly to a change in sentiment toward dollar-denominated assets. Of particular interest should be the change in the contribution to net capital inflows between official sources and private investors. Investors in the foreign exchange market should use caution if there is an excessive amount of foreign central bank intervention to support the dollar. Official efforts to bolster the dollar cannot be sustained if private investors are fundamentally bearish on the greenback. Traders will also zero in on the ratio between net capital inflows and trade deficits. A jump in the ratio, where dollars entering the U.S. is rising faster than the trade deficit, has been correlated with an increase in the value of the dollar. In contrast, a declining ratio portends trouble for U.S. currency and raises concerns about the future cost of capital in the U.S. and the economy's welfare.

CONSUMER PRICE INDEX (CPI)

Market Sensitivity: Very high.

What Is It: The most popular measure of price inflation in retail goods and
services.

News Release on the Internet: *www.bls.gov/cpi/*

Home Web Address: *www.bls.gov/*

Release Time: 8:30 a.m. (ET); released the second or third week following the
month being covered.

Frequency: Monthly.

Source: Bureau of Labor Statistics, Department of Labor.

Revisions: No monthly revisions. Only annual changes are introduced in
February with the release of the January CPI data. Revisions can go back five
years.

WHY IS IT IMPORTANT?

Along with the employment report, the Consumer Price Index (CPI) is another one of
those red-hot economic indicators that is carefully dissected by the financial markets. It's
fairly obvious why it gets so much attention. Inflation touches everyone. It determines
how much consumers pay for goods and services, affects the cost of doing business,
causes havoc with personal and corporate investments, and influences the quality of life
for retirees. Moreover, the outlook for inflation helps set labor contracts and government
fiscal policy.

Changes in the CPI also alter the benefits of 50 million Social Security recipients and
25 million people on food stamps. Landlords take inflation forecasts into account to lock
in future hikes in rental contracts. Judges even refer to the CPI to compute alimony and
child support payments. In short, the effects of inflation are ubiquitous. No one can
escape its reach.

Where it gets a little tricky is how to measure inflation. No less than half a dozen
economic indicators purport to gauge changes in prices. They include the personal consumption expenditures price index, producer prices, import prices, employment cost
index, unit labor costs, and GDP deflator. Each has its strengths and weaknesses. For
example, the GDP inflation indices cover a much broader range of items than the CPI, but
the former is released only quarterly, whereas the CPI is published monthly. And while
the producer price index is a monthly inflation measure, it reflects price changes mostly
at the wholesale business level and does not include the cost of most services. In contrast,
more than half of the CPI consists of services, which is the fastest-growing part of the
economy. This makes the CPI more relevant to consumers and workers.

What exactly is the CPI? In essence, it seeks to gauge the cost of living. But right away we run into a problem. The "cost of living" is just a theoretical concept because Americans do not all pursue the same lifestyle. Thus, the best the CPI can do is measure the average change in retail prices over time for a basket consisting of more than 200 categories of assorted goods and services. These categories are then divided into eight major groups. Each group is given a weight that represents its importance in the CPI calculation. The weights are determined by surveying thousands of families and individuals about what they actually bought in 2003 and 2004. Every two years, these weights get revised to adjust for people's changing tastes and priorities. The products in the CPI basket are eventually organized into eight major groups:

Group	Weight in the CPI
1. Housing	**42.4%**
Shelter 32.3%	
Fuel and utilities 5.4%	
Household furnishings and operations 4.7%	
2. Food and Beverages	**15.0%**
3. Transportation	**17.4%**
Private transportation 16.3%	
New vehicles 5.2%	
Motor fuel 4.2%	
Maintenance and repairs 1.1%	
Used cars and trucks 1.8%	
Public transportation 1.1%	
4. Medical Care	**6.2%**
5. Apparel	**3.8%**
6. Recreation	**5.6%**
7. Education and Communication	**6.0%**
8. Other Goods and Services	**3.5%**
Tobacco and smoking products 0.7%	

As you can see from the list, the biggest single component in the CPI is housing, with a 42% share (or weight). Transportation costs make up more than 17% of the index, and medical care just above 6%. When all the figures are compiled, the BLS puts out a CPI index number that represents the change in the total cost of these items during the latest month. The advantage of using an index number as opposed to a dollar figure is that it enables you to get a historical perspective of how inflation has performed over different time frames. Currently, the index base can be traced back to the years 1982–1984, where the average price in the basket has been assigned a value of 100. Thus, if the CPI index stood at 200 at the end of the year and increased in the first six months of the following year to 202, inflation rose 1% in the first half of the year. Or, if you annualize it, prices jumped at a 2% rate.

How does inflation get started in the first place, and is it really all that bad for the economy? There are two popular explanations for what causes inflation. One is based on the Monetarist view that excessive growth in the money supply is the culprit behind sharply rising prices. If the supply of money increases at a faster rate than the output of goods and services, you have a problem because ultimately it will mean that too much money will be chasing too few products. The result is that prices for these scarce but popular items are bid up and—voila!—you have inflation.

The second explanation puts less emphasis on the money supply and more on the overall demand for goods and services. This is the Keynesian view, known for its chief proponent, John Maynard Keynes. It argues that when overall demand (from consumers, businesses, the government, and foreign buyers who want American products) greatly exceeds the economy's ability to satisfy it, the resulting shortage in supply can drive up the price of goods and services and cause inflation to accelerate. How fast inflation increases depends on where the economy stands in the business cycle—or, more specifically, on how much production slack is left in the economy. A powerful pickup in the demand for goods and services immediately following a recession is not inflationary because there will likely be ample supplies and idle capacity to tap. It is only later in the cycle, when material and labor resources become increasingly scarce, that continued strong demand can fire up inflation pressures.

Equally interesting is the question of whether inflation is a bad thing. After all, higher prices allow companies to generate more revenues, which can boost stock prices and enrich investors large and small. Federal and state governments count on inflation to generate more tax revenues, which go to help balance the federal budget or finance new government spending programs. Large borrowers don't mind inflation because they can repay their loans with cheaper dollars.

So what's so awful about inflation? Plenty. Inflation creates a climate of instability and uncertainty and invites distortions in the economy. Sure, firms would love to see their revenues increase, but they prefer to accomplish this by selling more products, rather than by simply raising prices. Furthermore, companies can suffer like anyone else from inflation, especially if their own suppliers decide to bump up prices. Company employees also demand higher pay to offset the increased cost of living due to inflation. In addition, while Congress might quietly admit that inflation brings in more tax revenues, elected officials also know that rising inflation can anger voters who see their purchasing power eroding. That can cause them to take out their frustrations on Election Day. So is inflation harmful? Absolutely.

The only time inflation is deliberately sought is when an economy comes face to face with the threat of deflation, a phenomenon where prices across the board spiral downward. To be sure, falling prices initially sound great to shoppers. But make no mistake—

deflation can be as destructive to an economy as inflation. Tumbling prices slash corporate profits, which, in turn, can lead to job layoffs. Higher unemployment reduces household income, and that causes a retrenchment in consumer spending. As more consumers back away from shopping, prices drop further, and companies are forced to let go of additional workers. It's a vicious cycle of an economy in utter collapse. The U.S. suffered deflation during the Great Depression. Between 1929 and 1933, the CPI dropped 24%. As recently as 2001 and 2002, Japan was stuck in a deflationary spiral from which it could not recover, even though interest rates dropped to virtually zero. Its economy was unable to grow and joblessness rose to an all-time high.

Ideally, the goal of government—specifically, the Federal Reserve—is to avoid both harmful inflation and deflation by pursuing policies that promote price stability. In practical terms, that means tolerating only a modest level of inflation, with prices inching up no more than 1% to 2% a year.

HOW IS IT COMPUTED?

In the first three weeks of every month, agents from the Bureau of Labor Statistics (BLS) check out stores and conduct telephone interviews with about 23,000 retail outlets and other businesses located in 87 urban areas. Prices are collected on 80,000 items and services, including eyeglasses, hamburgers, dental exams, cars, gasoline, legal fees, beer, computers, cereal, funeral services, and rental units. Every month, the same basket of goods and services is analyzed to get a sense of how prices are behaving.

On the surface, the physical process of tracking prices looks fairly straightforward. You record the change in prices for more than 20,000 products each month to see if inflation has increased or not. However, in the real world it is rarely that easy. Sometimes data collectors in the field have to use their own judgment to determine whether the price of a particular item has gone up or down—even if that product's price tag hasn't changed at all. How could this be? The reason is that a change in packaging or advances in technology can alter a product's "effective price."

To illustrate this point, here are three typical scenarios the government confronts each month. Suppose a 5-fluid-ounce bottle of detergent cost $5 last month. Let's say the company that makes this detergent wants to attract more buyers and decides to add one more ounce to each bottle—without changing the price. You now get 6 fluid ounces of detergent, or 20% more, for the same $5. Government staffers will correctly view this as a *drop* in inflation and record the effective price as falling from $5 last month to $4 this month, a savings of 20%. After all, you're getting more for each dollar spent on detergent.

Here's a second example, and one especially irksome to consumers. You went shopping last month and bought a 10-ounce bag of potato chips for $5. This month you notice that while the packaging and price haven't changed, you're surprised (and upset) to see that the new bag holds just 8 ounces of chips, 20% less than last month. Though you're still paying $5 for that bag, the government classifies it as a price *increase* to $6, or an increase of 20%. Why? Because in this instance you receive less for each dollar spent.

The third example demonstrates how technological changes can influence a product's true cost. In this case, you spent $3 a month ago for a 100-watt light bulb that lasts about 50 hours. Let's say that during the course of the year, you replace that bulb three times to get 200 hours of usage for a total annual expense of $12. Now suppose the manufacturer discontinues that bulb and introduces a new high-tech 100-watt bulb that costs $6—twice as much as the old bulb—but the new one lasts 200 hours. Even though you will pay 100% more for each new 100-watt light bulb, when you take into account its technological improvement (it lasts four times as long as the older light bulb), the effective price of the new bulb actually drops by half and thus *lowers* inflation. Simply put, instead of spending $12 a year to get 200 hours of usage with the older bulb, you will now pay just $6 a year for the same duration. The point of this whole exercise is to show how computing changes in the CPI requires more than merely jotting down prices on thousands of products. Often other considerations have to be made to get the most accurate reading on how the cost of living has changed.

Once all the data is collected, seasonal adjustment factors are applied to correct for variations that can commonly occur during the year. For example, prices of oranges and other fruits typically edge higher in the winter because that's when supplies of such foods dwindle, even though demand remains strong. Seasonal adjustments try to iron out such abrupt shifts in prices, but the process is imperfect. For instance, oil prices can fluctuate wildly as a result of geopolitical shocks.

To reduce some of the statistical noise in the inflation data and to provide a better understanding of the genuine trend in inflation, the government publishes an index known as the core-CPI, which is the CPI without the unstable components of food and energy. Most economists see core-CPI as the best measure of the underlying inflation rate.

CPI-W Versus CPI-U

After receiving the raw data and subjecting it to seasonal adjustment factors, the BLS comes up with inflation figures for two different population groups. One index is called the CPI-W (with the "W" standing for wage earners and clerical workers). It covers 32% of the working population. While only one in three employees is covered, the CPI-W is still important to monitor because it's the benchmark used to figure out pay increases in collective bargaining agreements and for yearly cost-of-living adjustments on Social Security checks.

The other and much broader measure is the CPI-U (for all urban workers). It includes not only wage and clerical workers, but also professionals, the self-employed, managers, technical workers, and short-term workers. It's a broad-enough population to cover 87% of consumers. Because it comprises so many more people, the CPI-U gets most of the attention in the media and financial markets.

Geographic Coverage

Besides measuring how inflation behaved at the national level, the monthly CPI release also describes how prices changed in different regions of the country. This enables analysts to compare cost-of-living changes in a variety of communities. For example, the BLS publishes inflation data for 14 specific local areas. They were chosen because of their size and importance to the economy. Of the 14 regions, the BLS releases inflation data on three of them every month:

- Chicago-Gary-Kenosha, IL-IN-WI
- Los Angeles-Riverside-Orange County, CA
- New York-Northern NJ-Long Island, NY-NJ-CT-PA

Data for the other 11 metropolitan areas is published every other month to make the price collection process more manageable.

THE TABLES: CLUES ON WHAT'S AHEAD FOR THE ECONOMY

The CPI has only limited value as a forecasting tool. It can point to a couple of inflation hot spots that could become problematic for an economy down the road. This enables businesses to anticipate costs ahead of time. Evidence that inflation pressures are mounting can also help money managers reassess investment strategies. Union leaders rely on inflation forecasts to negotiate better pay terms for their rank and file. What the CPI cannot do, however, is function as a leading indicator of economic activity. If anything, the CPI is a lagging indicator. Price increases start to ease after a recession is well under way and don't accelerate again until a year or more after the recovery has begun. Therefore, the CPI has no real value as a predictor of turning points in the economy.

- **Table A**   Percent Changes in CPI for Urban Consumers (CPI-U)

3 ▼

Table A. Percent changes in CPI for Urban Consumers (CPI-U)

Expenditure Category	Seasonally adjusted							Compound annual rate 3-mos. ended Jan.'04	Un-adjusted 12-mos. ended Jan.'04
	Changes from preceding month						2004		
	2003								
	July	Aug.	Sep.	Oct.	Nov.	Dec.	Jan.		
All Items	.2	.4	.3	-.1	-.2	.2	.5	2.0	1.9
Food and beverages	.1	.3	.3	.4	.4	.5	-.1	3.6	3.5
Housing	.2	.1	.1	.2	-.1	.2	.4	2.2	2.2
Apparel	-.2	.1	.2	.2	-.5	-.3	-.3	-4.5	-1.9
Transportation	.1	1.2	.9	-1.4	-1.3	-.2	1.7	.5	1.0
Medical care	.4	.3	.4	.2	.3	.5	.2	4.2	3.8
Recreation	.1	.0	.1	-.1	.2	.1	.0	1.1	.9
Education and communication	.3	.4	.2	.0	.2	.2	.1	1.8	1.3
Other goods and services	.4	.2	.1	.1	.0	.2	.3	2.0	1.7
Special indexes:									
Energy	.3	3.1	3.3	-3.5	-3.0	.3	4.7	7.8	7.8
Food	.1	.4	.2	.5	.4	.5	.0	3.8	3.5
All items less food and energy	.2	.1	.1	.2	.0	.1	.2	.8	1.1

1 ▶
2 ▶

Every CPI release has two headline inflation numbers.

(1) *All items:* This lists the monthly percentage change in the CPI for all items.

(2) *Core-CPI:* This subset, known as core-CPI, is what the CPI would be if food and energy costs were excluded. The Federal Reserve prefers to monitor this subset of inflation when it deliberates on monetary policy.

Why subtract the food and energy components? Because these two items, which account for nearly 25% of the CPI, bounce around quite a lot month to month due to temporary factors such as crop failures or drops in global oil supplies. As a result, food and energy costs can potentially distort the true inflation picture in the U.S. By excluding these two commodities, it is possible to get a more accurate portrait of the inflationary pressures affecting the economy.

Of course, from a consumer's point of view, core-CPI has little significance. After all, food and energy are indispensable commodities in our economy. We can't simply ignore them, and it would be risky for anyone to make sweeping long-term forecasts about inflation and real economic growth that rely solely on core-CPI. In any event, the differential between these two CPI inflation measures over time is not that great. In the 10 years leading up to 2005, they were typically less than 1 percentage point apart annually.

(3) *Change in the CPI trend:* Don't rely on just one month's CPI data to tell you much about trends in inflation. It is far more useful to look at the annualized three-, six-, and 12-month percentage changes to get a better sense of how inflation is behaving. Table A presents the latest three-month and 12-month changes for the CPI and for each of the major CPI components.

- **Table 1** Consumer Price Index for All Urban Consumers (CPI-U): U.S. City Average, by Expenditure Category and Commodity and Service Group

Aside from the headline CPI number, it's helpful to look at how inflation has behaved for individual commodities and services, especially housing, transportation, and medical care. That's where the next two tables come in.

(4) *Medical care:* One of the biggest expenses for companies is paying for employee health care coverage. Firms planning their future budgets will want to set aside an amount for such expenditures, but how much? Executives can approximate such costs by looking at the medical care component in the CPI release, which itself is divided into four categories, including professional and hospital services. Monitoring the previous pace of price changes in these subcategories gives you some sense of where such costs may go in the months ahead.

(5) *Personal computers and peripheral equipment:* Given the pervasive use of PCs, software, and peripherals and their contribution to overall productivity growth in the U.S., the BLS regularly monitors price changes in these products. Faster computers and better software are constantly being introduced. This has led to

Table 1. Consumer Price Index for All Urban Consumers (CPI-U): U.S. city average, by expenditure category and commodity and service group

(1982-84=100, unless otherwise noted)

CPI-U	Relative importance, December 2003	Unadjusted indexes		Unadjusted percent change to Jan. 2004 from—		Seasonally adjusted percent change from—		
		Dec. 2003	Jan. 2004	Jan. 2003	Dec. 2003	Oct. to Nov.	Nov. to Dec.	Dec. to Jan.
Expenditure category								
All items	100.000	184.3	185.2	1.9	0.5	-0.2	0.2	0.5
All items (1967=100)	-	552.1	554.9	-	-	-	-	-
Food and beverages	15.384	184.1	184.3	3.5	.1	.4	.5	-.1
Food	14.383	183.6	183.8	3.5	.1	.4	.5	.0
Food at home	8.256	184.1	184.0	4.1	-.1	.6	.7	-.3
Cereals and bakery products	1.202	202.9	203.9	2.1	.5	.1	.1	.1
Meats, poultry, fish, and eggs	2.320	181.1	179.9	11.3	-.7	2.7	1.0	.0
Dairy and related products	.842	173.0	172.4	3.6	-.3	-.4	1.1	-.3
Fruits and vegetables	1.221	232.4	232.4	2.3	.0	.3	.3	-1.8
Nonalcoholic beverages and beverage materials	.905	139.3	140.7	.1	1.0	-.9	.7	.3
Other food at home	1.765	163.0	162.8	.6	-.1	-.5	.6	-.4
Sugar and sweets	.305	161.0	163.0	1.4	1.2	.4	-.5	-.3
Fats and oils	.251	157.7	160.7	3.1	1.9	-.1	.5	1.1
Other foods	1.210	179.6	178.0	-.1	-.9	-.8	.8	-.7
Other miscellaneous foods [1] [2]	.308	109.8	109.1	-.5	-.6	-1.5	.7	-.6
Food away from home [1]	6.127	184.3	184.9	2.8	.3	.3	.3	.3
Other food away from home [2]	.332	122.9	123.9	3.3	.8	.2	.3	1.0
Alcoholic beverages [1]	1.001	188.7	189.4	1.9	.4	.3	.1	.4
Housing	42.089	185.1	186.3	2.2	.6	-.1	.2	.4
Shelter	32.878	214.1	215.2	2.0	.5	.1	.2	.1
Rent of primary residence [3]	6.157	207.9	208.3	2.5	.2	.2	.2	.1
Lodging away from home [2]	2.954	112.9	117.2	2.5	3.8	-.7	1.1	-.2
Owners' equivalent rent of primary residence [3] [4]	23.383	222.2	222.6	1.9	.2	.1	.1	.1
Tenants' and household insurance [1] [2]	.385	114.3	114.8	.8	.4	-1.5	.0	.4
Fuels and utilities	4.741	153.6	156.3	7.0	1.8	-.7	.5	1.6
Fuels	3.830	136.5	139.2	7.5	2.0	-1.0	.4	1.9
Fuel oil and other fuels	.231	137.0	149.9	9.7	9.4	1.0	-.5	6.8
Gas (piped) and electricity [3]	3.599	143.3	145.5	7.3	1.5	-1.2	.6	1.6
Water and sewer and trash collection services [2]	.910	119.8	120.6	5.1	.7	.6	.3	.5
Household furnishings and operations	4.470	124.7	125.3	-1.6	.5	-.2	-.1	.4
Household operations [1] [2]	.704	122.6	122.7	1.6	.1	-.2	.2	.1
Apparel	3.975	119.0	115.8	-1.9	-2.7	-.5	-.3	-.3
Men's and boys' apparel	1.024	118.0	115.5	-.5	-2.1	.1	.0	-.1
Women's and girls' apparel	1.704	110.9	105.7	-1.8	-4.7	-.8	-.4	-.7
Infants' and toddlers' apparel	.195	119.2	117.7	-2.8	-1.3	-1.6	-.8	.2
Footwear	.778	118.5	115.9	-3.2	-2.2	-.3	-.3	-.8
Transportation	16.881	154.7	157.0	1.0	1.5	-1.3	-.2	1.7
Private transportation	15.817	150.8	153.2	.9	1.6	-1.4	-.2	1.9
New and used motor vehicles [2]	7.912	94.4	94.3	-4.0	-.1	-.4	-.5	-.1
New vehicles	4.817	138.0	138.0	-1.2	.0	-.1	-.1	-.1
Used cars and trucks [1]	2.007	131.0	130.8	-11.8	-.2	-2.3	-.8	-.2
Motor fuel	3.249	127.8	136.7	8.2	7.0	-5.1	.0	8.1
Gasoline (all types)	3.222	127.2	136.1	8.3	7.0	-5.1	.1	8.1
Motor vehicle parts and equipment [1]	.369	107.7	108.0	.2	.3	.0	-.2	.3
Motor vehicle maintenance and repair	1.349	198.0	198.2	2.3	.1	.2	.5	.1
Public transportation	1.064	205.6	206.3	2.0	.3	-.3	-.8	.2
Medical care	6.074	302.1	303.6	3.8	.5	.3	.5	.2
Medical care commodities	1.499	265.0	265.5	2.0	.2	-.1	.3	.1
Medical care services	4.575	311.9	313.8	4.3	.6	.5	.5	.3
Professional services	2.749	264.1	265.5	3.0	.5	.2	.5	.2
Hospital and related services [3]	1.489	407.0	409.7	6.2	.7	1.0	.5	.3

4 ▶

See footnotes at end of table.

significant price changes in computer technology, which is well documented in the CPI data. Firms that are budgeting to purchase new computer systems can get a sense of how prices might behave in the future by extrapolating recent trends.

Table 1. Consumer Price Index for All Urban Consumers (CPI-U): U.S. city average, by expenditure category and commodity and service group-Continued

(1982-84=100, unless otherwise noted)

CPI-U	Relative importance, December 2003	Unadjusted indexes		Unadjusted percent change to Jan. 2004 from—		Seasonally adjusted percent change from—		
		Dec. 2003	Jan. 2004	Jan. 2003	Dec. 2003	Oct. to Nov.	Nov. to Dec.	Dec. to Jan.
Expenditure category								
Recreation [2]	5.872	107.7	107.9	0.9	0.2	0.2	0.1	0.0
Video and audio [2]	1.736	103.3	103.6	.2	.3	.1	-.1	-.3
Education and communication [2]	5.948	110.9	111.1	1.3	.2	.2	.2	.1
Education [2]	2.841	139.4	140.1	7.3	.5	.4	.7	.5
Educational books and supplies	.219	342.8	345.4	4.8	.8	-.1	2.4	-.5
Tuition, other school fees, and childcare	2.623	401.7	403.6	7.5	.5	.5	.6	.6
Communication [2]	3.107	88.2	88.1	-4.2	-.1	-.1	-.3	-.3
Information and information processing [1] [2]	2.925	86.2	86.1	-4.7	-.1	-.2	.0	-.1
Telephone services [1] [2]	2.315	97.2	97.0	-3.4	-.2	.1	.0	-.2
Information technology, hardware and services [1] [5]	.610	15.3	15.3	-10.5	.0	-1.3	-.6	.0
Personal computers and peripheral equipment [1] [2]	.230	16.2	16.2	-16.9	.0	-1.2	-.6	.0
Other goods and services	3.776	300.2	301.4	1.7	.4	.0	.2	.3
Tobacco and smoking products [1]	.806	470.4	473.0	.1	.6	-.1	.3	.6
Personal care	2.970	179.0	179.7	2.2	.4	.0	.2	.2
Personal care products [1]	.680	153.4	153.8	.5	.3	-.3	.1	.3
Personal care services [1]	.650	194.3	194.6	2.1	.2	-.7	.1	.2
Miscellaneous personal services	1.448	287.1	288.8	3.8	.6	.5	.2	.3

5 ▶

• Table 3　Consumer Price Index for All Urban Consumers (CPI-U): Selected Areas, All Items Index

Table 3. Consumer Price Index for All Urban Consumers (CPI-U): Selected areas, all items index

(1982-84=100, unless otherwise noted)

CPI-U	Pricing schedule [1]	Indexes				Percent change to Jan.2004 from—			Percent change to Dec.2003 from—		
		Oct. 2003	Nov. 2003	Dec. 2003	Jan. 2004	Jan. 2003	Nov. 2003	Dec. 2003	Dec. 2002	Oct. 2003	Nov. 2003
U.S. city average	M	185.0	184.5	184.3	185.2	1.9	.4	.5	1.9	-0.4	-0.1
Region and area size[2]											
Northeast urban	M	195.4	195.1	194.9	195.9	2.8	.4	.5	2.8	-.3	-.1
Size A - More than 1,500,000	M	197.7	197.3	197.1	197.9	3.0	.3	.4	3.0	-.3	-.1
Size B/C - 50,000 to 1,500,000 [3]	M	115.2	115.3	115.0	116.0	2.6	.6	.9	2.1	-.2	-.3
Midwest urban	M	179.1	178.9	178.4	179.4	1.8	.3	.6	1.7	-.4	-.3
Size A - More than 1,500,000	M	181.7	181.4	180.9	181.8	2.0	.2	.5	1.7	-.4	-.3
Size B/C - 50,000 to 1,500,000 [3]	M	113.6	113.6	113.3	114.1	1.9	.4	.7	1.7	-.3	-.3
Size D - Nonmetropolitan (less than 50,000)	M	171.8	171.4	171.5	171.8	.6	.2	.2	1.2	-.2	.1
South urban	M	178.1	177.5	177.5	178.2	1.8	.4	.4	1.7	-.3	.0
Size A - More than 1,500,000	M	180.1	179.1	179.2	179.8	1.8	.4	.3	1.9	-.5	.1
Size B/C - 50,000 to 1,500,000 [3]	M	113.6	113.3	113.3	113.8	1.9	.4	.4	1.5	-.3	.0
Size D - Nonmetropolitan (less than 50,000)	M	175.6	175.4	175.1	175.3	1.2	-.1	.1	1.6	-.3	-.2
West urban	M	189.4	188.5	188.3	189.4	1.5	.5	.6	1.5	-.6	-.1
Size A - More than 1,500,000	M	191.9	191.0	190.6	191.7	1.3	.4	.6	1.4	-.7	-.2
Size B/C - 50,000 to 1,500,000 [3]	M	115.5	114.9	115.2	116.0	1.9	1.0	.7	1.9	-.3	.3
Size classes											
A [4]	M	169.5	168.9	168.7	169.4	2.0	.3	.4	2.0	-.5	-.1
B/C [3]	M	114.1	113.9	113.8	114.6	2.0	.6	.7	1.7	-.3	-.1
D	M	176.9	176.6	176.5	176.9	1.3	.2	.2	1.6	-.2	-.1
Selected local areas[5]											
Chicago-Gary-Kenosha, IL-IN-WI	M	185.8	185.6	185.5	185.4	1.5	-.1	-.1	1.7	-.2	-.1
Los Angeles-Riverside-Orange County, CA	M	187.8	187.1	187.0	188.5	1.8	.7	.8	1.8	-.4	-.1
New York-Northern N.J.-Long Island, NY-NJ-CT-PA	M	200.0	199.4	199.3	199.9	2.7	.3	.3	3.2	-.4	-.1
Boston-Brockton-Nashua, MA-NH-ME-CT	1	-	206.5	-	208.4	4.3	.9	-	-	-	-
Cleveland-Akron, OH	1	-	177.6	-	178.4	2.8	.5	-	-	-	-
Dallas-Fort Worth, TX	1	-	175.9	-	175.7	1.0	-.1	-	-	-	-
Washington-Baltimore, DC-MD-VA-WV [6]	1	-	116.7	-	117.1	2.2	.3	-	-	-	-
Atlanta, GA	2	180.1	-	179.0	-	-	-	-	1.0	-.6	-
Detroit-Ann Arbor-Flint, MI	2	183.3	-	181.3	-	-	-	-	.9	-1.1	-
Houston-Galveston-Brazoria, TX	2	166.1	-	164.1	-	-	-	-	2.7	-1.2	-
Miami-Fort Lauderdale, FL	2	181.6	-	181.6	-	-	-	-	2.1	.0	-
Philadelphia-Wilmington-Atlantic City, PA-NJ-DE-MD	2	190.3	-	189.0	-	-	-	-	2.0	-.7	-
San Francisco-Oakland-San Jose, CA	2	196.3	-	195.3	-	-	-	-	1.1	-.5	-
Seattle-Tacoma-Bremerton, WA	2	193.7	-	191.0	-	-	-	-	.5	-1.4	-

6 ▶

(6) *Selected local areas:* The inflation outlook can vary, depending on where you live or work in the country. Obviously, the rise in the cost of living in New York City is not expected to be the same for Cleveland. The CPI report breaks down the inflation rates by geographic regions and population-size areas. Why can this table be helpful? If you're interested in relocating your factory or are a retiree seeking a community with a lower cost of living, you can compare the rates of inflation for each of these regions and draw some conclusions about future price changes there. In addition to the areas listed in this table, the BLS publishes semiannual inflation rates of more than a dozen other metropolitan communities in its January and July issues of the CPI Detailed Report, which is separate from the monthly release but can be found on the same BLS Web site.

MARKET IMPACT

Bonds

An unexpected jump in the CPI can slash bond values and propel yields higher. Bond losses are likely to be even worse if the core-CPI surges as well because it represents a deterioration in the underlying rate of inflation. Conversely, a benign CPI report showing little or no inflation is bullish for fixed income securities, with bond prices generally rising and interest rates easing.

Stocks

Equity investors also detest sharp increases in the CPI, especially core-CPI, because it leads to higher bond rates, which raises the cost of corporate borrowing. While revenues and perhaps even profits might jump in an inflationary environment, that kind of income is worth much less to shareholders who prefer to see earnings improve from greater sales volume, not price hikes. Furthermore, the threat of inflation will almost certainly force the Federal Reserve to jump in and raise interest rates, which is also anathema to shareholders.

In contrast, if inflation is quiescent, it will keep interest rates from rising and buoy stock prices. Investors usually place a higher value on the stream of future earnings at such times because it will stem from greater sales and/or higher productivity.

Dollar

The effect inflation has on the dollar is less clear. As is often the case in a healthy economic expansion, rising U.S. interest rates can make the dollar attractive. But if rates surge primarily on account of growing inflation concerns, it can hurt the U.S. currency. Higher U.S. inflation erodes the value of dollar-based investments held by foreigners, so a sustained increase in the CPI can have a negative influence on the greenback.

Having said that, bear in mind that currency traders are also sensitive to other nuances. For instance, if players in the foreign exchange markets believe the Federal Reserve has moved quickly and deftly to smother inflation pressures, it's likely the dollar will hold its ground or even appreciate in value.

PRODUCER PRICE INDEX (PPI)

Market Sensitivity: Very high.

What Is It: Measures the change in prices paid by businesses.

News Release on the Internet: *www.bls.gov/ppi*

Home Web Address: *www.bls.gov*

Release Time: 8:30 a.m. (ET); announced two to three weeks after the reporting month ends.

Frequency: Monthly.

Source: Bureau of Labor Statistics, Department of Labor.

Revisions: The monthly data is subject to one revision that is published four months later. Annual revisions are published in February with the January data, and it can go back five years.

WHY IS IT IMPORTANT?

Inflation is public enemy number one to the financial markets. It can wipe out the value of bond portfolios, depress stock prices, and push interest rates higher. So when the first major inflation number of the month comes out, a distinction that belongs to the Producer Price Index (PPI), it should come as no surprise that everyone pounces on it. The PPI measures changes in prices that manufacturers and wholesalers pay for goods during various stages of production. Any whiff of inflation here could eventually be transmitted to the retail level. After all, if business has to pay more for goods, it is more likely to pass on some of those higher costs to consumers. (As we'll see later, the relationship between producer prices and consumer prices is actually not that simple.)

The producer price index is really not just one index, but a family of indexes. There are price indexes for each of the three progressive stages of production: crude goods, intermediate goods, and finished goods. The one that grabs all the headlines and most excites financial markets is the last one, the PPI for finished goods. It represents the final stage of processing just before these goods are shipped to wholesalers and retailers. Prices at this last stage of production are often determined by cost pressures encountered in the crude and intermediate steps, which is why it is important to monitor all three stages.

PPI Crude Goods

The crude goods index represents the cost of raw materials entering the market for the first time. Examples of crude food supplies are wheat, cattle, and soybeans. Non-food crude items include coal, crude petroleum, sand, and timber. Changes in the prices of these commodities are generally based on supplies, which can be subject to large swings as a result of droughts, animal disease, and geopolitical factors. A spurt in prices at this early stage will be felt at the intermediate stage.

PPI Intermediate Goods

The intermediate goods index reflects the cost of commodities that have undergone transitional processing before becoming the final product. Items like flour, certain animal feeds, paper, auto parts, leather, and fabric fall into this category. Again, changes in prices here can be transferred to the final stage, which is finished goods.

PPI Finished Goods

The finished goods index is the most closely watched measure in the entire PPI report. It consists of apparel, furniture, automobiles, meats, gasoline, and fuel oil. Any inflation at this stage is considered serious because these are the products retailers pay for and thus can influence the price tag consumers will see.

Do changes in the producer prices dictate what consumer prices will do? Many economists claim there is little correlation between the two. But that conclusion is not a fair one. Much depends on which of the three main PPI indexes is chosen as a predictive tool for future consumer price inflation. During the 1970s and 1980s, shifts in the price of crude and intermediate goods often preceded changes in the CPI. However, that relationship has been less reliable since the 1990s. What has stood the test of time is the link between PPI for finished goods and the CPI. Sure, they might diverge on a month-to-month basis, but they tend to move in tandem over the longer term, usually in the range of six to nine months. This complicated relationship exists because the two inflation measures have some important differences and similarities. One difference is that the PPI does not take into account the price of most services. In the CPI, services like housing and medical care make up more than half of the index. One area where both of these inflation gauges share common ground is in "consumer products." That sector accounts for 75% of the PPI for finished goods. So if prices leap higher here, chances are the CPI will also be under pressure to rise.

In addition to keeping a close eye on the PPI for finished goods, the investment community studies a subset known as core-PPI, a measure that excludes the bumpy categories of food and energy. Those two commodity groups make up a large 40% of the finished PPI, so any abnormal weather pattern or a temporary disruption in oil supplies can greatly distort the inflation numbers and mislead analysts. To get a more accurate reading of the underlying inflation trend, the core-PPI for finished goods is given equal and sometimes even greater consideration than the total index.

How Is It Computed?

The producer price series began in 1902, making it the nation's oldest inflation measure. The government computes the PPI as follows: Every month, around the week that includes the 13th, the Labor Department receives answers to questionnaires requesting prices on about 100,000 different items from nearly 30,000 firms around the country. A basket is formed of goods representing items at all stages of production: crude, intermediate, and finished. Which commodities are selected for the basket and what weight each has in the PPI depends on how much revenue these goods generate in the economy. The weights are reviewed and modified every five years or so to reflect changes in what industries are selling. Currently, the weights are determined based on sales patterns seen in 2002, and that led to a reassignment of the weights in the PPI in early 2007.

Certain categories are intentionally left out of the PPI basket. Among them are imported goods and most services. Excise taxes are also not included. However, the cost of special promotional programs, such as low-interest financing and rebates, is included to the extent it reduces the price for manufacturers.

To see how prices have changed over months and years, the government establishes a baseline using an index that starts at 100 and reflects the average price of goods in 1982. So, for example, if the index for finished goods prices rises to 120, it means that inflation for that category has climbed 20% since 1982. In a deflationary environment, where prices actually decline, the index may fall from 100 to 90, a drop of 10%.

A breakdown of the PPI for finished goods and their relative importance is as follows:

Finished consumer products	75.3%
Finished consumer foods (20.3%)	
Finished consumer goods (55%)	
Capital equipment	24.7%
	100%

THE TABLES: CLUES ON WHAT'S AHEAD FOR THE ECONOMY

- **Table A**   Monthly and Annual Percent Changes in Selected Stage-of-Processing Price Indexes

  A summary of major changes for the month in the producer price index can be found here:

  (1) Of particular interest are price changes along the production pipeline, from crude to intermediate to finished goods. You can easily locate trouble spots that show the greatest inflation (or deflation) pressures in each of the three stages of production. By knowing where price pressures originate, you can logically jump ahead and assume that some of it will be passed on to the next stage, and ultimately to consumer prices. But don't look at the PPI as an unfailing predictor of the CPI on a month-to-month basis. A correlation does exist, but over a six- to nine-month time frame.

(2) A longer-term perspective is a better way to view the PPI numbers. Table A lists how producer price inflation for finished goods has performed over the last 12 months. Corresponding annual changes for crude and intermediate levels are found in Table B of the report.

Table A. Monthly and annual percent changes in selected stage-of-processing price indexes, seasonally adjusted

| Month | Finished goods | | | | | Inter-mediate goods | Crude goods |
	Total	Foods	Energy	Except foods and energy	Change in finished goods from 12 months ago (unadj.)		
2002							
Sept.	0.3	-0.4	1.2	0.3	-1.8	0.5	2.2
Oct.	.8	.4	3.4	.3	.7	.7	2.2
Nov.	-.3	.4	-1.6	-.1	1.0	-.1	3.7
Dec.	-.3	.4	.2	-.6	1.2	-.1	2.0
2003							
Jan.	1.4	1.9	4.6	.3	2.5	1.2	7.6
Feb.	1.1	.4	7.4	-.1	3.3	2.0	5.2
Mar.	1.4	.2	5.4	.7	4.0	2.1	13.0
Apr.	-1.7	.8	-8.1	-.7	2.4	-2.3	-15.8
May	-.4	r .1	r -2.9	r .1	2.5	-.7	r 1.4
June	r .6	r .3	r 3.3	-.1	2.9	.5	r 4.6
July	.1	-.2	.3	.2	3.0	.2	-2.9
Aug.	.4	.7	1.2	.1	3.4	.5	-1.4
Sept.	.3	1.2	.1	0	3.5	-.1	3.4

▲1   ▲2

• **Table B** Monthly and Annual Percent Changes in Selected Price Indexes for Intermediate Goods and Crude Goods

(3) Here you can find the yearly changes in producer prices for the crude and intermediate stages of production for each of the last 12 months. What stands out is how volatile price changes can be. These wild fluctuations stem mostly from unpredictable swings in food and energy costs. Such commodities can rise or fall as a result of droughts, winter freezes, or tensions in the Middle East—factors that have nothing to do with the business cycle itself.

(4) Fortunately, the government also publishes the PPI for each stage of production, but without food and energy. This so-called core rate covers about two-thirds of the items in the PPI and is a more accurate portrayal of the underlying rate of inflation in the economy.

Here we see the monthly price changes for core-crude goods and for core-intermediate goods. (Price movements for core-finished goods are in Table A.)

Table B. Monthly and annual percent changes in selected price indexes for intermediate goods and crude goods, seasonally adjusted

	Intermediate goods				Crude goods			
Month	Foods	Energy	Except foods and energy	Change in intermediate goods from 12 months ago (unadj.)	Foods	Energy (unadj.)	Except foods and energy	Change in crude goods from 12 months ago (unadj.)
2002								
Sept.	1.1	2.2	0.1	-0.6	1.3	4.6	-0.2	3.1
Oct.	-.3	3.4	.2	1.6	.2	5.1	.3	15.4
Nov.	.5	-1.2	.1	2.4	1.1	7.8	1.4	13.7
Dec.	1.0	-.5	-.1	3.2	1.3	3.3	.2	24.7
2003								
Jan.	1.5	5.6	.4	4.5	5.3	13.0	1.3	28.7
Feb.	.7	7.9	.7	6.6	.7	9.9	3.4	36.7
Mar.	-.3	10.2	.4	8.0	-1.8	30.1	-.3	46.8
Apr.	.1	-11.0	-.2	4.6	1.2	-30.7	-1.1	18.2
May	r 1.1	r -4.4	0	4.2	r 2.0	r 1.9	r -.7	19.1
June	r 1.8	r 2.1	0	4.5	r -.7	r 11.7	r -.6	29.4
July	-.4	1.3	-.1	4.4	-3.0	-4.4	.8	24.5
Aug.	.2	2.4	.1	4.4	3.7	-7.4	3.7	20.9
Sept.	2.3	-2.3	.1	3.7	7.0	.6	2.3	22.3

(In the July row: ▲ 4 beside the "Except foods and energy" intermediate column and ▲ beside the intermediate "Change" column; ▲ 4 beside the "Except foods and energy" crude column and ▲ beside the crude "Change" column. Below the table: ▲ 3)

- **Table 1** Producer Price Indexes and Percent Changes by Stage of Processing

(5) To view how core-producer prices have performed over the last year and not just the previous month, you have to go to Table 1. Here's where the figures get interesting. One of the best but least followed leading economic indicators of U.S. and world growth can be found by tracking the monthly (Table A) and yearly (Table 1) inflation rates for the core rate of crude goods. Prices for this group have proven to be very sensitive to economic turning points. As an economy gears up production, demand for metals, paper boxes, and timber increases very early in the process, with accompanying jumps in prices that quickly move down the production pipeline. The opposite occurs when economic output turns down. Commodity prices fall months before an economy enters recession as purchases slow and unsold inventories accumulate. Because core-crude goods prices are quick to respond to shifts in economic activity, they are a valuable indicator for those who want to stay ahead of the business cycle curve.

Table 1. Producer price indexes and percent changes by stage of processing
(1982=100)

Grouping	Relative importance Dec. 2002 1/	Unadjusted index May 2003 2/	Unadjusted index Aug. 2003 2/	Unadjusted index Sept. 2003 2/	Unadjusted percent change to Sept.2003 from: Sept. 2002	Unadjusted percent change to Sept.2003 from: Aug. 2003	Seasonally adjusted percent change from: June to July	Seasonally adjusted percent change from: July to Aug.	Seasonally adjusted percent change from: Aug. to Sept.
Finished goods.................................	100.000	142.0	143.5	143.9	3.5	0.3	0.1	0.4	0.3
Finished consumer goods.....................	73.339	143.7	145.7	146.3	4.5	.4	.1	.6	.3
Finished consumer foods....................	20.672	144.6	146.2	147.9	6.6	1.2	-.2	.7	1.2
Crude..................................	1.333	133.1	127.8	136.8	15.0	7.0	1.0	5.6	5.5
Processed.............................	19.339	145.5	147.7	148.8	6.1	.7	-.3	.3	.8
Finished consumer goods, excluding foods.....	52.667	143.0	145.1	145.3	3.6	.1	.1	.5	.1
Nondurable goods less foods..............	36.364	146.3	149.7	150.2	5.2	.3	.2	.5	.1
Durable goods............................	16.303	132.4	131.6	131.1	0	-.4	.2	.2	-.1
Capital equipment...........................	26.661	139.0	139.3	139.1	.6	-.1	.4	.1	-.1
Manufacturing industries....................	7.839	139.5	140.5	140.4	.5	-.1	.4	.1	0
Nonmanufacturing industries.................	18.822	138.8	138.8	138.5	.6	-.2	.3	.1	-.1
Intermediate materials, supplies, and components..	100.000	132.5	134.0	134.1	3.7	.1	.2	.5	-.1
Materials and components for manufacturing.....	46.896	129.3	130.0	129.8	2.3	-.2	-.2	.5	-.2
Materials for food manufacturing.............	2.918	130.8	135.5	137.1	10.7	1.2	-.7	1.3	1.2
Materials for nondurable manufacturing.......	14.707	137.0	137.9	136.3	3.7	-1.2	-.3	1.1	-1.2
Materials for durable manufacturing..........	9.136	126.8	127.9	128.9	2.4	.8	-.2	.6	.9
Components for manufacturing.................	20.136	126.1	125.9	125.9	0	0	.1	-.1	0
Materials and components for construction......	12.772	152.9	153.8	155.1	2.0	.8	.3	.1	.9
Processed fuels and lubricants..............	16.110	108.0	113.6	113.3	12.6	-.3	.9	2.0	-1.6
Manufacturing industries	6.430	113.4	118.2	117.4	15.7	-.7	1.5	1.8	-1.3
Nonmanufacturing industries.................	9.680	104.8	110.7	110.7	10.6	0	.5	2.0	-1.7
Containers..................................	3.248	153.9	153.6	153.6	.7	0	-.1	-.1	0
Supplies....................................	20.974	141.5	141.4	141.7	1.5	.2	.1	-.1	.2
Manufacturing industries....................	4.589	146.8	147.0	146.7	1.3	-.2	.1	0	-.2
Nonmanufacturing industries.................	16.385	139.0	138.8	139.2	1.5	.3	.1	-.2	.3
Feeds..................................	1.097	104.6	101.8	107.4	3.1	5.5	.4	-2.8	5.5
Other supplies.........................	15.288	142.0	143.1	143.3	1.4	.1	.1	-.1	0
Crude materials for further processing...........	100.000	130.9	131.4	135.6	22.3	3.2	-2.9	-1.4	3.4
Foodstuffs and feedstuffs......................	38.685	111.0	111.5	118.7	17.9	6.5	-3.0	3.7	7.0
Nonfood materials..............................	61.315	142.4	142.9	144.5	25.2	1.1	-2.9	-4.2	1.1
Nonfood materials except fuel 3/..............	33.142	109.2	117.0	114.6	5.8	-2.1	.1	2.7	-2.1
Manufacturing 3/............................	32.295	100.3	107.6	105.3	5.9	-2.1	.1	2.8	-2.1
Construction................................	0.847	180.5	179.7	181.3	-.5	.9	-.3	1.0	.9
Crude fuel 4/..............................	28.173	183.7	171.8	180.1	56.1	4.8	-5.8	-11.2	4.8
Manufacturing industries...................	2.540	174.7	163.6	171.3	53.6	4.7	-5.8	-10.8	4.7
Nonmanufacturing industries...............	25.633	187.9	175.7	184.1	56.1	4.8	-5.9	-11.2	4.8

Special groupings

Grouping	Relative importance Dec. 2002 1/	May 2003 2/	Aug. 2003 2/	Sept. 2003 2/	Sept. 2002	Aug. 2003	June to July	July to Aug.	Aug. to Sept.
Finished goods, excluding foods..................	5/ 79.328	141.1	142.6	142.6	2.6	0	.3	.4	0
Intermediate materials less foods and feeds......	6/ 95.985	133.1	134.6	134.5	3.5	-.1	.1	.6	-.3
Intermediate foods and feeds....................	6/ 4.015	122.8	125.1	128.0	8.5	2.3	-.4	.2	2.3
Crude materials less agricultural products 3/ 7/..	8/ 59.316	145.0	145.0	146.4	25.6	1.0	-3.1	-4.6	1.0
Finished energy goods..........................	5/ 14.951	98.9	104.3	105.0	12.9	.7	.3	1.2	.1
Finished goods less energy......................	5/ 85.049	148.3	148.7	149.0	1.8	.2	.1	.3	.3
Finished consumer goods less energy.............	5/ 58.388	152.3	152.7	153.3	2.3	.4	0	.3	.5
Finished goods less foods and energy...........	5/ 64.377	150.0	149.9	149.7	.1	-.1	.2	.1	0
Finished consumer goods less foods and energy....	5/ 37.716	157.4	157.0	156.9	-.1	-.1	.1	.1	.1
Consumer nondurable goods less foods and energy..	5/ 21.413	177.6	177.6	177.8	-.3	.1	.1	.1	.1
Intermediate energy goods.......................	6/ 16.468	107.1	113.5	112.4	12.0	-1.0	1.3	2.4	-2.3
Intermediate materials less energy.............	6/ 83.532	137.5	137.7	138.0	2.0	.2	-.1	.1	.3
Intermediate materials less foods and energy.....	6/ 79.517	138.5	138.6	138.8	1.7	.1	-.1	.1	.1
Crude energy materials 3/......................	8/ 41.909	141.4	139.9	140.7	32.9	.6	-4.4	-7.4	.6
Crude materials less energy....................	8/ 58.093	120.0	121.7	127.9	15.6	5.1	-1.8	3.7	5.5
Crude nonfood materials less energy 4/...........	8/ 19.406	146.5	152.0	155.5	11.1	2.3	.8	3.7	2.3

5 ▶

While the core rate of producer prices can tell you something about future inflation pressures, you should not ignore the food and energy components. After all,
those two commodities are, in the final analysis, essential to the U.S. economy.
So a general rule is to look at the core rate to detect month-to-month changes in
inflation. But when longer projections of economic growth and inflation are
made, the core rate becomes less meaningful, since we ultimately pay for food
and energy. Thus, the core rate can serve as a proxy for near-term inflation,
while the total finished goods index can be helpful in determining the behavior
of consumer prices in the longer term.

MARKET IMPACT

Bonds

The PPI may not be an ideal leading indicator of consumer prices, but you'd never know
that from the way the bond market reacts. Producer price inflation is one of the hottest
economic indicators released by the government. Fixed income investors intuitively
believe that a jump in the PPI can be a wake-up call that consumer price inflation is
headed higher in the future. Second, since it is the first key inflation gauge the governments puts out every month, the market tends to view it with greater sensitivity. If the PPI
detects rising price pressures in the economy, it could depress bond prices and force interest rates higher. No change, or an actual decline in producer prices, is viewed favorably
by bond holders because it suggests the absence of any troublesome inflation.

Stocks

For the most part, equities respond much the same way bonds do to signs of inflation. A
jump in the PPI means higher production costs for companies, and this can erode profits
and endanger dividends. While some stock investors argue that a little inflation is a good
thing because it allows producers to charge more for goods, which bolsters revenues,
there is a point beyond which inflation pressures can do more harm than good to equities.
The problem is that there is no consensus on where that threshold is.

Dollar

A rise in the PPI is a tough call for participants in the foreign exchange market. Normally,
the dollar benefits from a little pickup in inflation, since this propels U.S. short-term
interest rates higher. A fast-rising inflation report, however, can hurt the dollar, because
the Federal Reserve can respond so aggressively as to jeopardize U.S. economic growth
altogether. By and large, a gradual rise in inflation that is accompanied by a well-timed
tightening of monetary policy is likely to lead to an appreciation of U.S. currency.

EMPLOYMENT COST INDEX

Market Sensitivity: Medium to high.

What Is It: The most comprehensive measure of labor costs.

News Release on the Internet: *www.stats.bls.gov/news.release/eci.toc.htm*

Home Web Address: *www.stats.bls.gov*

Release Time: 8:30 a.m. (ET); released the last Thursday of April, July, October, and January.

Frequency: Quarterly.

Source: Bureau of Labor Statistics, Department of Labor.

Revisions: Not on a quarterly basis. Revisions are announced annually with the release of first quarter data, and the changes can go back several years.

WHY IS IT IMPORTANT?

Inflation is the scourge of any economy. It drives interest rates higher and can punish stock prices. Thus, any indicator that serves as an early warning system of rising inflation pressures would be of great value to investors and business leaders. Topping the list as perhaps the best harbinger of pricing pressures is the Employment Cost Index (ECI). The ECI tracks changes in the cost of labor, the single biggest expense companies face. Labor-related outlays on wages, salaries, and the gamut of fringe benefits (such as vacations, health insurance, and social security) account for more than 70% of the cost of making a product. Employees make up such a huge proportion of operating expenses that any significant acceleration in compensation can quickly cut into corporate profits and pressure companies to pass on these additional costs to consumers in the form of higher prices.

Historically, once rising labor costs fuel inflation, they can unleash a vicious cycle that is hard to stop. As retailers hike their prices to offset rising employee expenses, workers will eventually demand bigger increases in wages and salaries just to keep up with inflation. Should employers again comply and pay workers more money, this soon brings about another jump in retail prices. This self-perpetuating escalation in inflation, known among economists as a wage-price spiral, is so destructive to an economy that it stands high on the Federal Reserve's enemy watch list.

To be fair, companies can respond to higher labor costs in ways other than raising prices. Firms might choose to absorb the extra expense and grudgingly accept less profit for the time being. Or they can decide that given how expensive labor has become, it makes more sense to simply dismiss a large number of employees and instead invest in new technology that would permit the same or even greater output but with fewer workers. Last, companies can simply decide to relocate their production facilities to other countries where labor is much cheaper. All of these responses to rising U.S. labor costs have significant consequences for the economy and the financial markets. By choosing to raise prices, firms can ignite inflation. At some point the Federal Reserve is likely to jump in and raise interest rates before a wage-price spiral gets out of hand. Should companies decide to absorb the extra costs, it will cut into earnings and adversely affect stock prices. Moving operations offshore can lead to higher joblessness in the U.S. and more government spending on unemployment insurance. For all these reasons, the ECI is monitored closely by Federal Reserve officials, money managers, business executives, and union leaders.

How Is It Computed?

The ECI is based on surveys of both private and public sectors (local and state only; the federal payroll is excluded). Every quarter, about 8,500 establishments in private industry, involving 37,000 occupational observations, and 800 establishments in state and local governments, public schools, and public hospitals, covering 3,700 occupational groupings, are queried on labor cost issues. The surveys are conducted for the pay period that includes the 12th day of the month in March, June, September, and December. All the information is then boiled down to 500 occupational classifications, which make up a fixed basket of job types.

Questions are asked about changes in wages, salaries, and benefits. Wage and salary data is collected on a straight-time hourly pay basis. For employees not paid on an hourly basis, a computation is made based on salary divided by the corresponding hours worked. Also included are production bonuses, incentive earnings, commission payments, and cost of living adjustments. Excluded from this calculation is premium pay for overtime and for work performed on weekends and holidays. Shift differentials are also excluded. Another major category not included in the ECI is stock options and restricted stocks.

Benefits covered by the ECI are paid vacations, sick leave, holidays, premium pay for overtime, shift differentials, insurance benefits, retirement and savings benefits, social security, Medicare, and federal- and state-mandated social insurance programs.

Changes in wages and salaries, as well as the cost of benefits, are then converted into an index (beginning with an index reference of 100 to reflect labor costs in 2005). Thus, if compensation costs stood at 105 at the end of one year and then rose to 110 by the close of the following year, labor costs increased by 4.8% over those 12 months. Separate indexes in this report show how these expenses changed in the private and public sectors, by labor union status, among industrial and occupational groups, and by geographic regions.

Figures are presented in both seasonal and nonseasonal adjustment form. The numbers for each quarter are not annualized.

THE TABLES: CLUES ON WHAT'S AHEAD FOR THE ECONOMY

- **Table A**   3-Month Percent Changes in Employment Cost Index

  Want to know how labor costs have behaved over the last two years? This is the place to begin. This table shows quarterly changes in compensation expenses—whether they've been climbing, falling, or holding steady. Besides listing total compensation costs, you can also see the percentage changes by the table's two basic components: wages and salaries, and benefit costs. Looking at the behavior of these two categories is important, for they can tell you whether it was pay hikes or a jump in benefits that most contributed to higher compensation costs. Detailed percentage changes are available for all civilian workers and their two principal groupings: private industry and state and local government.

Table A. 3-month percent changes in Employment Cost Index, seasonally adjusted

Compensation Component	Dec. 2001	Mar. 2002	June 2002	Sep. 2002	Dec. 2002	Mar. 2003	June 2003	Sep. 2003
Civilian workers								
Compensation costs	1.0	0.9	1.0	0.8	0.7	1.3	0.9	1.0
Wages and salaries	0.9	0.8	0.9	0.6	0.5	1.0	0.6	0.7
Benefit costs	1.2	1.0	1.3	1.2	1.3	2.2	1.4	1.5
Private industry								
Compensation costs	1.1	0.9	1.1	0.6	0.7	1.4	0.8	1.0
Wages and salaries	0.9	0.9	0.9	0.4	0.5	1.0	0.6	0.9
Benefit costs	1.3	1.1	1.3	1.1	1.2	2.4	1.3	1.4
State and local government								
Compensation costs	0.7	0.8	0.9	1.3	1.0	0.9	1.0	0.7
Wages and salaries	0.6	0.8	0.8	0.8	0.7	0.7	0.8	0.1
Benefit costs	0.9	1.0	1.1	2.2	1.7	1.5	1.3	2.0

- **Table B** 12-Month Percent Changes in Employment Cost Index

(1) Is the economy facing inflation pressures? It's simple enough to find out. Take the annual percentage change in compensation costs for private industry, and compare it with the annual change in non-farm productivity (see the section "Productivity and Costs") for the comparable period. Ideally, you want to see annual compensation costs rise no faster than the pace of annual productivity growth. Companies showing steady improvements in productivity can afford to give employees raises without hurting profits or raising prices. However, if employee compensation consistently climbs faster than productivity growth, the seeds have been sown for higher inflation down the road. This can spell trouble for consumers, companies, and the overall economy.

Some analysts consider average hourly earnings (AHE) data from the main employment report to be a better predictor of wage inflation because it is more timely. Average hourly earnings come out monthly, while the ECI is released quarterly. But timeliness is not everything. Average hourly earnings considers only workers who receive hourly pay, whereas ECI covers both hourly and salaried workers. Moreover, AHE does not include benefits costs; the ECI incorporates all major expenses (pay and benefits) that businesses incur as a result of their workforce.

Table B. 12-month percent changes in Employment Cost Index, not seasonally adjusted

Compensation Component	Sep. 1998	Sep. 1999	Sep. 2000	Sep. 2001	Sep. 2002	Sep. 2003
Civilian workers						
Compensation costs	3.7	3.1	4.3	4.1	3.7	3.9
Wages and salaries	4.0	3.3	4.0	3.6	3.2	2.9
Benefit costs	2.6	2.7	5.3	5.1	4.9	6.5
Private industry						
1 ▶ Compensation costs	3.8	3.1	4.6	4.0	3.7	4.0
Wages and salaries	4.3	3.2	4.1	3.6	3.2	3.0
Benefit costs	2.6	2.8	6.0	4.9	4.8	6.5
State and local government						
Compensation costs	3.0	2.9	3.3	4.4	3.8	3.6
Wages and salaries	3.0	3.3	3.5	3.9	3.1	2.3
Benefit costs	2.8	2.0	2.8	5.6	5.4	6.7

• **Table 6**   Employment Cost Index for Total Compensation for Private Industry Workers, by Bargaining Status, Region, and Area

(2) Highlighted here are the growth differences in compensation costs between union and nonunion workers. (Beginning in March 2007, however, the government will discontinue the series on "white-collar" and "blue-collar" workers because these classifications are no longer viewed as meaningful.)

(3) Interested in finding which region of the country shows the greatest increase or decrease in total compensation? The report segments labor cost changes by geographic area, quarterly and annually.

Table 6. Employment Cost Index for total compensation[1] for private industry workers, by bargaining status, region, and area

(Not seasonally adjusted data)

Bargaining status, region, and area	Indexes (June 1989=100)			Percent changes for—					
				3 months ended—			12 months ended—		
	Sep. 2002	Jun. 2003	Sep. 2003	Sep. 2002	Jun. 2003	Sep. 2003	Sep. 2002	Jun. 2003	Sep. 2003
Bargaining status									
▶Union	158.1	164.1	165.7	1.2	1.2	1.0	4.7	5.0	4.8
Blue-collar occupations	155.2	161.4	163.1	1.1	1.4	1.1	4.4	5.1	5.1
Goods-producing industries[2]	156.2	163.4	164.7	1.0	1.2	.8	3.7	5.6	5.4
Service-producing industries[3]	159.9	164.6	166.5	1.5	1.2	1.2	5.8	4.4	4.1
Manufacturing	155.9	163.8	165.0	.8	.9	.7	4.0	6.0	5.8
Blue-collar occupations	155.0	162.5	163.7	.8	.9	.7	3.7	5.7	5.6
Nonmanufacturing	158.8	163.7	165.5	1.4	1.4	1.1	5.1	4.5	4.2
▶Nonunion	162.2	166.8	168.4	.5	.8	1.0	3.5	3.3	3.8
Blue-collar occupations	156.9	161.3	162.6	.6	.9	.8	3.1	3.4	3.6
Goods-producing industries[2]	159.5	164.9	166.1	.6	.8	.7	3.6	4.0	4.1
Service-producing industries[3]	162.9	167.2	169.0	.4	.8	1.1	3.4	3.1	3.7
Manufacturing	160.1	165.8	166.9	.6	.8	.7	3.7	4.2	4.2
Blue-collar occupations	157.5	162.6	164.1	.5	.7	.9	3.6	3.8	4.2
Nonmanufacturing	162.4	166.7	168.5	.4	.8	1.1	3.4	3.1	3.8
Region[4]									
Northeast	160.5	165.2	166.9	.4	.9	1.0	3.4	3.3	4.0
South	158.9	161.6	163.2	.8	.6	1.0	3.5	2.5	2.7
Midwest	163.5	170.4	171.7	.6	.8	.8	3.9	4.8	5.0
West	163.8	169.5	171.4	.6	1.3	1.1	3.9	4.1	4.6
Area									
Metropolitan	161.8	166.6	168.3	.6	.8	1.0	3.7	3.5	4.0
Other	160.0	165.0	166.1	.9	.9	.7	3.4	4.1	3.8

MARKET IMPACT

Bonds

Bond traders react to the ECI much like they do for any forerunner of inflation. A larger-than-expected jump in the index is disconcerting to these investors and can provoke enough sales of fixed income securities to significantly drive up yields. Investors fear that rising labor costs without a concurrent increase in productivity can fire up price pressures and eventually force the Fed to raise interest rates before wage inflation firmly sets in. A stable or weaker-than-expected ECI is viewed as positive for the bond market.

Stocks

A sustained increase in labor costs is also bearish for the stock market. If wages and benefits climb faster than productivity, business costs swell, which then jeopardizes corporate profits. Moreover, this can compel the Fed to act. How quickly this all unfolds depends on where the economy stands in the business cycle and how vulnerable it is to an outbreak of inflation.

Dollar

No dependable pattern emerges between the ECI and the dollar's value in foreign exchange markets. Obviously, if labor costs pick up, this can propel interest rates higher, which normally would attract foreign investors to the dollar. However, higher labor costs can also erode the competitiveness of U.S. companies selling goods and services overseas and worsen the trade deficit—a distinct negative for the dollar. By and large, if players in the currency markets believe the Federal Reserve is successfully piloting the economy into a gentle slowdown and can forestall an outbreak of wage inflation, it would strengthen the dollar.

IMPORT AND EXPORT PRICES

Market Sensitivity: Low.

What Is It: Records price changes of goods bought and sold by the U.S. in foreign markets.

News Release on the Internet: *www.bls.gov/mxp*

Home Web Address: *www.bls.gov*

Release Time: 8:30 a.m. (ET); data is released about two weeks after the reported month.

Frequency: Monthly.

Source: Bureau of Labor Statistics, Department of Labor.

Revisions: Each release contains monthly revisions and corrections that go back three months. Changes affecting the weights of products in the basket of goods bought and sold in foreign markets are made every January and reflect shifts in trade patterns two years earlier.

WHY IS IT IMPORTANT?

When it comes to measuring inflation, the economic indicators that first come to mind are consumer prices, producer prices, and the personal consumption expenditure (PCE) deflators. Less well known is another series by the government—one that looks at the behavior of import and export prices. Why look at the cost of trade? Americans spend $2 trillion a year buying foreign products. These purchases make up more than 15% of GDP, so a major swing in import prices can have a palpable impact on inflation in this country. If the price of imported oil climbs sharply, consumers can end up paying more for gasoline and heating oil. A poor crop of coffee beans in Venezuela will effectively raise the price of a morning cup of caffeine. In addition, if the value of the dollar drops sharply against the major world currencies, it makes imports more expensive over a broad spectrum of goods and services.

Another reason to monitor import and export price indexes is that they have a direct bearing on the competitive position of the U.S. in foreign markets. Should American-made products get too pricey overseas because of inflation at home or a strengthening dollar, foreign buyers will stop ordering from the U.S. and seek other, cheaper suppliers. Since exports account for 10% of GDP, a significant drop in sales to other nations will reduce the earnings of major American companies and retard overall economic growth in this country.

The official reason for establishing these price indexes in the first place was to convert the monthly U.S. trade figures from current dollars into real dollars. Tracking trade flows in real terms is vital. If you simply tally all the sales in trade in current dollars, you're still left wondering whether America's higher import bill was the result of more products being purchased or because foreigners raised prices. The same applies to exports. If the value of U.S. shipments to other nations increased from one period to the next, was it because American firms actually sold more goods, or did they just hike prices? By using the information from this report, analysts can determine the real volume of imports and exports traded.

How Is It Computed?

Every month, information on export and import prices is collected on more than 20,000 products from over 6,000 companies and other sources. The Bureau of Labor Statistics asks these companies to report on the transaction price of trades that occur close to the beginning of every month. Most imports are priced on a "free on board" (FOB) basis and reflect the value of products at the foreign port of exportation. The seller is responsible for placing the goods on a boat or plane, but after that, the responsibility passes to the importer. The FOB price does not include the cost of insurance and duty taxes. On the export side, the majority of products are recorded with "free alongside ship" (FAS) prices, and represents their value before loading. The exporter is responsible only for placing the goods alongside the ship or plane. The price includes insurance and the cost of transporting everything up to the port of departure. However, the buyer pays the cost of actually loading the goods.

All prices collected are then weighed against a fixed market basket of goods that were imported and exported. Weights for the products in the basket are updated every year (beginning in 2004) and reflect changes in consumption patterns that occurred two years earlier.

Revisions are routine with each monthly release, and they can go back three months. The figures in the report are not seasonally adjusted.

The Tables: Clues on What's Ahead for the Economy

- **Cover Page**   Percent Changes in Import and Export Price Indexes

  This release deserves a close look because it tracks one of the most important economic forces to influence domestic inflation, growth, and corporate profits.

  (1) To begin with, the summary table permits a quick glance at the latest trend in import and export price movements by showing month-to-month percentage changes for the past year. If import prices are on the rise, it will put upward pressure on consumer price inflation, while a sustained fall in import prices can lead to disinflation (where the rate of inflation is decelerating) or, in rare instances, deflation (where the CPI is actually falling). Given the volatile nature of petroleum prices and how they can skew the total cost of imports, you should keep an eye on price patterns for both total imports and non-petroleum imports.

(2) Generally, a pickup in export prices, if sustained, can hurt U.S. foreign sales. However, there are a couple of caveats here. Much depends on how badly the rise in the price of U.S.-made goods hurts American competitiveness overseas. Often it does, especially if other foreign suppliers are offering similar quality products more cheaply. On the other hand, U.S. companies might successfully hold on to their foreign customers despite the higher price if the product is considered relatively unique or far superior in quality compared to its closest competitor.

Percent changes in import and export price indexes
by End Use category
- not seasonally adjusted -

Month	IMPORTS			EXPORTS		
	All Imports	Petroleum Imports	Non-petroleum Imports	All Exports	Agri-cultural Exports	Nonagri-cultural Exports
2002						
October	0.0	-0.1	0.0	-0.1	-1.8	0.1
November	-0.9	-8.2	-0.1	0.1	2.0	-0.1
December	0.6	5.6	0.2	-0.2	-0.5	-0.2
2003						
January	1.8	14.6	0.3	0.3	0.1	0.4
February	1.7	11.3	0.3	0.6	-0.4	0.6
March	0.6	-1.1	1.0	0.2	-0.4	0.3
April	-3.1	-18.8	-1.0	-0.1	0.4	-0.1
May	-0.7	-5.0	-0.2	0.1	2.5	-0.2
June	0.9	5.4	0.4	-0.2	-0.5	-0.1
July	0.5	5.2 r	0.0 r	-0.1	-0.1 r	-0.1
August	0.0 r	1.8 r	-0.3	0.0	-1.0 r	0.1
September	-0.4 r	-5.0 r	0.2	0.4	5.6 r	-0.1
October	0.1	2.3	-0.1	0.3	2.5	0.1
October 2001-02	1.9	32.2	-0.4	0.4	5.9	0.0
October 2002-03	0.9	3.4	0.7	1.4	10.5	0.6

r = revised to reflect late reports and corrections by respondents.

1   2

Looking at the export side of this table, most investors and economists focus on changes in non-agricultural export prices—a section that's made up mostly of manufactured goods and services. A drop in export prices will attract more foreign orders and thus raise U.S. corporate income.

The dominant factor behind changes in import and export prices is the rise and fall of the dollar's value in the currency market. A strengthening dollar reduces the price of imports but makes U.S. exports more expensive in foreign markets. A depreciating dollar raises the cost of imports. The flip side is that American exporters have an easier time getting foreign orders because their products drop in price outside the U.S. The following sections illustrate how changes in export and import prices can influence costs, profits, and growth in this country.

A Weak Dollar

Suppose France sells wine to the U.S. at a price of 25 euros per bottle. With an exchange rate of one dollar for each euro, the price of each bottle for American consumers is $25. Now let's say the dollar falls in value, and it now costs $1.25 to acquire each euro (that is, each U.S. dollar gets you only 0.80 euros). The price of the imported wine has now jumped from $25 to $31.25 (25 euros × $1.25 = $31.25), a 25% hike. Now imagine the broader inflationary implications of such a drop in the dollar's value, for in addition to wine, Americans also import from Europe cars, cheese, apparel, perfumes, art, and furniture. Moreover, with imports now pricier, domestic companies will be emboldened to lift their own prices as well because they have less to worry about from foreign competition.

A weaker dollar also enables exporters to sell products abroad at a lower, more competitive price. Here's how: Say an American firm sells jeans to Europeans for $25 a pair. Prior to the dollar's fall, foreigners would be able to pick up a pair of American jeans for 25 euros. But once the U.S. currency falls to $1.25 = 1 euro, the price of those jeans to Europeans drops from 25 euros to 20 euros ($25 ÷ $1.25 = 20), making them 20% cheaper. The lower price can spur more sales, lift earnings of U.S. exporters, and boost overall GDP growth.

A Strong Dollar

When the dollar's value climbs in currency markets, a different set of dynamics takes place for exporters and importers. Instead of having an equal exchange rate of $1 = 1 euro, let's say the U.S. currency jumps in value by 25%. Thus, Americans can now receive 1.25 euros for each U.S. dollar (or 1 euro = U.S. $ .80). This poses a serious problem for American exporters, for a jump in the dollar's value drives up the cost of those jeans for Europeans from 25 euros to 31.25 euros. U.S. firms, fearful that fewer people will buy jeans at that higher price, might decide to keep the European price unchanged at 25 euros just to stay competitive. However, that strategy will cost the company some revenue with each pair of jeans sold. By holding the price tag at 25 euros, the U.S. jeans producer is now getting just $20 for every pair of jeans sold, not the previous $25 (25 euros × U.S. $.80 = $20).

Importers and American consumers, on the other hand, are happy to see a muscular dollar because foreign products are now cheaper. When the value of the U.S. currency strengthened from U.S. $1 = 1 euro to U.S. $1 = 1.25 euros, the bottle of French wine for Americans fell from $25 to $20. However, what's great for U.S. shoppers can be awful for domestic producers, who now have to compete with lower-priced foreign goods entering this country. These American companies thus are now under immense pressure to keep their own prices down or face losing sales to imports. Multiply this by thousands of other commodities coming into the U.S., and you can begin to see how a strong U.S. currency can help reduce domestic inflation, but it can also hurt the earnings of many companies.

- **Table 3**   U.S. Import Price Indexes and Percent Changes for Selected Categories of Goods (Not Shown)

  This table contains a more detailed list of how import prices have fared for commodities, capital goods, foods, and other key categories of products. Equity analysts can seek out industries that thrive when import prices fall, and they can veer away from businesses that are threatened by low-price foreign goods being shipped to the U.S.

- **Table 4**   U.S. Export Price Indexes and Percent Changes for Selected Categories of Goods (Not Shown)

  Similar to Table 3, this page focuses on exports. Changes in exchange rates can provide economists and investors with better insights into how competitively priced U.S. products are in foreign markets. Keep in mind that nearly half the earnings of S&P 500 firms come from business generated outside the U.S.

- **Table 7**   U.S. Import Price Indexes and Percent Changes by Locality of Origin

  The prices of U.S. imports can drop precipitously if they originate from nations with ailing currencies. That's where Table 7 comes in. It looks at several of our most important trading partners—Canada, the European Union, Latin America, Japan, and Asia's Newly Industrialized Countries—and the change in import prices over time for each of these regions. U.S. importers prefer to deal with nations whose currencies are weak because they can purchase goods more cheaply from them than from stronger-currency nations. U.S. exporters, on the other hand, face serious hardships selling into a market whose local currency is slipping. For one thing, countries with weak currencies are usually in economic distress and are unlikely to buy much from the U.S. anyway. Secondly, the dollar's relative strength will probably price many American products out of that market.

Table 7 U.S. Import Price Indexes and Percent Changes by Locality of Origin
January 2006-January 2007   2000=100, unless otherwise noted

Description	Percentage of U.S. Imports 1/	Index		Percent Change				
				Annual	Monthly			
		December 2006	January 2007	Jan. 2006 to Jan. 2007	Sept. 2006 to Oct. 2006	Oct. 2006 to Nov. 2006	Nov. 2006 to Dec. 2006	Dec. 2006 to Jan. 2007
2/ Industrialized Countries.....................................	44.813	117.1	116.4	1.6	-2.2	1.5	0.9	-0.6
Nonmanufactured Articles........................	4.582	187.4	170.9	-13.8	-14.0	9.0	8.9	-8.8
Manufactured Articles..............................	39.766	111.7	112.1	3.5	-0.9	0.8	0.0	0.4
3/ Other Countries..	55.204	111.9	109.4	-1.6	-2.7	-0.1	1.0	-2.2
Nonmanufactured Articles........................	11.023	190.5	176.7	-9.2	-9.1	-1.1	3.6	-7.2
Manufactured Articles..............................	43.982	100.9	100.1	0.5	-0.7	0.1	0.3	-0.8
Canada...	17.052	129.6	127.5	-2.3	-4.4	2.6	1.9	-1.6
Nonmanufactured Articles........................	3.871	190.1	171.9	-16.6	-15.7	12.8	9.3	-9.6
Manufactured Articles..............................	12.851	118.7	119.5	2.3	-1.2	0.3	-0.1	0.7
4/ European Union..	17.908	120.6	121.2	4.4	-0.7	0.1	0.7	0.5
Nonmanufactured Articles........................	0.389	199.0	185.4	-13.1	-5.8	-5.1	1.2	-6.8
Manufactured Articles..............................	17.406	119.1	119.8	4.8	-0.5	0.4	0.7	0.6
France (Dec. 2003=100)................................	1.888	105.7	106.3	3.2	1.0	-0.1	0.7	0.6
Germany (Dec. 2003=100).............................	5.008	106.1	106.1	3.9	0.3	0.6	0.3	0.0
United Kingdom (Dec. 2003=100)...................	2.845	115.7	115.1	-0.4	-2.1	-0.9	0.3	-0.5
5/ Latin America...	17.619	136.3	133.5	-0.5	-2.8	-0.6	0.6	-2.1
Nonmanufactured Articles........................	4.822	195.9	183.0	-7.7	-8.0	-0.5	4.0	-6.6
Manufactured Articles..............................	12.721	125.9	125.7	2.4	-0.5	-0.7	-0.8	-0.2
Mexico (Dec. 2003=100)...............................	10.163	118.6	118.1	2.0	-1.9	-0.1	0.1	-0.4
6/ Pacific Rim (Dec. 2003=100).......................	33.452	98.5	98.3	-0.5	-0.3	-0.1	0.1	-0.2
China (Dec. 2003=100).................................	14.941	97.3	97.3	-0.8	-0.2	0.1	0.0	0.0
Japan...	8.308	94.1	94.2	-0.4	-0.2	-0.1	0.0	0.1
7/ Asian NICs...	6.124	89.1	88.7	-0.3	-0.1	-0.2	0.1	-0.4
8/ ASEAN (Dec. 2003=100).............................	5.993	98.0	96.6	0.1	-0.7	-0.3	0.0	-1.4
9/ Asia Near East (Dec. 2003=100).................	3.765	169.2	161.1	-4.4	-6.4	-1.0	3.2	-4.8

MARKET IMPACT

Bonds

The release on import and export prices is not a major market mover, though participants in the fixed income market might find some forward-looking signs of inflation pressures, or the lack thereof. Higher import prices can potentially unnerve bond investors who are hypersensitive to even the slightest scent of rising inflation. In contrast, a decline in the price of imports helps keep inflation under control, though this report alone is unlikely to significantly lift bond prices.

Stocks

Here, too, any response to this report is likely to be modest. That's not to say it's of minor importance to equity investors. Corporate profitability is very much affected by both import and export price movements. If the cost of imports drops, some U.S. firms—specifically, those that buy product components from other nations—stand to gain because this lowers production costs. Others will suffer from cheaper imports as foreign competitors threaten to grab a bigger share of the American market. Should imports become more expensive, the situation gives U.S. companies room to lift their own prices and increase profits. Yet other firms will feel the pinch of higher import costs.

In terms of exports, a drop in price can generate higher sales for U.S. firms selling abroad, while higher export prices can reduce foreign demand for U.S. goods and hurt corporate revenues. How this plays out in the stock market depends on the extent to which individual firms are exposed to the global marketplace. Generally speaking, the major equity indexes do not move much in response to this economic indicator, unless import prices surge to a level that fires up inflation pressures.

Dollar

The foreign exchange market normally does not spring into action as a result of this report. For these traders, much of the news on how exchange rate movements influence import and export prices has already been discounted. What alarms foreign investors is a situation in which the dollar's weakness or strength becomes so detrimental to the U.S. economy that it impels Washington to intervene in the currency market. Such actions are rare, but they cannot be totally dismissed among investors. What might trigger such a step? Several events can. Sharply higher import inflation, a significant deterioration in competitiveness, or an unacceptable widening of America's foreign trade deficit could at some point trigger remedial action by U.S. policymakers. That action can range from delicately crafted expressions of concern by administration officials about the dollar's value to direct intervention by the government in the currency markets.

PRODUCTIVITY AND COSTS

Market Sensitivity: Medium.

What Is It: Measures changes in the efficiency of workers who produce goods and services.

News Release on the Internet: *www.bls.gov/lpc/*

Home Web Address: *www.bls.gov*

Release Time: 8:30 a.m. (ET); the initial report is released about five weeks following the end of the quarter.

Frequency: Quarterly.

Source: Bureau of Labor Statistics, Department of Labor.

Revisions: Can be substantial. This first revision appears a month after the preliminary figures, and a second revision comes out 60 days after the initial revision. Subsequent changes to productivity data depend on revisions to GDP and employment data.

WHY IS IT IMPORTANT?

Here's a question: What single feat allows an economy to grow faster without any inflation, helps U.S. exporters win markets overseas, and enriches both households and corporations simultaneously? The answer is productivity growth. Productivity is the output in goods and services employees produce for each hour of labor worked. It serves as a way of measuring how well companies are using their employees and their physical capital (by which we mean land, material resources, and equipment).

Productivity is by far the most important determinant in the long-term health and prosperity of an economy. Here's why: Labor costs account for some 70% of all business expenses, so if companies are not using workers efficiently, it's an enormous waste of resources. With a productive workforce, however, an economy can produce enough supplies to meet the demands of consumers and businesses without causing shortages and higher prices. In addition, if workers produce more each hour, companies can increase sales and generate greater revenues. That will boost profits, which, in turn, can be used to distribute bigger dividends to shareholders, stimulate more business investment spending, or lead to greater pay for workers. Indeed, you might even be able do all three at the same time. On the other hand, poor productivity growth is a recipe for economic stagnation. It invites inflation, higher unemployment, weaker growth, and little or no gains in real income. The plain fact is that strong labor productivity growth is not just preferable, it's essential in an environment where U.S. companies face serious global competition.

That last point was painfully learned back in the 1970s and early 1980s, when productivity growth was close to flatlining. The U.S. economy at the time was reeling from soaring energy costs and several deep recessions. Moreover, American firms were losing customers overseas as well as in the United States as foreign competitors charged onto the scene with less-expensive, often better-quality cars, appliances, home electronics, and other products. Once overly confident that no nation could challenge America's post-World War II economic supremacy, companies here suddenly found themselves wholly unprepared to go up against their more agile foreign rivals.

After years of complacency, American industry finally awoke to the urgency of retooling their factories and operating more nimbly. Hundreds of plants were closed in the late 1980s and early 1990s. A wave of mergers, acquisitions, and consolidations followed, effectively burying companies that were no longer able to operate profitably. Just as corporate America began to work more efficiently, rapid technological innovation in the mid- and late 1990s contributed another large boost to productivity growth. These events have not only helped the U.S. regain its competitiveness in global trade, but also fundamentally altered the way Americans work and live. Cell phones, laptops, e-mail, high-speed telecommunication networks, and computer-based machine tools have spawned a true productivity revolution. But such major technology-driven breakthroughs in productivity are quite rare in history, occurring perhaps only once or twice every hundred years.

Far more common is the type of productivity swing that normally accompanies a business cycle. The ups and downs of cyclical productivity growth are better understood and tend to follow a predictable pattern. First, productivity typically falls when an economy approaches recession. The reason is that companies initially cut back production as demand shrinks, but they continue to hold on to employees—at least until it becomes clear that business will not turn up anytime soon. Thus, for a brief period of time, productivity plummets because output drops—but the number of people on payrolls remains unchanged. The next stage in the productivity cycle occurs when employers realize they have little choice but to begin layoffs. After all, with corporate revenues shrinking, it becomes too costly to keep idle or underutilized workers. As a result, during a recession companies try to get by with as few workers as possible. Third, as demand gradually picks up again and the economy starts to recover, productivity often surges because companies first rev up their production lines but hold off on hiring back workers. It's only when the economy begins to demonstrate sustainable growth that employers resume hiring. As more people are put back to work, the number of hours on the job increases, and productivity growth tapers off. This type of cyclical productivity has been faithfully observed for decades.

However, something quite bizarre occurred in the recession of 2001 and during the subsequent recovery. For the first time in modern history, productivity growth continued even during the economic downturn and further accelerated well into the recovery phase. Also unusual was that fewer workers were called back well after the economy rebounded.

The reason for this is still debated among economists. Many believe that companies invested heavily in new productivity-enhancing technologies in the 1990s, with particular emphasis on utilizing computers and software. There were also significant improvements in management techniques that enabled firms to operate more efficiently. Existing workers also underwent retraining to improve their skills. All these developments have had a profound impact on the economy. The streamlining of corporations allowed the U.S. to better compete in the international marketplace. But there was also a troubling side effect. The need for labor diminished. This prompted many to wonder whether the U.S. economy was now operating under a new paradigm where future increases in output could be achieved more easily and cheaply by relying on domestic and foreign capital (such as high-tech equipment, modern assembly lines, and outsourcing production) rather than by hiring more U.S. workers.

If true, this sounds wonderful to companies because they can satisfy consumer demand with a smaller, less costly, more efficient workforce. On the downside, though, is the prospect that sustained productivity growth can severely disrupt traditional patterns of job creation in the U.S. economy. Workers with outmoded skills will have far greater difficulty finding work in a period of high productivity growth and might have to relocate to another state, learn a new trade, or both.

Does productivity growth itself lead to a higher unemployment rate over the longer term? Conventional wisdom says no. Greater operating efficiencies produce more corporate profits, and this fosters higher investment spending by business. These outlays fuel the formation of new businesses, which leads to more employment opportunities. Indeed, the unemployment rate has remained near historic lows over the last decade.

Nevertheless, some economists still wonder whether the traditional relationship between economic growth, corporate profits, and employment has changed. If productivity can surge during both recessions and expansions, this could represent a historic shift in how the economy functions, specifically in terms of job creation. Meanwhile, as the debate continues, policymakers and economists are paying much more attention to the quarterly productivity data.

The report on productivity and costs contains three major components: output per hour (labor productivity), compensation per hour, and unit labor costs:

- *Output per hour of all persons:* Productivity reflects how efficient labor is at producing goods and services, normally referred to as output per hour. Calculating productivity is relatively straightforward. We look at how much labor and capital are put to work at companies. These represent the inputs. Next, we track how much is produced from these inputs. The relationship between input and output reflects the level of productivity. If a company can increase production (or output) with the same or fewer inputs, its productivity is on the rise. This will increase profit margins, improve earnings, and usually leads to higher wages. However, if a firm's inputs remain the same even as output is slowing, its productivity is slipping, and this will quickly reduce corporate profits and perhaps even lead to layoffs.

How is productivity calculated? It's a fairly simple formula. How much did the private, non-farm economy produce? Divide that number by the number of hours worked to make those goods and services. (For example, let's look at a kitchen appliance manufacturer. Productivity in this case would be based on how many toasters factory workers assembled in a single hour.)

• *Compensation per hour:* This is the average hourly rate of compensation given to employees in non-farm business. (Continuing with the example of toasters, how much did that company compensate its workers per hour?) Compensation includes wages and salaries, bonuses, commissions, exercised stock options, and the value of employee-paid benefits. These include health costs, social security funds, and private pensions. After total compensation is calculated, it is divided by the number of hours worked.

• *Unit labor costs:* Once we have the two components just described—output per hour and compensation per hour—we can determine the unit labor costs, which represent the cost of labor to produce a single unit of product. (Using the illustration of the company making toasters, unit labor costs would show how much the manufacturer pays its workers for each toaster they make.) Recall that labor is the greatest cost to production, representing more than two-thirds of all business expenses. As unit labor costs go up, employers will either pass on these additional expenses to consumers in the form of higher prices, or they will absorb them and take a cut in profits. Suppose compensation per hour jumps by 3%, but labor productivity (output per hour) increases by only 2%. In that case, the cost of labor (or unit labor costs) rises by 1%. There is a close statistical correlation between changes in unit labor costs and the behavior of consumer prices in the future. If unit labor costs ratchet up, prices at the retail level will eventually climb too.

Let's assume that instead of labor productivity increasing 2%, it actually jumps by 4%. Now, with labor output per hour greater than the increase in compensation per hour (3%), the result is a drop in unit labor costs of 1%. Whenever labor costs fall due to higher productivity, the economy benefits greatly. Corporate profits increase, which in turn buoys stock prices. Second, there's no need for companies to raise prices, and they might very well reward their workforce for their efficiency with higher compensation. The combination of higher pay and dormant inflation leads to a higher standard of living for workers.

How Is It Computed?

Non-farm productivity and labor costs are compiled from numerous sources. Data on hours worked comes from the monthly payroll employment report (see the section

"Employment Situation"). For output, the government uses total GDP minus the output generated by the government, nonprofit institutions, the employees of private households, the rental value of owner-occupied dwellings, and the farm sector. Strip out all these factors and you're still left with a hefty 80% of the GDP.

Labor compensation figures come from the Bureau of Labor Statistics and the Bureau of Economic Analysis. They include direct labor income from wages and salaries, tips, bonuses, commissions, and exercised stock options. Also added to labor compensation are indirect payments, such as employee-paid benefits for health care, social security funds, and private pensions. In this release, total compensation costs are presented in both current dollars and inflation-adjusted dollars.

Revisions tend to occur frequently with productivity data—and for obvious reasons. Many of the statistical sources that underlie this indicator, like GDP and hours worked, are themselves subject to periodic revisions. Thus, any change in those measures automatically leads to revisions in the productivity and cost data too.

THE TABLES: CLUES ON WHAT'S AHEAD FOR THE ECONOMY

- **Table 2** Non-Farm Business Sector: Productivity, Hourly Compensation, Unit Labor Costs, and Prices

  When it comes to monitoring productivity numbers, players in the financial markets prefer to track the non-farm business sector, which makes up 75% of the GDP and is the focus of this table.

  (1) The second column, formally labeled *output per hour of all persons*, is the best overall indicator of the economy's efficiency. It records the percentage change in labor productivity from one quarter to the next as well as over the past year. Labor productivity is considered a leading indicator of inflation in the economy. Higher output per hour is essential if the economy is to grow rapidly without inciting inflation.

  To figure out just how fast the economy can expand before inflationary pressures heat up, take the annual growth of labor productivity in this table and *add* that to the yearly increase in the labor force (or working age population). If *output per hour* has averaged a 2.5% annual rate in the last several quarters and the labor force increases by 1% a year, the economy generally can grow as fast as 3.5% annually in the long run without arousing price pressures.

Table 2. Nonfarm business sector: Productivity, hourly compensation, unit labor costs, and prices, seasonally adjusted

Year and quarter	Output per hour of all persons	Output	Hours of all persons	Compensation per hour (1)	Real compensation per hour (2)	Unit labor costs	Unit non-labor payments (3)	Implicit price deflator (4)
				Indexes 1992=100				
2001 I	116.9	140.7	120.3	136.7	111.3	117.0	113.5	115.7
II	117.4	139.7	119.0	137.4	111.0	117.1	114.9	116.3
III	118.3	139.4	117.8	138.2	111.4	116.8	116.8	116.8
IV	120.7	140.4	116.3	138.9	112.1	115.1	119.0	116.5
ANNUAL	118.3	140.1	118.4	137.8	111.4	116.5	116.1	116.3
2002 I	123.4	142.5	115.5	140.2	112.8	113.6	121.5	116.4
II	123.7	142.9	115.5	141.5	112.9	114.4	121.2	116.8
III	125.5	144.7	115.3	142.2	112.8	113.3	123.1	116.9
IV	126.0	145.3	115.3	142.8	112.7	113.3	124.3	117.3
ANNUAL	124.7	143.9	115.4	141.7	112.8	113.6	122.5	116.9
2003 I	126.7	145.8	115.1	r143.7	r112.4	r113.4	r125.2	117.7
II	r128.9	r147.5	114.4	r145.0	r113.2	r112.5	r127.5	117.9
III	131.4	150.6	114.6	146.1	113.4	111.2	131.0	118.4
				Percent change from previous quarter at annual rate(5)				
2001 I	-0.4	-0.9	-0.5	4.3	0.5	4.7	0.8	3.3
II	1.6	-2.7	-4.3	2.0	-1.2	0.3	5.0	2.0
III	3.4	-0.8	-4.1	2.4	1.5	-0.9	6.6	1.7
IV	8.3	2.9	-5.0	2.1	2.7	-5.7	7.7	-1.0
ANNUAL	1.9	-0.1	-2.0	3.6	0.8	1.7	2.4	1.9
2002 I	9.3	6.2	-2.9	3.7	2.4	-5.2	8.7	-0.2
II	1.0	0.9	0.0	3.9	0.3	2.9	-0.9	1.4
III	5.9	5.2	-0.6	2.0	-0.2	-3.7	6.6	0.1
IV	1.7	1.7	0.0	1.6	-0.4	-0.1	3.9	1.4
ANNUAL	5.4	2.7	-2.5	2.8	1.2	-2.4	5.6	0.5
2003 I	2.1	1.4	-0.7	r2.6	r-1.2	r0.4	r2.8	1.4
II	r7.0	r4.6	r-2.2	r3.6	r3.0	r-3.2	r7.4	r0.8
III	8.1	8.8	0.7	3.1	0.8	-4.6	11.6	1.5
				Percent change from corresponding quarter of previous year				
2001 I	2.0	1.4	-0.6	4.5	1.1	2.5	1.4	2.1
II	1.1	-0.6	-1.6	4.6	1.1	3.5	-0.3	2.1
III	1.7	-0.8	-2.5	3.0	0.3	1.3	3.7	2.2
IV	3.2	-0.4	-3.5	2.7	0.9	-0.5	5.0	1.5
ANNUAL	1.9	-0.1	-2.0	3.6	0.8	1.7	2.4	1.9
2002 I	5.6	1.3	-4.0	2.5	1.3	-2.9	7.0	0.6
II	5.4	2.3	-3.0	3.0	1.7	-2.3	5.4	0.5
III	6.1	3.8	-2.1	2.9	1.3	-3.0	5.4	0.1
IV	4.4	3.5	-0.9	2.8	0.5	-1.6	4.5	0.7
ANNUAL	5.4	2.7	-2.5	2.8	1.2	-2.4	5.6	0.5
2003 I	2.6	2.3	-0.3	r2.5	r-0.4	r-0.1	r3.1	1.1
II	4.1	3.2	-0.9	r2.4	r0.3	r-1.6	r5.2	0.9
III	4.7	4.1	-0.6	2.7	0.5	-1.9	6.4	1.3

This table can also offer some insights into future employment trends. If economic growth exceeds productivity growth, it will encourage more hiring. By adding more workers, companies hope to increase output to satisfy the economy's rising demand for goods and services.

(2) About midway across the page is a column called *compensation per hour*, and it provides some clues on emerging wage pressures. Because labor represents a significant portion of business costs, experts follow the compensation numbers closely, especially as they relate to productivity growth. The link between *compensation per hour* and *output per hour* shows up vividly in the nearby column titled *unit labor costs*, which is an excellent indicator of how painful labor costs are to business. As long as *output per hour* rises faster than *compensation per hour*, it will drive down the all-important *unit labor costs*. Should *unit labor costs* start to rise, which can happen when compensation expenses climb faster than productivity, it can unleash the destructive forces of inflation.

One interesting point here is that once productivity growth takes hold, it is likely to foster even more capital investment spending. The reason is that in a highly competitive global marketplace, the pressure is on for manufacturers, wholesalers, and retailers to keep their sales prices as low as necessary to hold on to customers. In this environment, companies will not be able improve profits simply by raising the price of their products. Otherwise, consumers here and abroad will react by quickly shopping elsewhere. Since it becomes increasingly difficult to rely on pricing as a way to fatten profits, the other option is to further reduce operating costs, and that can be accomplished by achieving even higher levels of productivity.

MARKET IMPACT

Bonds

Fixed income traders rarely get excited at quarterly releases, even for one as important as productivity. That's because some of the components, such as output and hours worked, have already been published in separate reports. Still, reaction in the bond market to the productivity report might vary, depending on how inflation and labor costs have been behaving in the background. The primary point here is that higher productivity levels keep inflation in check. However, a fall in productivity during times of rising wages will upset the bond market and lead to a sell-off, with prices falling and yields rising.

Stocks

The equity market in this instance will react much like bonds. Higher productivity growth translates into lower unit labor costs and bigger corporate profits—events that can propel stocks to higher prices. Flat or declining productivity is viewed as bearish for equity prices.

Dollar

The dollar will also be on better footing if there are firm gains in U.S. productivity. By operating efficiently, companies in this country will be in a better position to compete with foreigners, an important prerequisite to lowering the monthly trade and current account deficits.

EMPLOYER COSTS FOR EMPLOYEE COMPENSATION

Market Sensitivity: Low.

What Is It: Measures dollar cost per hour of having an employee on payroll.

News Release on the Internet: *www.bls.gov/news.release/ecec.toc.htm*

Home Web Address: *www.bls.gov*

Release Time: 10 a.m. (ET); released nearly three months after the end of the reported quarter.

Frequency: Quarterly.

Source: Bureau of Labor Statistics, Department of Labor.

Revisions: No revisions.

WHY IS IT IMPORTANT?

For years, economists have been clamoring for more information on labor costs. Employee compensation plays a pivotal role in determining future inflation and economic growth. A rise in wages can boost household confidence, fuel consumer spending, and keep the economy running smoothly. For business, however, a rise in the cost of labor can have adverse consequences on competitiveness and profits. If employee expenses, which account for about three-fourths of all business costs, climb too quickly, they can eventually ignite inflation. Given the enormous importance of compensation costs in the economy, it is easy to see why so much attention is focused on this subject. The Employment Cost Index does track changes for such expenses, but the results are put out in the form of an index. More helpful to some analysts would be labor cost data presented in actual dollar terms.

Now comes along a relatively new quarterly series that does precisely that. This release, which comes with the unfortunate appellation of Employer Costs for Employee Compensation (ECEC), looks at the average cost per hour in dollars of having an employee on payroll. It was originally put out just once a year, but the annual data quickly became outdated for those who tried to project future economic trends. As a result, starting in the fall of 2002, the Bureau of Labor Statistics began to publish it every quarter. Economists applauded the change, but the financial markets and the press have so far given this series surprisingly little notice even though it is easier to relate to. It's expected that the ECEC will shortly be recognized as an effective and reliable gauge of actual labor costs and possibly even become a leading indicator of consumer spending and inflation.

How Is It Computed?

The ECEC is based on a population survey involving both the private and public sector (local and state only; the federal payroll is excluded). Every quarter, the Bureau of Labor Statistics makes inquiries into labor costs at about 11,000 establishments in private industry involving 50,000 occupational observations. It also includes 800 establishments in state and local governments, public schools, and public hospitals covering 3,500 occupational groupings. The surveys are conducted for the pay period that includes the 12th day of the month in March, June, September, and December.

The same sampling is used to compute both the Employment Cost Index and the Employer Costs for Employee Compensation. After the raw data arrives, there is a slight difference in how these two labor cost measures are calculated, and this can cause them to diverge on an annual basis. The Employment Cost Index uses a fixed weight for different occupational groups that's updated about every 10 years, the last being in 2002. On the other hand, the ECEC reformulates its weights every quarter based on changes in the number of people at work for the jobs listed in the sampling data.

Wages and Salary

The data is collected on a straight-time hourly pay basis. For employees not paid on an hourly basis, a computation is made based on salary, which is then divided by the corresponding hours worked. Also included are production bonuses, incentive earnings, commission payments, and cost-of-living adjustments. Excluded from this calculation is premium pay for overtime and for work performed on weekends and holidays.

Benefits

Benefits covered by the ECEC are paid vacations, sick leave, holidays, premium pay for overtime, shift differentials, insurance benefits, retirement and savings benefits, social security, Medicare, and federal- and state-mandated social insurance programs.

The Tables: Clues on What's Ahead for the Economy

Labor cost measures, such as Average Hourly Earnings and the Employment Cost Index (ECI), have demonstrated some qualities as leading indicators of consumer spending and economic growth. The new quarterly ECEC series is expected have to similar predictive values. Precisely how well it correlates with these key variables in the economy has yet to be determined.

- **Table 1** Employer Costs Per Hour Worked for Employee Compensation and Costs as a Percent of Total Compensation

Want to know how much it costs on average for companies to have employees? You'll find all the key compensation figures in this table, along with their percentage of total labor expenses. For example, in September 2006, average total compensation (pay and benefits) for civilian workers came to $27.31 per hour. The table then breaks down that amount to show its two components: wages and salary at $19.12 per hour, and benefits expenses at $8.18 per hour. The latter is further segmented, listing the hourly cost to companies for providing paid leave, health and life insurance, retirement savings, and legally required benefits.

Table 1. Employer costs per hour worked for employee compensation and costs as a percent of total compensation: Civilian workers, by major occupational and industry group, September 2006

Compensation component	Occupational group							
	All workers[1]		Management, professional, and related		Sales and office		Service	
	Cost	Percent	Cost	Percent	Cost	Percent	Cost	Percent
Total compensation	$27.31	100.0	$45.77	100.0	$20.73	100.0	$14.97	100.0
Wages and salaries	19.12	70.0	32.46	70.9	14.78	71.3	10.63	71.0
Total benefits	8.18	30.0	13.31	29.1	5.95	28.7	4.34	29.0
Paid leave	1.91	7.0	3.67	8.0	1.40	6.8	0.87	5.8
Vacation	0.89	3.3	1.66	3.6	0.67	3.2	0.41	2.7
Holiday	0.63	2.3	1.18	2.6	0.47	2.3	0.27	1.8
Sick	0.29	1.1	0.62	1.3	0.20	1.0	0.14	0.9
Other	0.10	0.4	0.21	0.5	0.06	0.3	0.05	0.3
Supplemental pay	0.69	2.5	1.12	2.4	0.45	2.2	0.27	1.8
Overtime and premium[4]	0.25	0.9	0.16	0.3	0.13	0.6	0.15	1.0
Shift differentials	0.06	0.2	0.09	0.2	0.02	0.1	0.05	0.4
Nonproduction bonuses	0.37	1.4	0.87	1.9	0.29	1.4	0.06	0.4
Insurance	2.22	8.1	3.30	7.2	1.80	8.7	1.23	8.2
Life	0.05	0.2	0.08	0.2	0.03	0.2	0.02	0.1
Health	2.09	7.6	3.07	6.7	1.70	8.2	1.18	7.9
Short-term disability	0.05	0.2	0.07	0.2	0.03	0.2	0.02	0.1
Long-term disability	0.04	0.1	0.08	0.2	0.03	0.1	([5])	([6])
Retirement and savings	1.18	4.3	2.19	4.8	0.65	3.2	0.57	3.8
Defined benefit	0.74	2.7	1.33	2.9	0.31	1.5	0.46	3.1
Defined contribution	0.44	1.6	0.87	1.9	0.35	1.7	0.11	0.7
Legally required benefits	2.19	8.0	3.03	6.6	1.64	7.9	1.40	9.3
Social Security and Medicare	1.54	5.6	2.48	5.4	1.23	5.9	0.87	5.8
Social Security[7]	1.22	4.5	1.95	4.3	0.99	4.8	0.70	4.6
Medicare	0.31	1.1	0.53	1.2	0.24	1.2	0.17	1.2
Federal unemployment insurance	0.03	0.1	0.02	([6])	0.03	0.2	0.03	0.2
State unemployment insurance	0.15	0.5	0.14	0.3	0.14	0.7	0.12	0.8
Workers' compensation	0.48	1.8	0.39	0.8	0.25	1.2	0.37	2.5

This first table, however, is quite broad in that it encompasses all civilian workers in both private industry and state and local governments. Subsequent tables in this 24-page report, while not included in this book, list the costs for different segments of the active workforce. For example, Table 2 in the release shows labor costs in dollars for different occupational and industry groups.

Table 5 compares the compensation costs for union versus non-union employees.

Table 6 records labor expenses in the goods- versus service-producing sectors.

Table 7 quantifies how compensation expenses differ across regions of the country.

Table 8 notes labor costs at firms of various sizes. That is, it computes the average hourly expense for labor at companies with up to 99 employees, up to 500 employees, and more than 500 employees.

One question that arises here is which measure—the ECI or the ECEC—you should use to get a better sense of labor cost changes across American industry. The answer depends on what you're looking for. The ECEC gives you the average compensation in dollar terms during a certain period, while the ECI measures change in the cost of compensation from one period to the next. One problem with the ECEC release is that it does not contain any historical tables. To see changes in the dollar-based ECEC over several quarters and years, follow these steps:

1. Go to the Bureau of Labor Statistics Web site at *www.bls.gov/ncs/ect/home.htm*.

2. Click Get Detailed Statistics, located at the top line across the page.

3. You'll see a column titled "Create Customized Tables." Scroll down the page and click the category for Employer Costs for Employee Compensation (ECEC). A table appears, which allows you to pick and choose specific labor cost categories. Once you click "Get Data," it retrieves historical compensation costs that can go back quarterly or yearly—to the 1980s in some cases.

MARKET IMPACT

Again, this quarterly indicator is relatively new, so it hasn't received much notice from the investment community. That recognition will come once it develops a track record as a useful indicator that can anticipate future labor costs, corporate profit margins, and consumer spending.

REAL EARNINGS

Market Sensitivity: Low to medium.

What Is It: Measures the change in worker earnings after adjusting for inflation.

News Release on the Internet: *www.bls.gov/news.release/realer.toc.htm*

Home Web Address: *www.bls.gov/*

Release Time: 8:30 a.m. (ET); published in the middle of the month the same day the CPI is released and refers to earnings in the previous month.

Frequency: Monthly.

Source: Bureau of Labor Statistics, Department of Labor.

Revisions: Changes are made monthly and are the result of revisions in the previous month's employment report or the CPI.

WHY IS IT IMPORTANT?

Just how much do American workers earn these days after adjusting for inflation? This is a critical issue since people work hard for their money and rising prices can rob them of their purchasing power. If incomes fail to grow at or above the rate of inflation, Americans have less to spend on food, clothing, vacations, and gasoline. The result is lower living standards and discontented consumers. Labor unrest might follow as workers demand more pay to offset the corrosive effects of higher prices. On the other hand, if workers achieve true gains in real incomes, where earnings exceed the pace of inflation, more can be purchased with each paycheck, and that can promote further economic growth. Thus, tracking real earnings can be helpful in forecasting future trends in consumer spending.

Yet, the stock and bond markets do not react at all to this report. The reason is that the real earnings report simply combines two different sets of dated statistics. It's based on earnings from the previous employment release and then gets adjusted for inflation using the Consumer Price Index (CPI), which happens to be published at the same time as Real Earnings.

Another reason why this indicator fails to command much attention is that earnings from work represent just one source of household income. It does not include profit sharing or increases in household wealth due to capital gains from financial assets (like stocks and bonds) and real estate, all of which play a role in the psychology of spending.

How Is It Computed?

Data on average weekly earnings is collected from the monthly jobs release (see the section "Employment Situation")—specifically, the payroll reports of private non-farm establishments. Only workers holding full-time and part-time production and non-supervisory jobs, which represent more than two-thirds of the total workforce, are included here. To get the real average weekly earnings, economists take the current dollar earnings for the week and adjust it for changes in the Consumer Price Index for all workers (CPI-W). The outcome is real average weekly earnings based on 1982 dollars.

The Tables: Clues on What's Ahead for the Economy

- **Table A**   Composition of Change in Real Earnings of Production or Nonsupervisory Workers on Private Non-Farm Payrolls

  (1) This table lists the percentage change in real average weekly earnings for each month going back a year. The data is seasonally adjusted and can jump around wildly month to month—so much so that it's hard to detect an underlying trend at times. Nevertheless, it does provide useful data on how real earnings have performed in recent months.

Table A. Composition of change in real earnings of production or nonsupervisory workers[1] on private nonfarm payrolls

Year and month	Average hourly earnings	Average weekly hours	Average weekly earnings	The Consumer Price Index[2]	Real average weekly earnings
	Percent change from preceding month, seasonally adjusted				
2002:					
Oct.	0.3	-0.3	([3])	0.2	-0.1
Nov.	.3	.0	.3	.1	.2
Dec.	.4	.0	.4	.1	.3
2003:					
Jan.	.1	.0	.1	.3	-.2
Feb.	.5	-.3	.2	.7	-.5
Mar.	.0	.3	.3	.5	-.2
Apr.	.1	-.3	-.2	-.5	.3
May	.3	.0	.3	-.1	.5
June	.2	.0	.2	.2	([3])
July	.3	-.3	([3])	.1	-.1
Aug.	.1	.3	.4	.4	([3])
Sept. [p]	.0	.0	.0	.3	-.3
Oct. [p]	.1	.3	.4	-.2	.5 ◀1

• **Table B**   Percent Change in Earnings from the Same Month a Year Ago

(2) If you want to spot a pattern in real income growth, it's best to look at this table. Here you'll find the percentage change in real average hourly earnings and real weekly earnings over the past 12 months for each month. The information helps investors and economists forecast consumer expenditures and might even serve as an indicator of future labor turmoil, especially if there is a sustained decline in real earnings.

Table B. Percent change in earnings from the same month a year ago for production or nonsupervisory workers[1] on private nonfarm payrolls, seasonally adjusted

Year and month	Average hourly earnings		Average weekly earnings	
	Current dollars	Constant (1982) dollars[2]	Current dollars	Constant (1982) dollars[2]
2002:				
Oct.	3.1	1.2	3.4	1.5
Nov.	3.0	.9	3.0	.9
Dec.	3.2	.7	2.9	.4
2003:				
Jan.	3.3	.6	3.3	.6
Feb.	3.5	.4	2.9	-.2
Mar.	3.3	.0	3.0	-.3
Apr.	3.3	1.1	2.7	.4
May	3.3	1.2	2.7	.6
June	3.0	.9	2.1	([3])
July	3.1	1.1	2.5	.5
Aug.	2.9	.7	2.3	.1
Sept. [p]	2.7	.5	2.1	-.2
Oct. [p]	2.4	.4	2.4	.5

⬆   ⬆

▲
2

MARKET IMPACT

Bonds

The real earnings report does not have any effect on the fixed income market because it is overshadowed by the market-moving CPI, which is released simultaneously.

Stocks

The equity market does not react to this report.

Dollar

The U.S. currency is not sensitive to real earnings.

YIELD CURVE

Market Sensitivity: Medium.

What Is It: The range of yields on Treasury securities from short- to long-term
   maturities.

Web Addresses: *www.stockcharts.com/charts/YieldCurve.html*
   www.bloomberg.com/markets/rates/index.html

Frequency: Always available.

Source: Treasury markets.

WHY IS IT IMPORTANT?

When it comes to predicting the future course of the economy, only one indicator stands
above all others in terms of accuracy: the yield curve. No other measurement has demonstrated as much success in warning of upcoming turning points in business activity. The
yield curve is a collection of yields plotted on a graph that covers the entire spectrum of
maturities on U.S. Treasury securities. What distinguishes the yield curve from all other
economic indicators is that it's not something produced by a government agency or private group. Instead, it comes directly from the financial markets and is supposed to reflect
the collective wisdom of investors at any moment in time on the likely direction of the
economy and inflation. Best yet, you don't have to wait a week or a month for the results
of this indicator; you can check out Treasury yields anytime.

   All yield curve graphs have the same characteristics. They begin on the left with the
shortest maturities, which in most cases are three-month Treasuries, and then progress to
6 months, 1 year, 2, 5, 10, all the way up to 30-year bonds at the far right side of the
curve. What makes the yield curve such a powerful forecasting tool is its shape after you
plot the yields on a graph. The curve can slope up gradually or steeply, appear totally flat,
or be completely inverted. In a normal yield curve, the yield starts off low on short maturities and then gradually rises as the duration of the security lengthens (see Chart A). Why
is this considered normal? Because in a typical economic expansion, investors demand a
higher rate of return on longer maturing Treasury debt. After all, if they decide to purchase a 10- or 30-year bond, investors want extra compensation in the form of a higher
yield for all the unknown risks they face over the coming years. These risks can include
inflation swings, political turmoil, and war. In contrast, those investors buying short-term
Treasuries have far less risk to worry about and thus are willing to accept a lower yield.
It's much easier to foresee what will happen in the next few months than predict conditions two or three decades ahead.

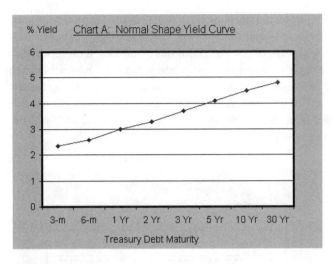

If a normal yield curve consists of a very gradual increase in interest rates over time, a steep yield curve is an extreme version of that, with yields climbing to higher levels much more rapidly than on a normal curve (see Chart B).

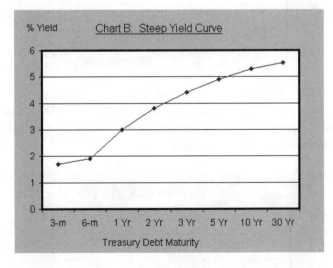

This can occur when the economy is starting to pick up speed, causing fresh anxieties that inflation can become more problematic in the near future. Such worries might provoke investors into selling longer-term Treasury securities, especially if they believe the Federal Reserve is moving too slowly to contain emerging price pressures. This will depress bond prices and drive longer-term yields higher. (On the other hand, if the Fed is perceived to be acting quickly to preempt an outbreak of inflation, investors could actually rush in to buy long-term Treasuries to lock in high yields while bond prices are still relatively cheap. In that case, a steep yield curve will not materialize. You can see how timely Federal Reserve intervention, or lack thereof, can greatly influence yields across the entire range of bond maturities.)

A flat yield curve exists when both short- and long-term securities provide nearly identical yields. It's the first major shot across the bow and warns that the economy is in trouble and in danger of slipping into recession (see Chart C), a scenario that markedly lessens the risk of inflation. Traders often buy bonds in such circumstances to capture higher longer-term yields. The result is that bonds prices appreciate and yields move down closer to short-term rates.

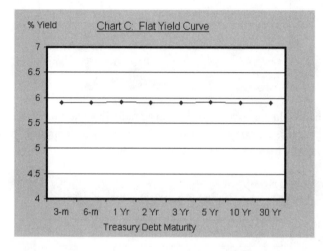

An inverted yield curve, where short-term rates are materially higher than long-term rates, is the siren call that a recession is in the offing (see Chart D). It reflects the view that the Fed is keeping short-term rates too high (with money getting scarce) and that an economic downturn is a virtual certainty.

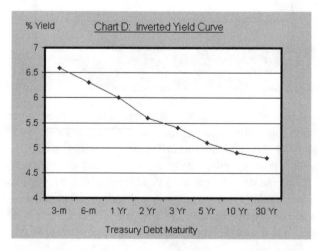

HOW IS IT COMPUTED?

Plotting a yield curve is easy enough. Several major newspapers (*New York Times*, *Wall Street Journal*, and *Investor's Business Daily*) as well as numerous financial sites on the Internet (see the Web locations listed at the beginning of this section) have a table listing the latest yields on Treasury debt. You don't have to graph them to determine whether the slope of the curve is normal, flat, or inverted. Simply jot down the published yields for the following Treasury securities:

- 3-month bill
- 6-month bill
- 1-year bill
- 2-year note
- 3-year note
- 5-year note
- 10-year note/bond
- 30-year bond

A normal yield curve has a spread, which is the difference in yield between the 30-year bond and the short 3-month bill, of about two and half percentage points. Anything greater than that would be considered a steep yield curve. A flat curve is where they all huddle close to the same rate, and an inverted curve is whenever the 3-month bill rate is higher than that of the 10- or 30-year bond. A key point to appreciate is that while the Federal Reserve sets yields at the shortest end of the curve by governing the overnight federal funds rate, it's the market that determines all other yields.

THE TABLES: CLUES ON WHAT'S AHEAD FOR THE ECONOMY

So what can you learn from the yield curve? After plotting the yields, determine the curve's shape. If the yield curve is flat or inverted, chances are that the economy is, or will soon become, sluggish. Indeed, once the curve is inverted, the odds greatly increase that a recession is unavoidable. Just how certain can we be a recession will occur? Let history be a guide. Since 1960, all six U.S. recessions have been preceded by an inverted yield curve months in advance. No other indicator has shown such consistency, not even the stock market. Once a recession is under way, short-term rates often plunge as the demand for money and credit dries up and the Federal Reserve pumps more funds into the economy to make borrowing even cheaper. Should the economy respond and start to turn up, the combination of very low yields on short-term Treasuries and a rebound in yields on 10- and 30-year bonds can produce a steep yield curve. It is symptomatic of an economy moving from recession to growth again. After healthy growth resumes, the Fed lifts short-term rates a little, and the yield curve returns to its more normal spread of about 2.5 percentage points.

Clearly, the yield curve has had an enviable track record of predicting turning points in the economy. But lately economists have been grappling with an unusual quandary. The yield curve had been inverted in both 2005 and 2006, yet the economy showed no sign of slipping into recession. Even more puzzling was that this inversion occurred against a backdrop of economic vitality, rising inflation, and higher short-term rates. Normally yields on longer-term Treasuries would jump on such occasions to produce a positively sloped curve. But that didn't happen. Instead, the curve inverted, with long-term rates remaining below those of much shorter maturities. This perverse behavior in the yield curve has bewildered many experts, including then-Federal Reserve Chairman Alan Greenspan, who characterized this peculiar behavior as a "conundrum."

Could it be that the yield curve is losing its value as a reliable predictor of economic weakness? This is the question many economists are presently wrestling with. At the very least, something has affected the shape of the yield curve, and we may have to reassess what it is trying to tell us.

One broad explanation for the recent inversion of the yield curve could be a fundamental shift in the demand for long-term Treasuries. In essence, American and foreign investors are buying government securities for reasons that have little to do with how the U.S. economy performs in the short run. For instance, oil exporters (both OPEC and non-OPEC producers) found themselves flush with petrodollars after the price of crude touched record high levels. Since oil is paid for in dollars all over the globe, oil-rich countries are acquiring more dollars than they know what to do with. Many have chosen to place a significant portion of that income in Treasuries, which are viewed as the safest and most liquid investment in the world.

In addition, countries such as China, Japan, and South Korea, which depend on exports for much of their economic growth, will take the surplus dollars they earn from their sales to the U.S. and buy Treasuries too. Such purchases enable these countries to better manage the value of their own currencies in foreign exchange markets. These countries do not want to have an overly strong currency because that can harm their exports. To keep their currency from significantly appreciating, they will buy more U.S. governments securities since that lifts the dollar's value.

Third, baby boomers, the wealthiest generation in U.S. history, are now preparing for retirement by gradually selling long-held stocks to lock up years of capital gains and are buying Treasuries for income and safety. This generational shift from stocks to bonds will become another significant source of demand for fixed income securities in the years ahead.

Finally, in an ironic twist, the whole "conundrum" of the inverted yield curve could be a by-product of the Federal Reserve's own success as an inflation fighter. Think about it. For two decades the U.S. central bank has been led by a tag team of skillful economists (Volcker, Greenspan, and Bernanke). Their aggressive stance against inflation has made U.S. Treasuries less risky and thus more appealing to domestic and foreign investors. All these factors have greatly fueled demand for government securities.

Does this mean the yield curve is becoming irrelevant? Not at all. It's just that in light of these recent developments, its future effectiveness as a forecasting measure will be based more on the *magnitude* of the inverted yield curve and its duration—not simply because it happens to be nominally inverted. One report by the Federal Reserve Bank of St. Louis calculated the probabilities of a recession based on the yield curve as follows: If the curve is normal so that the 10-year Treasury bond yield is more than 1.2 percentage points above the three-month bill, the chance of recession is less than 5%. Once the yield curve flattens and the two have essentially the same yield, the probability of recession rises to 25%. If the curve ends up inverted where the yield on three-month bills stands 2.4 percentage points *above* the 10-year bond, the odds leap to 90% that an economic downturn will materialize within the next 18 months.

MARKET IMPACT

Bonds

Expectations of future growth and inflation by fixed income traders determine which Treasury debt maturities are the most attractive to buy. Such preferences help shape the yield curve. However, since the outlook for economic activity and price behavior can change, the yield curve is constantly in a state of motion.

Stocks

The equity market has not taken the yield curve seriously in the past, despite its proven forecasting record. This is surprising because stock prices are based on expectations of future corporate earnings and overall business activity, both of which can be foreseen by the behavior of the yield curve. Indeed, studies have shown that the yield curve can serve as an effective market-timing strategy, yet it remains underappreciated among portfolio managers.

Dollar

Foreign investor reaction to a flat or inverted yield curve is difficult to predict. Much depends on the magnitude of the inverted yield curve, which is how much higher short-term rates are above long-term rates, and how U.S. short-term rates stack up against those of other countries. It is possible that active foreign traders might choose to avoid investing in the U.S. because a flat or inverted yield curve is a harbinger of anemic growth, if not recession. That will cause the dollar to depreciate in foreign exchange markets. However, if the yield curve is so inverted that U.S. short-term rates are markedly higher than those of other nations, it may attract an influx of "hot money" from overseas as foreign investors seek to take advantage of the greater returns they can receive here. What do we mean by "hot money"? It's fast-moving money from investors around the world who are constantly on the hunt for the highest possible short-term gains. The instant an investment loses its appeal (for example, when U.S. yields fall relative to their foreign counterparts), that "hot" money quickly leaves the borders of one country for another lucrative region of the world. Thus, the dollar might bounce up in value when there is an inverted yield curve, but its strength would be very tenuous.

A steep yield curves suggests stronger economic growth and rising short-term rates in the months ahead. This will likely attract foreign investors to purchase and hold dollar-based financial assets.

CHAPTER 4

International Economic Indicators: Why Are They So Important?

U.S. economic indicators help us understand what is happening in the domestic economy. However, to be a successful investor or an effective corporate leader in today's highly integrated global economy also requires knowledge of what is going on beyond U.S. borders. A CEO who wants to sell products overseas or an investor who seeks to achieve higher returns on stocks and bonds should be familiar with indicators that gauge the health of foreign economies.

Why place so much emphasis on the international business climate? One reason is that most of the growth in the world economy is taking place within the emerging countries, not the large industrial nations. Secondly, the performance of U.S. corporate profits, stocks and bonds, and the dollar is affected by foreign developments more than ever before. A recession in Europe harms not only companies on that continent, but many U.S.-based firms as well. Close to half of the earnings of S&P 500 firms originate from sales outside the U.S. Companies in the energy and technology sectors, for example, generate more than half of their revenues abroad. Moreover, it just makes good business sense to be aware of new opportunities that become available in markets outside the U.S. By diversifying into Europe, Asia, and Latin America, one is no longer bound to the economic swings of just one country. Indeed, there is much fertile territory to choose from in other markets. Equity investors, for example, can pick from more than 40,000 public companies that are listed on world stock exchanges, two-thirds of which are outside the U.S.

To be sure, there are additional risks to consider when investing overseas. One of the biggest is adverse movements in currencies. If you own securities or other assets in another country and their currency climbs in value against the dollar, great! The overall return on that investment gets an added lift because it is more valuable in dollar terms. However, should that currency happen to weaken relative to the dollar, the investment will be less valuable or perhaps even turn into a loss once it is sold and the proceeds converted back to dollars. Thus, shifts in foreign exchange values can potentially make or break a foreign investment.

Given the risks currencies pose, wouldn't it make more sense to simply shy away from international markets? Absolutely not. There is nothing inherently mysterious about the movement of the dollar, euro, yen, British pound, or any of the other major free-floating currencies in the foreign exchange markets, for ultimately, the long-term value of a currency is determined by a country's economic fundamentals. Is the economy growing? Does inflation remain under control? Are consumers and businesses confident about the future of their economy? Are government fiscal policies responsible? Does the country have adequate savings for investments? Is its international trade account in reasonable balance? These are the issues that have the greatest influence in determining currency values. Sure, exchange rates might fluctuate in the short term due to differences in interest rates or from occasional uncertainties born of economic or political instability. But, by and large, the true value of a currency is based on the economic soundness and vitality of the country behind it.

Another criticism heard about entering foreign markets is that the benefits of global diversification have been oversold. According to this argument, markets overseas increasingly appear to march in lockstep with those in the U.S., so why bother investing elsewhere, where the risks are greater? It is true that during periods of crises, whether they be economic, political, or military, markets around the world tend to move in unison. However, such moments of high global tension are uncommon, and these parallel movements in the value of assets around the world are usually very brief—a matter of days or weeks at most. Generally, foreign financial markets tend to pursue their own direction. Canada's stock market historically has a 65% correlation with the U.S.; for the U.K. it is 60%. German equities have a 45% correlation, and Japan has about a 25% relationship. Case in point: Just look at the best and worst performers by national stock markets over the last several years in Table 4.0.

Table 4.0   Ranking Stock Market Performance by Country (Based on Local Currencies)

	2002	**2003**	**2004**	**2005**	**2006**
Best Performers	Pakistan	Egypt	Egypt	Egypt	China
	Argentina	Thailand	Colombia	Colombia	Argentina
	Colombia	Peru	Indonesia	Russia	Indonesia
Worst Performers	Finland	Australia	Finland	Hong Kong	Turkey
	Sweden	Netherlands	Peru	U.S.	Israel
	Germany	Finland	Thailand	Malaysia	Jordan

Source: *Fidelity International, DataStream*

The first question that comes to mind after looking at this list is "Where is the U.S.?" It's not listed among the top performers. The reason for its absence is that U.S. stocks simply didn't perform well enough to earn that distinction, not even during the economic recovery that followed the 2001 recession. Indeed, the return on U.S. equities came in among the lowest in 2005 compared to other national markets. The point of this table is to underscore the importance of keeping an open mind about the opportunities as well as perils that come with international investments. No one can predict with certainty which economies and financial markets will outperform others. But there should be no dispute that the virtues of diversifying investments abroad remain as valid as ever.

This chapter is designed to take you to the next level, which is to identify the foreign indicators that provide the best read on current and future global economic conditions. Certain barometers of economic activity abroad should be followed with the same regularity and scrutiny as U.S. indicators so that investors and business managers have a chance of achieving success in international markets. The problem, much like with the U.S., is that there is a vast amount of foreign economic data in the public domain. Hundreds of countries churn out thousands of statistics on a regular basis. Even if you narrowed down the number of countries worth monitoring to two dozen, the task of following all the indicators that flow from these nations can still be overwhelming. Besides the sheer variety of international statistics, many of them are difficult to locate when needed. Often they are defined and computed differently than indicators in the U.S. and can vary greatly in quality. A large number are not even presented in English.

This chapter tries to overcome these problems. In the following pages, we select the most important foreign economic indicators for closer study. They represent the three major non-U.S. markets in the world: Europe, Asia, and Latin America. As is the case with U.S. economic statistics, these foreign indicators are released to the public on a predetermined schedule. Calendars of international economic releases can be found on the Web sites listed at the start of Chapter 6, "Best Web Sites for International Economic Indicators." All the international indicators presented here are available on the Internet. They originate either from official government or private association Web sites, are free to the public, and can be viewed in English.

Finally, note that international data is presented in different formats. Many countries use commas instead of decimal points and a period or a space instead of a comma to indicate the thousands place. For example, the U.S. and Germany both represent numbers using decimal points and commas, but sometimes the symbols are interchanged (2,325.77 versus 2.325,77). At other times, Germany (and France) might use a space as the digit-grouping symbol (2 325,77).

International dates are also displayed differently around the world. In the U.S., the month precedes the day; Europeans mostly use day-month-year, while Asian cultures use year-month-day. Why isn't there a single standard for all countries now that world economic and financial systems are so closely integrated? Tradition and politics. These two hurdles are difficult to overcome. Those favoring a uniform worldwide format will have a long wait. In the meantime, one has little choice but to get used to these local customs and move on.

GERMAN INDUSTRIAL PRODUCTION

What Is It: Industrial output in Europe's largest economy.

News Release on the Internet: *www.destatis.de/indicators/e/tkpi111x.htm*

Home Web Address: *www.destatis.de*

Release Time: 11 a.m. (Continental time); released the first or second week of the month and refers to activity two months earlier (so March data describes production in January).

Frequency: Monthly.

Source: Federal Statistics Office, Germany (Statistisches Bundesamt, Deutschland).

Revisions: Revisions can occur with each release and cover the two previous months.

Germany is Europe's richest and most populous country. Its output alone accounts for about a third of everything produced in Euroland, the name given to the region of 13 countries that use the euro currency.[*] Germany thus holds enormous sway over the Continent's economic well-being. However, the country's influence also extends far beyond Europe. Germany is the world's third-largest economy (preceded only by the U.S. and Japan) and the biggest exporter. It is also a key trading partner of the U.S. and an important investor. Trade between the two countries now exceeds $120 billion. The U.S. is the second-largest market for German products, while American exporters see Germany as their third-largest buyer. In terms of investing, German companies account for about 850,000 jobs in the U.S., while American firms have established roughly 500,000 positions in Germany.

   Given the dominance of its economy over Europe and the fact that it is a key player in the world as well, Germany's industrial production figure ranks at the top of the must-watch list. Though industrial output accounts for less than a quarter of the country's GDP, this indicator has been correlated with GDP changes in Euroland overall. Thus, investors and business executives who want to spot early signs of strength or weakness in Europe will find Germany's industrial production index a good leading indicator.

---

[*] As of this writing, 13 countries use the euro as their currency: Austria, Belgium, Finland, France, Germany, Greece, Ireland, Italy, Luxembourg, the Netherlands, Portugal, Slovenia, and Spain. Beginning in 2008, two more nations will join the group, Malta and Cyprus, enlarging the eurozone to 15 countries.

Federal Statistical Office Germany

Home | Contact | Press | Imprint | About us | Links | Deutsch | RSS

Production index - Production industries - Germany

DIISTATIS
wissen.nutzen.

Economic indicators
Please select

Time Series
Please select

⌐ Geography
⌐ Population
⌐ Employment
⌐ Elections
⌐ Education and culture
⌐ Social security schemes
⌐ Health
⌐ Justice
⌐ Construction and housing
⌐ Environment
⌐ Agriculture, fisheries
⌐ Industry, crafts
⌐ Domestic trade, hotel and restaurant industry, tourism
⌐ Transport
⌐ Money and banking, services
⌐ Foreign trade
⌐ Businesses, business notifications
⌐ Prices
⌐ Wages and salaries
⌐ Household budget surveys, time use
⌐ Finance and taxes
⌐ National accounts
▪ Microcensus
▪ Census
▪ Information society
▪ International data

Search

■Databases
▪GENESIS-Online
▪Federal Health Monitoring System

▪ Statistics-Shop

■Publications
Please select
■Library

▪ Scientific forum
Please select
■Events

21. Voorburg-Meeting
9 to 13 October 2006 in Wiesbaden
VOORBURG GROUP

Production index
Production industries
Germany

2000 = 100

Year	Month	Non-adjusted value		Working day and seasonally adjusted value (X-12-ARIMA)	
		Value	Change on the corresponding month of the previous year in %	Value	Change on the previous month in %
2006	Dec	105,1	1,3	111,7	-0,5
	Nov	121,7	6,3	112,3	2,0
	Oct	115,2	7,0	110,1	-1,1
	Sep	115,6	2,6	111,3	-0,5
	Aug	106,2	7,8	111,9	1,3
	Jul	108,5	5,8	110,5	0,9
	Jun	111,9	-0,1	109,5	0,1
	May	112,3	13,2	109,4	1,3
	Apr	101,6	-4,5	108,0	2,1
	Mar	116,5	11,4	105,8	-0,9
	Feb	99,3	5,6	106,8	0,7
	Jan	99,4	7,0	106,1	0,2
2005	Dec	103,8	4,4	105,9	0,3
	Nov	114,5	5,0	105,6	-0,8
	Oct	107,7	0,8	106,4	1,5
	Sep	112,7	3,7	104,8	1,3
	Aug	98,5	4,8	103,5	-1,0
	Jul	102,6	0,0	104,5	1,0
	Jun	112,0	5,1	103,5	1,2
	May	99,2	1,6	102,3	-0,2
	Apr	106,4	5,3	102,5	1,3
	Mar	104,6	-4,8	101,2	0,1
	Feb	94,0	0,0	101,1	-1,4
	Jan	92,9	2,9	102,5	1,3

Time series analysis by BV4.1

Table

Chart

GERMAN IFO BUSINESS SURVEY

What Is It: German business leaders assess the current and future economic climate.

News Release on the Internet: *www.ifo-business-climate-index.info*

Home Web Address: *www.ifo.de*

Release Time: 10:30 a.m. (Continental time); published the fourth week of the survey month.

Frequency: Monthly.

Source: IFO Institut für Wirtschaftsforschung (IFO Institute for Economic Research).

Revisions: Tend to be rare. Periodic revisions occur as a result of changes in seasonal adjustment factors.

Among the most anticipated economic statistics to come out in Europe every month is Germany's IFO Business Survey. It has been a very good leading indicator of how the German economy and, more broadly, the European economy will perform in the weeks ahead. Of course, a similar claim was made of the industrial production index. But what makes the IFO report such a sensitive one for investors is the timeliness of the data—the results are released the same month the survey is taken.

At the start of every month, the Institute questions more than 7,000 German business leaders and senior managers covering the manufacturing, construction, wholesale, and retailing industries. All are asked to appraise Germany's current business situation (good/satisfactory/poor) as well as their expectations over the next six months (more favorable/unchanged/more unfavorable). Their answers form the basis of the total IFO Business Climate Index and its two principal subcomponents: the present situations index, which assesses current economic conditions, and the expectations index, where those queried are asked to forecast what the business environment might be a half year later.

Of the three index results, European financial markets tune in more closely to the expectations series. History has shown that movements in the expectations index tend to lead changes in Euroland's industrial production by about two or three months. Thus, if the IFO expectations gauge turns up, odds are it will shortly be followed by an acceleration in factory output in Germany and perhaps much of Europe as well.

After the reunification of Germany, the IFO Institute initially published two separate business climate readings—one for eastern Germany and the other for western Germany. However, in 2004, the decision was made to combine the two sets of data to represent business activity in Germany as a whole. Economists at the IFO believed the business cycles for these two regions had by now largely converged, even though they were still operating at different output levels. Thus, the IFO Business Climate Survey now publishes a united German series for its headline index. Those who still want to see separate performance data for western and eastern Germany can do so by searching the more detailed IFO database on its Web sites.

Finally, it is interesting to note that the IFO Business Climate Survey appears to have a close correlation with the U.S.'s own Institute for Supply Management (ISM) manufacturing report. Over the years, a persistent rise in the ISM numbers has, after a six-month lag, been accompanied by an increase in the German IFO expectations index. Given the size and importance of the American economy in the world, this probably is not all that surprising. This linkage between the two surveys is yet another illustration of how interwoven the international economy has become.

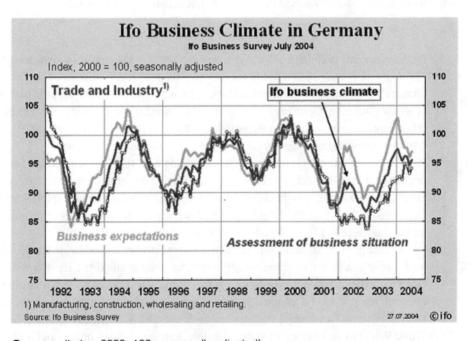

Germany (Index, 2000=100, seasonally adjusted)

	7/03	8/03	9/03	10/03	11/03	12/03	1/04	2/04	3/04	4/04	5/04	6/04	7/04
Climate	91.7	92.8	93.0	95.3	96.2	97.0	97.5	96.4	95.4	96.3	96.1	94.6	95.6
Situation	88.2	89.5	88.3	91.0	91.8	91.9	92.5	92.6	92.2	94.9	94.4	93.2	94.1
➤ Expectations	95.2	96.3	98.0	99.7	100.9	102.4	102.8	100.3	98.8	97.7	97.7	96.0	97.1

Source: IFO Institute for Economic Research, used with permission.

GERMAN CONSUMER PRICE INDEX (CPI)

What Is It: The main price inflation gauge for Europe's largest economy.

News Release on the Internet: *www.destatis.de/indicators/e/pre110je.htm*

Home Web Address: *www.destatis.de/e_home.htm*

Release Time: 7 a.m. (Continental time); the preliminary CPI is published around the 25th of every month. Final figures are released two weeks later.

Frequency: Monthly.

Source: Federal Statistics Office Germany (Statistisches Bundesamt Deutschland).

Revisions: Monthly report on the CPI might contain revisions for earlier months.

As the economic pillar of Europe, Germany can serve as the engine of growth for the Continent, or it can be responsible for dragging the region down. Which role Germany ultimately plays depends on many factors, but none more important than the performance of its own inflation. Germany's CPI can have a powerful impact on the economies of other European nations and on the policies of the European Central Bank (ECB), which sets short-term interest rates for all 13 countries using the euro currency.[*]

If German inflation is increasing at a troubling rate, the ECB will likely raise interest rates even if the other neighboring economies show their inflation to be relatively tame. On the other extreme, should Germany get caught up in a deflationary spiral where prices are consistently falling, the ECB is expected to jump in and lower rates to preempt a similar collapse in prices from spreading to the rest of the continent.

Germany's CPI has been on the radar screen of investors worldwide for decades. Its high profile can be traced to the country's oath to avoid at all costs a repetition of the catastrophic hyperinflation it experienced in the 1920s, when prices for essentials like bread and milk jumped several hundred percent every day, making its national currency essentially worthless. That painful memory led the Bundesbank (Germany's central bank) after World War II to set in stone a tough, inflexible, anti-inflationary policy, and it has never veered from that stance. For decades the Bundesbank showed zero tolerance for the slightest whiff of inflation beyond 2% a year. It made no difference whether the economy

---

[*] As of this writing, 13 countries use the euro as their currency: Austria, Belgium, Finland, France, Germany, Greece, Ireland, Italy, Luxembourg, the Netherlands, Portugal, Slovenia, and Spain. Beginning in 2008, two more nations will join the group, Malta and Cyprus, enlarging the eurozone to 15 countries.

was weak or unemployment was sky-high. The primary mandate of the central bank was to keep inflation close to zero and protect Germany's currency, the Deutsche Mark, at all costs, even if it meant lifting and holding rates at painfully high levels. While Germany's dogged defense against inflation contributed to years of chronically high joblessness, it also made its currency one of the most revered in the world.

During talks to establish the euro in the 1990s, Germany made clear to European negotiators that it would join the currency union only if the new European Central Bank agreed to pursue the same tough anti-inflationary position shown by the Bundesbank. German officials wanted the euro to have the kind of respectability in global currency markets that the mark had. That would mean keeping interest rate decisions for Eurozone nations out of the hands of politicians. Even today, Germany's influence on the ECB is palpable; Europe's central bank firmly toes the line that it will not permit inflation to exceed the 2% range for the Eurozone. Moreover, ECB policymakers place great weight on the outlook for German inflation to help formulate future monetary policy for the Eurozone.

Let's take a closer look at Germany's inflation measure itself. The CPI measures the average change in prices for all goods and services bought by households for the purpose of consumption. In the middle of the month, about 560 price collectors, working out of state government offices across Germany, collect prices on a basket of 750 specific goods and services. Overall, approximately 400,000 prices are obtained each month, including taxes (value-added and excise taxes) and price discounts (such as sales or rebates). The Federal Statistics Office (FSO) then compiles these price changes for six key German states (Baden-Württemberg, Bavaria, Brandenburg, Hesse, North Rhine-Westphalia, and Saxony) and announces the much-awaited preliminary inflation rate for the month, along with the latest 12-month change. The complete data on German CPI appears at different links within the FSO's Web site:

- The press release of Germany's CPI can be found here shortly after it's announced: *www.destatis.de/e_home.htm*

- Monthly trends in the CPI are located at this address: *www.destatis.de/indicators/e/pre110me.htm*

- Yearly changes for each month are published here: *www.destatis.de/indicators/e/pre110je.htm*

Federal Statistical Office Germany

Home | Contact | Press | Imprint | About us | Links | Deutsch

DESTATIS wissen.nutzen.

Price indices

Economic indicators

Please select

- Geography
- Population
- Employment
- Elections
- Education and culture
- Social security schemes
- Health
- Justice
- Construction and housing
- Environment
- Agriculture, fisheries
- Production industries, crafts
- Domestic trade, hotel and restaurant industry, tourism
- Transport
- Money and banking, services
- Foreign trade
- Businesses, business notifications
- Prices
- Wages and salaries
- Household budget surveys, time use
- Finance and taxes
- National accounts
- International data

▪ Values
▪ % change on the previous year

Price indices
Germany

Original value
% change on the previous month

		Consumer price index	Index of retail prices	Index of producer prices of industrial products 1)	Index of selling prices in wholesale trade	Foreign trade prices	
						Index of import prices	Index of export prices
2004	Apr	0,3	-	0,4	-	-	-
	Mar	0,3	0,4	0,6	1,3	-	-
	Feb	0,2	-0,1	0,1	0,3	-	-
	Jan	0,1	0,1	-0,2	0,5	-	-
2003	Dec	0,8	-	-	-0,1	-0,5	-0,2
	Nov	-0,2	-	-	-0,1	-	0,1
	Oct	-	0,1	-	0,1	0,1	-0,1
	Sep	-0,1	0,3	0,1	0,7	-0,2	0,2
	Aug	-	-0,2	-	0,4	0,8	0,1
	Jul	0,2	-0,2	0,2	-0,2	0,2	-
	Jun	0,3	0,1	-	-	-0,1	-0,2
	May	-0,2	-0,1	-0,3	-0,8	-1,4	-0,4
	Apr	-0,3	-0,2	-0,2	-1,1	-2,0	-0,1
	Mar	0,1	0,1	0,2	0,6	-0,6	-

Databases
- GENESIS-Online
- Federal Health Monitoring System

Statistics-Shop

Publications

Please select

- Library
- Microcensus

Scientific forum

Please select

- Events

Please select

- Geography
- Population
- Employment
- Elections
- Education and culture
- Social security schemes
- Health
- Justice
- Construction and housing
- Environment
- Agriculture, fisheries
- Production industries, crafts
- Domestic trade, hotel and restaurant industry, tourism
- Transport
- Money and banking, services
- Foreign trade
- Businesses, business notifications
- Prices
- Wages and salaries
- Household budget surveys, time use
- Finance and taxes
- National accounts
- International data

Search

▪ Values
▪ % change on the previous month

Price indices
Germany

Original value
% change on the previous year

		Consumer price index	Index of retail prices	Index of producer prices of industrial products 1)	Index of selling prices in wholesale trade	Foreign trade prices	
						Index of import prices	Index of export prices
2004	Apr	1,6	0,4	0,9	-	-	-
	Mar	1,1	0,2	0,3	0,8	-	-
	Feb	0,9	-0,1	-0,1	0,1	-	-
	Jan	1,2	0,3	0,2	0,4	-	-
2003	Dec	1,1	0,7	1,8	1,3	-2,5	-0,2
	Nov	1,3	0,8	2,0	1,5	-1,1	-
	Oct	1,2	0,7	1,7	0,8	-2,5	-0,2
	Sep	1,1	0,5	2,0	0,6	-2,6	-0,1
	Aug	1,1	0,4	2,0	0,8	-1,7	-0,2
	Jul	0,9	0,3	1,9	0,4	-2,0	-0,2
	Jun	1,0	0,3	1,4	0,5	-2,7	-0,3
	May	0,7	-0,1	1,4	-0,2	-3,8	-0,1
	Apr	1,0	-0,2	1,7	0,3	-3,0	0,3
	Mar	1,2	-	1,7	1,3	-0,8	0,6
	Feb	1,3	-	1,9	1,6	0,6	0,9
	Jan	1,1	-0,4	1,5	1,2	0,5	0,6

1) Domestic sale

Databases
- GENESIS-Online
- Federal Health Monitoring System

Statistics-Shop

Publications

Please select

- Library
- Microcensus

Scientific forum

Please select

- Events

Another virtue of the German CPI is how current it is. The government puts out a provisional estimate of inflation around mid-month. A final CPI is published two weeks later, between the 10th and 15th of the following month. It is the provisional figures, though, that traders in the financial markets react to the most, because the difference between the preliminary German CPI and the revised numbers tends to be negligible.

Without meaning to complicate this subject, it is necessary to know that the FSO also calculates another version of Germany's inflation every month, which is in the same press release. Why produce two CPI versions? The reason for the second version is to follow a standardized European formula for measuring the CPI. This allows business leaders, investors, and economists to more accurately compare Germany's inflation rates with those of its neighboring countries. Called the Harmonized Index of Consumer Prices (HICP), and dubbed "hiccup," it is the official inflation computation for the 15 member states of the European Union (EU), plus Norway and Iceland. When all is said and done, though, the difference between the national definition of the German CPI and the Harmonized CPI for Germany is not significant.

JAPAN'S TANKAN SURVEY

What Is It: A widely anticipated report on business confidence in Japan.

News Release on the Internet: *www.boj.or.jp/en/type/stat/boj_stat/tk/index.htm*

Home Web Address: *www.boj.or.jp/en/index.htm*

Release Time: 8:50 a.m. (local time); results are published at the start of April, July, and October, and in mid-December.

Frequency: Quarterly.

Source: Bank of Japan.

Revisions: Statistical corrections are rare. Revisions merely reflect changes in confidence and plans from one quarter to the next.

Aside from the U.S., Japan has arguably the most extensive collection of economic indicators in the world, much of it in English and freely available on the Web. Perhaps that's to be expected from the second-largest economy (after the United States). Among the reports Japan churns out is the Tankan survey, which has gained worldwide recognition for its sweeping coverage, forward-looking features, and quick release to the public. International investors and managers of multinational companies look to the Tankan report for the latest reading on the state of the Japanese economy and its forecasts of business activity in the months ahead. What gives this survey extra credibility is the agency behind it. The Tankan survey is produced by the Bank of Japan, the country's central bank, and its results can offer clues on the future course of monetary policy and interest rates.

Often described as a business confidence survey, the Tankan survey is really much more than that. Indeed, this report offers more insight into what the business community is thinking than does any comparable U.S. economic indicator. If you want to know about Japanese plans for future capital investments, employment, or expectations of pricing power, and predictions of where the yen will likely be valued in the future, this release covers all this and a lot more.

The survey itself is conducted quarterly by the Research and Statistics Department at the Bank of Japan. Questionnaires are sent out the last month of every quarter—March, June, September, and December—to about 9,000 firms. These companies are differentiated by their size—large (on average 24% of the sample), medium (27%), and small (49%)—and by industry type, with more going to non-manufacturers (58%) than to manufacturing (42%). Amazingly, the response rate of these surveys tends to be better than 98%.

Respondents are asked to respond to eight broad questions:

1. Business conditions (favorable or unfavorable?)

2. Supply-and-demand conditions (excessive demand or excessive supply?) and prices (rising or falling?)

3. Sales and current profits (% change)

4. Fixed investment at non-financial institutions (% change)

5. Fixed investments at financial institutions (%)

6. Employment (excessive employment or insufficient?)

7. Corporate finance (easy or tight monetary conditions?)

8. Business conditions at financial institutions (favorable or unfavorable?)

Of the eight topics, five seek qualitative assessments that require a judgment call (topics 1, 2, 6, 7, and 8). After these responses are collected, a diffusion index is computed by simply calculating the percentage of businesses reporting a negative tone and subtracting it from the percentage indicating a positive tone. The remaining three questions (3, 4, and 5) ask for quantitative changes in percentage terms regarding recent performance as well as expectations about how this will change in the future.

The following sections highlight a few of the most useful tables in the Tankan survey.

- **Business Conditions for Large Manufacturers**

  (1) Manufacturing is one of the main engines of growth in Japan because it includes the country's vital export industry. In this table, we see confidence improved in December (actual result) to a net 11, representing a 10 percentage-point gain in confidence from September's survey. However, these same manufacturers have predicted a slight deterioration in conditions in the next few months, because the diffusion index on the forecast dropped back to 8.

  Aside from the summary number at the top of the table, confidence levels are also broken down into broad industry categories such as motor vehicles and industrial machinery.

- **Business Conditions for Nonmanufacturers**

  (2) This section is a good measure of the strength of consumer demand in Japan. Large non-manufacturers conduct most of their business in the country and do not benefit much from strong export growth. One can look at the headline figure to get an idea of domestic demand, as well as how specific sectors are doing. For example, retailers noted that conditions have barely improved over the last quarter, moving from –14 to –13. Note, however, that more of them appear optimistic about conditions in the subsequent three months because the forecast index rose to –5.

Not to be released before 8:50 a.m. on Friday, December 12, 2003

December 12, 2003
Research and Statistics Department
Bank of Japan

TANKAN Summary (December 2003)

119th Short-Term Economic Survey of All Enterprises in Japan
186th Short-Term Economic Survey of Principal Enterprises in Japan

Number of sample enterprises

	Manufacturing	Nonmanufacturing	Total	Response rate
All Enterprises	3,561	4,643	8,204	98.3%
Large enterprises	738	627	1,365	99.2%
Medium-sized enterprises	1,036	1,576	2,612	98.4%
Small enterprises	1,787	2,440	4,227	97.9%
Principal Enterprises	369	291	660	99.8%
(Memo) Financial institutions	-	-	168	100.0%

Responding Period: November 10th to December 11th.

Memo: Average of predicted exchange rates expected by large manufacturing enterprises

(yen per US dollar)

	FY2002	FY2003	1H	2H	1H	2H
			(FY2002)	(FY2002)	(FY2003)	(FY2003)
June 2003 survey	122.37	123.74	117.88	117.99	117.97	117.79
Sept 2003 survey		121.06	117.99	118.47	118.47	117.53
Dec 2003 survey		114.68	118.08	111.40		

1. Business Conditions

(Net percentage of respondents who reported "Favorable")

Large enterprises

	Sept 2003 survey Actual result	Sept 2003 survey Forecast	Dec 2003 survey Actual result	Dec 2003 survey Changes in revision	Dec 2003 survey Forecast	Changes
Manufacturing	1	3	11	10	10	8
Textiles	-34	-14	-14	20	11	-3
Lumber & wood products	-11	-11	11	22	22	-22
Pulp & paper	21	29	29	8	8	0
Chemicals	6	5	13	7	9	-4
Petroleum & coal products	-29	-29	0	29	29	-15
Ceramics, stone & clay	-22	-26	-13	9	9	0
Iron & steel	15	19	23	12	12	-4
Nonferrous metals	-35	-25	10	45	45	-10
Food & beverages	0	6	2	2	2	4
Processed metals	-7	4	7	21	21	-7
Industrial machinery	15	14	14	4	19	0
Electrical machinery	-5	3	19	12	8	1
Shipbuilding & heavy machinery	-40	-60	-60	-20	-20	20
Motor vehicles	24	17	35	11	26	-9
Precision machinery	0	0	15	15	15	-11
Basic materials	-6	-3	9	15	15	4
Processing	2	6	11	9	10	-1
Nonmanufacturing	-13	-8	-9	4	4	2
Construction	-26	-30	-29	-3	-3	4
Real estate	20	20	20	0	0	0
Wholesaling	4	4	16	12	13	-3
Retailing	-14	0	-13	1	1	8
Transportation	-17	-12	-9	8	8	-6
Communications	40	20	22	-18	11	-11
Electric & gas utilities	-6	12	12	18	18	0
Services	-17	-10	-11	6	6	2
Leasing	-11	-11	11	22	22	0
All industries	-6	-2	1	7	7	1

Medium-sized enterprises

	Sept 2003 survey Actual result	Sept 2003 survey Forecast	Dec 2003 survey Actual result	Dec 2003 survey Changes in revision	Dec 2003 survey Forecast	Changes
Manufacturing	-10	-8	-1	9	9	-5
Textiles	-41	-41	-32	9	9	-33
Lumber & wood products	-14	-23	-10	4	4	-20
Pulp & paper	-20	-13	-7	13	13	-7
Chemicals	-12	-6	-4	8	8	-3
Petroleum & coal products	-10	-10	20	30	30	0
Ceramics, stone & clay	-32	-21	-24	8	8	-23
Iron & steel	11	0	8	-3	3	3
Nonferrous metals	0	-4	9	9	13	18
Food & beverages	-6	-4	-2	4	4	-3
Processed metals	-28	-17	-14	14	14	-11
Industrial machinery	-14	-14	-7	7	7	-10
Electrical machinery	-5	-7	6	11	11	-2
Shipbuilding & heavy machinery	25	33	33	0	17	-8
Motor vehicles	12	7	17	5	14	-3
Precision machinery	7	4	25	18	14	-11
Basic materials	-18	-14	-9	9	9	-10
Processing	-7	-7	2	9	9	-3
Nonmanufacturing	-22	-21	-20	4	4	-20
Construction	-27	-25	-29	-4	-4	-31
Real estate	0	4	0	-4	8	8
Wholesaling	-17	-20	-16	4	4	-15
Retailing	-22	-32	-28	4	4	-22
Transportation	-25	-26	-17	9	9	-24
Communications	-12	0	0	0	0	0
Electric & gas utilities	0	0	0	0	5	-19
Services	-24	-25	-20	5	5	-19
Leasing	-20	-15	-14	8	8	-15
All industries	-16	-20	-14	6	6	-13

Small enterprises

	Sept 2003 survey Actual result	Sept 2003 survey Forecast	Dec 2003 survey Actual result	Dec 2003 survey Changes in revision	Dec 2003 survey Forecast	Changes
Manufacturing	-23	-19	-13	10	10	-15
Textiles	-47	-43	-43	4	4	-37
Lumber & wood products	-26	-27	-17	9	9	-25
Pulp & paper	-22	-16	-12	10	10	-13
Chemicals	-13	-11	-5	8	8	-7
Petroleum & coal products	-19	-28	-15	4	4	-19
Ceramics, stone & clay	-55	-49	-49	6	6	-47
Iron & steel	-9	-11	-1	8	8	-11
Nonferrous metals	-4	-5	9	13	13	9
Food & beverages	-18	-12	-15	3	3	-16
Processed metals	-25	-21	-13	12	12	-16
Industrial machinery	-13	-10	0	13	13	0
Electrical machinery	-25	-18	-2	23	23	-7
Shipbuilding & heavy machinery	-35	-26	-36	-1	-1	-36
Motor vehicles	21	11	22	1	1	15
Precision machinery	-7	-7	3	10	10	-5
Basic materials	-30	-28	-23	7	7	-23
Processing	-18	-15	-8	10	10	-10
Nonmanufacturing	-31	-30	-28	3	3	-29
Construction	-36	-43	-36	0	0	-44
Real estate	-12	-11	-4	8	8	-4
Wholesaling	-35	-30	-31	4	4	-32
Retailing	-45	-40	-44	1	1	-40
Transportation	-28	-29	-22	6	6	-24
Communications	23	16	30	7	7	15
Electric & gas utilities	-15	-7	-4	11	11	-4
Services	-23	-20	-20	3	3	-22
Leasing	-27	-28	-20	7	7	-19
All industries	-28	-26	-22	6	6	-24

All Enterprises

	Actual result	Forecast	Actual result	Changes in revision	Forecast	Changes
Manufacturing	-15	-12	-5	10	10	-2
Nonmanufacturing	-27	-24	-23	4	4	-1
All industries	-21	-19	-15	6	6	-2

(Notes) 1. Response rate = The number of enterprises responding to the question of Business Conditions (or that of financial institutions responding to the question of Fixed Investment) / The number of sample enterprises * 100

2. Actual result: Judgement at the time of the survey, Forecast: Judgement at the time of three months hence.
Changes in revision of actual results = "Actual results of current survey" minus "Actual results of the previous survey".
Changes of forecast = "Forecast of current survey" minus "Actual results of current survey".

- Business Conditions at Small Enterprises

    (3) Are all businesses benefiting from economic growth, or just a few? How wide-spread is the recovery in Japan? By comparing the sentiment levels of large and small companies, one can tell whether businesses across the board are seeing an improvement in sales and profits—or if these gains are limited to mainly large enterprises.

- Average Exchange Rates Predicted by Large Manufacturers

    (4) Where the yen is valued in relation to other currencies can make all the differ-ence in how successful Japanese exporters are at selling products in foreign mar-kets. This table represents the best guess by major Japanese manufacturers what value the yen will average in the first and second halves of the year, as well as for the year as a whole. Indeed, there is a correlation between how cheap the yen is expected to be and the level of business confidence by large manufacturers. The lower the yen's value in foreign exchange markets, the more upbeat manu-facturers become because it effectively drops the price of Japanese-made goods abroad.

- Prices by Large Enterprises

    (5) Companies that can raise prices generally achieve higher earnings and hire more workers. However, there are times when businesses find it difficult to lift prices. Either competition prevents them from doing so, or the economy is undergoing a deflationary spiral where prices are under continuous pressure to fall. The latter has been a serious problem with Japan throughout the 1990s and beyond. This index represents the percentage of companies saying their prices had risen ver-sus those that lowered prices. The numbers show that slightly more firms in the latest survey have raised prices. The index for large manufacturers inched up from –23 in September to –21 in the December survey. But that might prove to be just a brief reprieve because the expectations index fell back to –24.

- Fixed Investment

    (6) Capital spending is another major contributor to economic growth. It serves as a marker of confidence that companies have about future business activity. Here we see large manufacturers planning to boost investment spending by 11.1% in Japan's 2003 fiscal year, compared to what was spent the previous year.

2. Supply and Demand Conditions, Inventories, and Prices

(% points)

		Large enterprises					
		Sept 2003 survey		Dec 2003 survey			
		Actual result	Forecast	Actual result	Changes in revision	Forecast	Changes
Supply and demand conditions for products and services	Manufacturing	-23	-23	-19	4	-20	-1
Diffusion index of "Excess demand" minus	Basic materials	-27	-28	-22	5	-21	1
"Excess supply"	Processing	-21	-21	-17	4	-20	-3
Overseas supply and demand conditions for products :	Manufacturing	-12	-12	-6	6	-7	-1
Diffusion index of "Excess demand" minus	Basic materials	-17	-17	-12	5	-11	1
"Excess supply"	Processing	-10	-10	-4	6	-5	-1
Inventory level of finished goods and merchandise:	Manufacturing	20	14	20	0	13	-7
Diffusion index of "Excessive or somewhat excessive"	Basic materials	23	17	24	1	17	-7
minus "Insufficient or somewhat insufficient"	Processing	19	12	18	-1	12	-6
Wholesalers' inventory level:	Manufacturing	22	19	18	-4	16	-2
Diffusion index of "Excessive or somewhat excessive"	Basic materials	24	21	25	1	19	-6
minus "Insufficient or somewhat insufficient"	Processing	21	17	16	-5	15	-1
Change in output prices:	Manufacturing	-23	-23	-21	2	-24	-3
Diffusion index of "Rise" minus "Fall"	Basic materials	-11	-10	-4	7	-11	-7
	Processing	-28	-28	-29	-1	-29	0
Change in input prices:	Manufacturing	-2	-4	-1	1	-1	0
Diffusion index of "Rise" minus "Fall"	Basic materials	8	6	12	4	9	-3
	Processing	-5	-8	-5	0	-6	-1

5 ▶

Fixed Investment   (Year-to-year growth rate, %)

		FY2002		FY2003	
			Adjustment ratio	(Forecast)	Adjustment ratio
Large enterprises	Manufacturing	-17.4	-	11.1	0.0
	Nonmanufacturing	-11.1	-	1.6	1.3
	All industries	-13.6	-	5.2	0.7
Medium-sized enterprises	Manufacturing	-11.5	-	4.8	3.0
	Nonmanufacturing	-2.0	-	2.8	-0.7
	All industries	-3.2	-	3.0	-0.3
Small enterprises	Manufacturing	-4.0	-	-1.7	7.1
	Nonmanufacturing	-2.5	-	1.2	5.9
	All industries	-2.9	-	0.5	6.2
All Enterprises	Manufacturing	-14.2	-	7.6	1.6
	Nonmanufacturing	-5.4	-	2.1	1.1
	All industries	-7.7	-	3.4	1.3

◀6

- **Production Capacity**

  (7) Lots of unused factory capacity poses problems for an economy. It will depress business spending in the future and perhaps even lead to plant closings and lay-offs. In contrast, a reduction in excess plant capacity suggests that customer orders are rising and more factories are being utilized to satisfy this demand. The diffusion index shows the net percentage of companies that claim to have too much excess capacity. Figures here show that fewer companies are experiencing idle assembly lines; the index for excessive capacity fell from 17 to 14. The forecast is for even greater use of existing capacity, since the number is expected to drop to 12.

Production Capacity   (Net percentage of respondents who reported "Excessive capacity")

		Sept 2003 survey		Dec 2003 survey			
		Actual result	Forecast	Actual result		Forecast	
					Changes in revision		Changes
7 ▶	Manufacturing	17	15	14	-3	12	-2
Large enterprises	Nonmanufacturing	7	6	6	-1	5	-1
	All industries	13	11	11	-2	9	-2
Medium-sized	Manufacturing	18	15	12	-6	11	-1
enterprises	Nonmanufacturing	4	1	4	0	2	-2
	All industries	9	7	7	-2	6	-1
	Manufacturing	18	15	15	-3	14	-1
Small enterprises	Nonmanufacturing	8	6	7	-1	5	-2
	All industries	12	10	10	-2	9	-1
	Manufacturing	19	15	14	-5	13	-1
All Enterprises	Nonmanufacturing	6	5	6	0	4	-2
	All industries	11	9	10	-1	8	-2

As rich as the Tankan survey is with information on the private business sector in Japan, there are two cautionary points to consider. Since the powerful Bank of Japan is behind this report, the firms queried are aware their responses might have a bearing on monetary policy by the central bank. Therefore, respondents could be tempted to shape their answers in a way that can result in a favorable interest rate policy. Secondly, a large part of the survey depends on forecasts, which might turn out to be inaccurate. Aside from these caveats, the Tankan survey is viewed by the international investment community as a valuable and well-regarded economic report.

JAPAN INDUSTRIAL PRODUCTION

What Is It: Measures the change in monthly industrial output.

News Release on the Internet: *www.meti.go.jp/english/statistics*

Home Web Address: *www.meti.go.jp/english*

Release Time: 8:50 a.m. (local time); a preliminary report is released in the final week of the next month. A revised report is published another two to three weeks later. (For example, data on October is announced during the last week in November, to be followed by another report on revisions in mid-December.)

Frequency: Monthly.

Source: Ministry of Economy, Trade, and Industry (METI).

Revisions: Monthly and annual revisions are frequent and can be substantial.

After achieving one of the highest growth rates in the world from the 1960s through the 1980s, Japan has struggled to regain its footing. Indeed, economists describe the 1990s as that country's lost decade. To get Japan back on its feet, the central bank lowered short-term rates to near zero, and the government put through a series of financial and regulatory reforms to encourage more borrowing, spending, and investment. The results have been encouraging. After several false starts earlier this decade, the economy appears to be on the mend. While Japan's woes are far from over, it still faces an aging population, high public debt, an excessive reliance on exports for economic growth, and it has to import nearly all the oil it needs, the country's importance to the international economy and its influence in global capital markets remains largely undiminished. Japan still holds title as the world's second-largest economy and is the biggest exporter of investment capital. It sells $550 billion worth of goods and services every year to the rest of the world. Moreover, the yen continues to stand alongside the U.S. dollar and the euro as one of the three most important currencies. For all these reasons, global investors and business leaders, especially those in the U.S., closely monitor Japan's economic health.

Also looming large for Americans is the fact that, outside the U.S., no other country owns more U.S. Treasury securities than Japan. As a result, Japanese banks, insurance companies, and government agencies have helped fund the U.S. government budget for years, lending hundreds of billions of dollars. However, this is also a cause for concern. If serious financial and economic problems were to erupt again in Japan, they could easily spill over into the U.S. Investors in Japan, for example, may decide to purchase less U.S. Treasury debt or even sell some of their holdings in dollar-based financial assets. They can also choose to manipulate the value of the yen to help export sales. Indeed, few countries in the world intervene in the currency markets as much as Japan.

Given the ability of Japan's economy to affect asset values in world capital markets and to sway currency markets, foreign investors know they have to stay informed about the soundness of the economy. That means paying particularly close attention to its industrial production, which many experts consider to be one of the best barometers of business activity in Japan. Analysts prefer to monitor industrial output over GDP because the former comes out sooner, responds faster to changes in the business climate, and is rich with information on the country's manufacturing and mining industries. In fact, Japan's industrial production release is more comprehensive in its coverage of the economy than its U.S counterpart. Case in point: Japan's monthly production report even includes forecasts of how key manufacturers are expected to perform in the next two months.

In view of all the attention paid to Japanese manufacturers, it might be surprising to learn that manufacturing activity makes up less than a quarter of the GDP. But this figure is very misleading because the actual impact that manufacturers have on the economy is much greater. For example, exports represent a primary engine of growth for Japan. Strong foreign demand for cars, digital cameras, HDTVs, and computer accessories feeds right through to the domestic economy by stimulating capital investment spending, employment, and overall output.

Japan started measuring industrial production in 1953, and it now includes virtually all privately owned companies in mining and manufacturing, regardless of size. The main task of the industrial production series is to compute monthly changes in output for 536 items. Figures are also given for the actual quantity of goods being produced, shipped, and kept in inventory for many commodities.

The initial release, called the "Preliminary Report on Indices of Industrial Production," is published a month after the period being covered ends. A revised release is issued about three weeks later. One can access the industrial production report in two ways. There is a summary report on the Web (*www.meti.go.jp/english/statistics/*). Inside that report is another link where you can download the full 78-page release as a PDF file. The tables shown in this section come from that detailed report. Data is presented in both English and Japanese and is well organized. Figures are seasonally adjusted with an index base of 100 that is tied to the year 2000. Keep in mind that revisions are frequent and can be very large.

- **Mining and Manufacturing: Industrial Production**

  (1) This is the summary page of the industrial production report. It provides the latest monthly and annual changes in output. (The release shows it was up 0.8% for the month of October and up 3.6% over the year.) A black triangle near a number indicates a decline. Other pages in the report (not included here) provide additional details on the strength and weakness of individual sectors.

- **Mining and Manufacturing: Shipments**

  (2) Industrial shipments represent actual sales and can be used to determine demand. If shipments are increasing, this will likely lead to further increases in production in the months ahead. Should shipments begin to slacken, it will cause inventory levels to swell and discourage future production. (In the table, shipments climbed 1.2% for the month and 5.1% over the year.)

- **Mining and Manufacturing: Inventories and Inventory Ratios**

  (3) This section sheds light on the supply-and-demand pressures in the industrial sector. A rise in the inventory index reflects the quantity of goods produced that remains unsold. The inventory ratio index is similar to the inventory-sales ratio in the U.S., except that it uses an index rather than months of supply on hand. The ratio, which represents inventories divided by shipments, can be a leading indicator of future industrial output.

- **Survey of Production Forecast**

  (4) Included in the industrial production release is a projection of what output is expected to be the next two months. It's a useful addition because the numbers provide a sense of where the economy may be heading. (The data in this table shows that production is predicted to increase 3.1% in November but drop 0.9% in December.) This page also breaks down the main components of production, enabling you to identify which sectors will help raise output and which will drag it down. (For example, General Machinery output is predicted to surge 18.7% in November and fall 8.8% in December.) However, you should view this forecast table with some skepticism. Projections historically tend to be on the high side.

〈1. 鉱工業 ；Mining and manufacturing 〉

平成12年 ＝100
index,2000= 100

	生産 Production				生産者出荷 Shipments					
	季節調整済指数 Seasonal Adjustment Index		原指数 Original Index		季節調整済指数 Seasonal Adjustment Index		原指数 Original Index			
		前月 期)比 %Change From Previous Month(Quarter)		前年 剰月期)比 %Change From Previous Year		前月 期)比 %Change From Previous Month(Quarter)		前年 剰月期)比 %Change From Previous Year		
平成 12 年			100.0	5.7			100.0	5.8	C.Y.	2000
13 年			93.2	▲ 6.8			93.7	▲ 6.3		2001
14 年			92.0	▲ 1.3			93.5	▲ 0.2		2002
平成12年度			99.9	4.3			100.0	4.4	F.Y.	2000
13年度			90.8	▲ 9.1			91.6	▲ 8.4		2001
14年度			93.3	2.8			94.8	3.5		2002
平成14年III期	93.4	1.7	93.9	3.3	94.6	1.0	95.5	3.4	Q3	2002
IV期	93.8	0.4	95.2	6.0	95.3	0.7	96.7	6.7	Q4	
平成15年 I 期	94.1	0.3	94.1	5.5	95.8	0.5	96.9	5.7	Q1	2003
II 期	93.4	▲ 0.7	91.9	2.2	96.0	0.2	92.8	3.0	Q2	
III期	94.6	1.3	94.7	0.9	96.8	0.8	97.5	2.1	Q3	
平成14年 8月	93.3	0.3	86.8	1.2	94.9	1.6	88.3	2.3	Aug.	2002
9月	94.0	0.8	97.4	5.2	95.4	0.5	101.1	4.9	Sep.	
10月	94.1	0.1	97.0	5.4	95.7	0.3	97.0	6.5	Oct.	
11月	93.7	▲ 0.4	95.2	5.4	95.6	▲ 0.1	97.5	7.0	Nov.	
12月	93.6	▲ 0.1	93.3	7.0	94.7	▲ 0.9	95.5	6.6	Dec.	
平成15年 1月	95.2	1.7	87.7	8.1	96.9	2.3	88.0	8.4	Jan.	2003
2月	93.5	▲ 1.8	90.9	4.6	96.4	▲ 0.5	93.6	6.0	Feb.	
3月	93.6	0.1	103.6	3.9	94.1	▲ 2.4	109.0	3.1	Mar.	
4月	92.2	▲ 1.5	90.7	3.0	95.0	1.0	91.3	3.3	Apr.	
5月	94.6	2.6	90.2	1.3	96.8	1.9	90.3	1.1	May	
6月	93.4	▲ 1.3	94.8	2.4	96.3	▲ 0.5	96.8	4.4	Jun.	
7月	93.9	0.5	97.1	▲ 0.3	95.3	▲ 1.0	97.8	0.7	Jul.	
8月	93.2	▲ 0.7	85.7	▲ 1.3	95.8	0.5	88.2	▲ 0.1	Aug.	
9月	96.7	3.8	101.4	4.1	99.4	3.8	106.5	5.3	Sep.	
10月	97.5	[0.8]	100.5	[3.6]	100.6	[1.2]	101.9	[5.1]	Oct.	

1 ▶   ◀ 2

	生産者在庫 Inventory				生産者在庫率 Inventory Ratio					
	季節調整済指数 Seasonal Adjustment Index		原指数 Original Index		季節調整済指数 Seasonal Adjustment Index		原指数 Original Index			
		前月 期)比 %Change From Previous Month(Quarter)		前年 剰月期)比 %Change From Previous Year		前月 期)比 %Change From Previous Month(Quarter)		前年 剰月期)比 %Change From Previous Year		
平成 12 年			99.0	2.1			100.0	▲ 3.2	C.Y.	2000
13 年			98.3	▲ 0.7			110.4	10.4		2001
14 年			90.4	▲ 8.0			102.0	▲ 7.6		2002
平成12年度			97.8	2.3			101.3	▲ 0.2	F.Y.	2000
13年度			91.8	▲ 6.1			111.4	10.0		2001
14年度			86.7	▲ 5.6			99.4	▲ 10.8		2002
平成14年III期	92.5	▲ 0.2	89.6	▲ 9.9	99.0	▲ 2.1	98.7	▲ 12.4	Q3	2002
IV期	92.3	▲ 0.2	90.4	▲ 8.0	98.7	▲ 0.3	96.1	▲ 12.6	Q4	
平成15年 I 期	90.9	▲ 1.5	86.7	▲ 5.6	98.9	0.2	99.8	▲ 9.3	Q1	2003
II 期	90.4	▲ 0.6	91.8	▲ 2.5	97.7	▲ 1.2	99.6	▲ 3.4	Q2	
III期	91.2	0.9	88.4	▲ 1.3	98.8	1.1	98.7	0.0	Q3	
平成14年 8月	92.1	▲ 0.8	93.7	▲ 11.4	98.5	▲ 0.2	105.6	▲ 12.4	Aug.	2002
9月	92.5	0.4	89.6	▲ 9.9	99.7	1.2	92.1	▲ 12.3	Sep.	
10月	93.0	0.5	93.2	▲ 8.7	98.9	▲ 0.8	97.4	▲ 12.3	Oct.	
11月	91.4	1.7	92.3	▲ 9.5	97.9	1.4	95.4	▲ 13.7	Nov.	
12月	92.3	1.0	90.4	▲ 8.0	99.4	1.5	95.5	▲ 11.9	Dec.	
平成15年 1月	93.5	1.3	95.5	▲ 5.5	100.0	0.6	112.5	▲ 9.2	Jan.	2003
2月	91.4	▲ 2.2	93.9	▲ 6.5	96.9	▲ 3.1	101.5	▲ 10.3	Feb.	
3月	90.9	▲ 0.5	86.7	▲ 5.6	99.9	3.1	85.3	▲ 8.2	Mar.	
4月	90.8	▲ 0.1	88.5	▲ 4.2	98.1	▲ 1.8	96.8	▲ 4.3	Apr.	
5月	91.2	0.4	91.6	▲ 3.2	96.9	▲ 1.2	102.4	▲ 2.7	May	
6月	90.4	▲ 0.9	91.8	▲ 2.5	98.1	1.2	99.7	▲ 3.1	Jun.	
7月	91.6	1.3	93.9	▲ 1.3	99.3	1.2	99.1	0.6	Jul.	
8月	90.6	▲ 1.1	92.2	▲ 1.6	100.0	0.7	107.2	1.5	Aug.	
9月	91.2	0.7	88.4	▲ 1.3	97.1	▲ 2.9	89.7	▲ 2.6	Sep.	
10月	90.9	[▲ 0.3]	91.1	[▲ 2.3]	94.0	[▲ 3.2]	92.6	[▲ 4.9]	Oct.	

(注) 生産者製品在庫の年、年度及び四半期の数値は期末値である。
　　各比率は、伸び率 (%)である。以下、28 頁まで同様。

▲ 3

平成15年11月の製造工業生産予測調査結果
Survey of Production Forecast, November 2003

(1)前月比 季節調整済)
Month to Month Percent Change (Seasonal Adjustment)

(2)実現率及び予測修正率
Realization Ratio and Amendment Ratio

(%)

業　　　　　　種	10月 Oct.　Last Month	11月 Nov. 見込み　This Month	12月 Dec. 見込み　Next Month	10月の実現率 Realization Ratio	11月の予測修正率 Amendment Ratio
4 ▶ 製　造　工　業　Manufacturing	(2.8)	3.1　(2.5)	▲ 0.9	▲ 1.1	▲ 0.5
鉄　　鋼　　業　Iron and Steel	(1.2)	▲ 1.7　(1.6)	▲ 1.1	4.0	0.6
非 鉄 金 属 工 業　Non-Ferrous Metals	(2.0)	▲ 0.4　(▲ 1.4)	0.4	1.4	2.5
金 属 製 品 工 業　Fabricated Metals	(2.8)	▲ 0.1　(1.1)	▲ 1.1	▲ 1.1	▲ 2.4
4 ▶ 一 般 機 械 工 業　General Machinery	(4.0)	18.7　(14.4)	▲ 8.8	▲ 7.2	▲ 3.7
電 気 機 械 工 業　Electrical Machinery	(▲ 3.2)	4.3　(▲ 1.1)	6.8	▲ 1.8	3.6
情 報 通 信 機 械 工 業　Information and Communication Electronics Equipment	(4.2)	▲ 2.3　(1.7)	2.0	▲ 1.4	▲ 5.2
電 子 部 品 ・ デ バ イ ス 工 業　Electronic Parts and Devices	(2.9)	7.7　(7.3)	2.2	▲ 3.8	▲ 3.4
輸 送 機 械 工 業　Transport Equipment	(1.0)	▲ 0.8　(▲ 0.2)	0.8	0.6	▲ 0.1
化　学　工　業　Chemicals	(3.5)	2.4　(1.6)	▲ 0.8	▲ 0.1	0.6
紙 ・ パ ル プ 工 業　Pulp and Paper	(2.7)	2.2　(▲ 0.1)	▲ 0.4	▲ 2.0	0.2
そ　の　他　Others	(▲ 0.6)	▲ 2.2　(▲ 4.3)	▲ 2.2	0.9	3.0
(特掲) 電 気 機 械 工 業 (旧分類)　Electrical Machinery(1995 Version)	(5.2)	4.4　(4.0)	2.1	▲ 2.7	▲ 2.3

(参考)			
製　造　工　業　Manufacturing　(原系列) Original	(▲ 0.8)	▲ 0.5　(▲ 0.2)	0.2

※ （）内は前月調査による前月比を示す。
　　 Parentheses indicates the month-to-month percent change in the previous survey

EUROZONE: MANUFACTURING PURCHASING MANAGERS INDEX (PMI)

GLOBAL: MANUFACTURING PURCHASING MANAGERS INDEX

What Is It: One measures changes in manufacturing activity in the Eurozone; the other looks at shifts in manufacturing globally.

Home Web Address: *www.ntc-research.com*
www.ntceconomics.com
www.ism.ws/ISMReport/index.cfm

Release Time:
Eurozone Manufacturing PMI: 9:30 a.m. (London time); released the first business day of the month.
Global Manufacturing PMI: 11 a.m. (New York time); released the first business day of the month.

Frequency: Monthly.

Source:
Eurozone PMI: RBS/NTC Economics
Global PMI: JP Morgan/NTC Economics

Revisions: They tend to be rare and minor in both surveys.

The popularity of the U.S. purchasing manager surveys has spawned a bunch of similar measures in other countries. The U.S. Purchasing Managers Index (PMI) for manufacturing, produced by the Institute for Supply Management, is one of the hottest economic indicators out every month. It has demonstrated a solid track record of anticipating turning points in the business cycle and for being way ahead of the curve in detecting a buildup of inflation pressures. Indeed, it is so highly regarded by investors, economists, and policymakers that more than two dozen nations have developed their own PMI series in recent years, all basically modeled after the U.S. The U.K. purchasing managers survey was launched in 1991, followed by Germany in 1996. France and Japan composed theirs in 1998 and 2002, respectively.

Now, three organizations have taken those international PMI polls a step further. The Royal Bank of Scotland (RBS), JP Morgan, and NTC Economics, a London-based purveyor of global economic data, have come up with another series that combines several national surveys to produce broader regional PMI reports. The result is two releases that are worthy of particular attention: The Eurozone Manufacturing PMI, which is a composite of eight of the 13 European countries that make up the euro currency group, and the Global Manufacturing PMI.[*] The latter consolidates the outcomes of purchasing manager surveys from 23 countries around the world. Both the Eurozone and the Global PMI are now closely monitored by money managers because these reports can have a direct bearing on fiscal and monetary policy. They are considered very good predictors of foreign economic trends.

The surprisingly quick public acceptance of these new regional PMI measures comes at a time when there is growing frustration with government economic indicators. Such statistics are often released after a long lag time. Some, like the GDP, are published 60 to 70 days after the quarter ends. Another complaint about official data is that countries use different methods to come up with the same indicators. This complicates efforts to make comparisons between economies. In addition, figures can be of such poor quality that they are frequently followed by substantial revisions.

In contrast, the Eurozone and Global PMI series employ the same methodology with all the countries, so comparisons are much easier to make. What's more, revisions to the data are also extremely rare. This is not to say that these international surveys are without shortcomings. One problem with both is that they make no effort to quantify the degree of change. For instance, if a large number of purchasing managers say they witnessed just a modest improvement in activity in the latest month, that alone is enough to propel the index sharply higher. A second criticism is that this series leaves out some of the world's most important economies, such as Canada and South Korea. Thus, viewing the 23-country PMI as a comprehensive indicator of international manufacturing trends might be a bit of a stretch. Nonetheless, many analysts still track the Global PMI because it contains enough major countries to warn of upcoming turning points in the world economy.

Eurozone PMI

Established in 1997, the Eurozone Manufacturing PMI is the first composite indicator out every month on conditions in eight countries: Germany, France, Spain, Italy, Ireland, Greece, Austria, and the Netherlands. They represent 92% of all manufacturing activity in the euro currency area. (Countries in the Eurozone not represented in this PMI series are Finland, Luxembourg, Portugal, Slovenia, and Belgium.) The report is based on responses from 3,000 purchasing executives. NTC Economics collects the data from the individual national surveys and then recomputes a regional index for each of the major questions asked. Finally, an overall headline index is calculated to reflect total manufacturing activity in the region.

At the heart of the surveys are questions to purchasing managers that cover six key themes:

1. Is the level of new orders received by your company higher than, the same as, or lower than one month ago?

   This addresses the issue of demand in the economy. If demand for goods increases, it will drive up manufacturing output.

---

[*] As of this writing, 13 countries use the euro as their currency: Austria, Belgium, Finland, France, Germany, Greece, Ireland, Italy, Luxembourg, the Netherlands, Portugal, Slovenia, and Spain. Beginning in 2008, two more nations will join the group, Malta and Cyprus, enlarging the eurozone to 15 countries.

2. Is the level of output in your company higher than, the same as, or lower than one month ago?

    The focus here is on whether there's been a shift in production to higher levels because of new orders.

3. Is the stock of items purchased by your company higher than, the same as, or lower than one month ago?

    For manufacturers to keep their production lines running smoothly, they need to have an ample supply of raw materials on hand. But as output accelerates, supplies typically diminish and purchasing managers need to reorder more stock. Thus, the purchase of new items is linked to the pace of production.

4. Are supplier delivery times experienced by your company longer than, the same as, or shorter than one month ago?

    Just because a purchasing manager places an order to replenish its stock of raw materials doesn't necessarily mean it will arrive overnight. Suppliers generally can ship raw materials to manufacturers faster in a slow economy. In a booming economy, however, when lots of orders for raw materials are coming in at the same time, suppliers can't instantly satisfy all the demand. Bottlenecks emerge, and even suppliers have their own production constraints. As a result, shipments to manufacturers slow and this leads to delays in deliveries. Thus, longer lead times between orders and deliveries of raw materials are a sign of faster economic growth, while rapid deliveries suggest slower business activity.

5. Is the average input price experienced by your company higher than, the same as, or lower than one month ago?

    It should come as no surprise that when many manufacturers increase orders simultaneously, demand for raw materials can outstrip supplies. This places upward pressure on factory input prices.

6. Is the level of employment at your company higher than, the same as, or lower than one month ago?

    There is a link between employment in manufacturing and production. Greater demand for new orders often leads to more employment. However, over time, the relationship between jobs and output turns more tenuous. Given the high cost of labor, manufacturers may try investing more in improving productivity than in expanding their workforce to raise output. Thus, production could increase at a faster pace than job growth in the long run.

Based on these questions, an answer of "higher" (or longer for delivery times) is given one point, the "same" is allocated half a point, and "lower" (or shorter) gets no points. NTC Economics compiles the numbers from individual European countries and comes up with regional composite indexes that are part of the Eurozone Manufacturing PMI. The methodology is standardized for all the countries, and the results are presented in the form of a diffusion index. A reading of less than 50 indicates a contraction of activity, above 50 points to an expansion, and an index of exactly 50 says that no change has occurred.

On top of that, a composite index is calculated. That index is made up of a weighted average of five (of the six) key topics and is based on the following formula: the new orders response is given a 30% weight, output 25%, employment 20%, supplier delivery times 15%, and stocks of items purchased 10%. You'll notice that the PMI index on prices is left out of the equation. Though input prices are a very good leading indicator of producer price inflation, changes in prices can occur for many reasons that have nothing to do with the business cycle. Strikes, currency movements, restrictions in supplies by foreign producers, and bizarre weather all influence input prices of raw materials regardless of the pace of economic activity. As a result, the change in price data is excluded from the total survey index.

Global Manufacturing PMI

First released in October 2003, the Global PMI series wants to be considered a gauge of world manufacturing trends. It functions the same way as the Eurozone purchasing managers report, except that it includes a larger sample. JP Morgan and NTC Economics collect responses from 7,000 purchasing managers in 23 countries that collectively represent 80% of the world's total manufacturing output. Because the methodology is identical for all these countries, their performances can be compared side by side. (See Table 4.7.)

Table 4.7 Countries in the Global Manufacturing PMI Series

Country	% share of global GDP
U.S.	27
Japan	17
Germany	8
France	5.3
UK	3.9
Italy	3.6
China	3.1
Spain	2.1
The Netherlands	1.5
Australia	1.4
Russia	1.1
Switzerland	1
Austria	0.8
Denmark	0.6
South Africa	0.5
Poland	0.5
Greece	0.4
Ireland	0.3

Singapore	0.3
Israel	0.3
Czech Republic	0.2
Hungary	0.2
New Zealand	0.2

In addition to a composite Global PMI, several other subindexes are tracked:

• Global manufacturing output index

• Global manufacturing new orders index

• Global manufacturing employment index

• Global supplier delivery times

• Global stock of items purchased

• Global manufacturing input prices index

Again, a reading of 50 indicates no change from the previous month. Below 50 is a sign of contraction, and above 50 points to an expansion.

National Manufacturing PMI Summary: December 2006

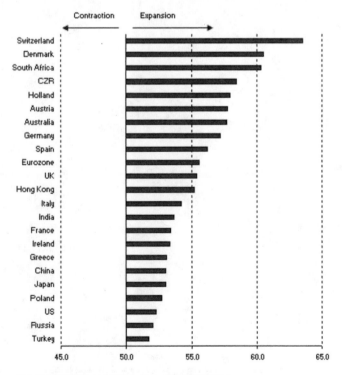

Source: NTC Economics, used with permission.

In addition to a manufacturing index, there are also separate releases on activity in the service sector for the Eurozone and Global PMIs. Services account for a predominant share of the GDP in most modern industrial economies. While that's not the case with emerging countries, even they have seen services grab an increasingly larger share of their economies in recent years. The central question is which PMI series—manufacturing or services—can better foreshadow economic turning points. For Europe the answer appears to be the purchasing managers index for services since there is evidence that this index has a better correlation with changes in GDP than the manufacturing PMI. But if you are trying to anticipate shifts in "global" economic activity, most investors still track the global manufacturing PMI. The reason is that the goods-producing sector tends to respond more quickly to changes in demand than services in the U.S. and in most developing countries. However, given the dynamic growth in services worldwide, you can expect the Global PMI Services Index to eventually outshine its manufacturing cousin in the next decade.

Getting Eurozone and Global PMI data from the Internet is relatively easy, though the amount of free information provided is limited. Details on both series are available primarily to clients. Still, there is some useful material on the Web that makes it worthwhile to check out. For instance, you can view the Global PMI index by simply by calling up its formal press release (*www.ism.ws/ISMReport/index.cfm*).

PRESS RELEASE Embargoed until 11:00am US Eastern Time   1 February 2007

JPMorgan Global PMI

Global Report on Manufacturing

Produced by JPMorgan and NTC Economics in association with ISM and IFPSM

Global manufacturing recorded a sluggish start to 2007, as production expanded at its least marked pace since mid-2003.

The global manufacturing economy lost noticeable momentum at the start of 2007. At 52.4 in January, the JPMorgan **Global Manufacturing PMI** remained above the no-change mark of 50.0 for a forty-third consecutive month, but fell to its lowest level since August 2005. Production growth slowed to a three-and-a-half year low.

The latest release saw some slight revision to the back data of the global manufacturing indexes. These revisions are the consequence of the application of an updated weighting structure to the global indicators and ISM's annual assessment of the seasonal adjustment factors applied to the US data.

Growth of the world manufacturing sector remained firmly centred on the Eurozone in January. However, latest national PMI data suggested that the upturn in this region has likely already passed its peak. Although still robust, production in the euro area expanded at its least marked rate for eleven months. New orders increased at their slowest pace in a year. In contrast, employment rose for the eleventh month running and at the fastest pace since November 2000. Within the Eurozone, Germany remained the principal growth engine.

The tentative recovery of the US manufacturing sector faltered at the start of 2007. The US PMI posted 49.3, its lowest reading since April 2003. Output declined for the second time in the past three months and new order growth slowed to a near-negligible pace. US manufacturing jobs declined for the third successive month.

There were slight improvements in the rates of expansion of Japanese manufacturing output and new orders, although growth was well below their respective averages for 2006.

At 53.0 in January, down from 54.3 in December, the **Global Manufacturing Output Index** signalled that growth of global IP had slipped to a level of around 2%-2.5% saar. The **Global Manufacturing New Orders Index** pointed to slower expansion in new order volumes, posting a twenty-month low of 53.1.

Growth of **international trade volumes** continued to ease in January, with the rate of increase at its lowest in over one-and-a-half years. Export orders for US manufactured goods rose at the weakest pace since last July. France saw a marked easing in the rate of expansion of new export business.

At 59.6 in January, the **Global Manufacturing Input Prices Index** signalled a slight pick up in the already elevated rate of increase in average input costs. Nevertheless, purchase price inflation remained well below the highs seen in mid-2006.

The **Global Manufacturing Employment Index** registered 52.0 in January, to point to a further incremental improvement in the rate of jobs growth. Employment increased in the Eurozone, Japan, China and the UK, but fell in the US.

Stocks of purchases contracted in January, ending a run of six successive months of marginal growth.

© Copyright and database rights in the compiled global PMI data owned by NTC Economics Limited

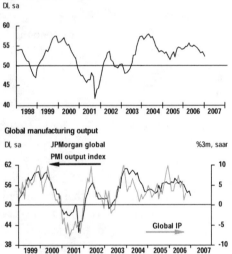

JPMorgan global manufacturing PMI
DI, sa

Global manufacturing output
DI, sa   JPMorgan global   %3m, saar
PMI output index
Global IP

Global Manufacturing PMI Summary
50 = no change on previous month.

	Dec	Jan	Change	Comparison with previous month
Global PMI	53.4	52.4	–	Expanding at slower rate
Output	54.3	53.0	–	Expanding at slower rate
New Orders	54.0	53.1	–	Expanding at slower rate
Input Prices	57.9	59.6	+	Increasing at faster rate
Employment	51.8	52.0	+	Expanding at faster rate

Commenting on the survey, David Hensley, Director of Global Economics Coordination at JPMorgan, said:

"PMI data suggest a sluggish start for the manufacturing sector in 2007, with IP growth expected at 2%-3% saar. The key forward looking new orders component also pointed to slower expansion. The good news is the survey's implication that the rate of inventory accumulation fell sharply. Traditionally, a rising ratio of new orders to inventory foreshadows a pickup in IP growth."

OECD COMPOSITE LEADING INDICATORS (CLI)

What Is It: A statistical guide to forecast business activity in the world's largest economies.

News Release on the Internet: *www.oecd.org/std/cli*

Home Web Address: *www.oecd.org*

Release Time: Noon (Continental time); data is released on the Friday of the first full week of the month and refers to activity two months earlier. (For example, January's release reports leading indicators for November.)

Frequency: Monthly.

Source: Organization for Economic Cooperation and Development (OECD).

Revisions: The previous month's data is frequently revised with each new release.

Investors and policymakers love to follow leading economic indicators because of their look-ahead qualities. They are supposed to predict short-term movements in an economy by using measures that are highly sensitive to upcoming changes in business conditions. The U.S. has its own set of domestic leading economic indicators from the Conference Board, a business research group in New York (see the section "Index of Leading Economic Indicators (LEI)" in Chapter 3, "The Most Influential U.S. Economic Indicators"). On a global scale, however, the best-known and most closely studied equivalent is the OECD's own Composite Leading Indicators (CLI). This Paris-based international organization computes a leading economic indicator index for 29 member countries and six major nonmember nations. The regional zones covered are Total OECD area, G-7, European Union (EU-15), Eurozone currency area, and the Big Five Asian economies. (See Table 4.8.) While some countries produce their own in-house leading indicators, it's the OECD's own indexes that make the big headlines and draw the greatest interest among money managers and policymakers.

Using economic data from its member countries, the OECD calculates CLI indexes designed to forecast what's ahead for industrial production in the OECD nations and regions. Why industrial production and not the more broad-based GDP? First, industrial output is seen as an effective proxy for GDP because, historically, turning points in industrial production have coincided with the overall economy. Second, using industrial production as a reference point is more practical because that data comes out every month, while the GDP is available only quarterly.

Table 4.8   OECD Composite Leading Indicators by Regions and Countries

---

1. OECD Total (29 countries)
Australia, Austria, Belgium, Canada, Czech Republic, Denmark, Finland, France, Germany, Greece, Hungary, Ireland, Italy, Japan, Korea, Luxembourg, Mexico, Netherlands, New Zealand, Norway, Poland, Portugal, Slovak Republic, Spain, Sweden, Switzerland, Turkey, United Kingdom, and United States

2. G7 (Major 7 Economies)
Canada, France, Germany, Italy, Japan, United Kingdom, and United States

3. Euro Currency Zone (12 countries)
Austria, Belgium, Finland, France, Germany, Greece, Ireland, Italy, Luxembourg, the Netherlands, Portugal, and Spain

4. European Union (EU) (15 countries)
Limited to 12 euro currency nations plus Denmark, Sweden, and United Kingdom

5. Major Five Asia Countries
China, India, Indonesia, Japan, and Korea

Slovenia, the newest member of the Eurocurrency zone, is not included in the EU–15 series at this time. Though total EU membership consists of 27 countries, of which 13 use the euro as their currency,* the Composite Leading Indicators series defines the regions only by the countries listed here.

Now for the obvious question: Does the OECD's CLI really work? Is it reliable in picking up signals of a pending slowdown or rebound in economic growth? Here we get one of those "Yes, but..." answers. To begin with, anticipating turning points is not easy. Signs are often elusive or ambiguous. Second, much depends on the quality of the underlying data from national governments, not to mention the judgment calls involved in setting up the leading indicator models and the assumptions behind them. By and large, the OECD's leading indicator series gets a thumbs-up from economists and large investors. Even central bankers review the CLI data when setting interest rate policy for the euro currency zone. Over the years, the CLI has proven to be an effective early-warning system, able to identify peaks and troughs in economic activity some nine months in advance.

The OECD has been publishing the CLI since 1981, and the methodology is fairly straightforward. Financial indicators with a reputation for being ahead of the economic curve are chosen as components of this indicator. Among the most common national components used by the OECD to calculate the CLI are stock prices, building permits, monetary data, and production orders. Indeed, more than 100 components are employed to come up with a monthly (Table 1) "Total OECD Composite Leading Indicator." However, the monthly index is not the one to watch. The better indicator is the six-month

---

* As of this writing, 13 countries use the euro as their currency: Austria, Belgium, Finland, France, Germany, Greece, Ireland, Italy, Luxembourg, the Netherlands, Portugal, Slovenia, and Spain. Beginning in 2008, two more nations will join the group, Malta and Cyprus, enlarging the eurozone to 15 countries.

annual rate of change in the CLI (Table 2) because it avoids some of the short-term noise and volatility found in economic statistics. If there are three consecutive months of negative or positive change in the six-month rate, chances are the economy or a region is within 6 to 12 months of reaching a high or low point in economic activity.

Table 1: Trend restored Composite Leading Indicators

	2005	2006											
	Dec	Jan	Feb	Mar	Apr	May	Jun	Jul	Aug	Sep	Oct	Nov	Dec
OECD Area	107.4	107.9	108.3	108.5	108.8	108.8	108.8	108.7	108.8	108.9	109.3	109.6	109.9
EU 15	106.2	106.5	107.0	107.3	107.8	108.1	108.1	108.1	108.2	108.3	108.5	108.7	108.7
Euro Area	106.6	107.0	107.4	107.7	108.2	108.6	108.7	108.6	108.8	108.8	109.1	109.3	109.3
Major Seven	104.3	104.6	104.9	105.0	105.1	105.1	104.9	104.8	104.9	104.9	105.2	105.4	105.6
Canada	99.5	99.7	99.6	99.5	99.4	99.7	100.5	101.2	101.1	101.6	102.4	103.0	103.4
France	105.8	105.9	106.0	106.1	106.5	106.6	106.5	106.6	107.1	107.3	107.7	107.7	107.2
Germany	110.3	111.1	111.9	112.5	113.3	113.8	113.9	113.9	114.0	114.0	114.5	115.0	115.3
Italy	97.1	96.9	97.0	96.9	97.2	97.6	97.7	97.2	96.9	96.8	96.5	96.0	95.9
Japan	101.9	102.1	102.3	102.3	102.3	102.0	101.3	100.6	100.7	100.7	100.7	100.7	100.9
United Kingdom	100.5	100.7	101.1	101.5	101.8	101.8	101.6	101.7	101.7	101.8	101.9	101.7	101.3
United States	105.6	106.1	106.4	106.4	106.4	106.1	105.9	106.1	106.1	106.1	106.5	106.9	107.3
Major Five Asia*	156.0	157.7	159.6	161.2	162.3	163.1	163.6	164.4	165.2	166.7	169.2	171.6	
Brazil	124.4	127.2	128.2	127.6	126.6	126.5	128.0	129.6	131.0	131.4	132.2	134.1	136.0
China	207.4	210.2	212.9	215.8	218.6	220.3	222.5	224.9	225.6	227.9	232.4	237.2	243.1
India	138.6	140.1	141.8	143.3	143.8	143.9	143.6	144.3	145.2	146.5	148.3	149.7	
Russia	134.1	135.4	136.2	137.4	139.3	139.8	140.4	139.6	139.5	136.2	134.2	133.3	134.8

Table 2: Six-month rate of change of the trend restored CLI (annualised)
Percentage change

	2005	2006											
	Dec	Jan	Feb	Mar	Apr	May	Jun	Jul	Aug	Sep	Oct	Nov	Dec
OECD Area	3.5	4.0	4.3	4.2	4.0	3.5	2.8	2.3	2.0	1.7	2.0	2.0	2.1
EU 15	3.4	3.7	4.0	4.2	4.5	4.4	3.8	3.1	2.7	2.3	2.2	2.0	1.6
Euro Area	3.7	4.0	4.4	4.4	4.8	4.8	4.2	3.4	3.0	2.5	2.4	2.2	1.9
Major Seven	3.1	3.4	3.7	3.4	3.2	2.6	1.8	1.3	1.1	0.8	1.0	1.1	1.2
Canada	1.1	1.5	1.2	0.9	0.6	1.2	2.5	3.5	3.1	3.7	4.7	5.1	5.2
France	2.8	2.8	2.7	2.8	3.2	2.9	2.2	1.8	2.1	2.0	2.4	2.0	1.0
Germany	5.8	6.6	7.4	7.6	7.9	7.6	6.5	5.4	4.6	3.7	3.7	3.7	3.5
Italy	0.3	0.1	0.4	0.2	0.7	1.5	1.5	0.5	-0.3	-0.6	-1.1	-2.0	-2.1
Japan	1.5	1.7	1.9	1.7	1.4	0.7	-0.9	-2.1	-1.8	-1.7	-1.6	-1.5	-1.0
United Kingdom	0.7	1.1	1.5	2.1	2.4	2.0	1.4	1.3	1.1	1.1	1.2	0.7	-0.2
United States	4.0	4.5	4.7	4.1	3.6	2.4	1.6	1.4	1.3	0.9	1.1	1.4	1.9
Major Five Asia*	9.9	10.6	11.3	11.7	11.3	10.6	9.6	8.9	8.3	8.7	10.1	11.3	
Brazil	6.8	10.3	10.8	8.7	6.1	5.0	6.6	8.2	9.1	8.3	7.9	9.3	10.5
China	14.9	15.3	15.5	15.8	15.8	14.8	14.4	14.3	12.5	12.4	14.4	16.3	18.9
India	7.2	8.2	9.6	10.3	9.7	8.4	6.6	6.4	6.5	7.2	8.3	8.8	
Russia	8.5	8.9	8.5	8.6	9.8	9.1	8.5	6.1	4.8	-0.6	-3.7	-5.0	-3.0

CHINA INDUSTRIAL PRODUCTION

What Is It: Measures the monthly change in China's industrial output.

News Release on the Internet:
   www.stats.gov.cn/english/statisticaldata/monthlydata

Home Web Address: *www.stats.gov.cn/english*

Release Time: Between 3:30 and 4:30 p.m. (local time); the report is first
   released in Chinese two weeks after the month ends, with a version in English
   published two weeks following the initial release.

Frequency: Monthly.

Source: National Bureau of Statistics of China (NBS).

Revisions: Corrections to data may occur more frequently in the future as China
   endeavors to improve the accuracy of its statistics.

China comes as close to the Promised Land as you can get for investors and business
executives. It is a nation with awesome growth rates and mind-boggling potential as an
economy. Depending on the measure you use, China is either the fourth-largest economy
in the world, as it is most commonly described, or the second-largest based on purchasing
power parity, which some economists prefer to use. (With purchasing power parity, GDP
values of two or more countries are readjusted so that prices for identical products are
effectively the same for consumers in these countries.) Whichever measure you choose,
the overall point is that China is buzzing with activity. No country in the world produces
more steel, cement, mobile phones, or color TVs. Auto production has exceeded that of
Germany's, making China the third-largest automaker, behind only the U.S. and Japan.
Indeed, one can argue that China's manufacturing capabilities can now be promoted to
the status of an industrial country.

   As a consumer market, the opportunities are limited only by imagination. Here is a
nation of 1.3 billion people and growing, including a labor force of 800 million, all eager
to work and spend money. Consumer demand has been climbing steadily the last two
decades as households are driven to improve their standard of living. That can be seen not
only by their larger and better-furnished residences, but also in the use of high-tech consumer products. Despite government controls on Internet access, more than 100 million
Chinese citizens surf the Web (as of early 2006), an exponential rise from just 620,000
users a decade earlier. In fact, China's Internet population has catapulted into second
place in the world, exceeding even Japan and closing in fast on the U.S. Moreover, the
potential market for the Internet alone is staggering because current users still represent
less than 10% of China's total population.

The broader question is, what intentions do China's top political leaders have for the country? Government officials talk about moving toward a "socialist market economy," a strange brew where socialist ideals can be met in conjunction with a more liberal, open, and capitalistic economy. Precisely what this means or how both can be achieved is anyone's guess. In any event, China's economic strategy can be more easily understood from the actions taken so far by its policymakers, and here there is reason for some encouragement. China is unmistakably evolving into a more market-oriented economy, with more than half of the business sector now in private hands. Concrete steps are being taken to shift economic decision-making away from a centralized, command-style system. What's more, China's ascension to the World Trade Organization in 2003 will bring its economic policies more in line with world standards.

The results so far have been nothing short of striking. For more than two decades, China's economic growth has consistently been among the fastest in the world, fueled mainly by explosive surges in industrial production, consumer demand, exports, and capital investments. Nothing seems to get in its way. This rapid expansion has continued irrespective of what else is going on in the rest of the world economy. It is little wonder that international investors and multinational business leaders are so eager to get a piece of this action. Foreign firms are pouring money into China, salivating at the chance to set up factories in a country where labor costs are still about one-tenth that of the developed world—though these costs have been accelerating in recent years. International money managers see more opportunities to add Chinese securities to their portfolios. Large foreign investment bankers see in China a rich source of new clients as an increasing number of companies there are being permitted to access global capital markets to raise funds. Credit ratings firms, such as Standard & Poor's, Fitch, and Moody's, are also charging into China to assess the credit-worthiness of its companies and government agencies. China itself has become a major player in the international community. With a war chest of more than $1 trillion in foreign exchange reserves, largest in the world thanks to its cumulative trade surpluses, China is in a position to buy huge chunks of foreign government bonds, stocks, real estate, and other types of assets.

And yet, even with all the attributes that make it a rising economic superpower, the country has at least one noticeable flaw: China has a reputation for putting out dubious statistics about its economy. This poses a genuine problem for foreign firms and investors who need to appraise the country's current and future well-being. Longtime observers have complained that China's economic numbers are less accurate than those of other industrialized countries, even going so far as to say that key officials "cook the books" to impress foreign investors and lenders. In recent years analysts have charged that China was overestimating its GDP growth to lure foreign capital. At other times, there were accusations that Chinese statisticians were intentionally underestimating growth to create the impression that the economy was not overheating. Amazingly, even top Chinese leaders acknowledged there was a problem with the integrity of the data. As recently as 2000, former premier Zhu Ronji said that Chinese economic reports suffered from "falsification and that exaggeration was rampant." One Chinese government study in 2002 concluded that 60,000 errors were committed in the collection of data over a five-month period.

Behind these statistical problems lies an antiquated data collection system, one that can be traced back to the old command economy days. During the 1950s and 1960s, Communist party headquarters relied extensively on production reports from local managers, who would often lie about output figures to curry favor with party leaders. Small-town Communist officials were often promoted based on the economic performance in their region, so it was in their best interest to embellish the figures. Thus, to some extent, the problem was not so much at the headquarters level in Beijing, but with the field reports from local and municipal managers. Today, China's National Bureau of Statistics (NBS) still gathers output figures much the same way as before, though the degree of fabrication is believed to be less widespread. Nevertheless, China still has no independent method in place to check the veracity of local production reports. This doesn't mean Beijing officials are sitting idle. They are well aware that without a trustworthy source of economic information, it will be hard for foreigners to make investment decisions or for Chinese leaders to carry out the right fiscal and monetary policies.

The NBS has been working in earnest to upgrade the quality of its economic reports and seek better ways to compile and estimate economic data. Among the modifications recently introduced was a change in the manner in which statistics are collected. For example, Chinese officials decided in March 2005 that data collectors should be placed under the authority of the NBS. This can help redress many of the statistical inaccuracies that originate from local municipalities. Second, the government revamped how GDP is computed. This redesign was critical. The traditional statistical reporting method failed to capture the growth under way in the expanding service industries, such as real estate agents, business consultants, and companies offering communication services. To correct this shortcoming, the government conducted its first-ever nationwide economic census in 2004, and the results were startling. At the end of 2005, China announced that its economy was actually much larger than previously thought. Virtually all of the upward revision came from services, which turned out to represent more than 40% of all economic activity, nearly 10 percentage points higher than its prerevision share. It was fresh evidence that China's economy is becoming more diversified than first believed.

Another way that China has moved to bring its economic reports up to global standards was to make the data more accessible to everyone in the world. China's NBS has a Web site with detailed information on economic output, inflation, and other measures of performance, and much of it is in English. Topping the list of perhaps the best and most timely measure of economic performance in China is its industrial production series. Industrial output and construction make up more than half of China's GDP. Every month, the NBS reports on industrial output, and much of the data can be seen on the Web (*www.stats.gov.cn/english/statisticaldata/monthlydata*), though it might take a few moments to learn how to navigate this site to arrive at the correct page. The only major complaint is that the English version of this report shows up on the NBS Web site about two weeks after it is released in Chinese. Government officials say they are working to accelerate that schedule.

Value added of Industry (2006.11)

National Bureau of Statistics of China   2006-11-15 09:13:11

Unit: 100 million yuan

	Accumulated	This month	Increase rate over the same period of last year %	
			Accumulated	This month
Output Value of Industry	**77890.99**	**7936.33**	**16.8**	**14.9**
Of which: Light Industry	23740.63	2428.98	14.2	11.2
Heavy Industry	54150.37	5507.35	17.9	16.6
Of which: State-owned and State-holding Industrial Enterprises	27813.99	2700.98	12.2	13.6
Of which: Private Enterprises	15003.09	1608.64	25.0	19.4
Of which: Collective Enterprises	2543.15	252.73	12.3	7.1
Share-holding Corporations Ltd.	882.93	92.88	16.5	14.4
Share-holding Enterprises	38895.02	3957.23	17.9	16.1
Foreign Funded, Hong Kong, Macao and Taiwan Funded Enterprises	22035.69	2250.75	17.2	14.7

The latest English version of the industrial production report can be seen both in summary form (see the following chart) and in greater detail by specific commodity.

A couple of pointers are needed to appreciate the industrial production numbers in the release. Unlike the U.S. series, the Chinese do not produce an index of industrial production, but instead estimate a value-added amount of what is produced each month. The process works as follows: Output data is compiled every month from all state-owned and stated-controlled enterprises. Also included are major private enterprises. After collecting the output data, the NBS converts the gross figures into a value-added price basis. Monthly changes in industrial output are calculated using current prices, while percentage change comparisons over the year are computed in constant prices (after being adjusted for producer price inflation).

Production is classified as being from either light industry or heavy industry. Light industry makes smaller products that are mainly for the consumer market. Heavy industry, as the term implies, involves output of capital goods, factory equipment, and automobiles. A more precise breakdown of industrial output for the month and cumulative year totals can be found elsewhere on the same Web site. It includes such commodities as telecom equipment, communication equipment, automobiles, large computers, PCs, electrical machinery, transportation equipment, mobile communication services, coal, gas, and electricity output. In addition to industrial production data, the NBS of China has many more economic indicators on its Web site. These include retail sales, consumer price inflation, and household income. Thus, it is well worth investing a little time to become familiar with this online government agency if you want to monitor the latest trends in China's economy.

中文简体 ▣ 中文繁体 ▣

National Bureau of Statistics of China

Jun.23, 2004 Wednesday

www.stats.gov.cn

| Home |
| Agency Information |
| Laws & Regulations |
| Statistical Standards |
| Survey Programs |
| Statistical Indicators |
| New Release |
| Statistical data |
| Int. Cooperation |
| News & Coming Events |
| Related Links |

Monthly Data

- Value added of Industry (2004.05)
- Value added of Industry by Region (2004.05)
- Ratio of Sales of Industrial Products by Region (2004.05)
- Output of Major Industrial Products (2004.05)
- Investment in Fixed Assets (2004.1-4)
- Investment in Fixed Assets by Industry (2004.1-4)
- Investment in Fixed Assets by Region (2004.1-4)
- Investment in Fixed Assets (2004.1-3)
- Investment in Fixed Assets by Industry (2004.1-3)
- Investment in Fixed Assets by Region (2004.1-3)
- Gross Domestic Product (GDP) (First Quarter 2004)
- Labor Rewards of Persons Employed in Urban Units (First Quarter 2004)
- Output Value of Farming, Forestry, Animal Husbandry, and Fishery (First Quarter 2004)
- Output Value of Farming, Forestry, Animal Husbandry, and Fishery by Region (First Quarter 2004)
- Major Indicators of Trade Markets with Sales over 100 million yuan (First quarter, 2004)
- Indicators of Trade Markets with Sales over 100 million yuan by Region (First quarter, 2004)
- Per Capita Cash Income of Rural Households by Region (First Quarter 2004)
- Business Climate Index (First Quarter 2004)
- Value added of Industry (2004.04)
- Value added of Industry by Region (2004.04)
- Ratio of Sales of Industrial Products by Region (2004.04)

INDIA: GDP AND WHOLESALE PRICE INDEX

What Is It: GDP measures India's national economic output; the Wholesale Price Index (WPI) is considered the country's best gauge of inflation pressures.

News Release on the Internet: *http://mospi.nic.in/mospi_nad_sdrs.htm*

Home Web Address: *http://mospi.nic.in/*

Release Time: GDP: Noon (local time); is published two months after the quarter ends. Wholesale Price Index: Noon (local time); comes out every Friday to report on price changes as of two weeks ago.

Frequency: Quarterly (GDP) and weekly (Wholesale Price Index).

Source: Central Statistical Organization, Ministry of Statistics.

Revisions: The quarterly GDP growth rates are revised only with the release of the fourth-quarter figures. As for the wholesale price index (WPI), each weekly release contains the final revision of the WPI for the week dated two months earlier.

India's emergence as an economic power often gets overshadowed by its giant neighbor to the east. That's unfortunate. Not only is India coming into its own, but many people believe the country could eventually surpass China in both population and total output. What's so compelling about India is that its stunning growth since the early 1990s can be traced to a strategy that sets it apart from other developing countries in the region. From the beginning, India cleverly positioned itself so that it did not have to compete head-to-head with China and the other Asian countries. Indeed, what India did was defy the text-book path toward economic development. Virtually all emerging countries in the 20th century used their cheap labor and whatever capital they could scrape together to build up their manufacturing or agricultural capabilities. Exports and construction became the key drivers of economic growth for these countries.

However, India followed a strikingly different road by capitalizing on its own unique comparative advantage. India, like China, enjoys a large population (1.1 billion versus 1.3 billion for China), but the characteristics of these two groups differ in important respects. India's labor force is younger, more traveled, and speaks English. Given these attributes, business leaders concluded that economic success would more likely come from services, not manufacturing. As a result, the country now offers a panoply of important services to the world, including banking, insurance, engineering, media, software, business outsourcing, medical diagnostics, telecommunications, and film entertainment. (India's film industry, for example, is the biggest in the world, in both the number of movies produced and the number of tickets sold.)

India has thus bucked the trend by choosing to rely on services, not manufacturing or natural resources, as a means to achieve healthy economic growth. This decision has propelled its $800 billion economy to be the third largest in Asia and the 10th largest in the world. Moreover, India's blistering growth rate has led to an escalation in wages among service sector employees, and especially for skilled workers. This has enhanced family income and stimulated domestic demand. To give you a sense of how rapidly the country is changing, back in 1991, India had a total of 5 million telephone lines in the country. Now it is adding that many phone lines each month!

One of the burning questions investors ask is whether India's economy can continue to race ahead as it has. Can it conceivably even overtake China in total output? The answer to both questions is yes, though the latter is probably a few decades away. India's prospects look bright for several reasons. First, the country has undertaken substantial political and economic reforms since 1991. It has rejected socialism, opened its economy to more imports, deregulated industries, allowed the Rupee to float more freely, and reduced barriers to trade.

Second, India's leaders also realized that the country cannot depend on services forever to keep its economy robust. And they certainly do not want the country to be viewed as simply a back-office operation for American companies that consists mainly of call centers, customer help lines, and computer programmers. So fresh domestic and foreign capital has also been directed to establish a sophisticated manufacturing industry, one that utilizes state-of-the-art technology and embraces the latest techniques of just-in-time inventory. The results have so far been impressive. India's annual growth in manufacturing is now accelerating at about the same pace as services.

Given the country's extraordinary economic accomplishments, international investors are making the inevitable comparisons with China. Though China's economy is three times the size of India's, the question often asked is, who really will have the edge in the years ahead?

Certainly both countries have enormous potential to grow and prosper. But there are some important differences between them that may shape their economic destiny:

- Cultural purists may yell and scream about it, but the fact remains that English is the language of international business. In this respect, India has a big advantage over China. The medium of communication in India's colleges and universities is English. Indeed, India is the world's largest English-speaking country. The ability of workers and management to effectively communicate with customers and investors around the world is critically important to attract foreign capital and to find new markets for Indian-made products.

- India has a long tradition of democracy and for having a transparent legal system. In contrast, China, while it has made some strides to decentralize its economy and allow more local autonomy, is still run by an autocratic Communist leadership. Its legal system is far from a model of transparency, and its courts are subject to political pressure. What's more, social unrest has increased in China, especially in rural farm areas. Such strife is symptomatic of a country that is struggling to pursue two inherently conflicting goals: allowing more market capitalism in the economy, and preserving its Communist political heritage and the ideologies that stem from it. The social tension that comes from pursuing two incongruous objectives is not expected to subside anytime soon. With so much uncertainty about China's long-term stability, investors may place greater faith in the future of a more open India.

• No economy can prosper unless it has a healthy banking system that can finance consumer and business activity. India's banking system, though much smaller than China's in terms of assets, is far healthier and better capitalized. India's loans, for example, are priced according to risk, so interest rates tend to be higher than those in China. China has chosen to keep rates artificially low, in part because policymakers want to keep its currency (the yuan) undervalued. However, that has also allowed Chinese banks to issue such artificially low interest rate loans to domestic borrowers, including failing state-owned enterprises, and that raises questions about the future viability of such loans. Keep in mind that China has had to bail out its banks more than once in the last decade. Meanwhile, India's regulators appear determined to keep its banks financially sound from the outset. They demand high capital requirements for lenders and make sure that these institutions have sufficient provisions set aside against bad loans.

• Unlike India, China faces a serious demographic squeeze in coming years. The Communist country has implemented a "one family, one child" policy, and Chinese households have mostly adhered to it. As a result, birthrates and family sizes have been shrinking since 1980. No such policy exists in India; consequently, its population is much younger on average and more dynamic. Experts predict that India will end up with a larger population than China in the next 15 years or so. If that trend materializes, it will have profound implications for both countries. As China struggles to service an aging workforce that draws down national savings, India will enjoy a more youthful, active, and prosperous labor force. This can help catapult India's economy past China by mid-century.

But it's not all smooth sailing for India. If the economy is ever to meet its full potential, India will first have to address some serious internal shortcomings. One is the critical need to upgrade its creaking infrastructure. India's road transportation system is in dismal shape. Highways make up less than 5% of its road network, and this makes it tough to transport goods around the country. In addition, there is a critical shortage of lodging facilities, and this has hurt both tourism and foreign business travel in the country. There were only 115,000 hotel rooms in all of India in 2006, while China had 10 times as many. Also in dire need of expansion are India's ports. There are not enough of them to handle all the merchant ships that arrive and leave with goods, and this has hampered the flow of both imports and exports. Government officials also have to beef up the nation's power generating system. Right now India does not have enough plants to satisfy the electrical demands of a fast-growing economy. Blackouts are not uncommon, even in Bangalore, where the country's high-tech computer and software industry is situated.

Aside from having a lagging infrastructure, India continues to be stigmatized by its stifling bureaucracy, red tape, corruption, and a set of rigid labor rules that makes it quite difficult for companies to lay off employees. Unless these deficiencies and administrative problems are corrected, India will have great difficulty achieving world-class economic status.

If the government fails to follow up with the needed public investments, it will stunt the economy's growth for years and probably bring higher rates of inflation. On the other hand, if officials allocate enough resources to improve roads, ports, electrical generation, and airports, as well as reduce bureaucratic delays, the benefits will be lasting and significant. Whichever course the country takes, the results will show up in the macroeconomic data, particularly in GDP and inflation. To monitor these and other key economic indicators of India, one can go online to the Ministry of Statistics—specifically, the Central Statistical Organization (CSO).

The latest data on the major indicators can be found on one page. It includes the following:

1. *GDP at current prices*

2. *GDP in constant dollars* (To view the entire press release of the latest quarterly GDP report, go to *http://mospi.nic.in/mospi_press_releases.htm.*)

3. *The key components of real GDP*

4. *Industrial production:* Total and broken down by its three major segments: mining, manufacturing, and electricity

5. *Inflation:* The CSO publishes five measures of inflation, and this has led to some confusion among investors as to which are worth following. Let's break down what these five are: the *GDP implicit price index*, three variants of *consumer prices* (each targeted to different groups of consumers), and the *Wholesale Price Index*.

   The *implicit price index* is a quarterly measure and thus is not especially timely. Of the three CPI measures, the most popular is the *CPI (IW)* for industrial workers, because it is meant to reflect the cost of living for those Indian households that are most likely to spend a major part of their income. But this series also has drawbacks. It's based on changes in the retail price for a selected basket of goods and services bought mainly by a homogenous group of consumers—namely, industrial workers. It is also released with a four-week lag. So, in a sense, none of the CPI measures here can be considered a price measure comparable to those used in developed countries. Most policymakers in India consider the *Wholesale Price Index* the one to watch.

6. *Wholesale Price Index (WPI):* India's WPI is similar to the Producer Price Index in other countries. It is sensitive to price changes in commodities and industrial

Unit of Description - Rupees (Rs.) in Crore.   1 Crore = 10 Million.

Advance Release Calendar

This page is updated periodically. Unless otherwise indicated, data are preliminary when first released. Data are not seasonally adjusted.

SDDS Data Category and Component	Unit of Description	Period of latest data	Latest Data	Previous data @	Percentage change from previous to latest period
1	2	3	4	5	6
National Accounts					
1 ▶ **GDP (at current prices)**	**Rs.Crore**	**Jul/06-Sep/06**	838367	735461	14.0
1. Agriculture, Forestry & Fishing	Rs.Crore		123419	114441	7.8
2. Mining & Quarrying	Rs.Crore		21231	18731	13.3
3. Manufacturing	Rs.Crore		143365	123473	16.1
4. Electricity, Gas & Water Supply.	Rs.Crore		17886	16569	7.9
5. Construction	Rs.Crore		59881	51928	15.3
6. Trade, Hotels, Transport and Communication	Rs.Crore		215982	185011	16.7
7. Financing, Insurance, Real Estate & Business Services.	Rs.Crore		130279	113413	14.9
8. Community, Social & Personal Services.	Rs.Crore		126325	111894	12.9
National Accounts					
2 ▶ **GDP[at Constant(1999-2000) prices]**	**Rs.Crore**	**Jul/06-Sep/06**	647290	592652	9.2
1. Agriculture, Forestry & Fishing	Rs.Crore		98589	96961	1.7
2. Mining & Quarrying	Rs.Crore		12254	11890	3.1
3. Manufacturing	Rs.Crore		106621	95318	11.9
4. Electricity, Gas & Water Supply.	Rs.Crore		14742	13688	7.7
3 ▶ 5. Construction	Rs.Crore		45676	41592	9.8
6. Trade, Hotels, Transport and Communication	Rs.Crore		178459	156721	13.9
7. Financing, Insurance, Real Estate & Business Services.	Rs.Crore		93825	85662	9.5
8. Community, Social & Personal Services.	Rs.Crore		97122	90821	6.9

National Accounts					
GDP (Implicit Price Index)	**1999-00=100**	**Jul/06-Sep/06**	129.5	124.1	4.4
1. Agriculture, Forestry & Fishing			125.2	118.0	6.1
2. Mining & Quarrying			173.2	157.5	10.0
3. Manufacturing			134.5	129.5	3.8
4. Electricity, Gas & Water Supply.			121.3	121.1	0.2
5. Construction			131.1	124.9	5.0
6. Trade, Hotels, Transport and Communication			121.0	118.1	2.5
7. Financing, Insurance, Real Estate & Business Services.			138.9	132.4	4.9
8. Community, Social & Personal Services.			130.1	123.2	5.6
4 ▶ **Production Index** **(Index of Industrial Production)**	**Index 93-94 =100**	**Dec/06**	258.3	232.5	11.1
1. Mining			171.4	165.2	3.8
2. Manufacturing			275.7	246.3	11.9
3. Electricity			211.8	193.8	9.3
5 ▶ **Consumer Price Index(CPI)**					
CPI-IW	2001=100	Dec/06	127	550 *	
CPI-AL	1986-87=100	Jan/07	391	357	9.52
CPI-RL	1986-87=100	Jan/07	391	359	8.91
CPI-UNME	1984-85=100	Jan/07	496	462	7.4
6 ▶ Wholesale Price Index(WPI)	1993-94=100	**Week ending Feb/10/07**	209.2	196.2	6.63
IW - Industrial Workers ; **AL** - Agricultural Labourers ; **RL** - Rural Labourers ; **UNME** - Urban Non-Manual Employees					

goods and has little representation in services. What makes the WPI the best inflation gauge for India is that it is updated *weekly* and that it assesses price changes that occurred just two weeks earlier. It therefore provides a fairly good indication of the current underlying rate of inflation in India's economy. The WPI is also the main inflation measure that India's central bank follows to conduct monetary policy. (To view the entire press release of the latest WPI, go to *www.eaindustry.nic.in/press_out.htm.*)

BRAZIL INDUSTRIAL PRODUCTION

What Is It: Tracks changes in Brazil's industrial output.

News Release on the Internet: *www.ibge.gov.br/english/*
www.bcb.gov.br/?INDICATORS

Release Time: 9:30 a.m. (local time); the report is released about 40 days after
the survey month ends. (Thus, January's release refers to industrial
performance in November.)

Frequency: Monthly.

Sources: Brazilian National Statistics Institute and the Brazilian Institute for
Geography and Statistics (IBGE).

Revisions: Monthly figures are subject to revisions.

The temptation for foreigners to invest in an emerging economy can be high given the
lucrative returns that are possible from a country with lots of growth potential. Two principal beneficiaries of such foreign investments have been China and India. However, many
investment managers look upon Brazil as possessing attributes that might match, if not
exceed, those two Asian giants. China may have matchless human assets with 1.3 billion
people, but it also is rapidly running out of accessible natural resources. In contrast, Brazil
is endowed with lots of physical resources; stands close to enjoying energy self-suffi-
ciency; occupies huge territory; is rich in minerals; has ample arable land, a benign climate, and thousands of miles of magnificent beaches; and is surrounded by other
democratically elected developing nations. With such characteristics, Brazil has all the pre-
requisites to become a prosperous leader among the emerging market economies.

The country is already a major player in the global arena. Brazil easily outweighs its
neighbors in economic size and alone accounts for more than 40% of Latin America's total
GDP. Over the years, the size of Brazil's economy in the world has shifted between eighth
and 13th place. These fluctuations exist not because of recessions in Brazil, but because of
movement in the exchange rates between its currency (the real) and the U.S. dollar.

What recently put Brazil back on the radar screen for many foreign investors were
not only its splendid resources, but also the political and economic reforms the country
has undertaken in the last two decades. After more than half a century of strong military
influence in the government, the country made a fateful transition to mass electoral
democracy in the mid-1980s. This shift was all the more remarkable because it occurred
smack in the middle of the Latin American debt crisis. In addition to political reforms,
Brazil's leaders have since liberalized the domestic capital markets. They allowed their

currency to float in foreign exchange markets, crafted a new fiscal spending plan, opened the economy to more competition, embarked on a privatization program, and passed legislation to further deregulate the economy.

The results for Brazil's economy have been palpable. After growing an average of 6% a year in the 1960s and nearly 9% in the 1970s, the economy was stuck at idle in the 1980s, squeaking out barely 1.5% growth annually, its worst 10-year economic performance since the 1930s. But it has bounced back nicely since. Brazil has weathered global economic downturns better than its neighbors. As the U.S. and Europe struggled with recession after the tech bubble burst and stock markets collapsed, economic activity in Brazil continued to expand without interruption, an accomplishment that did not escape the attention of foreign investors. At the core of Brazil's resilience and strength is a highly diversified export sector, one that ranges from shipments of orange juice and minerals to value-added manufactured products such as automobiles, planes, boats, and capital goods. Perhaps the most important benefit to Brazil from all the reforms is that for the first time in decades, the country is now capable of experiencing vibrant economic growth without necessarily suffering the previous side effects of huge trade deficits and soaring inflation.

Still, Brazil needs to do more. Its central bank, which carries out monetary policy, does not yet have full independence and thus can be subject to political influence. The country continues to have severe social problems due to sharp inequalities in its income distribution. It also has a creaky infrastructure that requires attention, and it needs to further reform its judicial system.

But make no mistake: Brazil's economy is on the move, and international investors have returned to help expand the country's industrial sector. In fact, the best barometer for measuring the health of Brazil's economy is industrial production, which represents 40% of its GDP (with services contributing 50% and agriculture 10%). To measure industrial output, the government surveys 8,500 establishments on the output of 944 different products. Brazil's Institute for Geography and Statistics compiles the data, announces the news, publishes an online press release in English, and provides relevant tables, though they are printed on different Web pages within the IBGE Web site. For instance, the headline news can be found on the home page (*www.ibge.gov.br/english*). A press release can be downloaded from the main industrial production news page. However, to get all the relevant tables, you have to return to the home page and click "indicators."

Another government agency, the Central Bank of Brazil, does a slightly better job of presenting the industrial production tables along with other important economic indicators—though without any accompanying commentary. What's more, the information has to be downloaded onto a spreadsheet (*www.bcb.gov.br/?INDICATORS*), but it's a step well worth the effort.

After the data is downloaded, the top part of the page notes the monthly value-added index of industrial production, while the bottom has all the percentage changes with the following time frames:

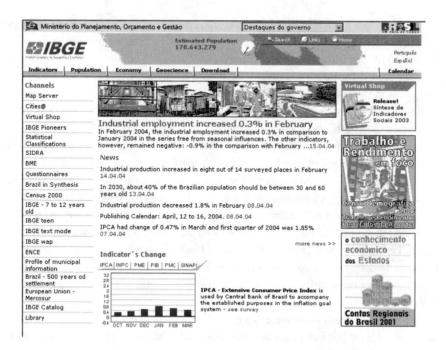

1. The latest monthly change (using seasonally adjusted figures)

2. The change over the last 12 months (using the observed data, not seasonally adjusted)

3. Change in the year so far versus the same period the previous year (using observed data)

4. Change in the last 12 months from the prior 12 months (using observed data)

The page also breaks down industrial production as follows:

• General industrial production index: Overall snapshot of industrial output

• Capital goods: An indicator that tells if companies are investing

• Intermediate goods: A helpful leading sign of future production

• Consumer durable goods: Consists of household appliances and home electronics

• Consumer nondurable goods: Food and clothing. Both consumer durable and non-durable goods output are linked to the growth in wages and personal income.

Economic indicators

Apr 14, 2004

I.23 - Industrial production (general and by category of use)

1992 = 100

Period		General		Capital goods		Intermediate goods		Consumer goods					
								Total		Durable		Nondurable and semidurable	
		Observed data	Seasonally adjusted[1/]	Observed data	Seasonally adjusted[1/]	Observed data	Seasonally adjusted[1/]	Observed data	Seasonally adjusted[1/]	Observed data	Seasonally adjusted[1/]	Observed data	Seasonally adjusted[1/]
2003	Jan	124.37	133.45	111.48	122.49	130.23	139.20	115.06	125.87	166.03	182.28	106.27	115.71
	Feb	121.43	132.56	117.44	120.28	124.97	138.45	111.79	123.15	170.08	173.57	102.04	115.20
	Mar	128.90	132.92	116.23	121.33	140.12	139.76	113.34	123.33	159.35	173.08	105.27	114.81
	Apr	128.16	132.99	119.84	122.98	136.05	138.43	114.69	123.43	177.63	171.80	104.24	115.15
	May	133.42	132.00	123.88	122.86	141.42	137.24	119.82	121.58	178.31	172.20	109.93	113.72
	Jun	128.16	130.26	117.96	119.20	135.99	133.72	114.21	120.13	161.63	172.83	105.93	110.79
	Jul	136.91	131.14	129.12	124.27	143.79	136.25	122.09	118.42	174.88	177.74	112.95	108.07
	Aug	138.07	133.03	128.36	127.18	143.50	138.42	125.01	120.44	176.03	174.71	116.07	110.00
	Sep	145.53	138.49	140.49	135.25	147.29	142.13	134.61	125.58	209.97	199.72	122.15	113.52
	Oct	153.66	142.20	157.68	143.24	151.81	142.84	144.82	126.54	231.72	208.18	130.58	113.53
	Nov	145.24	142.73	158.61	156.13	140.49	142.61	138.23	127.94	228.68	213.63	123.61	114.75
	Dec	132.19	139.79	134.94	144.27	131.29	143.61	126.40	130.43	185.07	208.93	116.37	118.02
2004	Jan	128.91	138.94	128.97	146.03	133.55	143.72	117.92	130.74	190.58	213.36	106.07	117.08
	Fev	123.59	136.42	129.66	142.54	130.34	142.57	109.54	126.20	174.37	201.91	98.91	114.75
1 ▶	% month	-4.13	-1.81	0.53	-2.39	-2.41	-0.80	-7.10	-3.47	-8.51	-5.37	-6.75	-1.99
	% month (-1)	-2.48	-0.61	-4.42	1.22	1.72	0.08	-6.71	0.23	2.98	2.12	-8.85	-0.79
	% month (-2)	-8.99	-2.06	-14.92	-7.60	-6.55	0.70	-8.56	1.95	-19.07	-2.20	-5.86	2.85
2 ▶	% month year (-1	1.78	2.92	10.41	18.50	4.30	2.98	-2.01	2.48	2.53	16.33	-3.06	-0.39
3 ▶	% year	2.73	3.52	12.98	18.87	3.41	3.11	0.27	3.18	8.58	16.70	-1.60	0.40
4 ▶	% 12 months	-0.03	0.47	3.94	5.65	1.88	2.07	-2.99	-1.80	2.66	5.39	-4.22	-3.28

CHAPTER 5

Best Web Sites for
U.S. Economic Indicators

Until the 1990s, large economic research firms would charge clients thousands of dollars to churn out statistics on the U.S. and international economies. Today, thanks to the Internet and the intense competition among financial services companies to attract customers, anyone can easily obtain economic or financial data directly from the Web at no cost. This chapter lists online resources that provide such information for free.

SCHEDULE OF RELEASES

- **Get a calendar of U.S. economic releases:**

  www.dailyfx.com/calendar/briefing/
  http://money.cnn.com/markets/IRC/economic.html
  www.nber.org/releases/
  http://fidweek.econoday.com/

ECONOMIC NEWS

- **Latest stories on the economy:**

  www.bloomberg.com/news/
  http://money.cnn.com/news/economy/
  www.cnbc.com
  http://cbs.marketwatch.com/news/
  http://news.yahoo.com/fc?tmpl=fc&cid=34&in=business&cat=us_economy

THE U.S. ECONOMY

- **Most recent GDP report:**

  www.bea.gov/newsreleases/national/gdp/gdpnewsrelease.htm

- **Historical data on the GDP and its components:**

  http://research.stlouisfed.org/fred2/categories/18

- **Industrial Production and Capacity Utilization:**

  www.federalreserve.gov/releases/g17/current

- **Factory Orders (formally known as Manufacturers' Shipments, Inventories, and Orders):**

  www.census.gov/indicator/www/m3/prel/index.htm

- **Advanced Report on Durable Goods Orders:**

  www.census.gov/indicator/www/m3/adv/

- **Chicago's Purchasing Managers Report (NAPM):**

  www.napm-chicago.org

- **Business Inventories (also known as Manufacturing and Trade Inventories and Sales):**

  www.census.gov/mtis/www/current.html

- **U.S. Leading Economic Indicators Index (as well as the Coincident and Lagging Indicators):**

  www.globalindicators.org/us/latestreleases/

- **Manufacturing activity from the Institute for Supply Management (ISM):**

  www.ism.ws/ISMReport/index.cfm

- **Non-manufacturing (service) activity from the Institute for Supply Management (ISM):**

  www.ism.ws/ISMReport/index.cfm

- **Dates and lengths of past recessions and expansions (business cycle data):**

  www.nber.org/cycles.html/

CONSUMER BEHAVIOR

- **Personal Income and Spending:**

  www.bea.gov/bea/newsrel/pinewsrelease.htm

- **Real Earnings:**

  www.bls.gov/news.release/realer.toc.htm

- **Retail Sales:**

  www.census.gov/svsd/www/advtable.html

- **E-Commerce Retail Sales:**
  www.census.gov/mrts/www/ecomm.html

- **Weekly Chain-Store Sales:**
  www.chainstoreage.com/csa/industrydata/pdfs/weeklysales.pdf

- **Consumer Debt (formally known as Consumer Credit Outstanding):**
  www.federalreserve.gov/releases/g19

- **Investor Confidence (UBS Index of Investor Optimism):**
  www.ubs.com/investoroptimism

- **ABC News/*Washington Post* Consumer Comfort Index:**
  http://abcnews.go.com/US/PollVault

- **Consumer Sentiment by the University of Michigan:**
  www.sca.isr.umich.edu/main.php

- **Consumer Confidence by the Conference Board:**
  www.conference-board.org/economics/consumerConfidence.cfm

- **Household Debt Device:**
  www.federalreserve.gov/releases/housedebt/default.htm

- **Credit Card Delinquencies:**
  www.aba.com/Press+Room/pr_releasesmenu.htm

- **Personal and Business Bankruptcy Filings:**
  www.abiworld.org/am/template.cfm?section=press_releases

EMPLOYMENT CONDITIONS

- **Employment Situation Report:**
  http://stats.bls.gov/news.release/empsit.toc.htm

- **Mass Layoffs:**
  www.bls.gov/mls

- **Weekly Claims for Unemployment Insurance:**
  www.ows.doleta.gov/unemploy/claims_arch

- **Help-Wanted Advertising Index:**
  www.conferenceboard.org/economics/helpwanted.cfm

- **ADP National Employment Report:**
  www.adpemploymentreport.com/report_analysis.aspx

HOME SALES AND CONSTRUCTION ACTIVITY

- **Housing Starts:**

  www.census.gov/const/www/newresconstindex.html

- **Housing Market Index—Builders' perception of the current and future market for new single-family homes (National Association of Home Builders):**

  www.nahb.org (type "HMI" in the search box)

- **Single-Family Existing Home Sales (National Association of Realtors):**

  www.realtor.org/research.nsf/pages/ehsdata

- **Pending Home Sales (for existing homes):**

  www.realtor.org/Research.nsf/Pages/PHSdata

- **New Home Sales:**

  www.census.gov/const/newressales.pdf

- **Construction Spending:**

  www.census.gov/c30

- **Weekly Mortgage Applications (Mortgage Bankers Association):**

  www.mortgagebankers.org/NewsandMedia

- **Home Affordability Index (National Association of Realtors):**

  www.realtor.org/research.nsf/pages/housinginx

INTERNATIONAL TRADE

- **International Trade:**

  www.bea.gov/newsreleases/international/trade/tradnewsrelease.htm

- **Export and Import Prices:**

  www.bls.gov/mxp

- **Current Account Balance (International Transactions):**

  http://bea.gov/newsreleases/international/transactions/transnewsrelease.htm

- **Treasury International Capital System (TIC):**

  www.treas.gov/press/international.html

INFLATION PRESSURES

- **Consumer Price Index (CPI):**

  www.bls.gov/cpi/

- **Producer Price Index (PPI):**

  www.bls.gov/ppi

- **Productivity and Costs:**

  www.bls.gov/lpc/

- **Employer Costs for Employee Compensation:**

  www.bls.gov/news.release/ecec.toc.htm

- **Employment Cost Index:**

  www.stats.bls.gov/news.release/eci.toc.htm

- **Historic rates of U.S. inflation (the CPI) going back to 1913:**

  http://woodrow.mpls.frb.fed.us/research/data/us/calc/hist1913.cfm

- **Estimates of U.S. inflation going back to 1800:**

  http://woodrow.mpls.frb.fed.us/research/data/us/calc/hist1800.cfm

- **Compute what inflation does to a dollar from one period to another:**

  http://woodrow.mpls.frb.fed.us/research/data/us/calc/
  www.eh.net/ehresources/howmuch/dollarq.php

FEDERAL RESERVE REPORTS

Surveys from regional Federal Reserve Banks:

- **Federal Reserve Bank of Philadelphia:**

  www.phil.frb.org/econ/bos/index.html

- **Federal Reserve Bank of Richmond:**

  www.richmondfed.org/research/regional_conditions/manufacturing_conditions/
  activity.cfm/

- **Federal Reserve Bank of Kansas City:**

  www.kc.frb.org/mfgsurv/mfgmain.htm

- **Federal Reserve Bank of New York:**

  www.ny.frb.org/research/regional_economy/empiresurvey_overview.html

- **Federal Reserve Bank of Chicago:**

  www.chicagofed.org/economic_research_and_data/cfnai.cfm

- **Federal Reserve Board's Beige Book:**

  www.federalreserve.gov/frbindex.htm

- **Federal Open Market Committee (FOMC) Statement:**

  www.federalreserve.gov/newsevents.htm

THE FEDERAL BUDGET

- **Current projections as well as historical data on the U.S. federal budget:**

  www.cbo.gov/

- **Latest proposed budget of the U.S.:**

  www.whitehouse.gov/omb/budget

INTEREST RATES

- **Latest interest rates on mortgages, mortgage refinancings, home equity loans, auto loans, and credit cards:**

  www.bankrate.com/brm/rate/avg_natl.asp

- **Historical interest rates on Federal funds and Treasury securities:**

  www.federalreserve.gov/releases/h15/data.htm

- **Current interest rates on Federal funds and Treasury securities:**

  www.federalreserve.gov/releases/h15/update/
  www.bloomberg.com/markets/rates/

MONEY AND CREDIT

- **Figures on the U.S. money supply:**

  www.federalreserve.gov/releases/h6/current

- **Data on U.S. bank reserves:**

  www.federalreserve.gov/releases/h3/

- **Historical figures on consumer loans by all commercial banks:**

  http://research.stlouisfed.org/fred2/series/CONSUMER/49

- **Current and historical numbers on commercial and industrial loans outstanding by commercial banks:**

  http://research.stlouisfed.org/fred2/series/BUSLOANS/49

U.S. DOLLAR

- **Dollar's exchange rate with virtually any currency in the world:**

  www.x-rates.com/
  www.xe.com/ucc/
  www.oanda.com/converter/classic

- **Historical foreign exchange rates:**

  www.federalreserve.gov/releases/h10/hist/
  www.oanda.com/converter/classic

- **Dollar's performance versus its major trading partners:**

  www.federalreserve.gov/releases/h10/summary

ONE-STOP SHOPPING FOR ECONOMIC STATISTICS

- **Locate common economic indicators:**

  www.economicindicators.gov

- **Raw data of U.S. economic statistics for graphing purposes:**

  www.economagic.com/

- **Economic Report of the President (which contains a comprehensive collection of economic indicators going back more than 50 years):**

  www.gpoaccess.gov/eop/index.html

- **Economic Indicators by the Joint Economic Committee (U.S. Congress):**

  www.gpoaccess.gov/indicators/

OTHER USEFUL ECONOMIC SOURCES ON THE WEB

- **Federal Reserve Board's Flow of Funds:**

  www.federalreserve.gov/releases/z1/

- **Glossary of economic and financial terms:**

  www.exchange-handbook.co.uk/glossary.cfm?
  www.digitaleconomist.com/glossary_macro.html

UNCONVENTIONAL ECONOMIC INDICATORS

- **Association of American Railroads:**

  Weekly press release on railroad freight traffic volume. It can tell us if factories and wholesalers are ordering more or fewer supplies.
  www.aar.org/ListContent.asp?ContentType_ID=4&ListCode=PR

- **Exhibitor Relations Co.:**

  Movie ticket sales. Helps track changes in discretionary spending by consumers.
  www.ercboxoffice.com/erc/reports/

- **Travel Industry Association:**

  Provides monthly data on air, rail, and road travel that can reflect business and consumer spending.
  www.tia.org/researchpubs/ipi_current_chart.html

- **GasBuddy Organization, Inc.:**

  Chart updates oil and gas prices around the U.S.
  www.gasbuddy.com/gb_retail_price_chart.aspx?time=24

- **American Staffing Association:**

  A weekly index that gauges the number of people hired for temporary or contract work.
  www.americanstaffing.net/statistics/staffing_index.cfm

- **National Restaurant Association:**

  A monthly report on current restaurant activity, as well as the latest outlook. Each report is released at the end of the month.
  www.restaurant.org/pressroom/releaselist.cfm

- **The Innovation Group:**

  Contains recent data on gaming activity around the country.
  www.theinnovationgroup.com/statistics.asp

- **American Hotel & Lodging Association:**

  Publishes a monthly report by Smith Travel Research on the lodging industry, including occupancy rates and average daily rates.
  http://ahlaradio.hsyndicate.com/index.html

CHAPTER 6

Best Web Sites for International Economic Indicators

(Only those available in English are listed here)

CALENDAR OF RELEASES FOR FOREIGN ECONOMIC DATA

www.fxstreet.com/nou/continguts/economiccal.asp

www.forexfactory.com/calendar.php

www.forexeconomiccalendar.com/

SOURCES OF GLOBAL ECONOMIC NEWS

http://news.bbc.co.uk/2/hi/business/default.stm

http://news.ft.com/business

www.fxstreet.com

www.reuters.com

www.iht.com/frontpage.html

www.bloomberg.com

ECONOMIC STATISTICS FROM OTHER COUNTRIES

- **Europe**
  - Albania: *www.instat.gov.al*
  - Austria: *www.statistik.at/index_englisch.shtml*
  - Belarus: *www.government.by/en/eng_analytics.html*
  - Belgium: *http://statbel.fgov.be/*
  - Bosnia and Herzegovina: *www.fzs.ba/Eng/index.htm*
  - Bulgaria: *www.nsi.bg/Index_e.htm*

- Croatia: *www.mingorp.hr/cacheeng.aspx?pg=*
                      defaulteng.asp&cache=1&id=6&glink
- Czech Republic: *www.czso.cz/eng/redakce.nsf/i/home*
- Denmark: *www.dst.dk/HomeUK.aspx*
- Estonia: *www.stat.ee/*
- Finland: *www.stat.fi/index_en.html*
- France: *www.insee.fr/en/home/home_page.asp*
- Germany: *www.destatis.de/indicators/e/iwf01.htm*
                      www.destatis.de/e_home.htm
                      www.ifo.de
                      www.ifo-business-climate-index.info
                      www.bundesbank.de/index.en.php
- Greece: *www.statistics.gr/Main_eng.asp*
- Hungary: *www2.pm.gov.hu/web/home.nsf/frames/english*
- Iceland: *http://eng.fjarmalaraduneyti.is/statistics/*
- Ireland: *www.cso.ie/*
- Italy: *www.istat.it/English/index.htm*
- Latvia: *www.csb.lv/avidus.cfm*
- Liechtenstein: *www.liechtenstein.li/*
- Lithuania: *www.std.lt/web/main.php*
- Luxembourg: *http://statec.gouvernement.lu/html_en/*
- Macedonia: *www.economy.gov.mk/*
- Malta: *www.nso.gov.mt/*
- Moldova: *www.statistica.md/*
- The Netherlands: *www.cbs.nl/en/*
                      www.cpb.nl/eng/
                      www.dnb.nl/dnb/homepage.jsp?lang=en
- Norway: *www.ssb.no/www-open/english/*
- Poland: *www.stat.gov.pl/english/*
- Portugal: *www.ine.pt/ajuda/mapa_eng.html*
- Romania: *www.insse.ro/indexe.htm*
- Russia: *www.cbr.ru/eng*
- Slovakia: *www.statistics.sk/webdata/english/index2_a.htm*
- Slovenia: *www.stat.si/eng/*
- Spain: *www.ine.es/welcoing.htm*
- Sweden: *www.scb.se/*
- Switzerland: *www.statistik.admin.ch/eindex.htm*
- Ukraine: *www.ukrstat.gov.ua/*
- United Kingdom: *www.statistics.gov.uk/*
                      www.bankofengland.co.uk

- **Asia**
  - Armenia: *www.armstat.am*
  - Azerbaijan: *www.azstat.org/indexen.php*
  - Bahrain: *www.mofne.gov.bh/English/eindex.asp*
  - Bangladesh: *www.bangladesh-bank.org/*
  - Cambodia: *www.nis.gov.kh/*
  - China: *http://ce.cei.gov.cn*
    www.china.org.cn/english
    http://english.peopledaily.com.cn/
    www.stats.gov.cn/english/index.htm
    www.stats.gov.cn/english/statisticaldata/index.htm
    www.stats.gov.cn/english/statisticaldata/monthlydata
    www.pbc.gov.cn/english/
    www.geoinvestor.com/countries/china/main.htm
    www.xinhuanet.com/english/business.htm
  - Cyprus: *www.centralbank.gov.cy/nqcontent.cfm?a_id= 1&lang=en*
  - Georgia: *www.nbg.gov.ge/eng/index.html*
  - Hong Kong: *www.info.gov.hk/censtatd/home.html*
  - India: *www.rbi.org.in/*
    http://mospi.nic.in/
    http://mospi.nic.in/mospi_nad_sdrs.htm
    http://finmin.nic.in/index.html
    www.censusindia.net/
  - Indonesia: *www.bps.go.id/index.shtml*
  - Iran: *www.cbi.ir/default_en.aspx*
  - Israel: *www.cbs.gov.il/engindex.htm*
    www.bankisrael.gov.il/firsteng.htm
  - Japan: *www.tse.or.jp/english/index.shtml*
    www.esri.cao.go.jp/index-e.html
    www.meti.go.jp/english
    www.meti.go.jp/english/statistics
    www.stat.go.jp/english/
    www5.cao.go.jp/keizai3/getsurei-e/index-e.html
    www.boj.or.jp/en/index.htm
    www.esri.cao.go.jp/en/sna/menu.html
    www.cao.go.jp/index-e.html
  - Jordan: *www.dos.gov.jo/dos_home_e/main/*
  - Korea (South): *www.korea.net/korea/kor_loca.asp?code=E0112*

- Kuwait: *www.cbk.gov.kw/WWW/index.html*
- Kyrgyzstan: *www.nbkr.kg/web/interfeis.builder_frame*
  ?language=ENG
- Laos: *www1.mot.gov.vn/laowebsite/default.asp*
- Lebanon: *www.cas.gov.lb/addsearch_en.asp*
- Macao: *www.dsec.gov.mo/e_index.html*
- Malaysia: *www.statistics.gov.my/*
- Maldives: *www.mma.gov.mv/statis.php*
- Mauritius: *http://bom.intnet.mu/*
- Mongolia: *www.mongolbank.mn/*
- Nepal: *www.cbs.gov.np/*
- Pakistan: *www.statpak.gov.pk/*
- Palestinian Authority: *www.pcbs.org/*
- Papua New Guinea: *www.nso.gov.pg*
- Philippines: *www.nscb.gov.ph/*
- Qatar: *www.planning.gov.qa/statistics.html*
- Saudi Arabia: *www.planning.gov.sa/indexe.htm*
  www.sama.gov.sa/indexe.htm
- Singapore: *www.singstat.gov.sg/*
- Sri Lanka: *www.statistics.gov.lk/index.asp*
- Syria: *www.syria-report.com/*
  www.syrecon.org/index.php?newlang=eng
- Taiwan: *http://english.www.gov.tw/e-Gov/index.jsp*
  ?categid=72
- Thailand: *http://web.nso.go.th/eng/index.htm*
- Turkey: *www.tcmb.gov.tr/yeni/eng/index.html*
- United Arab Emirates: *www.uae.gov.ae/mop/E_home.htm*
  www.uae.gov.ae/mofi/
- Vietnam: *www.gso.gov.vn/default_en.aspx?tabid=*
  494&itemid=1631
- Yemen: *www.economywatch.com/world_economy/*
  yemen/index.html

- **North America**
  - Anguilla: *http://gov.ai/statistics/statistics.htm*
  - Aruba: *www.aruba.com/extlinks/govs/cbstats.html*
  - Bahamas: *www.bahamascentralbank.com/*
  - Barbados: *www.centralbank.org.bb/*
  - Belize: *www.cso.gov.bz/*

- Bermuda: *www.bma.bm/*
- Canada: *www.statcan.ca*
                              www.bankofcanada.ca/en/
                              www.canadianeconomy.gc.ca/english/economy
- Cayman Islands: *www.cimoney.com.ky*
- El Salvador: *www.bcr.gob.sv/*
- Greenland: *www.statgreen.gl/english/*
- Guatemala: *www.banguat.gob.gt/en/*
- Jamaica: *www.statinja.com/*
- Mexico: *www.banxico.org.mx/sitioIngles/index.html/*
                              www.shcp.gob.mx/portada_english/ingles/
                              index_economic.html
- Netherlands Antilles: *www.centralbank.an/*
- St. Kitts and Nevis: *www.eccb-centralbank.org/*
- St. Lucia: *www.stats.gov.lc*
- Trinidad and Tobago: *www.cso.gov.tt/*

- **South America**
  - Argentina: *www.indec.mecon.ar/*
  - Brazil: *www.investebrasil.org*
                              www.ipeadata.gov.br/
                              www.ibge.gov.br/english/
                              www.bcb.gov.br/?INDICATORS
  - Chile: *www.bcentral.cl/eng/infoeconomic/*
  - Columbia: *www.banrep.gov.co/index_eng.html*
  - Peru: *www.mef.gob.pe/English/indexen.php*
  - Suriname: *www.cbvs.sr/english/over-de-cbvs.htm*
  - Uruguay: *www.bcu.gub.uy/indexe.html*
  - Venezuela: *www.bcv.org.ve/EnglishVersion/Index.asp*

- **Oceania**
  - Cook Islands: *www.mfem.gov.ck/*
  - Marshall Islands: *www.rmiembassyus.org/Economy.htm*
  - New Zealand: *www.treasury.govt.nz/*
                              www.rbnz.govt.nz/
                              www.stats.govt.nz/
  - Samoa: *www.cbs.gov.ws/*
  - Vanuatu: *www.vanuatustatistics.gov.vu*

- **Africa**
  - Algeria: *www.ons.dz/English/indexag.htm*
  - Benin: *www.gouv.bj/en/ministeres/mfe/index.php*
  - Botswana: *www.cso.gov.bw/*
  - Egypt: *www.capmas.gov.eg*
  - Ghana: *www.finance.gov.gh/*
  - Lesotho: *www.bos.gov.ls/*
  - Libya: *www.cbl.gov.ly/en/*
  - Malawi: *www.nso.malawi.net/*
  - Morocco: *www.bkam.ma/Anglais/Menu/Anex.asp*
  - Mozambique: *www.bancomoc.mz/index.php?menu=1&lang=uk*
  - Namibia: *www.npc.gov.na/cbs/*
  - Nigeria: *www.cenbank.org/*
  - Rwanda: *www.minecofin.gov.rw/*
  - Seychelles: *www.sey.net/gen_econ.htm*
  - Sierra Leone: *www.sierra-leone.org/cso2001-index.html*
  - South Africa: *www.statssa.gov.za/*
  - Swaziland: *www.gov.sz/home.asp?pid=75*
  - Tanzania: *www.tanzania.go.tz/statistics.html*
  - Uganda: *www.ubos.org/*
  - Zambia: *www.boz.zm/*

- **Australia**

     www.rba.gov.au
     www.abs.gov.au/

BEST MEGASITES FOR INTERNATIONAL ECONOMIC STATISTICS

www.worldbank.org/data/countrydata/countrydata.html
www.globalindicators.org
www.oecd.org
www.oecd.org/std/cli
www.ecb.int
www.ntc-research.com
http://europa.eu.int/comm/eurostat/
http://unstats.un.org/unsd/
http://datacentre.chass.utoronto.ca/pwt/
http://devdata.worldbank.org/data-query/
www.latin-focus.com/news

Index

D

F

G

S

T

U